Llewellyn's 98

MOON SIGN BOOK

YOUR KEY TO SUCCESS IN 2003

With Lunar Forecasts by Gloria Star

Copyright © 2002 Llewellyn Worldwide.
All rights reserved. Printed in the U.S.A.
Editor/Designer: Sharon Leah
Cover Design & Art: Kevin R. Brown
Illustration on page 222: Kathleen Sutherland, © 2001
Special thanks to Aina Allen
for astrological proofreading.
ISBN 0-7387-0070-3

LLEWELLYN WORLDWIDE
P.O. Box 64383 Dept. 0070-3
St. Paul, MN 55164-0383 U.S.A.

TABLE OF CONTENTS

Leisure & Recreation Section   181

Business & Legal Section   253

Farm, Garden, & Weather Section   299

Composting; Grafting; Harvesting Crops; Irrigation; Lawn
Mowing; Picking Mushrooms; Planting; Pruning; Spraying and
Weeding; and Weather

Gloria Star's Personal Lunar Forecasts for 2003   381

2003

JANUARY

S	M	T	W	T	F	S
			1	2	3	4
5	6	7	8	9	10	11
12	13	14	15	16	17	18
19	20	21	22	23	24	25
26	27	28	29	30	31	

FEBRUARY

S	M	T	W	T	F	S
						1
2	3	4	5	6	7	8
9	10	11	12	13	14	15
16	17	18	19	20	21	22
23	24	25	26	27	28	

MARCH

S	M	T	W	T	F	S
						1
2	3	4	5	6	7	8
9	10	11	12	13	14	15
16	17	18	19	20	21	22
23	24	25	26	27	28	29
30	31					

APRIL

S	M	T	W	T	F	S
		1	2	3	4	5
6	7	8	9	10	11	12
13	14	15	16	17	18	19
20	21	22	23	24	25	26
27	28	29	30			

MAY

S	M	T	W	T	F	S
				1	2	3
4	5	6	7	8	9	10
11	12	13	14	15	16	17
18	19	20	21	22	23	24
25	26	27	28	29	30	31

JUNE

S	M	T	W	T	F	S
1	2	3	4	5	6	7
8	9	10	11	12	13	14
15	16	17	18	19	20	21
22	23	24	25	26	27	28
29	30					

JULY

S	M	T	W	T	F	S
		1	2	3	4	5
6	7	8	9	10	11	12
13	14	15	16	17	18	19
20	21	22	23	24	25	26
27	28	29	30	31		

AUGUST

S	M	T	W	T	F	S
					1	2
3	4	5	6	7	8	9
10	11	12	13	14	15	16
17	18	19	20	21	22	23
24	25	26	27	28	29	30
31						

SEPTEMBER

S	M	T	W	T	F	S
	1	2	3	4	5	6
7	8	9	10	11	12	13
14	15	16	17	18	19	20
21	22	23	24	25	26	27
28	29	30				

OCTOBER

S	M	T	W	T	F	S
			1	2	3	4
5	6	7	8	9	10	11
12	13	14	15	16	17	18
19	20	21	22	23	24	25
26	27	28	29	30	31	

NOVEMBER

S	M	T	W	T	F	S
						1
2	3	4	5	6	7	8
9	10	11	12	13	14	15
16	17	18	19	20	21	22
23	24	25	26	27	28	29
30						

DECEMBER

S	M	T	W	T	F	S
	1	2	3	4	5	6
7	8	9	10	11	12	13
14	15	16	17	18	19	20
21	22	23	24	25	26	27
28	29	30	31			

To Readers

If you are among the rapidly increasing numbers who believe that the universe is operated upon a well-defined plan wherein each individual has a chance to advance and achieve success according to his or her degree of understanding and effort put forth toward that objective . . . this BIG little book may truly be for you a guide to victory.

Llewellyn George

Much has changed in our world since those words appeared in the *Moon Sign Book* in 1948, but we have the same basic needs, desires, and concerns today as that generation did. We want to realize success and advance as the result of our efforts, too. It is possible to achieve many of the things we want in our lives by using the knowledge of cycles within our universe that has been accumulated through the millenniums by men and women who have observed the correlation between events in the heavens and those on Earth. Their observations inform us about the best times to undertake important events, but it's up to us to understand and incorporate the knowledge of universal cycles into our daily lives. The *Moon Sign Book* provides you with essential tools that you can use to reap the benefits of timing events based on lunar cycles and the cycles of planets.

While the Sun is indeed the origin and sustainer of life on Earth, the exposure of the Sun's light and heat alone would not offer the stimulus to change and growth as do the tides that respond to lunar influences. Using astrological knowledge in our everyday lives will nurture and support us, just as the lunar cycle supports the growth of all living things on Earth.

From the very beginnings of life, Earth's two companions in the sky—the Sun and the Moon—established two separate rhythms that continue to this day: the Sun with its pattern of heat and light, and the setting of the seasons; the Moon raising and lowering the water in and with which life is nourished.

Twice each lunar day (a 24.8-hour period), the tides are high; and twice each lunar month (29.5 days) at Full and New Moons, there are higher tides. With each rise of the water, there is a new stirring of life in the waters, and with each retreat of the waters, life is left behind on the shores for other creatures to consume—thus setting the basic patterns of growth and harvest.

About Almanacs

If you wish to plan by the Moon, it is important to know how the *Moon Sign Book* differs from most almanacs, which list the placement of the Moon by the constellation. For example,

when the Moon is passing through the constellation of Capricorn, they list the Moon as being in Capricorn. The *Moon Sign Book*, however, lists the placement of the Moon in the zodiac by sign, not constellation.

The zodiac, consisting of twelve thirty-degree divisions, surrounds the Earth at the equator. Each segment houses one of the constellations—Leo, the lion, Sagittarius, the archer, and so on—and bears the name of that constellation. However, because of an astronomical phenomenon called the *precession of the equinoxes*, those constellations no longer match up with the segment of space named after them. In other words, the constellations and the signs don't "match up."

For astronomical calculations, the Moon's place is given as being in a constellation; but for astrological purposes the Moon's place should be figured in the zodiacal sign, which is its true place in the zodiac, and nearly one sign different from the astronomical constellation. The *Moon Sign Book* figures the Moon's placement for astrological purposes.

For example, if the common almanac gives the Moon's place in the constellation Taurus, its true place in the zodiac is in the zodiacal sign of Gemini. Thus it is readily seen that those who use the common almanac may be planting seeds when they think that the Moon is in a fruitful sign, while in reality it would be in one of the most barren signs of the zodiac. To obtain desired results, planning must be done according to sign.

Some almanacs confuse the issue further by inserting at the head of their columns "Moon's Sign," when what they really mean is "Moon's Constellation." In the *Moon Sign Book*, "Moon's sign" means "Moon's sign."

Tools for Timing

The *Moon Sign Book* contains five tools that can be used separately or in combination to help you achieve optimal results for your efforts. The first tool is our easy-to-use Astro Almanac, found on pages 19–27, which lists the best dates each month to begin important activities.

The dates provided are determined from the sign and phase of the Moon and the aspects the Moon makes to other planets. For example, the best time to apply for a new job would be when the Moon is in one of the earth signs of Taurus, Virgo, or Capricorn, and making favorable aspects to Jupiter or the Sun. If your personal Sun sign is involved, that's even better. However, when the Moon is in Capricorn you would want to avoid asking for a raise because those in positions of authority would not be as sensitive to your desires. (Capricorn energy

can be very somber, conservative, and structured.) To further increase the likelihood of getting the raise you seek, select a time between a New and Full Moon, the waxing phase.

While the dates in the Astro Almanac are approximate, you can fine-tune the timing of events by also taking into consideration your own Sun and Moon sign.

The Moon Tables and the tables on the opposite pages that contain the lunar aspectarian and favorable and unfavorable days found on pages 34–57; the tables of Gardening Dates found on pages 315–322, and the Best Dates to Destroy Weeds and Pests on pages 324–325, make up the second set of tools. The Moon Tables (on the even numbered pages) list the day, date, time, sign, phase, and element (air, earth, fire, or water) the Moon is in; the Lunar Aspectarian gives the aspects of the Moon to other planets, and the tables of favorable and unfavorable days take your Sun sign into consideration; the Gardening Date Tables provide dates and times for various gardening activities; and the last named table is useful for any occasion that calls for ridding yourself of unwanted circumstances, including garden pests, a bad relationship, or a bad habit, for example. New tables are compiled each year.

Of course, every day is important and brings its opportunities for doing good work, but some days are special days. By knowing the dates of favorable and unfavorable influences you have the opportunity to think before it's time to act, and to set a day in advance for any affair that will be most in keeping with the good results you desire. If you're unable to affect the timing of something, at the very least you will be aware of the potential energies, which will in turn afford you the chance to determine your actions ahead of time.

The *Moon Sign Book* offers you a third tool for working with lunar energies. The Personal Lunar Forecasts written by renowned astrologer Gloria Star tell you what is in store for you based on your Moon sign. This approach is different from Llewellyn's *Sun Sign Book*, which makes forecasts based on the Sun sign. While the Sun in an astrological chart represents the basic essence, or personality, the Moon represents the internal, or private you—your feelings, emotions, and subconscious. Knowing what's in store for your Moon can give you great insight for personal growth. If you don't know your Moon sign, you can figure it out using the Grant Lewi system outlined on page 65.

The fourth tool is informative articles on using the energy that is unique to each Moon. In addition to using the Moon's sign and phase to help you plant and maintain your garden, you can use the information to your advantage in your relationships at home, work, or place of business. The articles are written by people who successfully use the Moon to enhance their daily lives. We hope that they will enhance your knowledge about what the Moon can do for you, too.

A Note About Astrologers

Today, astrologers rely on ancient texts and incorporate new findings and research into their practice. However, astrology is an art, not a science. It is therefore possible for astrologers to vary, one from another, in their views and in the emphasis they chose to place on astrological components.

Understanding Lunar Astrology

The Moon's cycles and their correlation with everyday life are the foundation of the *Moon Sign Book*. By providing explicit tables and articles on the Moon's influence, we hope to bring a part of this valuable astrological knowledge within reach of everyone. Let us begin by looking at some basic astrological principles.

Everyone has seen the Moon wax and wane through a period of approximately twenty-nine and a half days. This circuit from New Moon to Full Moon and back again

PHINEAS PINCHBECK
SELLS
DOLLY-VARDEN ALARM-CLOCKS
FOR HUSBANDS,
APPRENTICES' TIMEKEEPERS
FOR MANUFACTURERS,
ELECTION REPEATERS
FOR POLITICIANS.

is called the *lunation cycle*. The cycle is divided into parts, called *quarters* or *phases*. The astrological system of naming the lunar phases does not always correspond to systems used in other almanacs and calendars. It is therefore important to follow only the *Moon Sign Book* or Llewellyn's *Astrological Calendar* for timing events.

First Quarter

The first quarter begins at the New Moon, when the Sun and Moon are conjunct (the Sun and Moon are in the same degree of the same zodiac sign). The Moon is not visible at first, since it rises at the same time as the Sun. The New Moon phase is a time for new

beginnings that favor growth, the externalization of activities, and the expansion of ideas. The first quarter is the time when things germinate and emerge; a time of beginnings, and outwardly directed activity.

Second Quarter

The second quarter begins halfway between the New Moon and the Full Moon, when the Sun and Moon are ninety degrees apart. This half Moon rises around noon and sets around midnight, so it can be seen in the western sky during the first half of the night. The second quarter is the time of growth, development, and articulation of things that already exist.

Third Quarter

The third quarter begins at the Full Moon, when the Sun is opposite the Moon and its full light can shine on the full sphere of the Moon. The round Moon can be seen rising in the east at sunset, and then rising a little later each evening. The Full Moon stands for illumination, fulfillment, completion, drawing inward, unrest, and emotional expressions. The third quarter is a time of maturity, fruition, and the assumption of the full form of expression.

Fourth Quarter

The fourth quarter begins about halfway between the Full Moon and

New Moon, when the Sun and Moon are again at ninety degrees, or square. This decreasing Moon rises at midnight, and can be seen in the east during the last half of the night, reaching the overhead position just about as the Sun rises. The fourth quarter is a time of disintegration, drawing back for reorganization, and for reflection.

Sign and Influence

Today, due to the movement of our solar system around the galaxy of stars, the signs and constellations no longer coincide. Except for a few fixed stars, astrology does not deal with the stars or constellations at all. We are only concerned with the planets, including the Sun and Moon, and their positions in the signs of the zodiac. These signs are divided into different categories to help us better understand their natures.

Element (Triplicity)

Each of the signs is classified as either fire, earth, air, or water. These are the four basic elements. The fire signs Aries, Sagittarius, and Leo are action oriented, outgoing, energetic, and spontaneous. The earth signs Taurus, Capricorn, and Virgo are more stable, conservative, practical, and oriented to the physical realm. The air signs Gemini, Aquarius, and Libra are sociable, critical, and tend to respond with intellect rather than feeling.

The water signs Cancer, Scorpio, and Pisces are emotional, receptive, intuitive, and can be very sensitive.

Quality (Quadruplicity)

Each zodiac sign is also classified as being either cardinal, mutable, or fixed. There are four signs in each quadruplicity, one sign of each element. The cardinal signs represent beginnings and initiate action. During the cycle of the year, the cardinal signs Aries, Capricorn, Libra, and Cancer initiate each new season. Fixed signs maintain the status quo through stubbornness and persistence. Taurus, Leo, Scorpio, and Aquarius represent the months when summer really is summer, that between time. Mutable signs adapt to change and tolerate situations. Pisces, Gemini, Sagittarius, and Virgo represent the last month of each season, when things are changing in preparation for the next season.

Nature and Fertility

In addition to a sign's element and quality, each sign is further classified as either fruitful, semi-fruitful, or barren. This classification is the most important for readers who use the gardening information in the *Moon Sign Book*, because the timing of most events depends on the fertility of the sign occupied by the Moon. The water signs—Cancer, Scorpio, and Pisces—are the most fruitful. The semi-fruitful signs are the feminine earth signs Taurus and Capricorn, and the masculine air sign Libra. The barren signs are the masculine fire signs Aries, Leo, and Sagittarius; the masculine air signs Gemini and Aquarius, and the feminine earth sign Virgo.

Rulerships

Each planet has one or two signs in which its characteristics are particularly enhanced. These planets are said to "rule" these signs. The Sun rules Leo, the Moon rules Cancer, Mercury rules Gemini and Virgo, Venus rules Taurus and Libra, Mars rules Aries, Jupiter rules Sagittarius, Saturn rules Capricorn, Uranus rules Aquarius, Neptune rules Pisces, and Pluto rules Scorpio.

The Moon in the Signs

Aries Moon

An Aries Moon has a masculine, dry, barren, fiery energy. It is an excellent time for starting things, but Aries lacks staying power. Use this assertive, outgoing sign for making changes, and for doing work that requires skillful, but not necessarily patient, use of tools. Things occur rapidly but also quickly pass. Aries rules the head and face.

Taurus Moon

A Taurus Moon personifies placid patience. The accent is on things that are long lasting and tend to increase in value. This is not a good time to seek change—especially in financial matters. While it is a good time to obtain a loan, bankers and others in charge of money are slow to make decisions. Things begun now tend to become habitual and hard to alter. Taurus rules the neck and throat.

Gemini Moon

A Gemini Moon favors intellectual pursuits and mental games over practical concerns. People are generally more changeable than usual. Because Gemini is a barren sign and primarily mental it is not favored for agricultural matters, although it is an excellent time to prepare for activities. Gemini rules the hands, arms, lungs, and nerves.

Cancer Moon

A Cancer Moon stimulates rapport between people and sharpens sensitivity. With it comes a strong drive toward self-indulgence, especially with food and drink. Because Cancer is traditionally the most fertile of the signs, it is associated with mothering. It can be a time of personal warmth and friendship, supporting growth and nurturance. Cancer rules the breasts and stomach.

Leo Moon

A Leo Moon has a masculine, hot, dry, fiery, barren energy. The accent here is on showmanship, playful activity, romance, and entertaining.

Leo types can be domineering and confident. It's an excellent time for charitable activities. Leo rules the heart and back.

Virgo Moon

A Virgo Moon is favorable for anything that requires painstaking attention, and for intellectual matters—especially those requiring exactness rather than innovation. Virgo is the sign of bargain hunting; and it's friendly toward agricultural matters with the greatest emphasis on harvesting vegetables. It is an excellent time to care for animals, especially training and veterinarian work. Virgo rules the intestines.

Libra Moon

A Libra Moon benefits anything that tends to beautify. Artistic work, especially involving color, is greatly enhanced in this sign. This Moon enjoys starting things of an intellectual nature, and because Libra is the sign of partnership and union, this transit can be good for forming partnerships of any kind, agreements, and negotiations. A Libra Moon accentuates teamwork—particularly teams of two. Libra rules the lower back and kidneys.

Scorpio Moon

A Scorpio Moon increases awareness of psychic power. Scorpio's energy is cold, fixed, and fruitful. This is the most intense sign, and when the Moon is here everything feels deeper—sometimes bordering on obsession. Now is a good time to do research, and to end connections thoroughly. Scorpio rules the sex organs.

Sagittarius Moon

A Sagittarius Moon encourages flights of imagination and confidence in the flow of life. Fiery, dry, and mutable, Sagittarius is the most philosophical of signs. Candor is enhanced at this time, as is honesty. This is an excellent time to "get things off your chest." Now is a time for dealing with institutions of higher learning, publishing companies, and the law. It's also a good time for sport and adventure. Sagittarius rules the hips and thighs.

Capricorn Moon

A Capricorn Moon increases awareness of the need for structure, discipline, and organization. Institutional activities are favored, but this Moon sign should be avoided if you're seeking favors as those in authority can be insensitive under this influence. This is a good time to set goals and plan for the future, tend to family business, taking care of details requiring patience or a businesslike manner. Capricorn rules the knees, bones, and skin.

Aquarius Moon

An Aquarius Moon favors activities that are unique and individualistic. It is concerned with humanitarian issues, society as a whole, and seeks to make improvements. It promotes the gathering of social groups for friendly exchanges. People tend to react and speak from an intellectual rather than emotional viewpoint. Aquarius rules the calves and ankles.

Pisces Moon

A Pisces Moon favors withdrawal into the self, making this an excellent time for retreat, meditation, sleep, prayer, or making that dreamed-of escape on a fantasy vacation. However, things are often not what they seem to be with the Moon in Pisces. Personal boundaries tend to be fuzzy. Pisces rules the feet.

Some Final Notes

We get a number of letters and phone calls every year from readers asking how to find certain information in the *Moon Sign Book* and how to use this information.

The best advice we can give is to read the entire introduction to each section. We provide examples using the current Moon and aspect tables so that you can follow along and get familiar with the process. At first, using the tables may seem confusing because there are several factors to take into account, but if you read the directions carefully and practice a little bit, you'll be a Moon sign pro in no time.

Retrogrades

When the planets cross the sky they occasionally appear to move backward as seen from Earth. When a planet appears to turn "backward" it is said to be retrograde. When it appears to turn forward again, it is said to "go direct." The point at which the movement changes from one direction to another is called a station.

When a planet is retrograde, its expression is delayed or out of kilter with the normal progression of events. Generally, it can be said that whatever is planned during this period will be delayed, but usually it will come to fruition when the retrograde is over. Of course, this only applies to activities ruled by the planet that is retrograde. Mercury retrogrades are easy to follow.

Mercury Retrograde

Mercury rules informal communications—reading, writing, and speaking; short errands or trips; and computers, for example. Whenever Mercury is retrograde, things ruled by Mercury tend to get fouled up or misunderstood. The general rule is: If Mercury is retrograde, avoid informal means of communication, or double-check everything twice.

Table of Retrograde Periods for 2003
(Times are listed in Eastern Standard Time)

Planet	Begin	EST	End	EST
Saturn	10/11/02	8:01 am	02/22/03	2:41 am
Jupiter	12/04/02	7:22 am	04/03/03	10:04 pm
Mercury	01/02/03	1:21 pm	01/22/03	8:08 pm
Pluto	03/23/03	12:12 pm	08/28/03	10:34 pm
Chiron	04/25/03	12:12 pm	09/18/03	12:33 am
Mercury	04/26/03	6:59 am	05/20/03	2:32 am
Neptune	05/15/03	7:48 pm	10/22/03	8:54 pm
Uranus	06/07/03	1:58 am	11/08/03	7:44 am
Mars	07/29/03	2:36 am	09/27/03	2:52 am
Mercury	08/28/03	8:41 am	09/20/03	3:51 am
Saturn	10/25/03	6:42 pm	03/07/04	11:51 am
Mercury	12/17/03	11:02 am	01/06/04	8:45 am

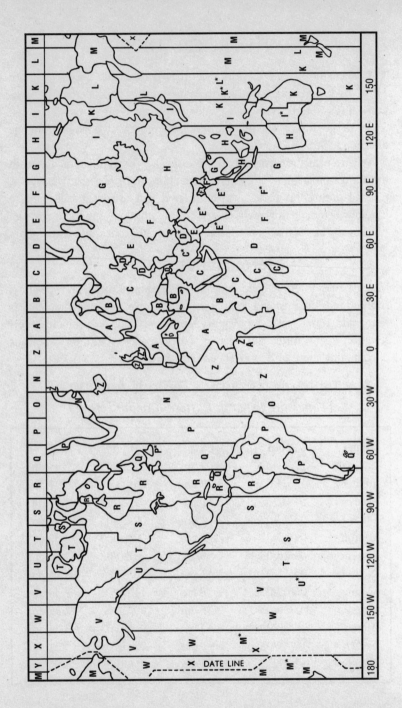

DATE LINE

TIME ZONE CONVERSIONS
World Time Zones
(Compared to Eastern Standard Time)

(R)	EST—Used	(C*)	Add 8½ hours
(S)	CST—Subtract 1 hour	(D)	Add 9 hours
(T)	MST—Subtract 2 hours	(D*)	Add 9½ hours
(U)	PST—Subtract 3 hours	(E)	Add 10 hours
(V)	Subtract 4 hours	(E*)	Add 10½ hours
(V*)	Subtract 4½ hours	(F)	Add 11 hours
(W)	Subtract 5 hours	(F*)	Add 11½ hours
(X)	Subtract 6 hours	(G)	Add 12 hours
(Y)	Subtract 7 hours	(H)	Add 13 hours
(Q)	Add 1 hour	(I)	Add 14 hours
(P)	Add 2 hours	(I*)	Add 14½ hours
(P*)	Add 2½ hours	(K)	Add 15 hours
(O)	Add 3 hours	(K*)	Add 15½ hours
(N)	Add 4 hours	(L)	Add 16 hours
(Z)	Add 5 hours	(L*)	Add 16½ hours
(A)	Add 6 hours	(M)	Add 17 hours
(B)	Add 7 hours	(M*)	Add 17½ hours
(C)	Add 8 hours		

Important!

All times given in the *Moon Sign Book* are set in Eastern Standard Time (EST). Use the time zone conversions chart and table to calculate the adjustment for your time zone. You must also adjust for Daylight Saving Time where applicable.

USING THE ASTRO ALMANAC

Llewellyn's Astro Almanac is a quick reference tool for finding the best dates for anything from asking for a raise to buying a car. The dates provided, which are approximate, are determined from the Moon's sign and phase, and the aspects to the Moon. We have removed dates that have long Moon void-of-course periods from the list. Although some of these dates may meet the criteria listed for your particular activity, the Moon void would nullify the positive influences of that day. We have not removed dates with short Moon voids, however, and we have not taken planetary retrogrades into account. To learn more about Moon void-of-course and planetary retrogrades, see pages 15 and 58–64.

We have also removed eclipse dates and days with lots of squares to the Moon. Like Moon voids, squares that occur late in the day could nullify the "good" influences of a given day. Eclipses lend an unpredictable energy to a day. We have removed eclipse dates so that you may begin your activities on the strongest footing possible.

Another thing to bear in mind when using the Astro Almanac is that sometimes the dates given may not be favorable for your Sun sign, or for your particular interests. The Astro Almanac does not take personal factors into account, such as your Sun and Moon sign, your schedule, etc. That's why it is important for you to learn how to use the entire process to come up with the most beneficial dates for you. To do this, read the instructions under Using the Moon Tables on pages 28–33. That way, you can get the most out of the power of the Moon!

Astro Almanac

Activity	Jan.	Feb.	Mar.	Apr.	May	Jun.	Jul.	Aug.	Sep.	Oct.	Nov.	Dec.
Advertise in print		8, 9, 10, 11	7, 9, 13	4, 14	3, 5, 11	1	4			12, 16	25	4, 27
Advertise on TV, radio, or Internet		11	10, 11	6, 7, 8	3, 5						25	4, 27
Apply for new job or promotion	3	8	8	4, 5, 13	2, 11	8	4	8, 27		29, 31	25, 26, 27	
Aquire art, supplies, or visit museum	3, 23, 24	7, 18, 22	7, 19	3, 4, 15	9, 23	9, 10, 24, 25	3, 12, 17, 23	3, 17, 18, 30	14, 15, 26, 27	12, 26	7, 8, 21	5, 6
Ask favor from one in authority	22, 23, 27	19, 23, 25	2, 8, 13, 22	20, 25	11, 25	9, 18	7, 23	3, 21, 22	14, 15	4, 15, 18, 19, 26	1, 6, 8	11
Ask favor from lawyer, clergy	14, 23	15, 23	14, 18	19	12, 16	13, 22, 23, 27	2, 11, 20, 25	8, 17, 21, 22		21	1, 13, 18, 26,	11, 24

Astro Almanac

Activity	Jan.	Feb.	Mar.	Apr.	May	Jun.	Jul.	Aug.	Sep.	Oct.	Nov.	Dec.
Automobile (buy or sell)	15, 27	24, 25	10, 22, 23	8	3, 20, 31	13, 14, 27, 28	22, 24, 25	22, 24	4, 6, 14	14, 20, 29	24, 25, 26	
Automobile (repair)	4, 5, 21, 22	1, 2, 17, 18	1, 27, 28	14, 25	10, 11, 12	6, 17, 18	3, 4, 15	1, 10, 11, 12	24	4, 5, 21, 22	1, 17, 18, 29	15, 16, 26
Beauty (cut hair-decrease growth)	20, 21	16, 17, 18	18, 27, 28	24	21, 22	17, 18, 26, 27, 28	14, 15, 24, 25	11, 12, 21, 25, 26	16, 17, 18, 21, 22, 23	14, 15, 19, 20, 21, 22	10, 11, 15, 16, 17, 18	8, 9, 12, 13, 14, 15, 16
Beauty (cut hair-increase growth)	6, 7, 16, 17	3, 4, 5, 12, 13, 14	11, 12	8, 9	5, 6, 7	2, 3, 30	8, 9	4, 5	28, 29	7, 8	3, 4, 31	1, 27, 28, 29
Beauty (remove superfluous hair)	2, 31	27, 28	1, 26, 27, 28			26, 27, 28	24, 25	25, 26	22, 23, 24	20, 21, 22, 23	19	
Brewing (begin process)	25, 26	22, 23	21, 22, 23	17, 18, 26, 27	23, 24	19, 20	16, 17, 26, 27, 28	23, 24	19, 20	16, 17	12, 13, 22, 23	10, 11, 19, 20

Astro Almanac

Activity	Jan.	Feb.	Mar.	Apr.	May	Jun.	Jul.	Aug.	Sep.	Oct.	Nov.	Dec.
Business (bid on contract)	11, 12	11	6, 7	3, 4	4, 30	1, 2, 12, 13	1, 2, 12, 13	8, 9, 10	5	2, 3	29, 30	8
Business (borrow money)	29, 31	2, 7, 15, 25	1, 8, 14	3, 21, 25	9, 22, 27, 28	4, 18, 23, 24	1, 2, 3, 21	17, 18	12	20, 29	8, 25, 26, 27	24, 25
Business (end partnership)		1, 28	28	28, 29, 30	26, 27	23	28, 29	25, 26	21, 22			
Business (form partnership)	14, 15	10, 11	10, 11	6, 7, 15	3, 4, 13, 31	1, 9, 10	6	2, 3, 8	5, 26, 27	2, 3, 4	26, 27	7, 8, 9, 23
Buy animals (household pets)	20, 21, 22	17, 18, 19	16, 17, 18	13, 14	10, 11, 12	6, 7,	3, 4, 5, 31	1, 27, 28, 29	23, 24, 25	21, 22, 23	17, 18, 19	15, 16
Buy animals (horses, cattle)	6, 7, 27, 28	2, 3, 23, 24, 25	2, 3, 4, 22, 23, 29, 31	19, 20, 25, 26, 27	16, 17, 23, 24	13, 14, 15, 19, 20	10, 11, 16, 17, 18	6, 7, 13, 14	2, 3, 4, 9, 10, 30	1, 6, 7, 8, 27, 28	2, 3, 4, 22, 23, 24, 25	1, 21, 22, 27, 28, 29

Astro Almanac

Activity	Jan.	Feb.	Mar.	Apr.	May	Jun.	Jul.	Aug.	Sep.	Oct.	Nov.	Dec.
Buy a house (to live in)	4	1, 2		3, 4	1, 2, 20	29, 30	1, 29, 30	27	25, 26, 27	26		25, 26
Buy real estate (investment)		6	5, 6	1, 2, 14, 15, 16		9, 10	6, 7, 12, 13	2, 3, 8, 9, 10	5, 6, 26, 27	2, 3, 10, 29, 30	5, 6, 26	3, 4, 24, 25, 30, 31
Clothing (buy new)	7, 9, 10, 13, 17, 22, 23	4, 17, 19, 20, 25	5, 8, 13, 16, 19, 23	1, 3, 4, 8, 9, 25	11, 12, 13, 16, 17, 23, 25, 26, 27	2, 3, 9, 10, 17, 18, 29, 30	4, 12, 16, 17, 20, 21, 22, 26	2, 3, 7, 17, 18, 22, 23, 27	13, 14, 15, 27, 28	7, 8, 11, 12, 15, 16, 24	3, 5, 6, 7, 13, 19, 25	1, 6, 11, 15, 21, 27
Clothing (dry clean)	22, 27, 28	17, 18, 23, 24	23, 24, 30, 31	19, 20, 26, 27	16, 17, 23, 24	19, 20, 26, 27, 28	16, 17, 23, 24, 25	13, 14, 20, 21	16, 17, 18, 24, 25	14, 15, 21, 22	10, 11, 17, 18	15, 16
Clothing (sew or repair)	11, 12, 13	7, 8, 9	8, 15, 16	3, 4, 12	7, 9, 11, 12, 13	4, 6, 9, 10	1, 3, 29	2, 3, 27	25, 26, 27	11	7, 8	5, 6
Dental (extract teeth)	14, 21	5, 10, 11	2, 10, 16	6, 14, 25, 26	3, 4, 5, 10, 11, 23, 24	1, 6, 7, 19, 20, 27, 28	4, 5, 17, 18, 24, 25, 31	1, 13, 14, 21, 22, 27, 29	11, 16, 17, 24, 25	7, 8, 14, 15, 22	3, 17, 18, 19	9, 15, 27, 28

Astro Almanac

Activity	Jan.	Feb.	Mar.	Apr.	May	Jun.	Jul.	Aug.	Sep.	Oct.	Nov.	Dec.
Dental (get teeth filled)	25	22, 28	20, 21, 27, 28	17, 18, 23, 24	16, 20, 21	17, 18, 19	14, 15, 28	12, 25, 26	21, 22, 23	19, 20	17, 21, 22	13, 19, 20
Finance (collect money)	29, 31	2, 7, 15, 25	1, 8, 14	3, 21, 25	9, 22, 27, 28	4, 18, 23, 24	1, 2, 3, 21	17, 18	12	20, 29	8, 25, 26, 27	24, 25
Finance (start savings)	3, 11, 29, 30, 31	7, 8, 9, 26	8, 25	3, 4, 5	18, 19, 20	24	13, 21, 22	8, 17, 18, 19	5, 6, 14, 15	2, 3, 11, 12, 29, 30, 31	7, 8, 9, 26	5, 6, 24
Finance (arrange to borrow money)	19, 25, 26, 27.	22, 23	22, 23	18, 19, 23, 24	16, 17, 25	18, 24, 25	15	11, 12, 18	14, 15, 22, 23	20	15, 16, 21, 22	12, 13, 19, 20, 21, 22
Household (buy appliance)	7, 22, 27	6, 11, 25	8, 13, 22, 27	20, 25	6, 11, 25	9, 10, 14, 18, 24	4, 20, 23, 26	2, 17, 22	5, 13, 15, 27	1, 4, 10, 15, 20, 29	19, 21, 29	4, 15, 18, 21, 27
Household (begin a decorating plan)	6, 23, 24	7, 15, 29	3, 9, 18, 25	9, 13, 14	7, 10, 28	3, 8, 20, 28	3, 8, 17, 28	2, 3, 17, 18, 22, 30	1, 6, 16	18, 20, 26	16, 21	5, 11, 16

Astro Almanac

Activity	Jan.	Feb.	Mar.	Apr.	May	Jun.	Jul.	Aug.	Sep.	Oct.	Nov.	Dec.
Household (begin new foundation)	19, 20		25	21, 22	18, 19, 20	15, 16, 17, 18	21, 22, 23	19, 25	21, 22	19, 20, 21	16, 17	
Household (begin new building)	4, 5, 11, 12	1, 2, 8, 9	7, 8, 14, 15	3, 4, 10, 11	1, 9	4, 5	1, 2, 29, 30		7, 8	4, 5, 31	1	5, 6, 13, 14
Household (begin to paint)	4, 5, 19, 24	1, 20	19, 23, 28	12, 16, 24	9, 13, 21	5, 9, 18	7, 15	3, 11, 30	26	5, 20, 24	1, 16, 17, 29	13, 18, 26
Household (begin to remodel)	12, 13, 16, 17	7	6, 8, 13	3, 4, 8, 9, 15	1, 5, 13	3, 9, 10, 30	1, 6	2, 3, 29, 30	26, 27	4, 5, 12	2, 7, 8, 14	5, 6, 9, 26
Household (scrub hardwood floors)	19-24, 27-31	17-20, 23-28	1, 19, 20, 23-28	19-24, 28-30	17-21, 25-31	15-18, 22-28	14, 15, 19-25	12, 16-21, 25-31	12-17, 22-24	11-15, 19-24	9-11, 15-20	8, 13-18
Household (begin to shingle a roof)		25, 26, 27, 28	1, 25, 26, 27, 28	21, 22, 23, 24, 26, 27, 28, 29, 30	19, 20, 21, 22, 25, 26, 27, 27, 28, 29	15, 16, 17, 18, 21, 22, 23, 24, 25	14, 15, 19, 20, 21, 22	15, 16, 17, 18, 19, 25, 26	11, 12, 13, 14, 15, 22, 23	11, 12, 13, 19, 20, 21	15, 16	12, 13, 14

Astro Almanac

Activity	Jan.	Feb.	Mar.	Apr.	May	Jun.	Jul.	Aug.	Sep.	Oct.	Nov.	Dec.
Household (sell items at garage sale)	21, 31	7, 12	22, 23, 27, 28	19, 20, 25, 26	17, 18, 22, 23	19, 20, 26, 27, 28	17, 18, 19, 23, 24, 25, 26	16, 17, 20, 21, 22	10, 11, 12, 13, 18, 19	14, 15, 24, 25	14, 15, 20, 21	
Household (set fence posts)	19, 20	16, 28	1, 27, 28	23, 24	20, 21, 22	17, 18, 24, 25	14, 15, 21, 22	11, 12, 18, 19	14, 15, 22, 23	12, 13, 29, 20	8, 9, 16, 17	13, 14
Personal (break habit)	28, 31	28	1, 28	24, 28, 29	25, 27	22, 27, 28	26	16	22, 23, 24	22, 23	22	20
Personal (entertain friends)	4, 5, 18, 19, 23, 24	1, 2, 15, 16, 19, 20	1, 2, 14, 15, 10, 11	10, 11, 15, 16, 23, 24	8, 9, 12, 13, 20, 21, 22	9, 10, 17, 18	1, 2, 3, 6, 7, 14, 15, 16, 28, 29, 30	2, 3, 10, 11, 12, 25, 26, 29, 30	7, 8, 9, 21, 22, 23, 26, 27	5, 19, 20, 23, 24	1, 2, 16, 17, 20, 21, 28, 29	12, 13, 14, 17, 18, 19, 25, 26, 27
Personal (join club)	4, 5, 18, 19, 23, 24	1, 2, 15, 16, 19, 20	1, 2, 14, 15, 10, 11	10, 11, 15, 16, 23, 24	8, 9, 12, 13, 20, 21, 22	9, 10, 17, 18	1, 2, 3, 6, 7, 14, 15, 16, 28, 29, 30	2, 3, 10, 11, 12, 25, 26, 29, 30	7, 8, 9, 21, 22, 23, 26, 27	5, 19, 20, 23, 24	1, 2, 16, 17, 20, 21, 28, 29	12, 13, 14, 17, 18, 19, 25, 26, 27
Personal (start a diet)	20, 21	16, 17, 18, 26	25, 26	21	18, 19	15, 16	12, 13, 31	25, 27	21, 22, 24	19, 20, 21	15, 16, 17, 18	12, 13, 14, 15

Astro Almanac

Activity	Jan.	Feb.	Mar.	Apr.	May	Jun.	Jul.	Aug.	Sep.	Oct.	Nov.	Dec.
Personal (start investing in stocks)		6	5, 6	1, 2, 14, 15, 16		9, 10	6, 7, 12, 13	2, 3, 8, 9, 10	5, 6, 26, 27	2, 3, 10, 29, 30	5, 6, 26	3, 4, 24, 25, 30, 31
Personal (start a lawsuit)	24, 31	2, 7, 15, 23	1, 8, 14, 15, 16	4, 11, 24, 25	2, 8, 9, 16, 18, 20, 25	13, 20, 22, 27, 30	3, 20, 25	3, 7, 8, 17, 21, 22, 31	14, 18, 19	10, 16, 26, 31	6, 7, 13, 21, 27, 30	5, 11, 12, 19, 21
Personal (begin to train an animal)	20, 21, 22	17, 18, 19	16, 17, 18	13, 14	10, 11, 12	6, 7,	3, 4, 5, 31	1, 27, 28, 29	23, 24, 25	21, 22, 23	17, 18, 19	15, 16
Personal (plan travel by air)		1, 2, 12, 19, 20, 28	1, 9, 19, 20, 21, 27	6, 8, 15, 16, 23, 24	3, 4, 12, 13, 20, 22, 31	1, 9, 10, 17, 18, 28	7, 15, 25	3, 11, 12, 22	18, 27	4, 5, 14, 15, 23, 25	1, 2, 11, 20, 21, 27, 29	18, 25, 26
Personal (plan travel by water)		3, 4, 5, 12, 13, 14	11, 12	8, 9	5, 6, 7	2, 3, 30	8, 9	4, 5	28, 29	7, 8	3, 4, 31	1, 27, 28, 29
Personal (travel by land)		7, 8, 9, 10, 11, 12	7, 8, 10, 11, 15	3, 4, 6, 7, 11	1, 2, 3, 4, 8, 9	1, 4, 6	1, 2, 3	2, 11		4, 5, 31	1, 2, 7, 8, 28, 29	5, 6, 7, 8, 9, 25, 26

Astro Almanac

Activity	Jan.	Feb.	Mar.	Apr.	May	Jun.	Jul.	Aug.	Sep.	Oct.	Nov.	Dec.
Personal (visit doctor or dentist)	14, 15, 20, 21, 27, 28	10, 11, 12, 17, 18, 24, 25	10, 17, 18, 24	6, 7, 13, 14, 19, 20	3, 4, 10, 11, 16, 17, 30, 31	7, 13, 14, 26, 27, 28	4, 5, 11, 12, 24, 25, 26, 31	1, 2, 6, 7, 20, 21, 22, 28, 29	17, 18, 24, 25, 30	1, 14, 15, 22, 23, 27, 28	10, 11, 12, 17, 18, 19, 24, 25	7, 8, 9, 15, 16, 21, 22, 23
Personal (wean children)	27, 28, 29, 30, 31	23, 24, 25, 26, 27, 28, 29	1	23, 24, 25, 26, 27, 28	19, 20, 21, 22, 23, 24	16, 17, 18, 19, 20, 21, 22	14, 15, 16, 17, 18	13, 14, 15	11, 12, 13	10, 11		22
Personal (work as volunteer)	6, 7, 16, 17, 18, 19, 20, 21, 22, 23, 24	13, 14, 15, 16, 17, 18, 19, 20	12, 13, 14, 15, 16, 17, 18, 19, 20	8, 9, 10, 11, 12, 13, 14, 15, 16	5, 6, 7, 8, 9, 10, 11, 12, 13	2, 3, 4, 5, 6, 7, 8, 9, 10, 29, 30	1, 2, 3, 4, 5, 6, 7, 16, 17, 27, 28, 29, 30, 31	1, 2, 3, 4, 11, 12, 13, 14, 23, 24, 25, 26, 27	7, 8, 9, 10, 19, 20, 21, 22, 23, 24, 25, 26, 27	5, 6, 7, 8, 17, 18, 19, 20, 21, 22, 23, 24, 25	1, 2, 3, 4, 5, 14, 15, 16, 17, 18, 19, 20, 21	1, 2, 10, 11, 12, 13, 14, 15, 16, 17, 18, 19
Well (digging)	6, 7, 8	3, 4	2, 3	8, 9	5, 6, 7	2, 3, 29, 30		5, 6	28, 29	25, 26	23, 30	1, 27, 28, 29
Wine (making)	6, 7, 12, 13	3, 4, 8, 9	2, 3, 4, 7, 8, 29, 30	3, 4,	1, 2, 22, 23, 24	19, 20, 24, 25	16, 17, 18, 21, 22	13, 17, 18, 19	9, 10, 14, 15	6, 7, 11, 12, 13	7, 8, 9, 30	1, 2, 5, 6
Wood (cutting)	21, 22, 29, 30, 31	17, 25, 26	26	21, 22, 28, 29	18, 19, 25, 26, 27	15, 16, 21, 22, 23	13, 14, 19, 20	15, 16, 17	24, 25	10, 11, 21, 22	17, 18, 19	15, 16

USING THE MOON TABLES

Timing activities is one of the most important things you can do to ensure their success. In many Eastern countries, timing by the planets is so important that practically no event takes place without first setting up a chart for it. Weddings have occurred in the middle of the night because that was when the influences were best. You may not want to take it that far, but you can still make use of the influences of the Moon whenever possible. It's easy and it works!

In the *Moon Sign Book* you will find the information you need to plan just about any activity: weddings, fishing, making purchases, cutting your hair, traveling, and more. Not all of the things you do will fall on favorable days, but we provide the guidelines you need to pick the best day out of the several from which you have to choose. The primary method in the *Moon Sign Book* for choosing your own

dates is to use the Moon Tables that begin on page 34. Following are instructions, examples, and directions on how to read the Moon Tables; and more advanced information on using the tables containing the lunar aspectarian and favorable and unfavorable days (found on odd numbered pages opposite the Moon Tables), Moon void-of-course, and retrograde information to choose the dates that are best for you personally.

To enhance your understanding of the directions given below, we highly recommend that you read the sections of this book called About Almanacs on page 7, Understanding Lunar Astrology on page 9, Retrogrades on page 15, and Moon Void-of-Course on page 58. It's not essential that you read these before you try the examples below, but reading them will deepen your understanding of the date-choosing process.

The Five Basic Steps

Step 1: Directions for Choosing Dates

Look up the directions for choosing dates for the activity that you wish to begin. The directions are listed at the beginning of the following sections of this book: Home, Health, & Beauty; Leisure & Recreation; Business & Legal; and Farm, Garden, & Weather. Check the Table of Contents to see in what section the directions for your specific activity are listed. The activities contained in each section are listed after the name of the section in the Table of Contents. For example, directions for choosing a good day for canning are listed in the Home, Health, & Beauty Section, and directions for choosing a good day to meet a new friend are in the Leisure Section. Read the directions for your activity, then go to step 2.

Step 2: Check the Moon Tables

You'll find two tables for each month of the year beginning on page 34. The Moon Tables on the left-hand pages include the day and date, the sign the Moon is in, the element of that sign, the nature of the sign, the Moon's phase, and the times that it changes sign or phase. If there is a time listed after a date, that time is the time when the Moon moves into that zodiac sign. Until then, the Moon is considered to be in the sign for the previous day.

The abbreviation *Full* signifies Full Moon and *New* signifies New Moon. The times listed directly after the abbreviation are the times when the Moon changes sign. The times listed after the phase indicate when the Moon changes phase.

If you know the month you would like to begin your activity, turn directly to that month. You will be using the Moon's sign and phase information most often when you begin choosing your own dates. All times are listed in Eastern Standard Time (EST). Use the Time Zone Conversions chart and table on page 16–17 to convert time to your own time zone.

When you have found some dates that meet the criteria for the correct Moon phase and sign for your activity, you may have completed the process. For certain simple activities, such as getting a haircut, the phase and sign information is all that is needed. If the directions for your activity include information on certain lunar aspects, however, you should consult the Lunar Aspectarian. An example of this would be if the directions told you not to perform a certain activity when the Moon is square (Q) Jupiter.

Step 3: Check the Lunar Aspectarian

On the pages opposite the Moon Tables you will find tables containing the lunar aspectarians and favorable and unfavorable days. The lunar aspectarian gives the aspects (or angles) of the Moon to the other planets. In a nutshell, it tells where the Moon is in relation to the other planets in the sky. Some placements of the Moon in relation to other planets are favorable, while others are not. To use the lunar aspectarian, which is the left half of this table, find the planet that the directions list as favorable for your activity, and run down the column to the date desired. For example, the Health & Beauty section says that you should avoid aspects to Mars if you are planning surgery. You would look for Mars across the top and then run down that column looking for days where there are no aspects to Mars (as signified by empty boxes). If you want to find a favorable aspect (sextile [X] or trine [T]) to Mercury, run your finger down the column under Mercury until you find an X or T. Adverse aspects to planets are squares [Q] or oppositions [O]. A conjunction [C] is sometimes beneficial, sometimes not, depending on the activity or planets involved.

Step 4: Favorable and Unfavorable Days

The tables listing favorable and unfavorable days are helpful in choosing your personal best dates, because they consider your Sun sign. All Sun signs are listed on the right half of the tables. Once you have determined which days meet the criteria for phase, sign, and aspects for your activity, you can determine whether or not those days are positive for you. To find out if a day is positive for you, find your Sun sign and then look down the column. If it is marked F, it is very favorable. If it is marked f, it is slightly favorable; U is very unfavorable; and u means slightly unfavorable. Once you have selected good dates for the activity you are about to begin, you can go straight to the examples section beginning on the next page. If you are up to the challenge, though, and would like to learn how to fine-tune your selections even further, read on.

Step 5: Void-of-Course Moon and Retrogrades

This last step is perhaps the most advanced portion of the procedure. It is generally considered poor timing to make decisions, sign important papers, or start special activities during a Moon void-of-course period or during a Mercury retrograde. Once you have chosen the best date for your activity based on steps one through four, you can check the Void-of-Course Table, beginning on page 59, to find out if any of the dates you have chosen have void periods.

The Moon is said to be void-of-course after it has made its last aspect to a planet within a particular sign, but before it has moved into the next sign. Put simply, the Moon is "resting" during the void-of-course period, so activities initiated at this time generally don't come to fruition. You will notice that there are many void periods during the year, and it is nearly impossible to avoid all of them. Some people choose to ignore these altogether and do not take them into consideration when planning activities.

Next, you can check the Table of Retrograde Periods on page 15 to see what planets are retrograde during your chosen date(s).

A planet is said to be retrograde when it appears to move backward in the sky as viewed from the Earth. Generally, the farther a planet is away from the Sun, the longer it can stay retrograde. Some planets will retrograde for several months at a time. Avoiding retrogrades is not as important in lunar planning as avoiding the Moon void-of-course, with the exception of the planet Mercury.

Mercury rules thought and communication, so it is advisable not to sign important papers, initiate important business or legal work, or make crucial decisions during these times. As with the Moon void-of-course, it is difficult to avoid all planetary retrogrades when beginning events, and you may choose to ignore this step of the process. Following are some examples using some or all of the steps outlined above.

Using What You've Learned

Let's say you need to make an appointment to have your hair cut. Your hair is thin and you would like it to look thicker. You look in the Table of Contents to find the section of the book with directions for hair care. You find that it is in the Home, Health, & Beauty section. Turning to that section you see that for thicker hair you should cut hair while the Moon is Full and in the sign of Taurus, Cancer, or Leo. You should avoid the Moon in Aries, Gemini, or Virgo. We'll say that it is the month of January. Look up January in the Moon Tables (page 34). The Full Moon falls on January 18 at 5:48 pm. The Moon moves into the sign of Leo January 18 at 9:29 am, and remains in Leo until January 20 at 1:32 pm, so January 18 meets both the phase and sign criteria.

Let's move on to a more difficult example using the sign and phase of the Moon. You want to buy a permanent home. After checking the Table of Contents and finding the house purchasing instructions located in the Home, Health, & Beauty section under "House Purchasing," you'll read that it says you should buy a home when the Moon is in Taurus, Cancer, or Leo. You need to get a loan, so you should also look in the Business & Legal section under "Loans." Here it says that the third and fourth Moon quarters favor the borrower (you). You are going to buy the house in June. Look up June in the Moon Tables. The Moon is in the third quarter June 14–20, the fourth quarter June 21–28. The Moon is in Taurus from 10:15 pm EST on June 23 until 11:13 am on June 26. The best days for obtaining a loan would be June 23–26, while the Moon is in Taurus.

Just match up the best signs and phases (quarters) to come up with the best dates. With all activities, be sure to check the Favorable and Unfavorable Days for your Sun sign in the table adjoining the Lunar Aspectarian. If there is a choice between several dates, pick the one most favorable for you (marked F under your Sun sign). Because buying a home is an important business decision, you may also wish to see if there are Moon voids or a Mercury retrograde during these dates.

Now let's look at an example that uses signs, phases, and aspects. Our example this time is starting new home construction. We will use March as the example month. Look in the Home, Health, & Beauty section under "Building." It says that the Moon should be in the first quarter of the fixed sign of Taurus or Leo. You should select a time when the Moon is not making unfavorable aspects to Saturn. (Good aspects are sextiles and trines, marked X and T. Conjunctions are usually considered good if they are not conjunctions to Mars, Saturn, or Neptune.) Look in the March Moon Table. You will see that the Moon is in the first quarter March 2–10. The Moon is in Taurus between 8:36 pm EST on March 6 and 9:38 am on March 9. Now, look to the lunar aspectarian for March (page 39). We see that there are no squares or oppositions to Saturn on March 6–8. In addition, there are no negative aspects to Mars on these dates. If you wanted to start building your house in March, the best dates would be March 6–8.

Use Common Sense

Some activities depend on outside factors. Obviously, you can't go out and plant when there is a foot of snow on the ground. You should adjust to the conditions at hand. If the weather was bad during the first quarter, when it was best to plant crops, do it during the second quarter while the Moon is in a fruitful sign. If the Moon is not in a fruitful sign during the first or second quarter, choose a day when it is in a semi-fruitful sign. The best advice is to choose either the sign or phase that is most favorable when the two don't coincide.

To Summarize

In order to make the most of your activities, check with the *Moon Sign Book*. First, look up the activity under the proper heading, then look for the information given in the tables (the Moon Tables, lunar aspectarian, or favorable and unfavorable days). Choose the best date considering the number of positive factors in effect. If most of the dates are favorable, there is no problem choosing the one that will fit your schedule. However, if there aren't any really good dates, pick the ones with the least number of negative influences.

Please keep in mind that the information found here applies in the broadest sense to the events you want to plan or are considering. To be the most effective, when you use electional astrology, you should also consider your own birth chart in relation to a chart drawn for the time or times you have under consideration.

Due to the general nature of this information, we do not guarantee any specific outcomes.

If you do not have a copy of your birth chart, you can obtain one by calling or writing Llewellyn's Customer Service at the address listed, or by going to Llewellyn's On Line Bookstore at www.llewellyn.com, and selecting "Astrological Readings." There is a shipping and handling charge. You can also go to www.astro.com to obtain a free chart.

Call Llewellyn's Customer Service at 1-800-843-6666 ext. 8345, or write to P.O. Box 64383, St. Paul, MN 55164-0383

January Moon Table

Date	Sign	Element	Nature	Phase
1 Wed. 6:42 pm	Capricorn	Earth	Semi-fruitful	4th
2 Thu.	Capricorn	Earth	Semi-fruitful	New 3:23 pm
3 Fri. 10:56 pm	Aquarius	Air	Barren	1st
4 Sat.	Aquarius	Air	Barren	1st
5 Sun.	Aquarius	Air	Barren	1st
6 Mon. 5:57 am	Pisces	Water	Fruitful	1st
7 Tue.	Pisces	Water	Fruitful	1st
8 Wed. 4:15 pm	Aries	Fire	Barren	1st
9 Thu.	Aries	Fire	Barren	1st
10 Fri.	Aries	Fire	Barren	2nd 8:15 am
11 Sat. 4:48 am	Taurus	Earth	Semi-fruitful	2nd
12 Sun.	Taurus	Earth	Semi-fruitful	2nd
13 Mon. 5:08 pm	Gemini	Air	Barren	2nd
14 Tue.	Gemini	Air	Barren	2nd
15 Wed.	Gemini	Air	Barren	2nd
16 Thu. 2:56 am	Cancer	Water	Fruitful	2nd
17 Fri.	Cancer	Water	Fruitful	2nd
18 Sat. 9:29 am	Leo	Fire	Barren	Full 5:48 am
19 Sun.	Leo	Fire	Barren	3rd
20 Mon. 1:32 pm	Virgo	Earth	Barren	3rd
21 Tue.	Virgo	Earth	Barren	3rd
22 Wed. 4:23 pm	Libra	Air	Semi-fruitful	3rd
23 Thu.	Libra	Air	Semi-fruitful	3rd
24 Fri. 7:09 pm	Scorpio	Water	Fruitful	3rd
25 Sat.	Scorpio	Water	Fruitful	4th 3:33 am
26 Sun. 10:26 pm	Sagittarius	Fire	Barren	4th
27 Mon.	Sagittarius	Fire	Barren	4th
28 Tue.	Sagittarius	Fire	Barren	4th
29 Wed. 2:30 am	Capricorn	Earth	Semi-fruitful	4th
30 Thu.	Capricorn	Earth	Semi-fruitful	4th
31 Fri. 7:44 am	Aquarius	Air	Barren	4th

January

Lunar Aspectarian   **Favorable and Unfavorable Days**

	Sun	Mercury	Venus	Mars	Jupiter	Saturn	Uranus	Neptune	Pluto	Aries	Taurus	Gemini	Cancer	Leo	Virgo	Libra	Scorpio	Sagittarius	Capricorn	Aquarius	Pisces
1						O	X			f		U		f	u	f		F		f	u
2	C									u	f		U		f	u	f		F		f
3		C	X	X						u	f		U		f	u	f		F		f
4								C		f	u	f		U		f	u	f		F	
5				Q	O	T	C		X	f	u	f		U		f	u	f		F	
6			Q							f	u	f		U		f	u	f		F	
7	X							Q		f	u	f		U		f	u	f			F
8		X	T	T		Q				f	u	f		U		f	u	f			F
9					T			X		F		f	u	f		U		f	u	f	
10	Q	Q			T	X	X		T	F		f	u	f		U		f	u	f	
11								Q		F		f	u	f		U		f	u	f	
12	T	T			Q			Q			F		f	u	f		U		f	u	f
13	T			O			Q				F		f	u	f		U		f	u	f
14			O		X			T		f		F		f	u	f		U		f	u
15						C	T		O	f		F		f	u	f		U		f	u
16										u	f		F		f	u	f		U		f
17		O								u	f		F		f	u	f		U		f
18	O			T						u	f		F		f	u	f		U		f
19			T		C	X		O	T	f	u	f		F		f	u	f		U	
20				Q		X	O			f	u	f		F		f	u	f		U	
21		T	Q						Q	f	u	f		F		f	u	f			U
22	T			X		Q				f	u	f		F		f	u	f			U
23		Q	X	X				T	X	U		f	u	f		F		f	u	f	
24						T	T		X	U		f	u	f		F		f	u	f	
25	Q	X			Q			Q			U		f	u	f		F		f	u	f
26								Q			U		f	u	f		F		f	u	f
27	X			C	T			X		f		U		f	u	f		F		f	u
28		C				O	X		C	f		U		f	u	f		F		f	u
29										u	f		U		f	u	f		F		f
30		C								u	f		U		f	u	f		F		f
31				X						u	f		U		f	u	f		F		f

February Moon Table

Date	Sign	Element	Nature	Phase
1 Sat.	Aquarius	Air	Barren	New 5:48 am
2 Sun. 2:55 pm	Pisces	Water	Fruitful	1st
3 Mon.	Pisces	Water	Fruitful	1st
4 Tue.	Pisces	Water	Fruitful	1st
5 Wed. 12:44 am	Aries	Fire	Barren	1st
6 Thu.	Aries	Fire	Barren	1st
7 Fri. 12:59 pm	Taurus	Earth	Semi-fruitful	1st
8 Sat.	Taurus	Earth	Semi-fruitful	1st
9 Sun.	Taurus	Earth	Semi-fruitful	2nd 6:11 am
10 Mon. 1:45 am	Gemini	Air	Barren	2nd
11 Tue.	Gemini	Air	Barren	2nd
12 Wed. 12:19 pm	Cancer	Water	Fruitful	2nd
13 Thu.	Cancer	Water	Fruitful	2nd
14 Fri. 7:04 pm	Leo	Fire	Barren	2nd
15 Sat.	Leo	Fire	Barren	2nd
16 Sun. 10:22 pm	Virgo	Earth	Barren	Full 6:51 pm
17 Mon.	Virgo	Earth	Barren	3rd
18 Tue. 11:48 pm	Libra	Air	Semi-fruitful	3rd
19 Wed.	Libra	Air	Semi-fruitful	3rd
20 Thu.	Libra	Air	Semi-fruitful	3rd
21 Fri. 1:09 am	Scorpio	Water	Fruitful	3rd
22 Sat.	Scorpio	Water	Fruitful	3rd
23 Sun. 3:46 am	Sagittarius	Fire	Barren	4th 11:46 am
24 Mon.	Sagittarius	Fire	Barren	4th
25 Tue. 8:11 am	Capricorn	Earth	Semi-fruitful	4th
26 Wed.	Capricorn	Earth	Semi-fruitful	4th
27 Thu. 2:24 pm	Aquarius	Air	Barren	4th
28 Fri.	Aquarius	Air	Barren	4th

February

Lunar Aspectarian   **Favorable and Unfavorable Days**

Day	Sun	Mercury	Venus	Mars	Jupiter	Saturn	Uranus	Neptune	Pluto	Aries	Taurus	Gemini	Cancer	Leo	Virgo	Libra	Scorpio	Sagittarius	Capricorn	Aquarius	Pisces
1	C			X	0	T		C	X	f	u	f		U		f	u	f		F	
2			X			T	C			f	u	f		U		f	u	f		F	
3				Q							f	u	f		U		f	u	f		F
4		X	Q			Q			Q		f	u	f		U		f	u	f		F
5			Q	T	T			X		F		f	u	f		U		f	u	f	
6	X	Q		T	T	X		T		F		f	u	f		U		f	u	f	
7			T					X		F		f	u	f		U		f	u	f	
8					Q			Q			F		f	u	f		U		f	u	f
9	Q	T						Q			F		f	u	f		U		f	u	f
10				X			T			f		F		f	u	f		U		f	u
11	T			0	X	C		0		f		F		f	u	f		U		f	u
12						T				f		F		f	u	f		U		f	u
13			0							u	f		F		f	u	f		U		f
14		0								u	f		F		f	u	f		U		f
15		0		C				0		f	u	f		F		f	u	f		U	
16	0			T	X	0		T		f	u	f		F		f	u	f		U	
17			T								f	u	f		F		f	u	f		U
18			T	Q	Q			Q			f	u	f		F		f	u	f		U
19		T			X			T		U		f	u	f		F		f	u	f	
20			Q	X		T	T	X		U		f	u	f		F		f	u	f	
21	T	Q			Q			Q			U		f	u	f		F		f	u	f
22			X			Q					U		f	u	f		F		f	u	f
23	Q				T	Q	X				U		f	u	f		F		f	u	f
24		X		C	0			C		f		U		f	u	f		F		f	u
25	X					X				f		U		f	u	f		F		f	u
26										u	f		U		f	u	f		F		f
27			C							u	f		U		f	u	f		F		f
28					0			C		f	u	f		U		f	u	f		F	

March Moon Table

Date	Sign	Element	Nature	Phase
1 Sat. 10:26 pm	Pisces	Water	Fruitful	4th
2 Sun.	Pisces	Water	Fruitful	New 9:35 pm
3 Mon.	Pisces	Water	Fruitful	1st
4 Tue. 8:30 am	Aries	Fire	Barren	1st
5 Wed.	Aries	Fire	Barren	1st
6 Thu. 8:36 pm	Taurus	Earth	Semi-fruitful	1st
7 Fri.	Taurus	Earth	Semi-fruitful	1st
8 Sat.	Taurus	Earth	Semi-fruitful	1st
9 Sun. 9:38 am	Gemini	Air	Barren	1st
10 Mon.	Gemini	Air	Barren	1st
11 Tue. 9:12 pm	Cancer	Water	Fruitful	2nd 2:15 am
12 Wed.	Cancer	Water	Fruitful	2nd
13 Thu.	Cancer	Water	Fruitful	2nd
14 Fri. 5:06 am	Leo	Fire	Barren	2nd
15 Sat.	Leo	Fire	Barren	2nd
16 Sun. 8:52 am	Virgo	Earth	Barren	2nd
17 Mon.	Virgo	Earth	Barren	2nd
18 Tue. 9:43 am	Libra	Air	Semi-fruitful	Full 5:35 am
19 Wed.	Libra	Air	Semi-fruitful	3rd
20 Thu. 9:38 am	Scorpio	Water	Fruitful	3rd
21 Fri.	Scorpio	Water	Fruitful	3rd
22 Sat.10:33 am	Sagittarius	Fire	Barren	3rd
23 Sun.	Sagittarius	Fire	Barren	3rd
24 Mon.1:48 pm	Capricorn	Earth	Semi-fruitful	4th 8:51 pm
25 Tue.	Capricorn	Earth	Semi-fruitful	4th
26 Wed. 7:51pm	Aquarius	Air	Barren	4th
27 Thu.	Aquarius	Air	Barren	4th
28 Fri.	Aquarius	Air	Barren	4th
29 Sat. 4:26 am	Pisces	Water	Fruitful	4th
30 Sun.	Pisces	Water	Fruitful	4th
31 Mon. 3:04pm	Aries	Fire	Barren	4th

March

Lunar Aspectarian   **Favorable and Unfavorable Days**

Day	Sun	Mercury	Venus	Mars	Jupiter	Saturn	Uranus	Neptune	Pluto	Aries	Taurus	Gemini	Cancer	Leo	Virgo	Libra	Scorpio	Sagittarius	Capricorn	Aquarius	Pisces
1		C		X		T	C		X	f	u	f		U		f	u	f		F	
2	C										f	u	f		U		f	u	f		F
3						Q			Q		f	u	f		U		f	u	f		F
4			X	Q							f	u	f		U		f	u	f		F
5					T			X	T	F		f	u	f		U		f	u	f	
6				T		X	X		T	F		f	u	f		U		f	u	f	
7		X	Q		Q			Q		F		f	u	f		U		f	u	f	
8	X									F		f	u	f		U		f	u	f	
9								Q		F		f	u	f		U		f	u	f	
10	Q	Q	T		X			T	0		F		f	u	f		U		f	u	f
11	Q					C	T		0		F		f	u	f		U		f	u	f
12		T		0						f		F		f	u	f		U		f	u
13	T	T								f		F		f	u	f		U		f	u
14					C			0		f		F		f	u	f		U		f	u
15			0		X			0	T	u	f		F		f	u	f		U		f
16				T				0		u	f		F		f	u	f		U		f
17		0				Q			Q	f	u	f		F		f	u	f		U	
18	0			Q	X					f	u	f		F		f	u	f		U	
19			T	Q		T		T	X	U		f	u	f		F		f	u	f	
20				X	Q	T				U		f	u	f		F		f	u	f	
21			Q	X				Q			U		f	u	f		F		f	u	f
22	T	T			T			Q			U		f	u	f		F		f	u	f
23					T	0		X	C	f		U		f	u	f		F		f	u
24	Q		X			0	X			f		U		f	u	f		F		f	u
25		Q		C						u	f		U		f	u	f		F		f
26										u	f		U		f	u	f		F		f
27	X	X			0			C		f	u	f		U		f	u	f		F	
28						T			X	f	u	f		U		f	u	f		F	
29			C				C			f	u	f		U		f	u	f		F	
30				X	Q				Q		f	u	f		U		f	u	f		F
31						Q					f	u	f		U		f	u	f		F

April Moon Table

Date	Sign	Element	Nature	Phase
1 Tue.	Aries	Fire	Barren	New 2:19 pm
2 Wed.	Aries	Fire	Barren	1st
3 Thu. 3:20 am	Taurus	Earth	Semi-fruitful	1st
4 Fri.	Taurus	Earth	Semi-fruitful	1st
5 Sat. 4:24 pm	Gemini	Air	Barren	1st
6 Sun.	Gemini	Air	Barren	1st
7 Mon.	Gemini	Air	Barren	1st
8 Tue. 4:36 am	Cancer	Water	Fruitful	1st
9 Wed.	Cancer	Water	Fruitful	2nd 6:40 pm
10 Thu. 1:54 pm	Leo	Fire	Barren	2nd
11 Fri.	Leo	Fire	Barren	2nd
12 Sat. 7:07 pm	Virgo	Earth	Barren	2nd
13 Sun.	Virgo	Earth	Barren	2nd
14 Mon. 8:42 pm	Libra	Air	Semi-fruitful	2nd
15 Tue.	Libra	Air	Semi-fruitful	2nd
16 Wed. 8:16 pm	Scorpio	Water	Fruitful	Full 2:36 pm
17 Thu.	Scorpio	Water	Fruitful	3rd
18 Fri. 7:51 pm	Sagittarius	Fire	Barren	3rd
19 Sat.	Sagittarius	Fire	Barren	3rd
20 Sun. 9:20 pm	Capricorn	Earth	Semi-fruitful	3rd
21 Mon.	Capricorn	Earth	Semi-fruitful	3rd
22 Tue.	Capricorn	Earth	Semi-fruitful	3rd
23 Wed. 1:58 am	Aquarius	Air	Barren	4th 7:18 am
24 Thu.	Aquarius	Air	Barren	4th
25 Fri. 10:02 am	Pisces	Water	Fruitful	4th
26 Sat.	Pisces	Water	Fruitful	4th
27 Sun. 8:54 pm	Aries	Fire	Barren	4th
28 Mon.	Aries	Fire	Barren	4th
29 Tue.	Aries	Fire	Barren	4th
30 Wed. 9:26 am	Taurus	Earth	Semi-fruitful	4th

April

Lunar Aspectarian **Favorable and Unfavorable Days**

	Sun	Mercury	Venus	Mars	Jupiter	Saturn	Uranus	Neptune	Pluto	Aries	Taurus	Gemini	Cancer	Leo	Virgo	Libra	Scorpio	Sagittarius	Capricorn	Aquarius	Pisces
1	C			Q	T			X		F		f	u	f		U		f	u	f	
2		C		Q		X			T	F		f	u	f		U		f	u	f	
3			X		Q		X			F		f	u	f		U		f	u	f	
4				T				Q			F		f	u	f		U		f	u	f
5						Q					F		f	u	f		U		f	u	f
6	X		Q		X			T		f		F	f	u	f			U		f	u
7	X					C			O	f		F	f	u	f			U		f	u
8		X					T			f		F	f	u	f			U		f	u
9	Q		T	O						u	f		F	f	u	f			U		f
10				O						u	f		F	f	u	f			U		f
11		Q				C		O	T	f	u	f		F	f	u	f		U		
12	T					X	O		T	f	u	f		F	f	u	f		U		
13		T									f	u	f		F	f	u	f			U
14			O	T		Q			Q		f	u	f		F	f	u	f			U
15						X		T		U		f	u	f	F		f	u	f		
16	O			Q		T	T		X	U		f	u	f	F		f	u	f		
17		O			Q			Q			U		f	u	f	F		f	u	f	
18			T	X				Q			U		f	u	f	F		f	u	f	
19					T			X		f		U	f	u	f		F		f		u
20	T		Q			O	X		C	f		U	f	u	f		F		f		u
21							X			u	f		U	f	u	f		F			f
22		T								u	f		U	f	u	f		F			f
23	Q		X	C	O			C		f	u	f		U	f	u	f		F		
24		Q				T		C	X	f	u	f		U	f	u	f		F		
25	X					T	C			f	u	f		U	f	u	f		F		
26		X							Q		f		u	f		U		f	u	f	F
27		X				Q			Q		f		u	f		U		f	u	f	F
28			C	X	T			X		F		f	u	f		U		f	u	f	
29						X			T	F		f	u	f		U		f	u	f	
30				Q		X	X			F		f	u	f		U		f	u	f	

May Moon Table

Date	Sign	Element	Nature	Phase
1 Thu.	Taurus	Earth	Semi-fruitful	New 7:15 am
2 Fri. 10:27 pm	Gemini	Air	Barren	1st
3 Sat.	Gemini	Air	Barren	1st
4 Sun.	Gemini	Air	Barren	1st
5 Mon. 10:42 am	Cancer	Water	Fruitful	1st
6 Tue.	Cancer	Water	Fruitful	1st
7 Wed. 8:46 pm	Leo	Fire	Barren	1st
8 Thu.	Leo	Fire	Barren	1st
9 Fri.	Leo	Fire	Barren	2nd 6:53 am
10 Sat. 3:31 am	Virgo	Earth	Barren	2nd
11 Sun.	Virgo	Earth	Barren	2nd
12 Mon. 6:42 am	Libra	Air	Semi-fruitful	2nd
13 Tue.	Libra	Air	Semi-fruitful	2nd
14 Wed. 7:14 am	Scorpio	Water	Fruitful	2nd
15 Thu.	Scorpio	Water	Fruitful	Full 10:36 pm
16 Fri. 6:43 am	Sagittarius	Fire	Barren	3rd
17 Sat.	Sagittarius	Fire	Barren	3rd
18 Sun. 7:03 am	Capricorn	Earth	Semi-fruitful	3rd
19 Mon.	Capricorn	Earth	Semi-fruitful	3rd
20 Tue. 10:01 am	Aquarius	Air	Barren	3rd
21 Wed.	Aquarius	Air	Barren	3rd
22 Thu. 4:41 pm	Pisces	Water	Fruitful	4th 7:31 pm
23 Fri.	Pisces	Water	Fruitful	4th
24 Sat.	Pisces	Water	Fruitful	4th
25 Sun. 2:59 am	Aries	Fire	Barren	4th
26 Mon.	Aries	Fire	Barren	4th
27 Tue. 3:32 pm	Taurus	Earth	Semi-fruitful	4th
28 Wed.	Taurus	Earth	Semi-fruitful	4th
29 Thu.	Taurus	Earth	Semi-fruitful	4th
30 Fri. 4:32 am	Gemini	Air	Barren	1st 11:20 pm
31 Sat.	Gemini	Air	Barren	1st

May

Lunar Aspectarian **Favorable and Unfavorable Days**

	Sun	Mercury	Venus	Mars	Jupiter	Saturn	Uranus	Neptune	Pluto	Aries	Taurus	Gemini	Cancer	Leo	Virgo	Libra	Scorpio	Sagittarius	Capricorn	Aquarius	Pisces
1	C	C			Q			Q			F		f	u	f		U		f	u	f
2		C									F		f	u	f		U		f	u	f
3				T	X			Q	T	f		F		f	u	f		U		f	u
4			X					T	0	f		F		f	u	f		U		f	u
5						C	T			f		F		f	u	f		U		f	u
6	X	X	Q							u	f		F		f	u	f		U		f
7										u	f		F		f	u	f		U		f
8		Q		0	C			0		f	u	f		F		f	u	f		U	
9	Q	Q	T			X			T	f	u	f		F		f	u	f		U	
10								0		f	u	f		F		f	u	f		U	
11	T	T				Q			Q		f	u	f		F		f	u	f		U
12				X	Q						f	u	f		F		f	u	f		U
13				T				T	X	U		f	u	f		F		f	u	f	
14		0	0		Q	T	T			U		f	u	f		F		f	u	f	
15	0	0		Q				Q			U		f	u	f		F		f	u	f
16						T		Q			U		f	u	f		F		f	u	f
17				X				X	C	f		U		f	u	f		F		f	u
18		T	T			0	X			f		U		f	u	f		F		f	u
19		T								u	f		U		f	u	f		F		f
20	T		Q							u	f		U		f	u	f		F		f
21		Q		C	0			C	X	f	u	f		U		f	u	f		F	
22	Q					T	C			f	u	f		U		f	u	f		F	
23		X	X								f	u	f		U		f	u	f		F
24						Q			Q		f	u	f		U		f	u	f		F
25	X				T	Q				F		f	u	f		U		f	u	f	
26				X	T			X	T	F		f	u	f		U		f	u	f	
27						X	X			F		f	u	f		U		f	u	f	
28		C	C		Q			Q			F		f	u	f		U		f	u	f
29			Q								F		f	u	f		U		f	u	f
30	C							Q			F		f	u	f		U		f	u	f
31				T	X			T	0	f		F		f	u	f		U		f	u

June Moon Table

Date	Sign	Element	Nature	Phase
1 Sun. 4:27 pm	Cancer	Water	Fruitful	1st
2 Mon.	Cancer	Water	Fruitful	1st
3 Tue.	Cancer	Water	Fruitful	1st
4 Wed. 2:25 am	Leo	Fire	Barren	1st
5 Thu.	Leo	Fire	Barren	1st
6 Fri. 9:51 am	Virgo	Earth	Barren	1st
7 Sat.	Virgo	Earth	Barren	2nd 3:28 pm
8 Sun. 2:30 pm	Libra	Air	Semi-fruitful	2nd
9 Mon.	Libra	Air	Semi-fruitful	2nd
10 Tue. 4:39 pm	Scorpio	Water	Fruitful	2nd
11 Wed.	Scorpio	Water	Fruitful	2nd
12 Thu. 5:12 pm	Sagittarius	Fire	Barren	2nd
13 Fri.	Sagittarius	Fire	Barren	2nd
14 Sat. 5:38 pm	Capricorn	Earth	Semi-fruitful	Full 6:16 am
15 Sun.	Capricorn	Earth	Semi-fruitful	3rd
16 Mon. 7:41 pm	Aquarius	Air	Barren	3rd
17 Tue.	Aquarius	Air	Barren	3rd
18 Wed.	Aquarius	Air	Barren	3rd
19 Thu. 12:57am	Pisces	Water	Fruitful	3rd
20 Fri.	Pisces	Water	Fruitful	3rd
21 Sat. 10:06 am	Aries	Fire	Barren	4th 9:45 am
22 Sun.	Aries	Fire	Barren	4th
23 Mon. 10:15 pm	Taurus	Earth	Semi-fruitful	4th
24 Tue.	Taurus	Earth	Semi-fruitful	4th
25 Wed.	Taurus	Earth	Semi-fruitful	4th
26 Thu. 11:13 am	Gemini	Air	Barren	4th
27 Fri.	Gemini	Air	Barren	4th
28 Sat. 10:52 pm	Cancer	Water	Fruitful	4th
29 Sun.	Cancer	Water	Fruitful	New 1:39 pm
30 Mon.	Cancer	Water	Fruitful	1st

June

Lunar Aspectarian | **Favorable and Unfavorable Days**

	Sun	Mercury	Venus	Mars	Jupiter	Saturn	Uranus	Neptune	Pluto	Aries	Taurus	Gemini	Cancer	Leo	Virgo	Libra	Scorpio	Sagittarius	Capricorn	Aquarius	Pisces
1				T		C	T			f		F		f	u	f		U		f	u
2						·				u	f		F		f	u	f		U		f
3		X	X							u	f		F		f	u	f		U		f
4								0		f	u	f		F		f	u	f		U	
5	X	Q	Q	0	C			0	T	f	u	f		F		f	u	f		U	
6			Q	0			X	0		f	u	f		F		f	u	f		U	
7	Q								Q	f	u	f		F		f	u	f			U
8		T	T			Q				f	u	f		F		f	u	f			U
9	T				X			T	X	U		f	u	f		F		f	u	f	
10				T		T	T			U		f	u	f		F		f	u	f	
11				Q				Q			U		f	u	f		F		f	u	f
12		0	0	Q		Q					U		f	u	f		F		f	u	f
13				T			X	C		f		U		f	u	f		F		f	u
14	0			X		0	X			f		U		f	u	f		F		f	u
15										u	f		U		f	u	f		F		f
16										u	f		U		f	u	f		F		f
17		T	T		0			C		f	u	f		U		f	u	f		F	
18	T			C				X		f	u	f		U		f	u	f		F	
19		Q	Q	C		T	C				f	u	f		U		f	u	f		F
20								Q			f	u	f		U		f	u	f		F
21	Q					Q					f	u	f		U		f	u	f		F
22		X	X		T			X	T	F		f	u	f		U		f	u	f	
23										F		f	u	f		U		f	u	f	
24	X			X		X	X	Q			F		f	u	f		U		f	u	f
25				Q			Q				F		f	u	f		U		f	u	f
26			Q			Q					F		f	u	f		U		f	u	f
27				X				T	0	f		F		f	u	f		U		f	u
28		C	C							f		F		f	u	f		U		f	u
29	C			T		C	T			u	f		F		f	u	f		U		f
30										u	f		F		f	u	f		U		f

July Moon Table

Date	Sign	Element	Nature	Phase
1 Tue. 8:13 am	Leo	Fire	Barren	1st
2 Wed.	Leo	Fire	Barren	1st
3 Thu. 3:16 pm	Virgo	Earth	Barren	1st
4 Fri.	Virgo	Earth	Barren	1st
5 Sat. 8:20 pm	Libra	Air	Semi-fruitful	1st
6 Sun.	Libra	Air	Semi-fruitful	2nd 9:32 pm
7 Mon. 11:43 pm	Scorpio	Water	Fruitful	2nd
8 Tue.	Scorpio	Water	Fruitful	2nd
9 Wed.	Scorpio	Water	Fruitful	2nd
10 Thu. 1:48 am	Sagittarius	Fire	Barren	2nd
11 Fri.	Sagittarius	Fire	Barren	2nd
12 Sat. 3:21 am	Capricorn	Earth	Semi-fruitful	2nd
13 Sun.	Capricorn	Earth	Semi-fruitful	Full 2:21 pm
14 Mon. 5:38 am	Aquarius	Air	Barren	3rd
15 Tue.	Aquarius	Air	Barren	3rd
16 Wed. 10:14 am	Pisces	Water	Fruitful	3rd
17 Thu.	Pisces	Water	Fruitful	3rd
18 Fri. 6:20 pm	Aries	Fire	Barren	3rd
19 Sat.	Aries	Fire	Barren	3rd
20 Sun.	Aries	Fire	Barren	3rd
21 Mon. 5:48 am	Taurus	Earth	Semi-fruitful	4th 2:01 am
22 Tue.	Taurus	Earth	Semi-fruitful	4th
23 Wed. 6:42 pm	Gemini	Air	Barren	4th
24 Thu.	Gemini	Air	Barren	4th
25 Fri.	Gemini	Air	Barren	4th
26 Sat. 6:23 am	Cancer	Water	Fruitful	4th
27 Sun.	Cancer	Water	Fruitful	4th
28 Mon. 3:17 pm	Leo	Fire	Barren	4th
29 Tue.	Leo	Fire	Barren	New 1:53 am
30 Wed. 9:27 pm	Virgo	Earth	Barren	1st
31 Thu.	Virgo	Earth	Barren	1st

July

Lunar Aspectarian   **Favorable and Unfavorable Days**

	Sun	Mercury	Venus	Mars	Jupiter	Saturn	Uranus	Neptune	Pluto	Aries	Taurus	Gemini	Cancer	Leo	Virgo	Libra	Scorpio	Sagittarius	Capricorn	Aquarius	Pisces
1										u	f		F		f	u	f		U		f
2						C		O	T	f	u	f		F		f	u	f		U	
3				X	0		X	0		f	u	f		F		f	u	f		U	
4	X	X			0				Q		f	u	f		F		f	u	f		U
5			Q								f	u	f		F		f	u	f		U
6	Q	Q				Q		T		U		f	u	f		F		f	u	f	
7		Q			X				X	U		f	u	f		F		f	u	f	
8			T	T			T	T	Q		U		f	u	f		F		f	u	f
9	T	T			Q						U		f	u	f		F		f	u	f
10				Q			Q	X		f		U		f	u	f		F		f	u
11					T				C	f		U		f	u	f		F		f	u
12			0	X		0	X			f		U		f	u	f		F		f	u
13	0									u	f		U		f	u	f		F		f
14		0						C		u	f		U		f	u	f		F		f
15					0			C	X	f	u	f		U		f	u	f		F	
16						T	C			f	u	f		U		f	u	f		F	
17			T	C					Q		f	u	f		U		f	u	f		F
18	T										f	u	f		U		f	u	f		F
19		T				Q		X		F		f	u	f		U		f	u	f	
20	Q		Q		T				T	F		f	u	f		U		f	u	f	
21	Q			X		X	X			F		f	u	f		U		f	u	f	
22		Q		X				Q			F		f	u	f		U		f	u	f
23	X		X		Q		Q				F		f	u	f		U		f	u	f
24				Q				T		f		F		f	u	f		U		f	u
25		X			X				0	f		F		f	u	f		U		f	u
26				T		C	T			f		F		f	u	f		U		f	u
27				T						u	f		F		f	u	f		U		f
28	C		C							u	f		F		f	u	f		U		f
29	C							0	T	f	u	f		F		f	u	f		U	
30		C				C	0			f	u	f		F		f	u	f		U	
31				0			X	0			f	u	f		F		f	u	f		U

August Moon Table

Date	Sign	Element	Nature	Phase
1 Fri.	Virgo	Earth	Barren	1st
2 Sat. 1:48 am	Libra	Air	Semi-fruitful	1st
3 Sun.	Libra	Air	Semi-fruitful	1st
4 Mon. 5:12 am	Scorpio	Water	Fruitful	1st
5 Tue.	Scorpio	Water	Fruitful	2nd 2:28 am
6 Wed. 8:11 am	Sagittarius	Fire	Barren	2nd
7 Thu.	Sagittarius	Fire	Barren	2nd
8 Fri. 11:02 am	Capricorn	Earth	Semi-fruitful	2nd
9 Sat.	Capricorn	Earth	Semi-fruitful	2nd
10 Sun. 2:23 pm	Aquarius	Air	Barren	2nd
11 Mon.	Aquarius	Air	Barren	Full 11:48 pm
12 Tue. 7:19 pm	Pisces	Water	Fruitful	3rd
13 Wed.	Pisces	Water	Fruitful	3rd
14 Thu.	Pisces	Water	Fruitful	3rd
15 Fri. 3:00 am	Aries	Fire	Barren	3rd
16 Sat.	Aries	Fire	Barren	3rd
17 Sun. 1:52 pm	Taurus	Earth	Semi-fruitful	3rd
18 Mon.	Taurus	Earth	Semi-fruitful	3rd
19 Tue.	Taurus	Earth	Semi-fruitful	4th 7:48 pm
20 Wed. 2:41 am	Gemini	Air	Barren	4th
21 Thu.	Gemini	Air	Barren	4th
22 Fri. 2:44 pm	Cancer	Water	Fruitful	4th
23 Sat.	Cancer	Water	Fruitful	4th
24 Sun. 11:48 pm	Leo	Fire	Barren	4th
25 Mon.	Leo	Fire	Barren	4th
26 Tue.	Leo	Fire	Barren	4th
27 Wed. 5:27 am	Virgo	Earth	Barren	New 12:26 pm
28 Thu.	Virgo	Earth	Barren	1st
29 Fri. 8:41 am	Libra	Air	Semi-fruitful	1st
30 Sat.	Libra	Air	Semi-fruitful	1st
31 Sun. 11:00 am	Scorpio	Water	Fruitful	1st

August

Lunar Aspectarian

Favorable and Unfavorable Days

Day	Sun	Mercury	Venus	Mars	Jupiter	Saturn	Uranus	Neptune	Pluto	Aries	Taurus	Gemini	Cancer	Leo	Virgo	Libra	Scorpio	Sagittarius	Capricorn	Aquarius	Pisces
1									Q		f	u	f		F		f	u	f		U
2	X		X			Q		T		U	f	u	f		F		f	u	f		
3					X				X	U	f	u	f		F		f	u	f		
4	Q	X	Q	T		T	T	T	Q	U	f	u	f		F		f	u	f		
5	Q				Q			Q			U	f	u	f		F		f	u		f
6		Q		Q	Q		Q				U	f	u	f		F		f	u		f
7	T	Q	T	Q				X	C	f		U	f	u	f		F		f		u
8				X	T	O	X			f		U	f	u	f		F		f		u
9		T		X		O				u	f		U	f	u	f		F			f
10										u	f		U	f	u	f		F			f
11	O		O					C	X	f	u	f		U	f	u	f		F		
12				O		C				f	u	f		U	f	u	f		F		
13			C		T					f	u	f		U	f	u	f				F
14		O							Q	f	u	f		U	f	u	f				F
15						Q	X			F		f	u	f		U	f	u	f		
16	T		T				X	T		F		f	u	f		U	f	u	f		
17	T		T		T		X			F		f	u	f		U	f	u	f		
18				X	X			Q			F	f	u	f			U	f	u	f	
19	Q	T	Q	Q							F	f	u	f			U	f	u	f	
20				Q		Q	T			f		F	f	u	f			U	f		u
21						T	O			f		F	f	u	f			U	f		u
22	X	Q	X	X		X	T			f		F	f	u	f			U	f		u
23				T	C					u	f		F	f	u	f			U	f	
24		X								u	f		F	f	u	f			U	f	
25								O		f	u	f		F	f	u	f			U	
26								T		f	u	f		F	f	u	f			U	
27	C		C	O	C	X	O			f	u	f		F	f	u	f			U	
28		C							Q	f	u	f			F	f	u	f			U
29		C				Q				f	u	f			F	f	u	f			U
30						Q		T	X	U	f	u	f		F		f	u	f		
31	X			T	X		T			U	f	u	f		F		f	u	f		

September Moon Table

Date	Sign	Element	Nature	Phase
1 Mon.	Scorpio	Water	Fruitful	1st
2 Tue. 1:32 pm	Sagittarius	Fire	Barren	1st
3 Wed.	Sagittarius	Fire	Barren	2nd 7:34 am
4 Thu. 4:51 pm	Capricorn	Earth	Semi-fruitful	2nd
5 Fri.	Capricorn	Earth	Semi-fruitful	2nd
6 Sat. 9:15 pm	Aquarius	Air	Barren	2nd
7 Sun.	Aquarius	Air	Barren	2nd
8 Mon.	Aquarius	Air	Barren	2nd
9 Tue. 3:07 am	Pisces	Water	Fruitful	2nd
10 Wed.	Pisces	Water	Fruitful	Full 11:36 am
11 Thu. 11:09 am	Aries	Fire	Barren	3rd
12 Fri.	Aries	Fire	Barren	3rd
13 Sat. 9:50 pm	Taurus	Earth	Semi-fruitful	3rd
14 Sun.	Taurus	Earth	Semi-fruitful	3rd
15 Mon.	Taurus	Earth	Semi-fruitful	3rd
16 Tue. 10:32 am	Gemini	Air	Barren	3rd
17 Wed.	Gemini	Air	Barren	3rd
18 Thu. 11:07 pm	Cancer	Water	Fruitful	4th 2:03 pm
19 Fri.	Cancer	Water	Fruitful	4th
20 Sat.	Cancer	Water	Fruitful	4th
21 Sun. 9:02 am	Leo	Fire	Barren	4th
22 Mon.	Leo	Fire	Barren	4th
23 Tue. 3:04 pm	Virgo	Earth	Barren	4th
24 Wed.	Virgo	Earth	Barren	4th
25 Thu. 5:49 pm	Libra	Air	Semi-fruitful	New 10:09 pm
26 Fri.	Libra	Air	Semi-fruitful	1st
27 Sat. 6:52 pm	Scorpio	Water	Fruitful	1st
28 Sun.	Scorpio	Water	Fruitful	1st
29 Mon. 7:57 pm	Sagittarius	Fire	Barren	1st
30 Tue.	Sagittarius	Fire	Barren	1st

September

Lunar Aspectarian   **Favorable and Unfavorable Days**

	Sun	Mercury	Venus	Mars	Jupiter	Saturn	Uranus	Neptune	Pluto	Aries	Taurus	Gemini	Cancer	Leo	Virgo	Libra	Scorpio	Sagittarius	Capricorn	Aquarius	Pisces
1	X		X			T		Q			U		f	u	f		F		f	u	f
2		X		Q	Q			Q			U		f	u	f		F		f	u	f
3	Q		Q					X	C	f		U		f	u	f		F		f	u
4		Q		X	T		X			f		U		f	u	f		F		f	u
5	T		T			0				u	f		U		f	u	f		F		f
6		T	T							u	f		U		f	u	f		F		f
7								C		f	u	f		U		f	u	f		F	
8								X		f	u	f		U		f	u	f		F	
9				C	0	T	C			f	u	f		U		f	u	f		F	
10	0	0	0			T			Q		f	u	f		U		f	u	f		F
11			0								f	u	f		U		f	u	f		F
12						Q		X	T	F		f	u	f		U		f	u	f	
13			X				X			F		f	u	f		U		f	u	f	
14		T		X	T	X		Q			F		f	u	f		U		f	u	f
15	T	T									F		f	u	f		U		f	u	f
16			T	Q	Q			Q			F		f	u	f		U		f	u	f
17		Q						T	0	f		F		f	u	f		U		f	u
18	Q			T			T			f		F		f	u	f		U		f	u
19		X	Q	T	X	C				u	f		F		f	u	f		U		f
20										u	f		F		f	u	f		U		f
21	X		X							u	f		F		f	u	f		U		f
22			X					0	T	f	u	f		F		f	u	f		U	
23				0	C		0			f	u	f		F		f	u	f		U	
24		C			C	X			Q	f	u	f			F	f	u	f			U
25	C									f	u	f			F	f	u	f			U
26			C			Q		T	X	U		f	u	f		F		f	u	f	
27				T			T			U		f	u	f		F		f	u	f	
28		X		X	T			Q			U		f	u	f		F		f	u	f
29		X		Q				Q			U		f	u	f		F		f	u	f
30	X				Q			X	C	f		U		f	u	f		F		f	u

October Moon Table

Date	Sign	Element	Nature	Phase
1 Wed. 10:21 pm	Capricorn	Earth	Semi-fruitful	1st
2 Thu.	Capricorn	Earth	Semi-fruitful	2nd 2:09 pm
3 Fri.	Capricorn	Earth	Semi-fruitful	2nd
4 Sat. 2:45 am	Aquarius	Air	Barren	2nd
5 Sun.	Aquarius	Air	Barren	2nd
6 Mon. 9:20 am	Pisces	Water	Fruitful	2nd
7 Tue.	Pisces	Water	Fruitful	2nd
8 Wed. 6:07 pm	Aries	Fire	Barren	2nd
9 Thu.	Aries	Fire	Barren	2nd
10 Fri.	Aries	Fire	Barren	Full 2:27 am
11 Sat. 5:05 am	Taurus	Earth	Semi-fruitful	3rd
12 Sun.	Taurus	Earth	Semi-fruitful	3rd
13 Mon. 5:45 pm	Gemini	Air	Barren	3rd
14 Tue.	Gemini	Air	Barren	3rd
15 Wed.	Gemini	Air	Barren	3rd
16 Thu. 6:41 am	Cancer	Water	Fruitful	3rd
17 Fri.	Cancer	Water	Fruitful	3rd
18 Sat. 5:41 pm	Leo	Fire	Barren	4th 7:31 am
19 Sun.	Leo	Fire	Barren	4th
20 Mon.	Leo	Fire	Barren	4th
21 Tue. 1:01 am	Virgo	Earth	Barren	4th
22 Wed.	Virgo	Earth	Barren	4th
23 Thu. 4:27 am	Libra	Air	Semi-fruitful	4th
24 Fri.	Libra	Air	Semi-fruitful	4th
25 Sat. 5:08 am	Scorpio	Water	Fruitful	New 7:50 am
26 Sun.	Scorpio	Water	Fruitful	1st
27 Mon. 4:55 am	Sagittarius	Fire	Barren	1st
28 Tue.	Sagittarius	Fire	Barren	1st
29 Wed. 5:37 am	Capricorn	Earth	Semi-fruitful	1st
30 Thu.	Capricorn	Earth	Semi-fruitful	1st
31 Fri. 8:41 am	Aquarius	Air	Barren	2nd 11:25 pm

October

Lunar Aspectarian

Favorable and Unfavorable Days

	Sun	Mercury	Venus	Mars	Jupiter	Saturn	Uranus	Neptune	Pluto	Aries	Taurus	Gemini	Cancer	Leo	Virgo	Libra	Scorpio	Sagittarius	Capricorn	Aquarius	Pisces
1		Q	X	X			X		C	f		U		f	u	f		F		f	u
2	Q				T	0				u	f		U		f	u	f		F		f
3		T	Q							u	f		U		f	u	f		F		f
4	T							C		f	u	f		U		f	u	f		F	
5			T						X	f	u	f		U		f	u	f		F	
6		T	C	0		C				f	u	f		U		f	u	f		F	
7				0	T				Q		f	u	f		U		f	u	f		F
8	0										f	u	f		U		f	u	f		F
9	0	0			Q		X			F		f	u	f		U		f	u	f	
10	0							T		F		f	u	f		U		f	u	f	
11		0	X	T		X	Q			F		f	u	f		U		f	u	f	
12				T	X		Q				F		f	u	f		U		f	u	f
13		Q			Q						F		f	u	f		U		f	u	f
14	T			Q			T			f		F		f	u	f		U		f	u
15	T							0		f		F		f	u	f		U		f	u
16		T	T			T				f		F		f	u	f		U		f	u
17	Q	T		X	C					u	f		F		f	u	f		U		f
18	Q									u	f		F		f	u	f		U		f
19		Q					0			f	u	f		F		f	u	f		U	
20	X	X				0		T		f	u	f		F		f	u	f		U	
21		0	C	X							f	u	f		F		f	u	f		U
22	X		X		X			Q			f	u	f		F		f	u	f		U
23		Q	T							f	u	f		F		f	u	f		U
24		Q				X			Aries U		f	u	f		F		f	u	f	
25	C	C	T	X	T	T	Q		U		f	u	f		F		f	u	f	
26	C	X	T					U		f	u	f		F		f	u	f
27	Q	Q	Q	X			U		f	u	f		F		f	u	f
28	Q			C	f		U		f	u	f		F		f	u
29	X	X	X	X		f		U		f	u	f		F		f	u
30	T	0		u	f		U		f	u	f		F		f
31	Q	X		u	f		U		f	u	f		F		f

Using the Moon Tables 53

November Moon Table

Date	Sign	Element	Nature	Phase
1 Sat.	Aquarius	Air	Barren	2nd
2 Sun. 2:52 pm	Pisces	Water	Fruitful	2nd
3 Mon.	Pisces	Water	Fruitful	2nd
4 Tue.	Pisces	Water	Fruitful	2nd
5 Wed. 12:02 am	Aries	Fire	Barren	2nd
6 Thu.	Aries	Fire	Barren	2nd
7 Fri. 11:29 am	Taurus	Earth	Semi-fruitful	2nd
8 Sat.	Taurus	Earth	Semi-fruitful	Full 8:13 pm
9 Sun.	Taurus	Earth	Semi-fruitful	3rd
10 Mon. 12:14 am	Gemini	Air	Barren	3rd
11 Tue.	Gemini	Air	Barren	3rd
12 Wed. 1:10 pm	Cancer	Water	Fruitful	3rd
13 Thu.	Cancer	Water	Fruitful	3rd
14 Fri.	Cancer	Water	Fruitful	3rd
15 Sat. 12:48 am	Leo	Fire	Barren	3rd
16 Sun.	Leo	Fire	Barren	4th 11:15 pm
17 Mon. 9:36 am	Virgo	Earth	Barren	4th
18 Tue.	Virgo	Earth	Barren	4th
19 Wed. 2:42 pm	Libra	Air	Semi-fruitful	4th
20 Thu.	Libra	Air	Semi-fruitful	4th
21 Fri. 4:24 pm	Scorpio	Water	Fruitful	4th
22 Sat.	Scorpio	Water	Fruitful	4th
23 Sun. 4:02 pm	Sagittarius	Fire	Barren	New 5:59 pm
24 Mon.	Sagittarius	Fire	Barren	1st
25 Tue. 3:31 pm	Capricorn	Earth	Semi-fruitful	1st
26 Wed.	Capricorn	Earth	Semi-fruitful	1st
27 Thu. 4:48 pm	Aquarius	Air	Barren	1st
28 Fri.	Aquarius	Air	Barren	1st
29 Sat. 9:25 pm	Pisces	Water	Fruitful	1st
30 Sun.	Pisces	Water	Fruitful	2nd 12:16 pm

November

Lunar Aspectarian — Favorable and Unfavorable Days

Day	Sun	Mercury	Venus	Mars	Jupiter	Saturn	Uranus	Neptune	Pluto	Aries	Taurus	Gemini	Cancer	Leo	Virgo	Libra	Scorpio	Sagittarius	Capricorn	Aquarius	Pisces
1		Q						C	X	f	u	f		U		f	u	f		F	
2			Q					C		f	u	f		U		f	u	f		F	
3	T	T		C	0	T			Q		f	u	f		U		f	u	f		F
4									Q		f	u	f		U		f	u	f		F
5			T			Q		X		F		f	u	f		U		f	u	f	
6						Q			T	F		f	u	f		U		f	u	f	
7								X		F		f	u	f		U		f	u	f	
8	0			X	T	X			Q		F		f	u	f		U		f	u	f
9		0						Q			F		f	u	f		U		f	u	f
10			0	Q				T		f		F		f	u	f		U		f	u
11				Q					0	f		F		f	u	f		U		f	u
12						T				f		F		f	u	f		U		f	u
13				T	X	C				u	f		F		f	u	f		U		f
14	T									u	f		F		f	u	f		U		f
15		T						0		f	u	f		F		f	u	f		U	
16	Q		T						T	f	u	f		F		f	u	f		U	
17		Q						0		f	u	f		F		f	u	f		U	
18		Q	Q	0	C	X			Q		f	u	f		F		f	u	f		U
19	X										f	u	f		F		f	u	f		U
20		X				Q		T	X	U		f	u	f		F		f	u	f	
21			X					T		U		f	u	f		F		f	u	f	
22				T	X	T		Q			U		f	u	f		F		f	u	f
23	C					Q					U		f	u	f		F		f	u	f
24		C		Q	Q			X	C	f		U		f	u	f		F		f	u
25			C			X				f		U		f	u	f		F		f	u
26				X	T	0				u	f		U		f	u	f		F		f
27	X									u	f		U		f	u	f		F		f
28	X							C	X	f	u	f		U		f	u	f		F	
29		X						C	X	f	u	f		U		f	u	f		F	
30	Q		X			T					f	u	f		U		f	u	f		F

December Moon Table

Date	Sign	Element	Nature	Phase
1 Mon.	Pisces	Water	Fruitful	2nd
2 Tue. 5:56 am	Aries	Fire	Barren	2nd
3 Wed.	Aries	Fire	Barren	2nd
4 Thu. 5:30 pm	Taurus	Earth	Semi-fruitful	2nd
5 Fri.	Taurus	Earth	Semi-fruitful	2nd
6 Sat.	Taurus	Earth	Semi-fruitful	2nd
7 Sun. 6:26 am	Gemini	Air	Barren	2nd
8 Mon.	Gemini	Air	Barren	Full 3:37 pm
9 Tue. 7:11 pm	Cancer	Water	Fruitful	3rd
10 Wed.	Cancer	Water	Fruitful	3rd
11 Thu.	Cancer	Water	Fruitful	3rd
12 Fri. 6:40 am	Leo	Fire	Barren	3rd
13 Sat.	Leo	Fire	Barren	3rd
14 Sun. 4:07 pm	Virgo	Earth	Barren	3rd
15 Mon.	Virgo	Earth	Barren	3rd
16 Tue. 10:46 pm	Libra	Air	Semi-fruitful	4th 12:42 pm
17 Wed.	Libra	Air	Semi-fruitful	4th
18 Thu.	Libra	Air	Semi-fruitful	4th
19 Fri. 2:20 am	Scorpio	Water	Fruitful	4th
20 Sat.	Scorpio	Water	Fruitful	4th
21 Sun. 3:16 am	Sagittarius	Fire	Barren	4th
22 Mon.	Sagittarius	Fire	Barren	4th
23 Tue. 2:55 am	Capricorn	Earth	Semi-fruitful	New 4:43 am
24 Wed.	Capricorn	Earth	Semi-fruitful	1st
25 Thu. 3:13 am	Aquarius	Air	Barren	1st
26 Fri.	Aquarius	Air	Barren	1st
27 Sat. 6:10 am	Pisces	Water	Fruitful	1st
28 Sun.	Pisces	Water	Fruitful	1st
29 Mon. 1:08 pm	Aries	Fire	Barren	1st
30 Tue.	Aries	Fire	Barren	2nd 5:03 am
31 Wed.	Aries	Fire	Barren	2nd

December

Lunar Aspectarian

Favorable and Unfavorable Days

	Sun	Mercury	Venus	Mars	Jupiter	Saturn	Uranus	Neptune	Pluto	Aries	Taurus	Gemini	Cancer	Leo	Virgo	Libra	Scorpio	Sagittarius	Capricorn	Aquarius	Pisces
1				C	0				Q		f	u	f		U		f	u	f		F
2	T	Q	Q								f	u	f		U		f	u	f		F
3	T					Q		X	T	F		f	u	f		U		f	u	f	
4		T						X		F		f	u	f		U		f	u	f	
5			T		X		Q			F		f	u	f		U		f	u	f	
6				X	T						F		f	u	f		U		f	u	f
7								Q			F		f	u	f		U		f	u	f
8	0				Q			T	0	f		F		f	u	f		U		f	u
9			Q					T		f		F		f	u	f		U		f	u
10		0				C				u	f		F		f	u	f		U		f
11			0	T	X					u	f		F		f	u	f		U		f
12			T							u	f		F		f	u	f		U		f
13	T							0	T	f	u	f		F		f	u	f		U	
14	T							0		f	u	f		F		f	u	f		U	
15		T			C	X					f	u	f		F		f	u	f		U
16	Q		T	0	C				Q		f	u	f		F		f	u	f		U
17		Q				Q		T		U		f	u	f		F		f	u	f	
18	X		Q					T	X	U		f	u	f		F		f	u	f	
19		X			T	T		Q			U		f	u	f		F		f	u	f
20				X		Q					U		f	u	f		F		f	u	f
21			X	T				Q	X		U		f	u	f		F		f	u	f
22				Q		X			C	f		U		f	u	f		F		f	u
23	C	C		Q		0	X			u	f		U		f	u	f		F		f
24						T				u	f		U		f	u	f		F		f
25			C	X				C		u	f		U		f	u	f		F		f
26									X	f	u	f		U		f	u	f		F	
27	X	X				T	C			f	u	f		U		f	u	f		F	
28				0	T				Q		f	u	f		U		f	u	f		F
29		Q									f	u	f		U		f	u	f		F
30	Q		X	C		Q		X		F		f	u	f		U		f	u	f	
31		T						X		F		f	u	f		U		f	u	f	

MOON VOID-OF-COURSE

By Kim Rogers-Gallagher

The Moon makes a loop around the Earth in about twenty-eight days, moving through each of the signs in two-and-a-half days (or so). As she passes through the thirty degrees of each sign, she "visits" with the planets in numerical order by forming angles or aspects with them. Because she moves one degree in just two to two-and-a-half hours, her influence on each planet lasts only a few hours, then she moves along. As she approaches the late degrees of the sign she's passing through, she eventually reaches the planet that's in the highest degree of any sign, and forms what will be her final aspect before leaving the sign. From this point until she actually enters the new sign, she is referred to as void-of-course, or void.

Think of it this way: the Moon is the emotional "tone" of the day, carrying feelings with her particular to the sign she's "wearing" at the moment. After she has contacted each of the planets, she symbolically "rests" before changing her costume, so her instinct is temporarily on hold. It's during this time that many people feel "fuzzy" or "vague"—scattered, even. Plans or decisions we make now will usually not pan out. Without the instinctual "knowing" the Moon provides as she touches each planet, we tend to be unrealistic or exercise poor judgment. The traditional definition of the void Moon is that "nothing will come of this," and it seems to be true. Actions initiated under a void Moon are often wasted, irrelevant, or incorrect—usually because information is hidden, missing, or has been overlooked.

Although it's not a good time to initiate plans, routine tasks seem to go along just fine. However, this period is really ideal for what the Moon does best: reflection. It's at this time that we can assimilate what the world has tossed at us over the past few days.

On the lighter side, remember that there are other good uses for the void Moon. This is the time period when the universe seems to be most open to loopholes. It's a great time to make plans you don't want to fulfill or schedule things you don't want to do. See the table on pages 59–64 for a schedule of the 2003 Moon void-of-course times.

Moon Void-of-Course

Last Aspect		Moon Enters New Sign		
Date	Time	Date	Sign	Time
January				
1	12:23 pm	1	Capricorn	6:42 pm
3	7:56 pm	3	Aquarius	10:56 pm
6	3:44 am	6	Pisces	5:57 am
8	6:55 am	8	Aries	4:15 pm
10	10:10 pm	11	Taurus	4:48 am
13	12:44 pm	13	Gemini	5:08 pm
15	9:16 pm	16	Cancer	2:56 am
18	5:48 am	18	Leo	9:29 am
20	8:46 am	20	Virgo	1:32 pm
22	4:34 am	22	Libra	4:23 pm
24	2:48 pm	24	Scorpio	7:09 pm
26	6:14 pm	26	Sagittarius	10:26 pm
28	10:26 pm	29	Capricorn	2:30 am
30	5:34 am	31	Aquarius	7:44 am
February				
2	11:02 am	2	Pisces	2:55 pm
4	9:53 am	5	Aries	12:44 am
7	9:22 am	7	Taurus	12:59 pm
9	10:28 pm	10	Gemini	1:45 am
12	9:29 am	12	Cancer	12:19 pm
13	7:22 am	14	Leo	7:04 pm
16	8:18 pm	16	Virgo	10:22 pm
18	10:56 am	18	Libra	11:48 pm
20	11:29 pm	21	Scorpio	1:09 am
23	2:15 am	23	Sagittarius	3:46 am
25	6:50 am	25	Capricorn	8:11 am
27	7:58 am	27	Aquarius	2:24 pm
March				
1	9:30 pm	1	Pisces	10:26 pm

Moon Void-of-Course

Last Aspect		Moon Enters New Sign		
Date	**Time**	**Date**	**Sign**	**Time**
4	8:04 am	4	Aries	8:30 am
6	8:10 pm	6	Taurus	8:36 pm
9	9:29 am	9	Gemini	9:38 am
11	6:24 am	11	Cancer	9:12 pm
13	4:13 pm	14	Leo	5:06 am
15	8:24 pm	16	Virgo	8:52 am
18	5:35 am	18	Libra	9:43 am
19	10:02 pm	20	Scorpio	9:38 am
21	11:30 pm	22	Sagittarius	10:33 am
24	6:58 am	24	Capricorn	1:48 pm
25	1:16 pm	26	Aquarius	7:51 pm
28	3:27 pm	29	Pisces	4:26 am
31	1:59 am	31	Aries	3:04 pm
		April		
2	5:05 pm	3	Taurus	3:20 am
4	7:15 pm	5	Gemini	4:24 pm
7	4:34 pm	8	Cancer	4:36 am
10	12:34 am	10	Leo	1:54 pm
12	9:18 am	12	Virgo	7:07 pm
14	1:38 pm	14	Libra	8:42 pm
16	3:22 pm	16	Scorpio	8:16 pm
18	4:52 pm	18	Sagittarius	7:51 pm
20	8:02 pm	20	Capricorn	9:20 pm
22	7:40 am	23	Aquarius	1:58 am
25	1:19 am	25	Pisces	10:02 am
27	12:18 pm	27	Aries	8:54 pm
30	1:12 am	30	Taurus	9:26 am
		May		
2	12:27 am	2	Gemini	10:27 pm
5	3:43 am	5	Cancer	10:42 am

Moon Void-of-Course

Last Aspect		Moon Enters New Sign		
Date	**Time**	**Date**	**Sign**	**Time**
6	11:21 pm	7	Leo	8:46 pm
9	10:13 pm	10	Virgo	3:31 am
12	2:09 am	12	Libra	6:42 am
14	3:13 am	14	Scorpio	7:14 am
15	10:36 pm	16	Sagittarius	6:43 am
18	3:41 am	18	Capricorn	7:03 am
20	8:29 am	20	Aquarius	10:01 am
22	1:49 pm	22	Pisces	4:41 pm
25	12:33 am	25	Aries	2:59 am
27	1:41 pm	27	Taurus	3:32 pm
29	10:53 am	30	Gemini	4:32 am
		June		
1	3:55 pm	1	Cancer	4:27 pm
3	11:27 am	4	Leo	2:25 am
6	1:18 am	6	Virgo	9:51 am
8	11:27 am	8	Libra	2:30 pm
10	12:00 pm	10	Scorpio	4:39 pm
12	4:51 pm	12	Sagittarius	5:12 pm
14	4:05 pm	14	Capricorn	5:38 pm
14	10:12 pm	16	Aquarius	7:41 pm
18	8:08 pm	19	Pisces	12:57 am
21	9:45 am	21	Aries	10:06 am
22	10:28 pm	23	Taurus	10:15 pm
25	8:41 am	26	Gemini	11:13 am
28	9:31 pm	28	Cancer	10:52 pm
29	1:39 pm	1	Leo	8:13 am
		July		
3	1:06 pm	3	Virgo	3:16 pm
4	11:15 pm	5	Libra	8:20 pm
7	5:23 am	7	Scorpio	11:43 pm

Moon Void-of-Course

Last Aspect		Moon Enters New Sign		
Date	Time	Date	Sign	Time
9	12:58 pm	10	Sagittarius	1:48 am
11	10:53 am	12	Capricorn	3:21 am
13	2:21 pm	14	Aquarius	5:38 am
15	5:57 pm	16	Pisces	10:14 am
18	9:49 am	18	Aries	6:20 pm
21	2:01 am	21	Taurus	5:48 am
23	4:14 am	23	Gemini	6:42 pm
25	4:38 am	26	Cancer	6:23 am
28	2:25 pm	28	Leo	3:17 pm
30	10:46 am	30	Virgo	9:27 pm
August				
1	4:02 am	2	Libra	1:48 am
3	8:33 pm	4	Scorpio	5:12 am
6	12:22 am	6	Sagittarius	8:11 am
8	4:01 am	8	Capricorn	11:02 am
9	9:57 am	10	Aquarius	2:23 pm
12	1:35 pm	12	Pisces	7:19 pm
14	5:29 am	15	Aries	3:00 am
17	9:36 am	17	Taurus	1:52 pm
19	11:29 pm	20	Gemini	2:41 am
22	1:15 pm	22	Cancer	2:44 pm
24	3:51 pm	24	Leo	11:48 pm
26	7:00 am	27	Virgo	5:27 am
29	2:26 am	29	Libra	8:41 am
30	1:37 pm	31	Scorpio	11:00 am
September				
2	5:18 am	2	Sagittarius	1:32 pm
4	6:23 am	4	Capricorn	4:51 pm
6	7:43 am	6	Aquarius	9:15 pm
8	4:01 am	9	Pisces	3:07 am

Moon Void-of-Course

Last Aspect		Moon Enters New Sign		
Date	Time	Date	Sign	Time
11	12:41 am	11	Aries	11:09 am
12	8:40 pm	13	Taurus	9:50 pm
16	10:25 am	16	Gemini	10:32 am
18	10:50 pm	18	Cancer	11:07 pm
21	5:21 am	21	Leo	9:02 am
23	2:33 pm	23	Virgo	3:04 pm
24	8:52 pm	25	Libra	5:49 pm
27	6:10 pm	27	Scorpio	6:52 pm
29	7:09 pm	29	Sagittarius	7:57 pm
October				
1	9:25 pm	1	Capricorn	10:21 pm
3	5:40 pm	4	Aquarius	2:45 am
6	8:06 am	6	Pisces	9:20 am
7	6:30 pm	8	Aries	6:07 pm
11	3:31 am	11	Taurus	5:05 am
13	4:02 pm	13	Gemini	5:45 pm
16	4:54 am	16	Cancer	6:41 am
18	7:31 am	18	Leo	5:41 pm
20	11:18 pm	21	Virgo	1:01 am
22	8:19 am	23	Libra	4:27 am
25	3:31 am	25	Scorpio	5:08 am
27	3:15 am	27	Sagittarius	4:55 am
29	3:51 am	29	Capricorn	5:37 am
31	3:07 am	31	Aquarius	8:41 am
November				
2	2:40 pm	2	Pisces	2:52 pm
4	1:36 am	5	Aries	12:02 am
7	9:16 am	7	Taurus	11:29 am
9	10:00 pm	10	Gemini	12:14 am
12	10:57 am	12	Cancer	1:10 pm

Moon Void-of-Course

Last Aspect		Moon Enters New Sign		
Date	Time	Date	Sign	Time
14	8:39 am	15	Leo	12:48 am
17	7:38 am	17	Virgo	9:36 am
19	9:15 am	19	Libra	2:42 pm
21	2:44 pm	21	Scorpio	4:24 pm
23	2:28 pm	23	Sagittarius	4:02 pm
25	1:57 pm	25	Capricorn	3:31 pm
26	10:52 pm	27	Aquarius	4:48 pm
29	7:46 pm	29	Pisces	9:25 pm
		December		
2	4:39 am	2	Aries	5:56 am
4	3:52 pm	4	Taurus	5:30 pm
7	4:54 am	7	Gemini	6:26 am
9	5:48 pm	9	Cancer	7:11 pm
12	1:53 am	12	Leo	6:40 am
14	3:05 pm	14	Virgo	4:07 pm
16	12:49 pm	16	Libra	10:46 pm
19	1:39 am	19	Scorpio	2:20 am
21	2:43 am	21	Sagittarius	3:16 am
23	2:29 am	23	Capricorn	2:55 am
24	8:52 am	25	Aquarius	3:13 am
27	5:58 am	27	Pisces	6:10 am
28	7:03 pm	29	Aries	1:08 pm

FIND YOUR MOON SIGN

Every year we give tables for the position of the Moon during that year, but it is more complicated to provide tables for the Moon's position in any given year because of its continuous movement. However, the problem was solved by Grant Lewi in *Astrology for the Millions* (available from Llewellyn Worldwide).

Grant Lewi's System

Step 1:
Find your birth year in the Natal Moon Tables located on pages 68–78.

Step 2:
Run down the left-hand column and see if your birth date is there.

Step 3:
If your birth date is in the left-hand column, run over this line until you come to the column under your birth year. Here you will find a number. This is your base number. Write it down, and go directly to the direction under the heading "What to Do with Your Base Number" on page 66.

Step 4:
If your birth date is not in the left-hand column, get a pencil and paper. Your birth date falls between two numbers in the left-hand column. Look at the date closest after your birth date; run across this line to your birth year. Write down the number you find there, and label it "top number." Directly beneath it on your piece of paper write the number printed just above it in the table. Label this "bottom number." Subtract the bottom number from the top number. If the top number is smaller, add 360 and subtract. The result is your difference.

Step 5:
Go back to the left-hand column and find the date before your birth date. Determine the number of days between this date and your birth date. Write this down and label it "intervening days."

Step 6:

Note which group your difference (found at step 4) falls in.

Difference	Daily Motion
80–87	12 degrees
88–94	13 degrees
95–101	14 degrees
102–106	15 degrees

Note: If you were born in a leap year and use the difference between February 26 and March 5, then the daily motion is slightly different. If you fall into this category and your difference use the figures below.

Difference	Daily Motion
94–99	12 degrees
100–108	13 degrees
109–115	14 degrees
115–122	15 degrees

Step 7:

Write down the "daily motion" corresponding to your place in the proper table of difference above. Multiply daily motion by the number labeled "intervening days" (found at step 5).

Step 8:

Add the result of step 7 to your bottom number (under step 4). This is your base number. If it is more than 360, subtract 360 from it and call the result your base number.

What to Do with Your Base Number

Turn to the Table of Base Numbers on page 67 and locate your base number in it. At the top of the column you will find the sign your Moon was in. In the far left-hand column you will find the degree the Moon occupied at 7:00 am of your birth date if you were born under Eastern Standard Time (EST). Refer to the Time Zone Conversions chart and table on pages 16–17 to adjust information for your time zone.

If you don't know the hour of your birth, accept this as your Moon's sign and degree. If you do know the hour of your birth, get the exact degree as follows:

If you were born after 7:00 am EST, determine the number of hours after the time that you were born. Divide this by two, rounding up if necessary. Add this to your base number, and the result in the table will be the exact degree and sign of the Moon on the year, month, date, and hour of your birth.

If you were born before 7:00 am EST, determine the number of hours before the time that you were born. Divide this by two. Subtract this from your base number, and the result in the table will be the exact degree and sign of the Moon on the year, month, date, and hour of your birth.

Table of Base Numbers

	♈ (13)	♉ (14)	♊ (15)	♋ (16)	♌ (17)	♍ (18)	♎ (19)	♏ (20)	♐ (21)	♑ (22)	♒ (23)	♓ (24)
0°	0	30	60	90	120	150	180	210	240	270	300	330
1°	1	31	61	91	121	151	181	211	241	271	301	331
2°	2	32	62	92	122	152	182	212	242	272	302	332
3°	3	33	63	93	123	153	183	213	243	273	303	333
4°	4	34	64	94	124	154	184	214	244	274	304	334
5°	5	35	65	95	125	155	185	215	245	275	305	335
6°	6	36	66	96	126	156	186	216	246	276	306	336
7°	7	37	67	97	127	157	187	217	247	277	307	337
8°	8	38	68	98	128	158	188	218	248	278	308	338
9°	9	39	69	99	129	159	189	219	249	279	309	339
10°	10	40	70	100	130	160	190	220	250	280	310	340
11°	11	41	71	101	131	161	191	221	251	281	311	341
12°	12	42	72	102	132	162	192	222	252	282	312	342
13°	13	43	73	103	133	163	193	223	253	283	313	343
14°	14	44	74	104	134	164	194	224	254	284	314	344
15°	15	45	75	105	135	165	195	225	255	285	315	345
16°	16	46	76	106	136	166	196	226	256	286	316	346
17°	17	47	77	107	137	167	197	227	257	287	317	347
18°	18	48	78	108	138	168	198	228	258	288	318	248
19°	19	49	79	109	139	169	199	229	259	289	319	349
20°	20	50	80	110	140	170	200	230	260	290	320	350
21°	21	51	81	111	141	171	201	231	261	291	321	351
22°	22	52	82	112	142	172	202	232	262	292	322	352
23°	23	53	83	113	143	173	203	233	263	293	323	353
24°	24	54	84	114	144	174	204	234	264	294	324	354
25°	25	55	85	115	145	175	205	235	265	295	325	355
26°	26	56	86	116	146	176	206	236	266	296	326	356
27°	27	57	87	117	147	177	207	237	267	297	327	357
28°	28	58	88	118	148	178	208	238	268	298	328	358
29°	29	59	89	119	149	179	209	239	269	299	329	359

Month	Date	1901	1902	1903	1904	1905	1906	1907	1908	1909	1910
Jan.	1	55	188	308	76	227	358	119	246	39	168
Jan.	8	149	272	37	179	319	82	208	350	129	252
Jan.	15	234	2	141	270	43	174	311	81	213	346
Jan.	22	327	101	234	353	138	273	44	164	309	84
Jan.	29	66	196	317	84	238	6	128	255	50	175
Feb.	5	158	280	46	188	328	90	219	359	138	259
Feb.	12	241	12	149	279	51	184	319	90	221	356
Feb.	19	335	111	242	2	146	283	52	173	317	94
Feb.	26	76	204	326	92	248	13	136	264	60	184
Mar.	5	166	288	57	211	336	98	229	21	147	267
Mar.	12	249	22	157	300	60	194	328	110	230	5
Mar.	19	344	121	250	24	154	293	60	195	325	105
Mar.	26	86	212	334	116	258	22	144	288	69	192
Apr.	2	175	296	68	219	345	106	240	29	155	276
Apr.	9	258	31	167	309	69	202	338	118	240	13
Apr.	16	352	132	258	33	163	304	68	204	334	115
Apr.	23	96	220	342	127	267	31	152	299	77	201
Apr.	30	184	304	78	227	354	114	250	38	164	285
May	7	267	40	177	317	78	210	348	126	249	21
May	14	1	142	266	42	172	313	76	212	344	124
May	21	104	229	350	138	275	40	160	310	85	210
May	28	193	313	87	236	2	123	259	47	172	294
Jun.	4	277	48	187	324	88	219	358	134	258	30
Jun.	11	11	151	275	50	182	322	85	220	355	132
Jun.	18	112	238	359	149	283	48	169	320	93	218
Jun.	25	201	322	96	245	11	133	267	57	180	304
Jul.	2	286	57	197	333	97	228	8	142	267	40
Jul.	9	21	160	283	58	193	330	94	228	6	140
Jul.	16	121	247	7	159	291	57	178	330	102	226
Jul.	23	209	332	105	255	18	143	276	66	188	314
Jul.	30	295	66	206	341	105	239	17	151	275	51
Aug.	6	32	168	292	66	204	338	103	237	17	148
Aug.	13	130	255	17	168	301	65	188	339	111	234
Aug.	20	217	341	113	265	27	152	285	76	197	323
Aug.	27	303	77	215	350	113	250	25	160	283	62
Sep.	3	43	176	301	75	215	346	111	246	27	157
Sep.	10	139	263	27	176	310	73	198	347	121	242
Sep.	17	225	350	123	274	35	161	294	85	205	331
Sep.	24	311	88	223	358	122	261	33	169	292	73
Oct.	1	53	185	309	85	224	355	119	256	35	166
Oct.	8	149	271	36	185	320	81	207	356	130	250
Oct.	15	233	359	133	283	44	169	305	93	214	339
Oct.	22	319	99	231	7	130	271	42	177	301	83
Oct.	29	62	194	317	95	233	5	127	266	44	176
Nov.	5	158	279	45	193	329	89	216	5	139	259
Nov.	12	242	6	144	291	53	177	316	101	223	347
Nov.	19	328	109	239	15	140	280	50	185	311	91
Nov.	26	70	203	325	105	241	14	135	276	52	185
Dec.	3	168	288	54	203	338	98	224	15	148	268
Dec.	10	251	14	155	299	61	185	327	109	231	356
Dec.	17	338	118	248	23	150	289	59	193	322	99
Dec.	24	78	213	333	115	249	23	143	286	61	194
Dec.	31	176	296	61	213	346	107	232	26	155	277

Month	Date	1911	1912	1913	1914	1915	1916	1917	1918	1919	1920
Jan.	1	289	57	211	337	100	228	23	147	270	39
Jan.	8	20	162	299	61	192	332	110	231	5	143
Jan.	15	122	251	23	158	293	61	193	329	103	231
Jan.	22	214	335	120	256	23	145	290	68	193	316
Jan.	29	298	66	221	345	108	237	32	155	278	49
Feb.	5	31	170	308	69	203	340	118	239	16	150
Feb.	12	130	260	32	167	302	70	203	338	113	239
Feb.	19	222	344	128	266	31	154	298	78	201	325
Feb.	26	306	75	231	353	116	248	41	164	286	60
Mar.	5	42	192	317	77	214	2	127	248	26	172
Mar.	12	140	280	41	176	311	89	212	346	123	259
Mar.	19	230	5	136	276	39	176	308	87	209	346
Mar.	26	314	100	239	2	124	273	49	173	294	85
Apr.	2	52	200	326	86	223	10	135	257	35	181
Apr.	9	150	288	51	184	321	97	222	355	133	267
Apr.	16	238	14	146	286	48	184	318	96	218	355
Apr.	23	322	111	247	11	132	284	57	181	303	96
Apr.	30	61	208	334	96	232	19	143	267	43	190
May	7	160	296	60	192	331	105	231	4	142	275
May	14	246	22	156	294	56	192	329	104	227	3
May	21	331	122	255	20	141	294	66	190	312	105
May	28	69	218	342	106	240	29	151	277	51	200
Jun.	4	170	304	69	202	341	114	240	14	151	284
Jun.	11	255	30	167	302	65	200	340	112	235	11
Jun.	18	340	132	264	28	151	304	74	198	322	114
Jun.	25	78	228	350	115	249	39	159	286	60	209
Jul.	2	179	312	78	212	349	122	248	25	159	293
Jul.	9	264	39	178	310	74	209	350	120	244	20
Jul.	16	349	141	273	36	161	312	84	206	332	123
Jul.	23	87	237	358	125	258	48	168	295	70	218
Jul.	30	187	321	86	223	357	131	256	36	167	302
Aug.	6	272	48	188	319	82	219	360	129	252	31
Aug.	13	359	150	282	44	171	320	93	214	342	131
Aug.	20	96	246	6	133	268	57	177	303	81	226
Aug.	27	195	330	94	234	5	140	265	46	175	310
Sep.	3	281	57	198	328	90	229	9	138	260	41
Sep.	10	9	158	292	52	180	329	102	222	351	140
Sep.	17	107	255	15	141	279	65	186	312	91	234
Sep.	24	203	339	103	244	13	149	274	56	184	319
Oct.	1	288	68	206	337	98	240	17	148	268	52
Oct.	8	18	167	301	61	189	338	111	231	360	150
Oct.	15	118	263	24	149	290	73.	195	320	102	242
Oct.	22	212	347	113	254	22	157	284	65	193	326
Oct.	29	296	78	214	346	106	250	25	157	276	61
Nov.	5	26	177	309	70	197	348	119	240	7	161
Nov.	12	129	271	33	158	300	81	203	329	112	250
Nov.	19	221	355	123	262	31	164	295	73	202	334
Nov.	26	305	88	223	355	115	259	34	165	285	70
Dec.	3	34	187	317	79	205	359	127	249	16	171
Dec.	10	138	279	41	168	310	89	211	340	120	259
Dec.	17	230	3	134	270	40	172	305	81	211	343
Dec.	24	313	97	232	3	124	267	44	173	294	78
Dec.	31	42	198	325	87	214	9	135	257	25	181

Month	Date	1921	1922	1923	1924	1925	1926	1927	1928	1929	1930
Jan.	1	194	317	80	211	5	127	250	23	176	297
Jan.	8	280	41	177	313	90	211	349	123	260	22
Jan.	15	4	141	275	41	175	312	86	211	346	123
Jan.	22	101	239	3	127	272	51	172	297	83	222
Jan.	29	203	325	88	222	13	135	258	34	184	306
Feb.	5	289	49	188	321	99	220	359	131	269	31
Feb.	12	14	149	284	49	185	320	95	219	356	131
Feb.	19	110	249	11	135	281	60	181	305	93	230
Feb.	26	211	334	96	233	21	144	266	45	191	314
Mar.	5	297	58	197	343	107	230	8	153	276	41
Mar.	12	23	157	294	69	194	328	105	238	6	140
Mar.	19	119	258	19	157	292	68	190	327	104	238
Mar.	26	219	343	104	258	29	153	275	70	200	323
Apr.	2	305	68	205	352	115	240	16	163	284	51
Apr.	9	33	166	304	77	204	337	114	247	14	149
Apr.	16	130	266	28	164	303	76	198	335	115	246
Apr.	23	227	351	114	268	38	161	285	79	208	331
Apr.	30	313	78	214	1	123	250	25	172	292	61
May	7	42	176	313	85	212	348	123	256	23	160
May	14	141	274	37	173	314	84	207	344	125	254
May	21	236	359	123	277	47	169	295	88	217	339
May	28	321	88	222	11	131	259	34	181	301	70
Jun.	4	50	186	321	94	220	358	131	264	31	171
Jun.	11	152	282	45	182	324	93	215	354	135	263
Jun.	18	245	7	134	285	56	177	305	96	226	347
Jun.	25	330	97	232	20	139	268	44	190	310	78
Jul.	2	58	197	329	103	229	9	139	273	40	181
Jul.	9	162	291	54	192	333	101	223	4	144	272
Jul.	16	254	15	144	294	65	185	315	104	236	355
Jul.	23	338	106	242	28	148	276	54	198	319	87
Jul.	30	67	208	337	112	238	20	147	282	49	191
Aug.	6	171	300	62	202	341	110	231	15	152	281
Aug.	13	264	24	153	302	74	194	324	114	244	4
Aug.	20	347	114	253	36	157	285	65	206	328	95
Aug.	27	76	218	346	120	248	29	156	290	59	200
Sep.	3	179	309	70	213	350	119	239	25	161	290
Sep.	10	273	32	162	312	83	203	332	124	252	13
Sep.	17	356	122	264	44	166	293	75	214	337	105
Sep.	24	86	227	354	128	258	38	165	298	70	208
Oct.	1	187	318	78	223	358	128	248	35	169	298
Oct.	8	281	41	170	322	91	212	340	134	260	23
Oct.	15	5	132	274	52	175	303	85	222	345	115
Oct.	22	97	235	3	136	269	46	174	306	81	216
Oct.	29	196	327	87	232	7	137	257	44	179	307
Nov.	5	289	50	178	332	99	221	349	144	268	31
Nov.	12	13	142	283	61	183	313	93	231	353	126
Nov.	19	107	243	12	144	279	54	183	315	91	225
Nov.	26	206	335	96	241	17	145	266	52	189	314
Dec.	3	297	59	187	343	107	230	359	154	276	39
Dec.	10	21	152	291	70	191	324	101	240	1	137
Dec.	17	117	252	21	153	289	63	191	324	99	234
Dec.	24	216	343	105	249	28	152	275	60	199	322
Dec.	31	305	67	197	352	115	237	9	162	285	47

Month	Date	1931	1932	1933	1934	1935	1936	1937	1938	1939	1940
Jan.	1	60	196	346	107	231	8	156	277	41	181
Jan.	8	162	294	70	193	333	104	240	4	144	275
Jan.	15	257	20	158	294	68	190	329	104	239	360
Jan.	22	342	108	255	32	152	278	67	202	323	88
Jan.	29	68	207	353	116	239	19	163	286	49	191
Feb.	5	171	302	78	203	342	113	248	14	153	284
Feb.	12	267	28	168	302	78	198	339	113	248	8
Feb.	19	351	116	266	40	161	286	78	210	332	96
Feb.	26	77	217	1	124	248	29	171	294	59	200
Mar.	5	179	324	86	213	350	135	256	25	161	306
Mar.	12	276	48	176	311	86	218	347	123	256	29
Mar.	19	360	137	277	48	170	308	89	218	340	119
Mar.	26	86	241	10	132	258	52	180	302	69	223
Apr.	2	187	334	94	223	358	144	264	34	169	315
Apr.	9	285	57	185	321	95	227	355	133	264	38
Apr.	16	9	146	287	56	178	317	99	226	349	128
Apr.	23	96	250	18	140	268	61	189	310	80	231
Apr.	30	196	343	102	232	7	153	273	43	179	323
May	7	293	66	193	332	103	237	4	144	272	47
May	14	17	155	297	64	187	327	108	235	357	139
May	21	107	258	28	148	278	69	198	318	90	239
May	28	205	351	111	241	17	161	282	51	189	331
Jun.	4	301	75	201	343	111	245	13	154	280	55
Jun.	11	25	165	306	73	195	337	117	244	5	150
Jun.	18	117	267	37	157	288	78	207	327	99	248
Jun.	25	215	360	120	249	28	169	291	60	200	339
Jul.	2	309	84	211	353	119	254	23	164	289	64
Jul.	9	33	176	315	82	203	348	125	253	13	160
Jul.	16	126	276	46	165	297	87	216	336	108	258
Jul.	23	226	8	130	258	38	177	300	69	210	347
Jul.	30	317	92	221	2	128	262	33	173	298	72
Aug.	6	41	187	323	91	211	359	133	261	21	170
Aug.	13	135	285	54	175	305	97	224	346	116	268
Aug.	20	237	16	138	267	49	185	308	78	220	355
Aug.	27	326	100	232	10	136	270	44	181	307	80
Sep.	3	49	197	331	100	220	8	142	270	31	179
Sep.	10	143	295	62	184	314	107	232	355	125	278
Sep.	17	247	24	147	277	58	194	317	89	228	4
Sep.	24	335	108	243	18	145	278	55	189	316	88
Oct.	1	58	206	341	108	229	17	152	278	40	188
Oct.	8	151	306	70	193	322	117	240	4	134	288
Oct.	15	256	32	155	287	66	203	324	100	236	13
Oct.	22	344	116	253	27	154	287	64	198	324	98
Oct.	29	68	214	350	116	239	25	162	286	49	196
Nov.	5	161	316	78	201	332	126	248	12	145	297
Nov.	12	264	41	162	298	74	212	333	111	244	22
Nov.	19	353	125	262	36	162	296	73	207	332	108
Nov.	26	77	222	0	124	248	33	172	294	58	205
Dec.	3	171	325	87	209	343	135	257	19	156	305
Dec.	10	272	50	171	309	82	220	341	120	253	30
Dec.	17	1	135	271	45	170	306	81	217	340	118
Dec.	24	86	231	10	132	256	43	181	302	66	214
Dec.	31	182	333	95	217	354	142	265	27	167	313

Month	Date	1941	1942	1943	1944	1945	1946	1947	1948	1949	1950
Jan.	1	325	88	211	353	135	258	22	165	305	68
Jan.	8	50	176	315	85	219	348	126	256	29	160
Jan.	15	141	276	50	169	312	87	220	340	123	258
Jan.	22	239	12	133	258	52	182	303	69	224	352
Jan.	29	333	96	221	2	143	266	32	174	314	75
Feb.	5	57	186	323	95	227	358	134	265	37	170
Feb.	12	150	285	58	178	320	96	228	349	131	268
Feb.	19	250	20	142	267	62	190	312	78	234	359
Feb.	26	342	104	231	11	152	274	43	182	323	83
Mar.	5	65	196	331	116	236	8	142	286	46	179
Mar.	12	158	295	66	199	328	107	236	10	139	279
Mar.	19	261	28	150	290	72	198	320	102	243	8
Mar.	26	351	112	242	34	161	281	53	204	332	91
Apr.	2	74	205	340	125	244	16	152	294	55	187
Apr.	9	166	306	74	208	337	117	244	19	148	289
Apr.	16	270	36	158	300	81	206	328	112	252	17
Apr.	23	360	120	252	42	170	290	63	212	340	100
Apr.	30	83	214	350	133	254	25	162	302	64	195
May	7	174	316	82	217	346	127	252	27	158	299
May	14	279	45	166	311	90	215	336	123	260	26
May	21	9	128	261	50	179	299	72	221	349	110
May	28	92	222	1	141	263	33	173	310	73	204
Jun.	4	184	326	91	226	356	137	261	36	168	307
Jun.	11	287	54	174	322	98	224	344	134	268	34
Jun.	18	17	137	270	60	187	308	81	231	357	119
Jun.	25	102	231	11	149	272	42	183	318	82	213
Jul.	2	194	335	99	234	7	145	269	44	179	316
Jul.	9	296	63	183	332	106	233	353	144	277	43
Jul.	16	25	147	279	70	195	318	89	241	5	129
Jul.	23	110	240	21	157	280	52	192	327	91	224
Jul.	30	205	343	108	242	18	153	278	52	190	324
Aug.	6	304	71	192	341	115	241	3	153	286	51
Aug.	13	33	156	287	80	203	327	98	251	13	138
Aug.	20	119	250	30	165	289	63	201	336	99	235
Aug.	27	216	351	117	250	28	162	287	61	200	332
Sep.	3	314	80	201	350	125	249	13	161	296	59
Sep.	10	41	165	296	90	211	336	108	260	21	146
Sep.	17	127	261	39	174	297	74	209	345	107	246
Sep.	24	226	359	126	259	38	170	295	70	209	341
Oct.	1	323	88	211	358	135	257	22	170	306	67
Oct.	8	49	174	306	99	220	344	118	269	30	154
Oct.	15	135	272	47	183	305	84	217	353	116	256
Oct.	22	236	8	134	269	47	180	303	80	217	351
Oct.	29	333	95	220	7	144	265	31	179	315	75
Nov.	5	58	181	317	107	229	352	129	277	39	162
Nov.	12	143	283	55	192	314	94	225	1	125	265
Nov.	19	244	18	141	279	55	189	311	90	225	0
Nov.	26	343	104	229	16	153	274	39	189	323	84
Dec.	3	67	189	328	115	237	360	140	284	47	171
Dec.	10	153	292	64	200	324	103	234	9	136	274
Dec.	17	252	28	149	289	63	199	319	100	234	9
Dec.	24	351	112	237	27	161	282	47	199	331	93
Dec.	31	76	198	338	123	246	9	150	293	55	180

Month	Date	1951	1952	1953	1954	1955	1956	1957	1958	1959	1960
Jan.	1	194	336	115	238	6	147	285	47	178	317
Jan.	8	297	67	199	331	107	237	9	143	278	47
Jan.	15	30	150	294	70	200	320	104	242	9	131
Jan.	22	114	240	35	161	284	51	207	331	94	223
Jan.	29	204	344	124	245	17	155	294	55	189	325
Feb.	5	305	76	207	341	116	246	18	152	287	56
Feb.	12	38	159	302	80	208	330	112	252	17	140
Feb.	19	122	249	45	169	292	61	216	340	102	233
Feb.	26	215	352	133	253	27	163	303	63	199	333
Mar.	5	314	96	216	350	125	266	27	161	297	75
Mar.	12	46	180	310	91	216	351	121	262	25	161
Mar.	19	130	274	54	178	300	86	224	349	110	259
Mar.	26	225	14	142	262	37	185	312	72	208	356
Apr.	2	324	104	226	358	135	274	37	169	307	83
Apr.	9	54	189	319	100	224	360	131	271	34	170
Apr.	16	138	285	62	187	308	97	232	357	118	269
Apr.	23	235	23	150	271	46	194	320	82	217	5
Apr.	30	334	112	235	6	146	282	48	177	317	91
May	7	62	197	330	109	232	8	142	279	42	177
May	14	146	296	70	196	316	107	240	6	127	279
May	21	243	32	158	280	54	204	328	91	225	15
May	28	344	120	244	15	155	290	55	187	326	100
Jun.	4	71	205	341	117	241	16	153	288	51	186
Jun.	11	155	306	79	204	325	117	249	14	137	288
Jun.	18	252	42	166	290	63	214	336	101	234	25
Jun.	25	354	128	253	26	164	298	63	198	335	109
Jul.	2	80	214	351	125	250	24	164	296	60	195
Jul.	9	164	315	88	212	335	126	259	22	147	297
Jul.	16	260	52	174	299	72	223	344	110	243	34
Jul.	23	3	137	261	37	173	307	71	209	343	118
Jul.	30	89	222	2	134	258	33	174	304	68	205
Aug.	6	174	324	97	220	345	134	268	30	156	305
Aug.	13	270	62	182	308	82	232	353	118	254	42
Aug.	20	11	146	269	48	181	316	79	220	351	126
Aug.	27	97	232	11	143	267	43	183	314	76	215
Sep.	3	184	332	107	228	355	143	278	38	166	314
Sep.	10	280	71	191	316	92	241	2	127	265	50
Sep.	17	19	155	278	58	189	325	88	230	359	135
Sep.	24	105	242	20	152	274	54	191	323	84	225
Oct.	1	193	341	116	237	4	152	287	47	174	324
Oct.	8	291	79	200	324	103	249	11	135	276	58
Oct.	15	27	163	287	68	198	333	98	239	8	143
Oct.	22	113	252	28	162	282	64	199	332	92	235
Oct.	29	201	350	125	245	12	162	295	56	182	334
Nov.	5	302	87	209	333	114	256	19	144	286	66
Nov.	12	36	171	297	76	207	341	109	247	17	150
Nov.	19	121	262	37	171	291	73	208	341	101	244
Nov.	26	209	0	133	254	20	173	303	65	190	345
Dec.	3	312	95	217	342	124	265	27	154	295	75
Dec.	10	45	179	307	84	216	348	119	255	27	158
Dec.	17	129	271	46	180	299	82	218	350	110	252
Dec.	24	217	11	141	263	28	184	311	73	199	355
Dec.	31	321	103	225	352	132	273	35	164	303	84

Month	Date	1961	1962	1963	1964	1965	1966	1967	1968	1969	1970
Jan.	1	96	217	350	128	266	27	163	298	76	197
Jan.	8	179	315	89	217	350	126	260	27	161	297
Jan.	15	275	54	179	302	86	225	349	112	257	36
Jan.	22	18	141	264	35	189	311	74	207	359	122
Jan.	29	105	225	1	136	275	35	173	306	85	206
Feb.	5	188	323	99	225	360	134	270	35	171	305
Feb.	12	284	64	187	310	95	235	357	121	267	45
Feb.	19	26	150	272	46	197	320	81	218	7	130
Feb.	26	113	234	11	144	283	45	182	315	93	216
Mar.	5	198	331	109	245	9	142	280	54	180	313
Mar.	12	293	73	195	332	105	244	5	142	277	54
Mar.	19	34	159	280	71	205	329	90	243	15	139
Mar.	26	122	243	19	167	291	54	190	338	101	226
Apr.	2	208	340	119	253	18	151	290	63	189	323
Apr.	9	303	82	204	340	116	252	14	150	288	62
Apr.	16	42	167	288	81	213	337	99	253	23	147
Apr.	23	130	253	28	176	299	64	198	347	109	235
Apr.	30	216	349	128	261	27	161	298	71	197	333
May	7	314	90	213	348	127	260	23	158	299	70
May	14	51	176	298	91	222	345	109	262	32	155
May	21	137	263	36	186	307	74	207	357	117	245
May	28	225	359	137	270	35	172	307	80	205	344
Jun.	4	325	98	222	357	137	268	31	168	309	78
Jun.	11	60	184	308	99	231	353	119	270	42	163
Jun.	18	146	272	45	195	315	82	217	6	126	253
Jun.	25	233	10	145	279	43	183	315	89	214	355
Jul.	2	336	106	230	6	147	276	40	178	318	87
Jul.	9	70	191	318	108	241	1	129	279	51	171
Jul.	16	154	281	56	204	324	91	227	14	135	261
Jul.	23	241	21	153	288	52	193	323	98	223	5
Jul.	30	345	115	238	16	156	286	47	188	327	97
Aug.	6	79	200	327	116	250	10	138	288	60	180
Aug.	13	163	289	66	212	333	99	238	22	144	270
Aug.	20	250	32	161	296	61	203	331	106	233	14
Aug.	27	353	124	246	27	164	295	55	199	335	106
Sep.	3	88	208	336	126	259	19	147	297	68	189
Sep.	10	172	297	77	220	342	108	249	30	152	279
Sep.	17	260	41	170	304	72	212	340	114	244	23
Sep.	24	1	134	254	37	172	304	64	208	344	115
Oct.	1	97	217	344	136	267	28	155	308	76	198
Oct.	8	180	306	88	228	351	117	259	38	161	289
Oct.	15	270	50	179	312	82	220	350	122	254	31
Oct.	22	10	143	262	47	182	313	73	217	353	123
Oct.	29	105	226	352	146	275	37	163	318	84	207
Nov.	5	189	315	97	237	359	127	268	47	168	299
Nov.	12	281	58	188	320	93	228	359	130	264	39
Nov.	19	19	151	271	55	191	321	82	225	3	131
Nov.	26	113	235	1	157	282	45	172	328	92	215
Dec.	3	197	326	105	245	7	138	276	55	176	310
Dec.	10	291	66	197	328	102	237	7	139	273	48
Dec.	17	30	159	280	63	202	329	91	234	13	139
Dec.	24	121	243	11	167	291	53	183	337	101	223
Dec.	31	204	336	113	254	14	149	284	64	184	320

Month	Date	1971	1972	1973	1974	1975	1976	1977	1978	1979	1980
Jan.	1	335	109	246	8	147	279	56	179	318	90
Jan.	8	71	197	332	108	243	6	144	278	54	176
Jan.	15	158	283	69	207	328	93	240	18	139	263
Jan.	22	244	20	169	292	54	192	339	102	224	4
Jan.	29	344	117	255	17	156	288	64	188	327	99
Feb.	5	81	204	342	116	253	14	153	287	63	184
Feb.	12	167	291	79	216	337	101	251	26	147	271
Feb.	19	252	31	177	300	62	203	347	110	233	14
Feb.	26	353	126	263	27	164	297	72	199	334	109
Mar.	5	91	224	351	124	262	34	162	296	72	204
Mar.	12	176	312	90	224	346	122	262	34	156	203
Mar.	19	261	55	185	309	72	226	356	118	243	37
Mar.	26	1	149	270	37	172	320	80	208	343	130
Apr.	2	100	233	360	134	270	43	170	307	80	213
Apr.	9	184	320	101	232	355	131	273	42	164	302
Apr.	16	271	64	194	317	82	235	5	126	254	46
Apr.	23	9	158	278	47	181	329	88	217	352	139
Apr.	30	109	242	8	145	278	52	178	318	88	222
May	7	193	329	111	240	3	141	282	50	173	312
May	14	281	73	203	324	92	243	14	134	264	54
May	21	19	167	287	55	191	337	97	226	3	147
May	28	117	251	16	156	286	61	187	328	96	231
Jun.	4	201	339	120	249	11	151	291	59	180	323
Jun.	11	291	81	213	333	102	252	23	143	273	63
Jun.	18	29	176	296	64	201	346	106	234	13	155
Jun.	25	125	260	25	167	295	69	196	338	105	239
Jul.	2	209	349	129	258	19	162	299	68	188	334
Jul.	9	300	90	222	341	111	261	32	152	282	72
Jul.	16	40	184	305	72	212	354	115	243	24	163
Jul.	23	133	268	35	176	303	78	206	347	114	248
Jul.	30	217	0	137	267	27	172	308	77	197	344
Aug.	6	309	99	230	350	120	271	40	161	290	83
Aug.	13	51	192	314	81	223	2	124	252	34	171
Aug.	20	142	276	45	185	312	86	217	356	123	256
Aug.	27	225	10	146	276	36	182	317	86	206	353
Sep.	3	317	109	238	360	128	281	48	170	299	93
Sep.	10	61	200	322	90	232	10	132	262	43	180
Sep.	17	151	284	56	193	321	94	228	4	132	264
Sep.	24	234	20	155	284	45	191	326	94	215	2
Oct.	1	325	120	246	9	136	291	56	179	308	103
Oct.	8	70	208	330	101	241	19	140	273	51	189
Oct.	15	160	292	66	202	330	102	238	12	140	273
Oct.	22	243	28	165	292	54	199	336	102	225	10
Oct.	29	334	130	254	17	146	301	64	187	318	112
Nov.	5	79	217	338	112	249	27	148	284	59	197
Nov.	12	169	300	76	210	339	111	247	21	148	282
Nov.	19	253	36	175	300	63	207	347	110	234	18
Nov.	26	344	139	262	25	156	310	73	195	329	120
Dec.	3	87	226	346	122	257	36	157	294	67	206
Dec.	10	177	310	84	220	347	121	255	31	156	292
Dec.	17	261	45	185	308	72	216	356	118	242	28
Dec.	24	355	148	271	33	167	318	81	203	340	128
Dec.	31	95	235	355	132	265	44	166	303	76	214

Month	Date	1981	1982	1983	1984	1985	1986	1987	1988	1989	1990
Jan.	1	226	350	129	260	36	162	300	71	205	333
Jan.	8	315	89	225	346	126	260	36	156	297	72
Jan.	15	53	188	309	73	225	358	119	243	37	168
Jan.	22	149	272	35	176	319	82	206	348	129	252
Jan.	29	234	0	137	270	43	172	308	81	213	343
Feb.	5	324	98	234	354	135	270	44	164	306	82
Feb.	12	64	196	317	81	236	6	128	252	48	175
Feb.	19	157	280	45	185	328	90	217	356	138	260
Feb.	26	242	10	145	279	51	182	316	90	222	353
Mar.	5	332	108	242	15	143	280	52	185	313	93
Mar.	12	74	204	326	104	246	14	136	275	57	184
Mar.	19	166	288	55	208	337	97	227	19	147	268
Mar.	26	250	20	154	300	60	191	326	111	230	1
Apr.	2	340	119	250	24	151	291	60	194	322	103
Apr.	9	84	212	334	114	255	22	144	286	66	192
Apr.	16	175	296	66	216	346	106	237	27	156	276
Apr.	23	259	28	164	309	69	199	336	119	240	9
Apr.	30	349	130	258	33	160	302	68	203	331	113
May	7	93	221	342	124	264	31	152	297	75	201
May	14	184	304	75	225	355	114	246	36	165	285
May	21	268	36	175	317	78	207	347	127	249	18
May	28	358	140	266	41	170	311	76	211	341	122
Jun.	4	102	230	350	135	272	40	160	307	83	210
Jun.	11	193	313	84	234	3	123	255	45	173	294
Jun.	18	277	45	185	325	87	216	357	135	258	27
Jun.	25	8	149	275	49	180	320	85	219	352	130
Jul.	2	110	239	359	146	281	49	169	317	92	219
Jul.	9	201	322	93	244	11	133	263	55	181	304
Jul.	16	286	54	196	333	96	225	7	143	266	37
Jul.	23	19	158	284	57	191	328	94	227	3	138
Jul.	30	119	248	7	155	290	57	178	327	101	227
Aug.	6	210	331	101	254	19	142	272	66	189	313
Aug.	13	294	64	205	341	104	236	16	152	274	48
Aug.	20	30	166	293	66	202	337	103	236	13	147
Aug.	27	128	256	17	164	299	65	187	335	111	235
Sep.	3	218	340	110	264	27	151	281	75	197	321
Sep.	10	302	75	214	350	112	247	24	160	282	59
Sep.	17	40	174	302	74	212	345	112	245	23	156
Sep.	24	138	264	26	172	309	73	197	343	121	243
Oct.	1	226	349	119	274	36	159	292	84	206	329
Oct.	8	310	86	222	359	120	258	32	169	291	70
Oct.	15	50	183	310	84	220	354	120	255	31	165
Oct.	22	148	272	35	181	319	81	206	352	130	251
Oct.	29	234	357	130	282	44	167	303	92	214	337
Nov.	5	318	86	230	8	129	268	40	178	300	79
Nov.	12	58	193	318	93	229	4	128	265	39	175
Nov.	19	158	280	44	190	329	90	214	2	139	260
Nov.	26	243	5	141	290	53	175	314	100	223	345
Dec.	3	327	106	238	16	139	277	49	185	310	88
Dec.	10	66	203	326	103	237	14	136	274	48	185
Dec.	17	167	288	52	200	337	98	222	12	147	269
Dec.	24	252	13	152	298	62	184	324	108	232	355
Dec.	31	337	114	248	24	149	285	59	193	320	96

Month	Date	1991	1992	1993	1994	1995	1996	1997	1998	1999	2000
Jan.	1	111	242	15	145	281	53	185	317	92	223
Jan.	8	206	326	108	244	16	136	279	56	186	307
Jan.	15	289	54	210	337	99	225	21	147	270	37
Jan.	22	18	158	299	61	190	329	110	231	2	140
Jan.	29	119	252	23	155	290	62	193	326	101	232
Feb.	5	214	335	116	254	24	145	287	66	193	315
Feb.	12	298	63	220	345	108	235	31	155	278	47
Feb.	19	29	166	308	69	201	337	119	239	12	148
Feb.	26	128	260	32	164	299	70	202	335	111	240
Mar.	5	222	356	124	265	32	166	295	76	201	337
Mar.	12	306	87	229	354	116	259	39	164	285	72
Mar.	19	39	189	317	77	211	360	128	248	22	170
Mar.	26	138	280	41	172	310	90	212	343	121	260
Apr.	2	230	5	133	275	40	175	305	86	210	345
Apr.	9	314	98	237	3	123	270	47	173	294	83
Apr.	16	49	198	326	86	220	9	136	257	31	180
Apr.	23	148	288	50	180	320	98	221	351	132	268
Apr.	30	238	13	143	284	48	183	315	95	218	353
May	7	322	109	245	12	132	281	55	182	302	93
May	14	57	207	335	95	228	18	144	267	39	190
May	21	158	296	59	189	330	106	230	1	141	276
May	28	247	21	154	292	57	191	326	103	227	1
Jun.	4	330	119	253	21	141	291	64	190	311	102
Jun.	11	66	217	343	105	236	28	152	276	48	199
Jun.	18	168	304	68	199	340	114	238	11	150	285
Jun.	25	256	29	165	300	66	199	337	111	236	10
Jul.	2	339	129	262	29	150	300	73	198	321	111
Jul.	9	74	227	351	114	245	38	160	285	57	209
Jul.	16	177	313	76	210	348	123	246	22	158	293
Jul.	23	265	38	175	309	75	208	347	120	245	19
Jul.	30	349	137	272	37	160	308	83	206	331	119
Aug.	6	83	237	359	123	255	48	169	293	67	218
Aug.	13	186	322	84	221	356	132	254	33	166	302
Aug.	20	273	47	185	318	83	218	356	129	253	29
Aug.	27	358	146	282	45	169	317	93	214	340	128
Sep.	3	93	246	7	131	265	56	177	301	78	226
Sep.	10	194	331	92	231	4	141	263	43	174	311
Sep.	17	281	56	194	327	91	228	5	138	261	39
Sep.	24	8	154	292	53	178	326	102	223	349	137
Oct.	1	104	254	16	139	276	64	186	310	89	234
Oct.	8	202	339	101	241	13	149	273	53	183	319
Oct.	15	289	66	202	337	99	238	13	148	269	49
Oct.	22	16	164	301	61	187	336	111	231	357	148
Oct.	29	115	262	25	148	287	72	195	318	100	242
Nov.	5	211	347	111	250	22	157	283	61	193	326
Nov.	12	297	76	211	346	107	247	22	157	277	58
Nov.	19	24	174	309	70	194	346	119	240	5	159
Nov.	26	126	270	33	156	297	80	203	328	109	251
Dec.	3	220	355	121	258	31	165	293	69	202	334
Dec.	10	305	85	220	355	115	256	31	165	286	67
Dec.	17	32	185	317	79	203	357	127	249	13	169
Dec.	24	135	278	41	166	306	89	211	338	117	260
Dec.	31	230	3	131	266	41	173	303	78	211	343

Month	Year	2001	2002	2003	2004	2005	2006	2007	2008	2009	2010
Jan.	1	355	128	263	33	165	300	74	203	336	111
Jan.	8	89	228	355	117	260	39	165	288	71	211
Jan.	15	193	317	79	209	4	127	249	20	174	297
Jan.	22	280	41	174	310	91	211	346	121	261	21
Jan.	29	4	137	273	42	175	308	84	211	345	119
Feb.	5	97	238	3	126	268	49	173	296	80	221
Feb.	12	202	326	87	219	12	136	257	31	182	306
Feb.	19	289	49	184	319	99	220	356	130	269	31
Feb.	26	13	145	283	49	184	316	94	219	355	127
Mar.	5	106	248	11	147	278	59	181	317	90	229
Mar.	12	210	334	95	244	20	145	265	56	190	315
Mar.	19	298	58	193	342	107	229	4	153	277	40
Mar.	26	23	153	293	69	193	325	104	239	4	136
Apr.	2	116	257	20	155	289	67	190	325	101	237
Apr.	9	218	343	104	255	28	154	274	67	198	323
Apr.	16	306	68	202	351	115	239	12	162	285	50
Apr.	23	32	162	303	77	202	334	114	247	12	146
Apr.	30	127	265	29	163	300	75	199	333	112	245
May	7	226	352	113	264	37	162	284	76	207	331
May	14	314	77	210	1	123	248	21	172	293	59
May	21	40	173	312	86	210	345	122	256	20	157
May	28	138	273	38	171	311	83	207	342	123	254
Jun.	4	235	0	122	273	46	170	294	84	217	339
Jun.	11	322	87	219	11	132	257	30	181	302	68
Jun.	18	48	183	320	95	218	356	130	265	29	168
Jun.	25	149	281	46	181	321	92	216	352	132	262
Jul.	2	245	8	132	281	56	178	304	93	227	347
Jul.	9	330	95	229	20	140	266	41	190	310	76
Jul.	16	56	195	328	104	227	7	138	274	38	179
Jul.	23	158	290	54	191	330	101	224	2	140	272
Jul.	30	254	16	142	290	65	186	313	101	236	356
Aug.	6	339	103	239	28	149	274	52	198	319	84
Aug.	13	65	205	336	112	236	17	147	282	47	188
Aug.	20	167	299	62	201	338	110	232	12	149	281
Aug.	27	264	24	151	299	74	194	321	111	245	5
Sep.	3	348	112	250	36	158	282	63	206	328	93
Sep.	10	74	215	345	120	246	26	156	290	58	197
Sep.	17	176	309	70	211	347	120	240	22	157	290
Sep.	24	273	33	159	309	83	203	330	122	253	14
Oct.	1	356	120	261	44	167	291	73	214	336	103
Oct.	8	84	224	354	128	256	34	165	298	68	205
Oct.	15	184	318	78	220	355	129	248	31	167	299
Oct.	22	281	42	167	320	91	212	338	132	261	23
Oct.	29	5	129	271	52	175	301	82	222	344	113
Nov.	5	95	232	4	136	266	42	174	306	78	213
Nov.	12	193	327	87	229	5	137	257	40	177	307
Nov.	19	289	51	176	331	99	221	346	143	268	31
Nov.	26	13	139	280	61	183	312	91	231	352	123
Dec.	3	105	240	13	144	276	51	183	315	87	223
Dec.	10	203	335	96	237	15	145	267	48	188	315
Dec.	17	297	59	185	341	107	229	356	152	277	39
Dec.	24	21	150	288	70	190	322	98	240	0	134
Dec.	31	114	249	22	153	285	60	191	324	96	232

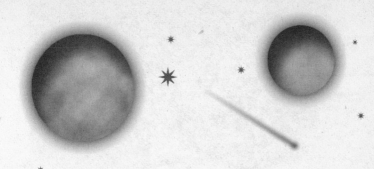

Home, Health, & Beauty Section

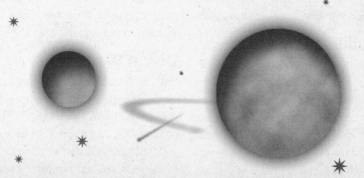

How To Choose the Best Dates for Home, Health, & Beauty Activities

Automobiles

When buying an automobile, select a time when the Moon is conjunct, sextile, or trine to Mercury, Saturn, or Uranus; and in the sign Gemini or Capricorn.

Brewing

It is best to start brewing during the third or fourth quarter, when the Moon is in Cancer, Scorpio, or Pisces.

Building

Turning the first sod for the foundation marks the beginning of the building. For best results excavate the site when the Moon is in the first quarter of the fixed sign Taurus or Leo, and making favorable aspects to Saturn.

Canning

Can fruits and vegetables when the Moon is in either the third or fourth quarter and in the water sign of Cancer or Pisces. Preserves and jellies use the same quarters and the signs Cancer, Pisces, or Taurus.

Concrete

Pour concrete when the Moon is in the third quarter of the fixed signs of Taurus, Leo, or Aquarius.

Dental Work

Visit the dentist when the Moon is in Virgo, or pick a day marked favorable for your Sun sign. Mars should be marked X, T, or C; Saturn, Uranus, and Jupiter should not be marked Q or O. Teeth are best removed when the Moon is in Gemini, Virgo, Sagittarius, or Pisces, and during the first or second quarter. Avoid the Full Moon! The day should be favorable for your lunar cycle, and Mars and Saturn should be marked C, T, or X. Fillings should be done in the third or fourth quarters in the sign of Taurus, Leo, Scorpio, or Pisces. The same applies for plates.

Dressmaking

William Lilly wrote in 1676: "Make no new clothes, or first put them on when the Moon is in Scorpio or afflicted by Mars, for they will be apt to be torn and quickly worn out." Design, repair, and sew clothes in the first and second quarters of Taurus, Leo, or Libra on a day marked favorable for your Sun sign. Venus, Jupiter, and Mercury should be aspected, but avoid hard aspects to Mars or Saturn.

Eyes and Eyeglasses

Have your eyes tested and glasses fitted on a day marked favorable for your Sun sign, and on a day that falls during your favorable lunar cycle. Mars should not be in aspect with the Moon. The same applies for any treatment of the eyes, which should also be started during the Moon's first or second quarter.

Fence Posts

Set the posts when the Moon is in the third or fourth quarter of the fixed sign Taurus or Leo.

Habits

To bring an end to an undesirable habit, including smoking, start on a day when the Moon is in the fourth quarter and in the barren sign of Gemini, Leo, or Aquarius. Aries, Virgo, and Capricorn may be suitable as well, depending on the habit you want to be rid of. Make sure that your lunar cycle is favorable. Avoid lunar aspects to Mars or Jupiter. However, favorable aspcets to Pluto are helpful.

Hair Care

Haircuts are best when the Moon is in mutable Gemini, Sagittarius, or Pisces; or earthy Taurus or Capricorn, but not in barren Virgo. Look for favorable aspects to Venus. For faster growth, hair should be cut when the Moon is in Cancer or Pisces in the first or second quarter. To make hair grow thicker, cut it when the Moon is Full or in opposition to the Sun (marked O in the Lunar Aspectarian) in the signs of Taurus, Cancer, or Leo up to and at, but not after, the Full Moon. However, if you want your hair to grow more slowly, the Moon should be in Aries, Gemini, or Virgo in the third or fourth quarter, with Saturn square or opposing the Moon.

BEAUTY
SALON

Permanents, straightening, and hair coloring will take well if the Moon is in Taurus or Leo and Venus is marked T or X. You should avoid hair treatments if Mars is marked Q or O, especially if heat is to be used. For permanents, a trine to Jupiter is helpful. The Moon also should be in the first quarter, and check the lunar cycle for a favorable day in relation to your Sun sign.

Health

A diagnosis is more likely to be successful when the Moon is in the cardinal signs: Aries, Cancer, Libra, or Capricorn; and less so when in air signs: Gemini, Sagittarius, Pisces, or Virgo. Begin a recuperation program when the Moon is in a cardinal or fixed sign and the day is favorable to your sign. Enter hospitals at these times, too. For surgery, see "Surgical Procedures." Buy medicines when the Moon is in Virgo or Scorpio.

Home Furnishings

Saturn days (Saturday) are good for buying, and Jupiter days (Thursday) are good for selling. Items bought on days when Saturn is well aspected tend to wear longer and purchases tend to be more conservative.

House Purchasing

If you desire a permanent home, buy when the New Moon is in Taurus, Cancer, or Leo. Each sign will affect choice in a different way. For example, a home bought when the Moon is in Taurus is likely to be more practical and have a country look—right down to the split-rail fence—while a house purchased when the Moon is in Leo is more likely to be a showplace.

If you're buying for speculation and a quick turnover, be certain that the Moon is in a cardinal sign: Aries, Cancer, Libra, or Capricorn. Avoid buying in a fixed sign.

Lost Articles

Search for lost articles during the first quarter and when your Sun sign is marked favorable. Also check to see that the planet ruling the lost item is trine, sextile, or conjunct the Moon. The Moon governs household utensils; Mercury letters and books; and Venus clothing, jewelry, and money.

Marriage

The best time for marriage to take place is during the time when the Moon is increasing; just after it has past the first quarter, but is not yet a Full Moon. Good signs for the Moon to be in are Taurus, Cancer, Leo, and Libra.

The Moon in Taurus produces the most steadfast marriages, but if the partners later want to separate they may have a difficult time. Make sure that the Moon is well aspected (X or T), especially to Venus or Jupiter. Avoid aspects to Mars, Uranus, or Pluto, and the signs Aries, Gemini, Virgo, Scorpio, and Aquarius.

Moving

Make sure that Mars is not aspecting the Moon. Move on a day favorable to your Sun sign, or when the Moon is conjunct, sextile, or trine the Sun.

Mowing the Lawn

Mow the lawn in the first or second quarter to increase growth. If you wish to retard growth, mow in the third or fourth quarter.

Painting

The best time to paint buildings is during the waning phase of the Moon, and in the sign Libra. If the weather is hot, do the painting while the Moon is in Taurus; if the weather is cold, paint while the Moon is in Leo. Another good sign for painting is Aquarius. Schedule the painting for the fourth quarter as the wood is drier and the paint will penetrate. Around the New Moon the wood is likely to be damp, and the paint is subject to scalding when hot weather hits it. It is not advisable to paint while the Moon is in Cancer, Scorpio, or Pisces if the temperature is below 70°F, as the paint is apt to creep, check, or run.

Pets

Take home new pets when the day is favorable to your Sun sign or the Moon is trine, sextile, or conjunct Mercury, Venus, or Jupiter, or in the sign of Virgo or Pisces. However, avoid days when the Moon is either square or opposing the Sun, Mars, Saturn, Uranus, Neptune, or Pluto. When selecting a pet, have the Moon well aspected by the planet that rules the animal. Cats are ruled by the Sun, dogs by Mercury, birds by Venus, horses by Jupiter, and fish by Neptune.

Train pets when the Moon is in Virgo, or when the Moon trines Mercury.

Neuter or spay animals when the Moon is in Sagittarius, Capricorn, or Pisces, when it has passed beyond the body part affected, in this case, Scorpio. Avoid the week before and after the Full Moon. Declaw cats in the dark of the Moon. Avoid the week before and after the Full Moon and the sign of Pisces.

Romance

The same principles hold true for starting a relationship as for marriage. However, since there is less control of when a romance starts, it is sometimes necessary to study it after the fact. Romances begun under an increasing Moon are more likely to be permanent or satisfying, while those begun during the decreasing Moon will tend to transform the participants. The tone of the relationship can be guessed from the sign the Moon is in. Romances begun with the Moon in Aries may be impulsive. Those begun in Capricorn will take greater effort to bring to a desirable conclusion, but they may be very rewarding. Good aspects between the Moon and Venus are good influences. Avoid unfavorable apsects to Mars, Uranus, and Pluto. Ending relationships is facilitated by a decreasing Moon, particularly in the fourth quarter. This causes the least pain and attachment.

Sauerkraut

The best tasting sauerkraut is made just after the Full Moon in the fruitful signs of Cancer, Scorpio, or Pisces.

Selecting a Child's Sex

Count from the last day of menstruation to the day of its next beginning, and divide the interval between the two dates into halves. Pregnancy in the first half produces females, but copulation should take place with the Moon in a feminine sign. Pregnancy in the latter half, up to three days of the beginning of menstruation, produces males, but copulation should take place with the Moon in a masculine sign. The three-day period before the next period again produces females.

Shingling

Begin roofing a building in the decrease of the Moon (third or fourth quarter), when the Moon is in Aries or Aquarius. However, shingles laid during the New Moon have a tendency to curl at the edges.

Surgical Procedures

The flow of blood, like ocean tides, appears to be related to Moon phases. To reduce hemorrhage after a surgery, schedule it within one week before or after a New Moon.

Schedule surgery to occur during the increase of the Moon if possible, as wounds heal better and vitality is greater than during the decrease of the Moon. Avoid surgery within one week before or after the Full Moon. Select a date when the Moon is past the sign governing the part of the body involved in the operation. For example, abdominal operations should be done when the Moon is in Sagittarius, Capricorn, or Aquarius. To find the signs and the body parts they rule, turn to the chart on page 86. The further removed the Moon sign is from the sign ruling the afflicted part of the body, the better.

For successful operations, avoid lunar aspects to Mars, and look for favorable aspects to Venus and Jupiter. Do not operate when the Moon is applying to any aspect of Mars (this tends to promote inflammation and complications). See the lunar aspectarian (pages 35–57) to determine days with negative Mars aspects and positive Venus and Jupiter aspects. Never operate with the Moon in the same sign as a person's Sun sign or Ascendant. Let the Moon be in a fixed sign and avoid square or opposing aspects. The Moon should not be void-of-course. Avoid amputations when the Moon is conjunct or opposed the Sun (C or O), or opposed by Mars.

Cosmetic surgery should be done in the increase of the Moon, when the Moon is not square or in opposition to Mars. Avoid days when the Moon is square or opposing Saturn or the Sun.

Weaning Children

To wean a child successfully, do so when the Moon is in Sagittarius, Capricorn, Aquarius, or Pisces—signs that do not rule vital human organs. By observing this astrological rule, much trouble for parents and child may be avoided.

Weight, Losing

If you want to lose weight, the best time to get started is when the Moon is in the third or fourth quarter, and the barren sign of Virgo. Review the section on Using the Moon Tables beginning on page 34 to help you select a date that is favorable to begin your weight loss program.

Wine and Drinks Other Than Beer

It is best to start brewing when the Moon is in Pisces or Taurus. Sextiles or trines to Venus are favorable, but avoid aspects to Mars or Saturn.

Zodiac Signs & Their Corresponding Body Parts

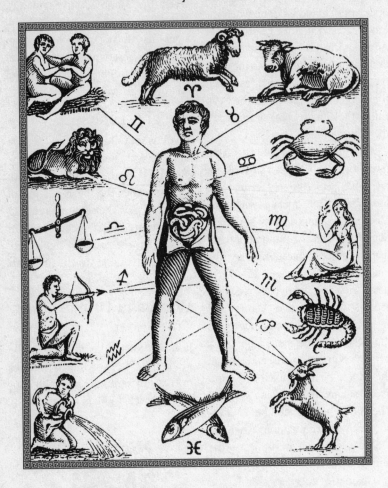

♈ = Aries   ♎ = Libra
♉ = Taurus   ♏ = Scorpio
♊ = Gemini   ♐ = Sagittarius
♋ = Cancer   ♑ = Capricorn
♌ = Leo   ♒ = Aquarius
♍ = Virgo   ♓ = Pisces

Autumn Salad Gardens

By Penny Kelly

You may dream of eating delicious summer salads made from greens grown in your own garden, but did you know that the best time to grow salad greens is in the autumn, when the cool weather turns lettuces and greens sweet and succulent? These tender vegetables taste much too bitter to enjoy when grown in the hot summer months. Greens love cool—even cold—weather. Even without a greenhouse, you can often get delicious greens long after the rest of the garden has gone to sleep. And eating salad greens well into fall helps postpone the return to the heavy, cooked winter fare. Salads made from fresh greens and a variety of chopped, raw vegetables do not make as many demands on the digestive system either. The result is a combination of rest and detoxification for your system.

Out of Sight is Out of Mind

Plant your autumn salad garden close to your house, and on those cool, wet days, when you lack the energy to go out and harvest anything, your autumn salad garden won't seem too far away. A raised bed right outside the backdoor of your house is a good option. If your yard has a spot that gets good Sun in autumn and winter—next to the foundation of your house or outdoor deck, for example—plant your autumn garden there. Of course, a small greenhouse is also an option, as are a dozen large flower-pots. The flowerpots should be at least twelve inches wide and twelve inches deep, though.

Once you have chosen a place you can easily get to for small harvests on a daily basis, go to your hardware store or local garden center and buy several bags of compost. This is a critical step if you want your greens to survive early frosts. If you want to make sure your soil is really balanced and has the correct pH, you can buy a pH meter and test the soil. Like most vegetables, salad greens prefer a pH that is somewhere between 6.5 and 6.9, although cabbage, broccoli, and cauliflower prefer a pH of 7.0 or even a bit higher. If your soil is too acidic (less than 6.5) you can amend it with lime or greens. If it is too alkaline, add peat moss. And any time you can get some crushed paramagnetic rock to add, do so. It boosts the soil's ability to carry small electrical charges, facilitating the chemical reactions necessary in a growing plant. It also adds minerals for healthy plant structure, and cuts down on susceptibility to fungus diseases. Regardless of what you add to the soil, mix it in well, water it, and let it sit for a few days to normalize.

What and How Much to Plant

When it's time to plant, figure that about fifteen to twenty plants will keep a family of four people in salads for months. Plant a combination like spinach, Bibb lettuce, leaf lettuces, mustard greens, collards, kale, romaine lettuce, cabbage, parsley, thyme, peas, buttercrunch lettuce, a colorful chard or two, cauliflower, broccoli, some lovage, and maybe even a few beets, turnips, and carrots. Except for the carrots, all are cold weather plants. If you are going to put your seeds directly in the garden, have them in the ground by mid-August, and a few days before the Full Moon if you can. August 1 is not too early, however, and September 1 is not too late, so don't get hung up over time and calendars. Just get the seeds planted, and let Mother Nature do the rest.

If you are going to seed a flat of greens and transplant them, do your seeding by mid-July or early August. Transplant them as soon as they have enough of a root system to withstand handling without falling apart. When your seedlings are coming up, or have been transplanted, keep a watchful eye on them. If you are planting in large flowerpots, they can dry out quickly, so keep them in a partly shady place. Even in a garden plot, too much Sun and high temperatures can wilt young plants beyond recovery. If you happen to have a few days of unusually high temperatures, keep the garden moist and find a way to shade the young plants. Sometimes an old bed sheet will do the job, or you can turn cardboard boxes or wooden crates upside down over the plants in the hottest part of the day. You can also stand a couple of cement blocks at each end of the garden bed and lay a few boards, or a piece of plywood, across the blocks to provide the young plants relief from the Sun's heat.

When October arrives, you will have to keep an eye on night temperatures. The same tricks that worked to protect your salad garden against too much Sun will also work to keep it safe from frost. If you are using large pots, move them on to the porch up against the wall of the house. It is at this time that the compost will prove to be most valuable. If your plants are growing in healthy soil with plenty of minerals, they will withstand some pretty cold temperatures, even a number of hard frosts. Just don't touch them when they have been frozen. As the day warms up, they will restore themselves and keep growing.

The rule of thumb for watering during the chilly autumn season is: keep watering to a minimum. If the plants suck up too much water, then freeze, the expanding crystals of ice in their leaves will destroy leaf and stem cells, doing tremendous damage. If the plant has not been watered, natural oils in the plant act as an antifreeze. They get sluggish but don't expand, thus no damage occurs and the plant keeps growing. When the plants are good-sized, you can begin picking their leaves.

My harvesting policy is to select one or two, maybe three, leaves from every third plant, alternating the plants I pick from. I select the biggest leaves, from the bottom of the plants, and allow the tops to keep producing more leaves. This way, you can have a continuous supply of fresh greens for weeks. By managing your autumn salad garden well and protecting it from frost, fresh salads on Thanksgiving and Christmas are almost guaranteed, and a true gift to be thankful for.

About the Author

Penny Kelly has earned a degree in naturopathic medicine. She lives with her husband on a fifty-seven-acre farm, where they are in the process of restoring two vineyards. Penny is the author of *The Elves of Lily Hill Farm* (Llewellyn, 1997).

Moon's Sign is the Key to Understanding a Child's Emotional Nature

By Gloria Star

The experience of raising a child brings unmeasured joy along with unexpected challenges. There's simply nothing like it! Each child is different, and as every parent will attest, sometimes figuring out what your child needs is like solving an ever-changing mystery. Your child's personal horoscope—the astrological chart calculated from the precise date, time, and place of birth—provides marvelous clues to solving the mystery of your child's needs, and can be a helpful guide to understanding the best ways to nurture each child. The horoscope shows the positions of the Sun, Moon, and planets at the time of birth, and each chart is unique. During the early years of childhood, the Moon is an especially important factor. In fact, a child's Moon sign is much more significant than the Sun sign when it comes to personality drives and needs. Childhood is the time when each person develops the basic matrix of the personality, and each quality in the horoscope unfolds at a different period during childhood. The Moon is the first noticeable quality of the personality expressed by a child.

In astrology, the Moon signifies how an individual needs to be nurtured; it represents the space in the psyche where each person stores all feelings. The Moon operates from a subconscious level, and we know from our study of psychology that the experiences stored in the psyche from this impressionable period of infancy and youth form the matrix of an individual's emotional make-up. In fact, the Moon is a key factor in identifying what we've come to know as the "EQ" (Emotional Intelligence) of an individual. A child's Moon sign (the zodiac sign the Moon is in at birth) shows how these early feelings and experiences are filtered in that young psyche. In addition, the Moon illustrates what feels good and what might be especially important to help a child feel secure and safe, and what he or she needs most when comfort is required.

The intuitive link between parents and children, especially that between mother and baby, helps guide them through the stormy waters of upsetting moments and sharing simple pleasures. The Moon in your child's chart illustrates what your child may need from those who nurture him or her to strengthen that intuitive connection. The Moon also shows how a child is likely to perceive mother. Also, if you have more than one child, you'll be likely to see the differences in the way each child relates to mother by exploring the meaning of the Moon in the chart of each child.

The Moon is strongly linked to the soul, and for many, the Moon represents what the soul seeks to develop over the course of a lifetime. Of course, a child may not be conscious of this process, but for the parent guiding a child, understanding that the Moon's significance in the chart represents these needs can help the parent to choose experiences and opportunities to further enhance the spiritual elements of personal growth. Children have not yet developed the many blocks that can get in the way of the unity between self and spirit, so feeding the "lunar" nature will help a child maintain this strong connection.

Since the Moon is the most outstanding quality seen in the personality of an infant and toddler, the qualities represented by the Moon and her sign will overshadow the qualities of the Sun sign during these early years. As a child matures, other energies, drives, and needs will begin to emerge. Even though the Moon is prominent in the first few years, it's always there—like the heartbeat of the personality.

From the Moon's sign, you can learn about your child's strongest emotional sensitivities and most prominent needs. Think of the Moon as the representative of your child's most "pressing" needs. Once you understand the basic quality of these needs, you can then create an environment and daily routine that might be most comfortable for your child—plus you'll have an inside track when it comes to understanding his or her personal preferences! Don't forget—the Moon also shows you what a child looks for in his or her mother. Let's look at the twelve different Moon signs from the perspective of childhood, or "developmental astrology."

As I describe each Moon sign, I'm choosing to use only one gender per sign, just for ease of reading. Please realize that boys and girls are both included.

Moon in Aries

Make room! An urge for independence is evident for a child with an Aries Moon. In fact, this quality can be seen in the earliest weeks of life! The most significant thing you're likely to notice is strong impatience—punctuated by higher levels of physical activity or even more aggressive behavior if anything takes too long. When it's time for cuddling, Aries Moon can demand immediate satisfaction, and gives warm hugs, but might not like it if he feels too restrained in the process. (That's what you feel when he's pushing away!) During toddler years, expect the potential for a love of teasing games and a desire to be active. Flares of temper may extend well beyond the "terrible twos," and it's important to help this child find healthy outlets for his need to be assertive. The more negative emotions are most likely to occur when he is overtired or bored.

Although testing physical strength may be an obvious drive, he will also enjoy mental challenges. Once in school, this is the kid who's eager to learn new things. Just remember that the basic impatience can extend into this arena, and as subjects (or sports) become more complex, teach him to accept that more effort may be required to grasp an idea or meet a physical challenge. Throughout life, this child hungers to express what may seem to be an endless mental creativity. He is likely to always have ideas—and will need plenty of room to express them. In some instances this expression will be through physical means (since there's a strong competitive drive). After all, the most successful athletes may be those who harness the power of the mind and direct it through a physical means!

He may love bright colors, a room with plenty of light, and toys that help develop coordination. This child needs encouragement from mother when it comes to exercising that independent spirit. He needs to see her as a leader, since the seed within his own heart is a desire to lead. Remember, even if mother is not always "out front," this child will look for evidence that she is—at least some of the time. During early teen years, he is also likely to present a more-than-expected challenge to the rules mom has established. He needs to understand cause and effect, and may have trouble developing awareness of the impact of his actions and words upon others in the world. If mom can illustrate a positive balance between self-assertiveness and consideration for others—the child with an Aries Moon may get the point more quickly!

Moon in Taurus

Underneath it all, the child with a Taurus Moon loves feeling mellow. In fact, this baby may even have a mellowing influence on the family. Within her heart of hearts, there is a deep desire for consistency, comfort, and stability. Her sweet nature almost begs for touching and closeness. During infancy, she may seem to fall into a predictable routine quite early. Yet, the innate stubborn streak that becomes readily apparent by the age of two may even show itself during her first year. Dietary preferences are likely to emerge in a marked way, and adding new foods to her diet can be a bit of a challenge. For this child, too much variety can seem intimidating—and unexpected changes can stir resistance and feelings of insecurity. If parents are considering changes, like a move, providing ample notice and giving her time to adapt before the change happens will make the transition smoother. Also, before this child starts school, a visit to the campus or classroom beforehand can save both the parents and the child tearful moments.

On the plus side, developing focus is almost second nature to this child. An environment rich with earthy warmth can enhance her creative abilities. Building blocks, modeling clay, finger paints, or musical toys are likely to be her favorite toys. Music and singing may be especially significant for this child, and the comfort of mother's voice can work wonders when she is upset. In addition, a steady, gentle tone of voice will capture her attention much more effectively than shrill shouts. Lasting emotional connections are important to this child, and she may form some of these connections in early childhood or during her teen years. She is likely to view mother as stable, but possessive, and may look to mother to learn about the importance of developing strong connections to people and places while maintaining the capacity to let go when change is necessary.

Moon in Gemini

That inquisitive look in the eyes of a child with a Gemini Moon gives a hint about the fact that this little mind is constantly in motion. Ever-changing sights and sounds are usually welcome, since the more input, the happier this baby is likely to be. Multicolored mobiles hanging over the crib can be a delight. Moods can change like the wind, and preferences may change just as quickly. This can be quite evident when parents are trying to identify a toddler's favorite foods—since what was yummy yesterday may be deemed yucky today. You may notice that this child is fascinated with language, and he may talk early (even if it is a language only you understand). There's simply a powerful need to connect on a mental level. In fact, it is that mental connection that is most significant for this child's emotional security. When he feels understood, he feels safe and at home. This child may see mother as the primary communication link, and will look to her to explain what he cannot easily understand. So, Mom, if you're asked to teach the math you always found daunting, maybe this is your chance to learn it once and for all by sorting through it with your inquisitive child!

There's also a strong desire to explore and know as many things as possible—or at least it will seem that way. The need for diversity is intense, and if he is bored, there is a tendency to be too easily distracted, and focus can be a problem. In early learning, this may not be noticeable, but once subject material requires greater discipline to master, this child can lose focus unless he is interested in the subject itself. Be sure to include story time as a regular part of your child's routine from the earliest days, and encourage him to join you reading as soon as he shows an interest. Later, encourage him to write and tell stories of his own. Books and reading tools

can be favorites, but toys or instruments that develop manual dexterity can also be great. At home, a bright, airy room will feel most comfy, but to encourage sleep, keeping his room quiet and free of excess light may be necessary. Keep stimuli to a minimum when it's near time to rest, since once this child is school age, he may find it difficult to drift into sleep immediately following a bout of video-game playing or watching television.

Moon in Cancer

Your emotionally sensitive Cancer Moon baby can be the ultimate cuddler, and feels right at home strapped close to mother. In fact, letting go of mother is difficult. This is the young child you might see standing and peering out from behind the safe shield of Mom's skirt—especially when being introduced to someone new. This child needs to feel the protection of family and security, and may require something she can touch to keep this feeling alive. Early on, an attachment to a blanket or soft toy is likely to be evident. As this child grows, she may enjoy spending time helping at home, and is likely to search out ways to take care of something or someone. Care and tending of a family pet can help fill the need to nurture, but play-acting in ways that elicit tender loving care can be just as important. Even a Cancer Moon boy needs to develop his nurturing sensibilities, but this by no means indicates that he is weak. He may become the best gardener (or cook) in the family, so give him room to try it.

This child looks to mother for the model of nurturing protector, but as she grows up she may see her mother as too protective. The need for emotional shielding is definitely present with this Moon sign, since this child can sense and feel what's happening and may feel extra vulnerable when surrounded by emotional turmoil. Parents can spell words in an attempt to keep this young child from understanding, but she will get the meaning anyway. There's a keen intuitive capacity, and if developing trust in intuition is encouraged, this child will be blessed. A warm, cozy environment filled with favorite memorabilia helps her to feel secure, and she will enjoy toys that feel good to touch. Singing can be a favorite activity, especially if someone else is singing along. This child might also enjoy keeping a scrapbook or collecting things. Just be sure that every scrap is not crammed somewhere beneath the bed, since letting go is one of the big lessons to learn for this child.

Moon in Leo

Get the cameras ready. Set the lights just right. The child with a Leo Moon loves to be noticed—when he wants to be noticed, that is. He can be quite comfortable as the center of attention, and might occasionally insist on it. Frequently, he simply draws attention, and has a radiant smile to boot. Even a quiet Leo Moon child might be at ease performing on stage. If you have access to opportunities for this child to sing, act, dance, or perform in any capacity, he is likely to enjoy cultivating these talents. This does not necessarily mean he is destined to be an actor, but developing the capacity to bring a positive focus, to take on leadership roles, or to simply be in front of others can be useful in a number of situations throughout life.

At the heart of Leo Moon children, mom is a queen, although when she's busy running the carpool and getting him to all those lessons she may wonder about that. He will need to take pride in mom, and may brag about the oddest things, i.e., "My mom can talk a lot louder than yours!" The downside is this child's strong tendency to be lazy, and that can certainly be irritating if he also exhibits what you might call the "little prince" complex. Early on, it's necessary to help him learn that it's fine to be in command when it's earned, but that demanding power for its own sake is not particularly endearing. At home, he will appreciate a sunny room, plenty of entertaining toys, lots of games, and a time when family gathers to share talents and games. After all, learning to applaud others can feel just as good as taking one's own bows under the spotlight.

Moon in Virgo

A Virgo Moon adds a deep curiosity to a child's personality. Even as a baby, quizzical looks or a studious gaze may be quite noticeable when she is interested in something. From a very young age, she begins to express certain preferences, something parents will see when adding new foods to the diet. While she might try something once or twice, if it does not pass muster, trying it again may not meet with much success until some time has passed. She also loves to learn and will feel quite satisfied when mom or dad issue confirmation that the right answer or an excellent result has been accomplished. Too often, though, she goes about quietly doing ordinary things in extraordinary ways, and may feel unappreciated. Part of the reason for that is that she develops a discriminating sensibility fairly early, and she can see imperfections. This can lead to a feeling that she simply does not measure up to standards, and parents need to take extra care to reassure this child that she is okay.

This child will prefer to stay busy, and might enjoy having plenty of toys around that help her learn how things work. Tools will be appreciated, too—including electronic gadgets and computers. mother may be seen as the one who does everything correctly, and this child will definitely look to mother as the first line of defense when defining what is or is not acceptable (or perfect). Although these babies are not born organizers, as a child, Virgo Moon will definitely respond to learning the positive attributes of tidiness and organization. Just don't expect every closet or drawer to meet standards all the time. She may also like to lend a helping hand, and should be encouraged to take part in family tasks or community projects, since making a difference adds a positive sense of accomplishment.

Moon in Libra

A child with the Moon in Libra is usually highly aware of color and may have a special sensibility when it comes to the influence of color. He may show a distinct desire to wear "favorite" colors, and may appreciate an invitation to participate in choosing color preferences in his personal surroundings. Peaceful surroundings will encourage feelings of security, and color has a special impact for this child. Baby may be more sensitive than parents first realize. Harsh surroundings or rough surfaces can easily irritate him. Fussiness can arise when baby is simply in an awkward position or if too much light is streaming through the window. You may notice that this child has a very gentle nature, and that being around other people is important. The drive from Libra is to relate—even before he has mastered the ability to speak. Reaching out and feeling connected is one of the most powerful motivators for this child. Playtime and toys that incorporate artistic self-expression will be most enjoyable. Always keep crayons and art supplies on hand, but remember that this child might also enjoy music, any type of design (including dressing up all the bears and dolls in the house), and he will want to participate in decorating his room at an age that may surprise you.

One of the greatest challenges he may face is that of developing self-confidence. While he may look up to others, or admire friends and their abilities, it can be difficult for him to acknowledge his personal strengths. In the company of family, and later with special friends, he may feel more confident about sharing special talents and abilities. Simply stepping onto a stage without that support can leave him feeling too vulnerable. (It will help to have mom standing in the wings—or in visible range.) "Rehearsing" can be great preparation when Libra Moon is being tested, so take the time to go over that spelling list with your elementary school age child! He will also be sensitive to peer pressure, and talking over concerns he may have can help build confidence in his approach to dealing with school friends. He needs to see mother as the ultimate negotiator and peacemaker, and he learns his model for relationships from mom. The most profound drive for this child is the need to experience partnership, and the way mother handles her connections with friends or spouse will form the pattern he is likely to follow. Help this child discover the power of self-assertiveness and confidence.

Moon in Scorpio

With the Moon in Scorpio, emotions run deep and are felt intensely. As a baby, this child may be extra sensitive to environmental stimuli, especially loud noises, or changes in temperature. There may be a very strong attachment to mother, and the need for closeness, cuddling, and tenderness is quite marked. Once she gets a little older, a stubbornness can be very apparent. This can range from refusal to give up "blankie," when it needs to be washed, to reluctance to share a toy with a sibling or friend. This may simply be the beginning development of her negotiating skills, but parents are likely to wonder if they ever have a chance to win. Extreme stubbornness is most likely to arise if she feels threatened or has witnessed that when some things are taken away, they fail to return. With reassurance, she can be much more cooperative.

A room or space that's definitely "mine" will be a must for her, and lots of comfy bedcovers will be appreciated. She is likely to enjoy music and the arts, and may love mysteries and tall tales. Nature is particularly appealing, and a studious nature can be cultivated during school years. This child may also seem to be secretive, and does need to know that her privacy is honored. A secret treasure box may be a favorite possession, but only if that privacy is not violated. The same is true when it comes to sharing feelings. This child may hide emotions, too, and needs to know that sharing deep feelings or fears is okay. Once trust is established, this is not such a problem, but if trust is broken, regaining it will be very difficult indeed. Scorpio Moon's view of mother is usually rather profound, and she may really feel that mom has eyes in the back of her head.

Moon in Sagittarius

"Let's get moving!" may be the message you get from a child with a Sagittarius Moon. Even as a baby, motion feels great, and going somewhere can rank high on the list of favorite things to do. As soon as he learns to crawl, you'll realize that there's an adventurer in the house. Playpens will not be appreciated, since feeling fenced in runs against his nature. This child may be a giggler, and laughter is likely to become one of his trademarks.

The drives and needs of Sagittarius prompt a child to be game for just about anything, although learning about limits can be tough. Parents may wonder if this kid understands the word "No." Of course he does. He just may not accept it! In fact, limits, focus, and discipline might be most easily taught through sports, games, and stories. This child has a natural optimism, and may be willing to try again while others are stuck or held back by fear of failure. In school, mental discipline and concentration can be problematic, particularly if the subjects have lost their luster. Since he views mother as the quintessential teacher, she can become his best inspiration to strive to do better or to learn more. Mom also needs to understand that the platitudes she speaks are considered ultimate truths to this child—until the world proves otherwise, that is! Expect this child to ask questions. In other words, buy that encyclopedia or reference software as soon as he is talking. You'll be glad you did!

Moon in Capricorn

If any child appreciates and needs consistency, it's the child with a Capricorn Moon. The drives and needs from this Moon sign are rooted in structure. Without it, this child will feel insecure and uncertain. Although excessive scheduling may not be appreciated, some sense of routine will work nicely for all concerned. In fact, lax attitudes from those in authority will leave her feeling a lack of trust. It's important to encourage this child to appreciate and to express feelings, since the tendency is to try to control emotions, or to bury them in feelings of guilt. Certainly, learning right from wrong is necessary, and taking responsibility is paramount, however if too much responsibility is foisted on her at too young an age, she may feel that childhood was simply lost. This can be especially important if she is the older sibling, since although she might love helping take care of baby, she might grow to resent responsibilities that get in the way of developing her own needs.

On the lighter side, this child sees the humor in life, and a keen, wry wit is likely to be expressed even in early childhood. In some ways, this child appreciates spending time with adults, and may need to approval and guidance of a mentor to help her forge a sense of self confidence. Mother represents control, discipline, and is the ultimate authority for this child, although mom will be tested once this child enters early adolescence. She will enjoy spending time in nature, and might appreciate a room filled with things she has collected from these explorations. One thing this child needs to see in life is the true association between cause and effect, and sometimes nature is the best teacher.

Moon in Aquarius

One of the first things you may notice about an Aquarius Moon baby is that his eyes have a cool, sparkling beauty. This child can seem to look right through you, but in a way that makes you feel good about yourself. In many ways, that's what he seeks to find about himself as he grows up. In childhood, he has a powerful need to feel truly unique. However, it's also possible that this child may feel too different, or that the things making him special are not appreciated. As he grows, he'll look for friends and peers who have their own uniqueness. Friends and social connections may even seem to be the most important reason to go to school every day. Fortunately, he also loves to explore ideas, and might enjoy learning for its own sake.

At home, this child will prefer an airy room with plenty of room to play, and he might enjoy gadgets and toys that are a bit of a puzzle to figure out. Aquarius Moon babies will have fun with interactive toys and games. Computers and electronic toys and games may be favorites. Encourage this child to develop strong communication skills, since he probably has a lot to say, and may have quite an interesting take on some old (or new) ideas! Aquarius Moon sees mother as a special individual in her own right, but he needs to learn from mother how to make emotional connections. There is a tendency to be emotionally detached (or to try to make feelings "sensible"), and if mother helps him feel special, warm, and alive, he'll learn the difference between healthy objectivity and detachment.

Moon in Pisces

For the child with a Pisces Moon, tranquility is almost a necessity. The impressionable quality of Pisces brings an extrasensitive filter to her emotions. You may see a special mesmerizing quality in the eyes of this child, since the deepest part of her being reflects a powerful imagination, as a baby she will appreciate a serene environment. Soothing music can be a sure way to lull her into sleep or calm her when she is upset or ill. You may also notice that this child is like a barometer for the emotions of others in the household. When tension is in the air, she will reflect those feelings.

During childhood, this child needs plenty of room to exercise imaginative creativity. Story time is a must, and play-acting can be second nature. Despite a tendency toward shy behavior, this child may also be a ham on stage. It's a good idea to keep a trunk or box in the closet filled with possibilities for costumes—scarves, hats, funny glasses, old shirts or jackets—anything that will aid her to become a character. If she shows an interest in singing or performing arts, encouragement and support can make a world of difference.

In the eyes of a child with a Pisces Moon, mother may be seen as the spiritual anchor for the family. This child's need to establish a deep bond with mother is quite powerful, but mother also needs to be aware that her child may soak up moods more readily than mom realized. This child may want to help others, or can be very connected to the family pet. You may also observe that she enjoys being part of any activities that fall in the category of care-taking. Special attention to television and other images is necessary, since her impressionable psyche may take things too personally. Make time to talk about her concerns, and help her learn about personal emotional boundaries, learning to distinguish what she feels and needs and what others are feeling and needing.

About the Author

Gloria Star has been a contributing author of the *Moon Sign Book* since 1995. She is the author of *Astrology & Your Child* (Llewellyn, 2000), *Astrology: Woman to Woman* (Llewellyn, 1999), and *Astrology for Women: Roles and Relationships* (Llewellyn, 1997), which she coauthored. Her column "Astrology News" is a feature in *The Mountain Astrologer* magazine, and she has also written online for several large websites.

Listed in *Who's Who of American Women* and *Who's Who in the East*, Gloria is active within the astrological community. She has served on the faculty of the United Astrology Congress (UAC) since its inception in 1986, and has lectured for groups and conferences throughout the U.S. and abroad. She is a member of the Advisory Board for the National Council for Geocosmic Research (NCGR), and is now on the Association for Astrological Networking (AFAN) Advisory Board. She currently resides in the shoreline township of Clinton, Connecticut.

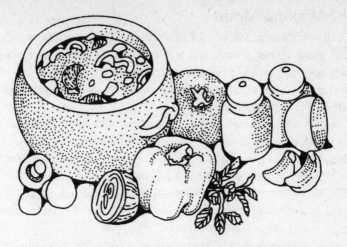

Cooking By Moonlight

By Karri Ann Allrich

Those of us attuned to the Moon and her cyclic monthly guises do more than simply moon-gaze in dreamy fascination. We are well aware of our own body's natural affinity to the Moon's waxing and waning influence. We pay attention to the changing needs of our body. As any woman knows, our bodies are made up of approximately 50 percent water, which can be all too apparent as the Full Moon approaches.

Using lunar influences to enhance our cooking is a delicious way to invite magic and healing into our daily life. By following along with the Moon phases, we can develop our inborn intuition and work everyday magic. Food is energy, after all. By taking advantage of the lunar properties of certain foods, herbs, and spices, we are capable of stirring up enchantment, healing, and intention everyday.

Tuning in to Body, Mind, and Pantry

Each night the starlit sky provides a constantly revolving show. The waxing and waning phases of the Moon become a visual meditation on the cycle of growth, fruition, decline, and renewal. By opening ourselves to the Moon's cycles, we may follow her example, inviting her wisdom and magic into our hearts, minds, and bodies, as well as our kitchens.

The Waxing Moon

The slender crescent Moon is full of promise and increasing potential. This lunar phase invites growth and renewal; it is a time for strengthening, energizing, and creating new things and experiences. During this phase, select natural tonics that will help tone the body, and seasonal foods that will build up your strength.

In the kitchen, try new recipes, experiment with seasonings, gather staples for the pantry, and hone your cooking skills. This is the time to choose foods that build up strength, invigorate the mind, and revitalize body and spirit. Hearty, rustic recipes featuring poultry, meat, and fish are the ideal centerpiece for any waxing Moon meal. Whether roasted, baked, or simmered in a slow-cooker, be sure to include the strengthening accents of onions and curative garlic in your cooking.

Fresh vegetables such as broccoli, carrots, corn, and sweet potatoes are chockfull of immune boosting vitamins. Use them liberally, not only as side dishes, but also in soups, stews, oven-roasted dinners, and creative stir-fries.

If you have a sweet tooth, puddings, ice creams, and yogurt smoothies are calcium rich. Baked fruit pies and cobblers, spiced with cinnamon for luck and prosperity help invite the bountiful into your life. Even if you are watching your calorie intake, don't deny yourself sweets altogether. Starving yourself only slows down your metabolism. Choose a modest treat once a day, and enjoy every morsel with a hot mug of ginger-cinnamon tea. It will keep you from feeling deprived, and the fiery elements in the tea will help aid your digestion.

Herbs like basil, parsley, and thyme invigorate the system and awaken the taste buds. Ginger, turmeric, and curry act as tonics and stimulate digestion. If the waxing Moon falls during damp and chilly weather, use these warming spices to add the fire element to our cooking, and help us to cope with the chill. If it is hot and dry, use less garlic, onions, and fiery spices. Try cooking with cumin, cilantro, mint, or dill instead.

The Full Moon

The luminous Full Moon inspires lovers, poets, and the wild and crazy. During the Full Moon, celebrate! Create meals that are sensual, romantic, and inviting. This can be a sacred time that is full of energy, magic, and celebration. Foods at this Moon phase reflect motherhood and full potential, so they should be rich, abundant, and celebratory. This is the time to share your table by inviting friendship, warmth, and romance into your life.

A lemon-roasted turkey; baked or broiled salmon; egg dishes such as quiches, potato frittatas, or omelets stuffed with cheeses and veggies; and bowls of steaming pasta topped with abundant sauces are perfect main dish choices to serve on the Full Moon.

For side dishes to accompany your Full Moon menu, try sensuous tomatoes; or mushrooms, potatoes, cabbage, or snowy cauliflower bathed in creamy sauces. Add a dash of wine, and sprinkle of chopped fresh basil or mint.

For desserts, think sensual. Serve generous platters of ripened juicy fruits with nuts, mild cheeses, dessert wine, and anything chocolate. Finger foods, such as fresh strawberries dipped in chocolate fondue, are romantic and playful. Or slice up pound cake and smother it with fresh peach slices and whipped cream.

Herbs and spices for the Full Moon should be lively and uplifting. Include mint, thyme, fresh basil, marjoram, and oregano; add chili peppers and garlic for their passion inducing qualities. Sweet spices—cinnamon, nutmeg, and vanilla—are subtly sensual and inviting. Accent your foods with zest of lemon for love, or a twist of orange for happiness and fidelity.

The Waning Moon and Dark Moon

The waning Moon invites us to turn inward, to finalize details, and to clear away what we have outgrown or no longer need. It is a time to foster wisdom in the quiet, a time to let go. This phase of the Moon teaches patience, and urges us to pay attention to our intuition. Choose foods that cleanse the system, and fortify protection for your mind, body, and spirit.

In the kitchen, clear out, finish up leftovers, and organize your pantry. During the dark Moon, center yourself and eat simply. Invite dreams.

Foods that help clear the body and aid in cleansing accumulated energy include lemon, grapefruit, cabbage, barley, and bitter greens. Make a waning Moon soup featuring shredded cabbage, barley, carrots, and onions. Start your mornings with a mug of hot water and fresh squeezed lemon. This will help your liver eliminate toxins from your body.

During the waning Moon, choose lighter proteins, such as baked seasoned tofu, or stir-fried chicken, for your main dish. Substitute turkey for meat in your favorite meatloaf recipe. Try going veggie one night and create a Southwestern dinner that features hand wrapped burritos stuffed with beans, salsa, and rice. Broth-based soup with plenty of vitamin-rich vegetables, or angel hair pasta that has been tossed lightly in a mixture of virgin olive oil, lemon, and garlic make a simple, satisfying meal during the waning phase. Or, you could try roasting assorted root vegetables in an olive oil and balsamic vinegar mixture. Serve the roasted vegetables with thick slices of crusty bread spread with soft goat cheese. Top cucumbers with dressing made from yogurt, dill, and mint for a refreshing side dish. Or serve bowls of sliced seasonal fruits topped with a dollop of lemon yogurt.

Naturally sweet desserts, such as crisp Granny Smith apples or wedges of chilled watermelon, are perfect waning Moon food. Think astringent! Lemon sorbet or a classic key lime pie will be welcome treats at your table.

Cleansing and purifying herbs, such as cilantro and parsley, may be added to soups, risottos, and pastas. For a perfect waning phase salad, try fresh herbs and Mesclun (a mixture of lettuce, greens, and herbs) tossed in balsamic vinaigrette and sprinkled with fresh lemon thyme and cracked pepper. Rosemary adds a heady fragrance to breads, biscuits, pizza, and roasted vegetables. Nettle, cranberry, and raspberry leaf teas are very supportive during the waning Moon. White sage tea has antibiotic and protective properties. It also provides wise and calming support during a woman's own menstral cycle. Visualize those elements you need to remove from your life as you sip your herbal infusion.

Using Herbs and Spices for Your Moonlit Cookery

Using herbs and spices in your cooking does not have to be complicated. Follow your intuition, and consider the properties of the most commonly used herbs and spices when you make your choices. Their fragrance and taste will tell you much of what you need to know. What are the properties of cinnamon? Inviting, warm, soft, and spicy-sweet. It makes you feel like smiling. According to folklore, cinnamon attracts luck, prosperity, and love. Sprinkle it into dishes intended to invite abundance, luck, love, friendship, and pleasure.

Following is a short list of culinary herbs and spices to get you in the mood for cooking by moonlight.

Basil

Basil is uplifting. Think of it as inducing feelings of love, passion, mental clarity, and harmony into your life. Appropriate for all Moon phases, basil is associated with the fire element, and is a must for any moonlit pantry. Infuse tomato dishes with this lively, peppery, aromatic herb. Use basil in tomato sauces, pesto, pizza, egg dishes, and salads.

Caraway

The distinctive flavor of caraway adds flavorful dimension to quick breads, potato salads, and many Moon vegetables, such as cauliflower, cabbage, and potatoes. Associated with air, caraway imparts the qualities of fidelity and protection, and it is said that caraway enhances memory.

Cardamom

This sweet, delectable spice is a lovely addition to breads, cakes, and biscuits baked for love, sensuality, and passion. Its delicate flavor quickly fades, though, so buy only very fresh cardamom from a good spice store. It is especially useful for cooking during the waxing Moon and Full Moon phases.

Chili Pepper

Chilies add the fire element to pastas, pizza, cornbreads, Southwestern dishes, eggs, and beans. They have curative, preventative, and passion-inducing qualities. Use chili peppers during all Moon phases.

Cilantro

The leaves of corriander are used to make cilantro, which are used as flavoring and a garnish. Associated with the fire element, cilantro's refreshing leaves are the perfect addition to spicy foods, salsas, and salads. Cilantro is useful for waxing and Full Moon cooking.

Cinnamon

Associated with both air and fire, cinnamon complements both sweet and spicy dishes. It is believed to attract success and induce passion, enhance feelings of love into our lives, and attract abundance. Cinnamon makes a perfect complement to recipes made during the waxing or Full Moon.

Cloves

Cloves spice up teas and ciders, curries, pies, and quick breads. This fragrant spice is associated with the fire element, and in addition to its usefulness in the kitchen, it can be used to clear away negative energies as well as bring protection and peace of mind. Cloves is a perfect spice for use during the waning and dark Moon phases.

Coriander

These orange-scented seeds add the fire element to dishes crafted for health, passion, protection, gain, and fertility. Coriander is useful to liven up vegetable dishes and curries, and it is wonderful added to pickles. Use liberally during any lunar phase.

Cumin

Cumin brings the elements of fire and earth to chili, soups, salsas, chicken dishes, potato salads, and egg dishes. Its scent is very sexy! Cumin is appropriate for use during the waxing and full phases to increase passion, and during the waning and dark phases to invite protection.

Dill

The distinctive scent of dill is associated with both the air and fire elements, and is most often used for love and protection. Add dill to potato salad, cream cheese omelets, or baked fish, to bring blessings, protection, and confidence to your table. It is appropriate for use in all Moon phases.

Garlic

The lore and history surrounding garlic goes back centuries. This bulbous herb is associated with the fire element. A necessity in every kitchen, it is believed to bring protection, passion, and magic into our lives. Use daily.

Parsley

This natural breath freshener is associated with the air element. Use parsley as an accent in rice dishes, pastas, vegetables, omelets, and herb butters. It's especially lovely when paired with lemon and garlic. Add it to your dish at the very end of cooking to retain its bright green color. You can also use parsley for cleansing and purification, psychic development, and divination.

Peppermint

Peppermint is such a freshening, beneficial herb that I love to grow many varieties. Associated with both the air and earth element, mint is cleansing, healing, and reviving. Use it fresh in salads, couscous, rice dishes, and pastas laced with lemon and garlic. Dried mint does not have nearly the flavor of freshly picked mint, but used in tea, it calms digestion and soothes nerves.

Sage

Culinary rubbed sage is linked to the earth element, and it enhances roasted poultry and meat. What would traditional turkey stuffing be without it? When you need to feel more grounded, add sage to roasted root vegetables, and enjoy its dusky, earthy fragrance. Use sage for cleansing, healing, longevity, and wisdom. Sage is also said to invite domestic harmony, making it the perfect herb for the holidays.

Salt

I love the coarser texture and sweeter flavor of natural sea salt, and prefer to use it in my cooking. Salt is commonly associated with the earth element, but some believe that, due to its oceanic source, it invokes the water element as well. Use it in all foods to enhance flavors and invite protection to your home. A handful of sea salt dissolved in your bath will help to energetically and physically purify your body.

Thyme

Linked to both the elements air and earth, thyme is a sturdy grower in the garden. I enjoy planting it in several varieties, keeping small pots of different thymes in my kitchen window gives me flavorful options right at my fingertips. Use thyme in vegetable, egg, and poultry dishes to invite divination, dreams, love, money, and happiness.

About the Author

Karri Ann Allrich is an artist, creative cook, and dream-worker. She shares her Massachusetts home and studio with her husband, artist and author Steve Allrich, and their two sons. Published books include Llewellyn titles: *Recipes From a Vegetarian Goddess*, *A Witches' Book of Dreams*, and *Cooking By Moonlight* (forthcoming in February 2003).

The Moon and Spirituality

By Stephanie J. Clement

Some of life's most difficult questions concern our spiritual lives. Many of us are taught to believe in a certain religion, attend a certain church, and know about God in a certain way. So when we discover the richness of spiritual possibility, we may feel a bit guilty. We observe that what our parents taught us was not enough.

Our families teach us many of the basic tenets that make up our individual belief system, and the set of cultural and social circumstances we grew up with form a large part of our permanent belief systems. But there are more avenues to a satisfying spiritual life than there are churches, or even religions. Each of us is an individual, and therefore each of us has a unique perspective when it comes to our spiritual—core—beliefs.

So how do you identify the differences between what you believe, and what others have taught you? How do you form your own set of beliefs and practices? How can you pursue your spiritual path, keeping what is useful from everything you have been taught, and gathering other ideas and practices that support the core of what you are about as a spiritual person? The Moon can help.

The Moon

The Moon in your birth chart reflects your soul. It shows the inner, private part of your mind—the part that other people seldom see. It also reflects your imagination. The Moon relates to memory—how you organize and store information. Its placement by element and sign reveals the personal side of your spiritual belief system; it indicates core beliefs that are significant throughout your life.

The Moon in the Elements

If you have your birth chart, you know what sign your Moon occupies.[1] The signs are organized into four groupings according to the elements fire, earth, air and water. The chart below shows which signs are related to each element.

Elements	Signs
Fire	Aries, Leo, Sagittarius
Earth	Taurus, Virgo, Capricorn
Air	Gemini, Libra, Aquarius
Water	Cancer, Scorpio, Pisces

We'll look at the elements first, to get a general idea of the four ways people approach their spiritual lives.

Moon in Fire

People with a fire sign Moon take an intuitive approach to life. They will ask: Does this particular belief work for me? How will my future change if I pursue this belief? How will the future be different if I take up a different set of beliefs? Do I owe anything to my family and culture? Do I have to continue to believe what I have been taught? If I continue along the path I have been following, will I achieve a sense of satisfaction and fulfillment on the spiritual level?

Their questions will relate to the future, and core spiritual beliefs will relate to how circumstances will be later in life, or after life. Actions today are based on intuitions about the future.

---

1. To obtain a birth chart, contact Llewellyn's Chart Services at 1-877-NEWWRLD, or go to Llewellyn's Online Bookstore, and link to "Astrology Readings." You can also get a chart by going to www.patterns.com or www.astro.com

If you have a fire sign Moon, you are likely to experience a spiritual initiation that relates to this element. The sacrament of confirmation, for example, symbolizes the descent of the Holy Spirit, which is symbolized by a fire or flame. A fire initiation could involve actual contact with fire, such as fire-walking, meditation using a candle or fire as the focus, or rituals involving fire. Some people who have suffered severe burns find that they are transformed by the event, which leads them to take on different or more serious spiritual tasks. People have been burned at the stake, a particularly intense fire initiation, for their beliefs. If your Moon is in a fire sign, you may want to consciously evaluate your relationship to fire as a spiritual teacher.

Moon in Earth

People with an earth sign Moon, in stark contrast to those whose Moon is in a fire sign, tend to think about the present moment—not the future. They take a practical approach to life, and for them spirituality has to have some practical application if it is going to make sense. They'll ask: Will attending church services help me to be a better person right now? Am I more confident because I meditate or perform other rituals that support my core beliefs?

When you question core beliefs, you look for answers on the physical level. Today's actions are considered in the light of today's beliefs. You focus on living each day as it comes, and finding joy in doing the best you can each day in each situation encountered.

The most obvious earth initiation is birth. Entering the physical body is a profound experience. The planet Earth emanates energies, and as spiritual beings we each relate to these energies in a personal way. With the Moon in an earth sign, you relate through the physical body. In Gestalt therapy, this relationship is called a "felt sense." It is the capacity to feel answers to your questions somewhere in your physical body. You tend to sink roots deep into the earth itself to find answers, and to understand your spiritual path. You have the capacity to bring your imagination and spirit into manifestation through any physical medium that appeals to you.

Moon in Air

People with an air sign Moon are thinkers. All sorts of information comes in from family, school, culture—wherever they go in life. The information is stored away to be considered, even pondered at some later date. Their core beliefs are arrived at in a logical, rational way. They'll ask: Does this belief actually make sense, given where I am in life? Is there a better system of beliefs? Can I discard a belief that doesn't fit, or accept a new one that does?

When beliefs are examined, it is with the desire to make everything fit together logically. One part of logic is to have things fit into a pattern of timing. Another is to fit personal beliefs into a logical pattern, so that actions are based on reason.

One way of being initiated into the air element is by acquiring language. Through initiation onto language, you find access to all the knowledge that is stored symbolically in words

Moon in Water

People with their Moon in a water sign tend to evaluate beliefs on a gut level. They have to feel right about their beliefs. They'll ask: Can I swallow this belief? Can I assimilate this new idea into the spiritual model I have developed for myself? Is it all right for someone else to believe differently from the way I do?

Core beliefs need to flow seamlessly together. There should be no holes in the system, but neither will there be a lid that is so tightly sealed that no new ideas can enter. One may change his or her mind, but not unless the new idea "flows."

The Moon in the Signs

Now that we have looked at the how the four different elements are experienced, we'll consider the individual signs. Just as you have a particular way of expressing your individuality, moods, intellect, and other human traits, there are specific attributes of your spiritual life. The Moon reflects a wide range of possibilities, depending on what part of your life you are considering. The sign reveals a lot about the internal process you use to examine the core of beliefs you have been taught, and it helps you to revise those beliefs based on what you perceive, through the senses, through thought, through intuition, or through personal feelings, to be the best path for your unique spiritual life.

Moon in Aries

Your progress on the spiritual path is largely a matter of applying your will to the process. You have the inherent power to make progress, and you also have a very strong will. This combination is great for spiritual progress, or they can combine to your detriment. You have the choice.

With the Moon in Aries, you are sensitive to the energies reflected by the planet Mars. Your imagination and thought process are stimulated by ideas, and your intuition plays a strong role in all your life decisions. As you develop your will power, you become more effective in the spiritual realm. You are more effective because you control your impulses more successfully. You may have been rather willful as a child, but as an adult you become strong-willed. There is a big difference. Instead of simply saying, "I am," you now say "I am a spiritual being who ..." and you fill in the blank.

Some religions believe that the Holy Spirit—the emissary of god or goddess—comes to us in fire. Thus, you may be in a direct, comfortable relationship to whatever divinity you have chosen for your own.

Moon in Taurus

Desire is a key to your spiritual path. You have skills that aid you in getting the material and emotional things you want. This serves you well in the spiritual arena, as long as you don't demand everything right now. You have hopes for your future spiritual life, and you will find that spiritual aspirations become more and more important to you.

With the Moon in Taurus, you find that taking care of your physical body is an element of your core belief system. This is a practical decision. We each do only get one physical vehicle per lifetime, and your life will be richer and, yes, easier, if the vehicle is well oiled and fueled. Then there are intellectual decisions to make. Your core beliefs have to fit into a logical system that is based on the practical. For example, you may have made decisions about marriage and children, based on what you believe will keep you comfortable and content. Core spiritual values need to "fit" as well. No spiritual system will work for you if it rubs you the wrong way on the comfort (physical) level.

By the same token, your spirituality runs very deep. When you have exhausted your physical resources, when you are emotionally worn down, when logic no longer seems to apply, your spiritual beliefs will get you through. This is your spiritual will at work, and it transcends the will to acquire material and emotional wealth. You don't usually exhibit this depth in your daily activities, but your life will rest in the confidence that your spiritual values will never fail you.

Moon in Gemini

The fundamental belief that guides your entire life, spiritual or otherwise, is that things change. You love to have multiple activities going on, and you can manage multiple careers. In your spiritual beliefs, this core attitude is both a help and a hindrance.

With the Moon in Gemini, you are willing to try out different spiritual belief systems to see if they work for you. In fact, you have no problem working with two or more systems at the same time. You are well positioned to provide a bridge between cultures because of your willingness to embrace the new and different. You penetrate to the essential meaning of spiritual systems, and find that they are all compatible once you get past the specific words each system uses. You have a deep understanding of the connection between mental processes and spiritual beliefs. You can often see where other people get caught up in a mental attitude that affects their spiritual progress, and, generally, you are able to see the spiritual value in everything around you, so you don't limit yourself.

The very breadth of your interests may keep you from going deeply into one practice or belief system. As you come to appreciate the common themes in different spiritual systems, you develop greater depth of personal purpose, then greater understanding comes naturally.

Moon in Cancer

More than any other Moon sign, you have an instinctual understanding of your core values and beliefs. You were born into the flow of spirit, and return to the center of that current more easily than most people. This doesn't mean that everything is easy, it just means that you know it is possible.

With the Moon in Cancer, you have an obvious set of beliefs that are largely consistent with the people around you. You follow along with family and tradition. Beneath the surface, however, is a far richer spiritual resource that you don't talk about much, as it is deeply personal. This resource is like the vast underground river that supports the larger stream that we can see. It is this way with your spiritual resource.

Your instincts lead you to the spiritual path that is right for you. When you are asked, you may not even be able to articulate just how you came to a certain belief. You simply know that it is right for you. Ultimately, this may lead you to abandon the core beliefs of your family, in order to pursue your individual path in life.

Moon on Leo

You are deeply intuitive, and your intuition allows you to see into your future—an ability may lead you away from many of the core beliefs of your family and culture. Unlike the Cancer Moon person, who finds the flow and stays in it, you are likely to undergo major shifts in your spiritual awareness. You will stand in the metaphorical fire of your beliefs, purging attachments to old values that do not suit your sense of your self and your spiritual path.

With the Moon in Leo, you achieve purification of your beliefs through the burning away of the old. You also pursue your path with the zeal of fire. You are passionate on both the physical and emotional levels, and that passion drives your intellectual pursuits. It is important for you to remember that your path is not for everyone. In your zeal to share, you may offend others who do not share your beliefs. It is better for you to "cook" your own beliefs in a well-insulated oven than to let the fire run wild in your life. This way, your spirituality will be well done at the end of your life, and you won't have singed others in the process.

As your intuition develops, you will likely find that you get hints, or even very clear pictures, about the future. This visionary capacity doesn't necessarily provide you with a way to affect the future. It does, however, prepare you to handle changes and to help others whose vision is less certain.

Moon in Virgo

Whether male or female, your spirituality rests most comfortably in a belief in the Virgin or the goddess. The fruitful quality of the Earth is an essential component of your values. There are three expressions of the feminine that may attract your spiritual thought.

With the Moon in Virgo, you may be attracted to scientific disciplines that allow you to investigate and study spiritual ideas, much the way you pursue career or other activities. You get into the details to see how the system is constructed, and to find the flaws. Instead of discarding beliefs because of illogical bits within the system, you may dismantle the system and put the parts back together so they work better than before. This may mean trimming of a rough edge or two, but you are able to save all the spiritual elements you value. The third expression is that of the Cosmic Mother. You may find that people come to you for advice, and leave feeling spiritually nurtured and valued.

An essential core belief for you is that you are open and receptive to spiritual impulses that come primarily from the physical world. You are a person well grounded in the material world, so it is no surprise that your spiritual values come from the physical world. You appreciate the period of gestation of spirit that precedes any visible change.

Moon in Libra

The spiritual belief that is central to your life has to do with balance. You like for your home, family, career, and studies—everything—to be balanced. It is important to remember that when one area is out of balance, there is more than one way to re-create the comfortable equilibrium you desire.

With the Moon in Libra, your desires are strong, but you tend not to act them out in the world. Thus, a passionate response to your partner may be happening on the inside, while on the outside you have a ho-hum look. Balance, in this case, may be overvalued. It is important for you to reach out to others and to experience the extremes of desire, at least occasionally. Only through experience can you fully appreciate the value of balance. To know great joy, you may need to contrast it to great sorrow, and to know great love, you may need to experience fear. And to gain the trust of a partner, you may have to display your feelings—even when they are not in balance.

Your strong intellect leads you to collect knowledge throughout your life. This collected knowledge becomes wisdom when you can distinguish your own core beliefs from those imposed upon you by family and society. Wisdom deepens as you allow yourself to experience the profound depth of love for another human being.

Moon in Scorpio

Physical and sexual appetites are the basic building blocks of your life, but they are not the only ones. You have profound spiritual desires as well.

With the Moon in Scorpio, you desire to know everything about another person, and then you desire to transcend mere knowing. You also desire to know everything about yourself, and then to transcend any faults by aspiring to the heights of your greatest strengths. Your life, even in childhood, may have been filled with disruptions. Spiritual beliefs often form more easily when life follows a consistent path, so you may have been derailed more than once just when you were reaching out to a new spiritual perspective. You don't need to enter a monastery, you just need to focus for a few minutes each day on what is truly valuable in your spiritual life. If you develop a contemplative practice, you will find that the outer disruptions do little to shake the foundation of your core spiritual beliefs.

Because you have experienced so much change, your capacity for compassion is large. You understand what it means to lose the people and things you felt were most important. You understand that an idea, in itself, is nothing without the courage and persistence to see it through. Therefore you understand the pain of others and can help them simply by acknowledging it, and encouraging them to transform their own spiritual lives.

Moon in Sagittarius

Spiritual aspirations drive your life, even from early childhood. The material world may be somewhat uncomfortable, whether because of illness, material deprivation, or the restrictions of an overly dogmatic family and culture. Your mind is always seeking a way out of the limitations you face.

With the Moon in Sagittarius, you have a lively imagination and a rich inner life. Others often seek to understand what is going on inside your mind, and sometimes you oblige them with the straightest version of the truth imaginable. This is not always a successful tactic. Many times your whole truth is far more than the other person asked for. Because you are also intuitive, you need to avoid being boxed in by intellectual pursuits. The intuitive side of your spirit needs to be cultivated without the limits of practical or logical considerations. Not everything you envision has to be reasonable. If it is important, you will find a way to manifest it in concrete reality. In the beginning it is enough to simply have the vision.

As your spiritual awareness grows, it is very important to be certain the path you take is of your own choosing. It can be very comforting to simply follow along someone else's path without giving it much thought. You need to think for yourself in every area of your life, not the least in your spiritual life.

Moon in Capricorn

You possess a strong sense of direction in life. You have strong desires for material success, but the comfort of this success is largely a tool for your personal growth.

With the Moon in Capricorn, you will do well to search out a teacher who can give you orderly, step-by-step instruction in spiritual matters. This could be a priest, minister, monk, yoga instructor, or peer counselor. The idea is to study a course of spiritual development. There are two reasons for this. First, you have a tendency to start one thing, and then go to the next before you are finished. Learning one spiritual path all the way through will be good discipline. Second, once you have done this, you can benefit from considering other practices, and you will have a sense of what "all the way through" means. Thus, you will learn quickly if the current path will work for you, and if it fits into the one path you have pursued fully.

You have spent part of your life seeking material success, and much of your belief system is based on what works in the material world. The same skills can be applied to your spiritual pursuits. You will very likely be more goal oriented than some people, so it will be wise to choose a path that includes some instruction concerning fruition will be useful to you.

Moon in Aquarius

Even before you considered your spiritual path, you had gathered together ideas and feelings about what satisfies your aspirations. You have found that your ideas don't always mesh with your family and social circle, yet you have been willing to pursue your own path. Intuition has played a strong role in all your choices.

With the Moon in Aquarius, you are willing to consider new ideas. You take them in so that you can assimilate and evaluate them. It may be somewhat difficult to get rid of an idea that does not fit, as you may have swallowed it whole in order to experience it. When you come to a sticking point—when there is a tenet of the belief system that you cannot accept—you may disgorge the whole system and begin a search for a new one. Because this procedure is somewhat traumatic, you will benefit from

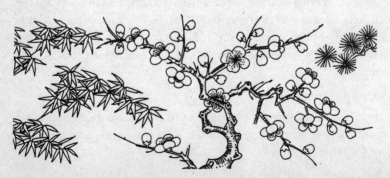

some analysis at arms length before you jump into a new spiritual adventure. Use your intellect and intuition to evaluate the surface of the new path. Also, develop a way to try the new ideas without immersing yourself too quickly.

You tend to put your best effort into whatever you do, and this is certainly true of your spiritual endeavors. You don't show everything to the people around you, so they are sometimes surprised when you announce a major step in your learning. What seems like a natural outgrowth of your experience may be a big surprise for family and friends.

Moon in Pisces

You are the classic empath, understanding what others are feeling with very little effort. You may sense or even see auras. It is important for you to establish boundaries so that other people don't overwhelm you with their energies.

With the Moon in Pisces, you are able to consider many paths, and you find the elements of each path that resonate with your being. Even as a child you could identify the difference between what people said or did, and what they were feeling. By observing the energy it takes to be inconsistent, you may have learned that every area of your life has to fit together harmoniously. When you identify a core belief that is not compatible, you are able to examine it, keep what is of value, and discard the portion that doesn't work for you. As you work with each belief, you develop a core that sustains you throughout your life and that supports family and friends as well.

Sometimes you are aware that you are actually reclaiming values that you established in previous lifetimes, or that were presented to you in childhood and forgotten. Your learning style is different from most of your peers, yet you are successful in any pursuit that you truly value. You fit into groups because you don't judge others—you generally accept their beliefs, and you ignore or avoid those ideas that don't work for you.

What the Aspects to the Moon Can Tell You

If you know your astrological birth chart, you will want to consider the aspects the Moon makes. The closest aspect (the most exact one) reveals the feeling tone you experience most often when you are undergoing changes. The planet involved in this aspect shows you the direction your thinking takes when you are presented with a new path, and it also shows the way you evaluate new ideas. You may want to study this planet in order to recognize traits and develop skills that maximize the benefit of this lunar aspect. Here is a list of qualities that relate to spiritual development, including the planet and the sign(s) associated with it.

Sun (Leo)

The connection between conscious and unconscious mind should be cultivated. Listen to dream messages.

Mercury (Gemini and Virgo)

Measure thought by paying attention to feelings. Learn factual knowledge, and then check to see how it feels. What is your gut response?

Venus (Taurus and Libra)

You have a deep capacity for love, and this includes compassionate response as well as physical love. Cultivate relationships with sympathetic women.

Mars (Aries and Scorpio)

Your excitable emotions guide you into difficult circumstances, yet your emotions are the barometer of spiritual action.

Jupiter (Sagittarius and Pisces)

You may seek a traditional religious path, although it may not be the path of your family and society. Focus on kindness in all your activities, even when you have to say no to others.

Saturn (Capricorn and Aquarius)

Your path demands self-control. You will have deep feelings, but they may not be evident in your outer demeanor. Learn to communicate your ideas and feelings, as this will relieve moments of depression.

Uranus (Aquarius)

There is a strong tension between intuition and feelings. You get ideas from nowhere and you learn how to manage them skillfully. You act on your own convictions, even when it may not be comfortable to do so.

Neptune (Pisces)

You are very sensitive to the energies around you. Learn to focus on them when it is appropriate, and close off you ability to see them when it is too distracting or painful. Your dream life can be a valuable source of ideas.

Pluto

The power of your emotions can overtake you, yet they are a profound source of spiritual guidance. If something upsets you greatly, consider that as a measure of the value of the thing. This intellectual approach helps to moderate your response.

Because the Moon is associated with the sign Cancer, this sign is not covered in the list of planets. Each aspect of the Moon relates to this sign indirectly. The Moon indicates the soul and its direction, as discussed in this article. Its relationship to other planets modifies or guides the spiritual expression and path.

About the Author

Stephanie Clement, an astrologer and author with twenty-five years of professional experience, has had numerous articles published in astrological magazines, and has written several books including *Charting Your Spiritual Path with Astrology* (Llewellyn 2002), *What Astrology Can Do for You* (Llewellyn 2000), *Charting Your Career* (Llewellyn 2000), *Power of the Midheaven* (Llewellyn 2001), and *Dreams: Working Interactive* (Llewellyn 2001). Stephanie is on the board of the American Federation of Astrology (AFA) and has degrees in English literature, humanistic psychology, and transpersonal psychology. She also serves on the faculty of Kepler College.

Lunar World of Children and Mothers

By Valerie Vaughn

There's a lot that Sun sign astrology can't tell us about young children, because children do not come into the full expression of their Sun sign until about the age of seven. Up to that time, the Moon sign is much more descriptive of the general nature of the child's personality. This makes sense if we examine what the Moon represents astrologically.

The Moon and Cancer are symbolic representations of mothering, nurturing, dependence, and the home. Usually, children spend their first years within the home, close to mother, and surrounded by the protective lunar influence. Even if mother works, the daycare site is designed to imitate this homey, lunar atmosphere. During their early years, children develop their receptive, emotional, lunar nature. By the age of six or seven, children are prepared to leave this Cancer shell, and enter into the societal world of school. Now, their father or teachers take on a more influential role in their lives. At this juncture, children begin to mature, moving from dependence to independence, and their Sun sign becomes more prominent.

However, no one ever loses his or her Moon sign personality; it simply recedes to a more instinctual place behind the front-and-center light show of the Sun sign. Eventually, the Moon sign comes to represent the "inner child" of an adult, and it remains an important factor in the "at-home" self. This is why the Moon sign shows up in someone's daily habits, what a person eats (how he or she nurtures himself or herself), what makes him feel comfortable, and how he or she functions when on "automatic pilot."

Development of the Lunar Personality

How do we get to be the way we are? Modern psychology attempts to explain this as "child development," but such theories are merely elaborate variations on what astrology has been describing for centuries. Nearly 2,000 years ago, the great astrologer Ptolemy described the seven ages of man, each ruled by a planet. His first stage, from birth through the third year of life, was assigned to the Moon. Ptolemy explained that the Moon was suitable as a ruler of this stage because it "produces the suppleness and lack of fixity in the body, the child's quick growth and the moist nature of his food, the changeability of his condition, and the unformed and inarticulate state of his mind," all of which he noted was in accordance with the astrological nature of the Moon.

Modern psychologists have not discovered anything that contradicts this description; they've simply created more scientific-sounding terms for what are basically astrological descriptors of the Moon. Sigmund Freud called it the "oral" stage; Jean Piaget called it "sensory-motor"; Erik Erikson described it as the stage that develops trust; Ken Wilber says it's the emotional self; for Rudolf Steiner, it is a stage of "assimilation"; Robert Kegan uses the term "impulsive." The general view of modern psychologists is that the first three years of life are characterized as a time when consciousness is more generalized and when the sense of being a unique self is not yet known. It is a time when bonding with the mother is crucial for the development of trust. Also, this stage is generally recognized as setting the foundation for all the other stages.

In traditional astrology, the Moon represents nurturance, caretaking, and providing (the traditional female role of mother). On a biological level, the Moon is the symbol for the primitive needs for touch and oral gratification. These lunar qualities are most apparent in the behaviors and attitudes of people born with a prominent, strong Moon. The typical body type of such people is usually heavy, fluid, and soft. Many lunar types are overweight, while others express the feeding-nurturing quality by becoming involved in some aspect of the food business. The Moon in a birth chart can also describe the feeding patterns of early childhood, which may explain the development of obesity. Mothers who use food to quiet a crying infant may be giving the message that stress and anxiety can be diminished by oral gratification. This association of food with security is thus thought to be a factor that leads to obesity.

The Moon Tells a Touching Story

The classic connection of Moon-oral-food-obesity needs some qualification, however. Babies cry for many reasons, and a major one is to express their very great need (actually a requirement for survival) to be physically close to mom, i.e., right next to her body, either held or carried. Unlike many other species, human infants are born somewhat prematurely, emerging from the womb before they are completely ready to deal with their environment. To ease this transition, they need their immediate environment to be as much like the womb as possible (warm and enfolded), and to simulate this experience, they want to be constantly held close to a warm human. The womb is, of course, ruled by the Moon, and basically, human infants require a lunar-like environment to survive.

A sensitive mother is in tune with her lunar role. She can hear the different kinds of communication sounds that her baby makes, especially one that is voiced often, which is "Hold me." A natural extension of being close to mom is the convenience of breast-feeding, and the breasts are another part of the anatomy traditionally ruled by the Moon. The purpose of breastfeeding is not just to provide food, however; it satisfies the need for touch. There is nothing wrong with oral nurturing per se; it is the indiscriminate use of oral gratification, often as a substitute for touch, that may eventually lead to obesity. It is possible that eating disorders are less common among people who were breast-fed.

Grasping the Importance of the Moon

Because the Moon is the astrological indicator of the mouth, breast, stomach, and food, many people interpret this to mean that the Moon is "oral." It is very counterproductive, however, to assume that the Moon (and its associated stage in life, infancy) is only oral. That kind of thinking can lead to inappropriate responses to the needs of babies. Early infancy is not just oral, it is very much about touch, too.

After all, what are the first things one experiences at birth? Suddenly being surrounded by air instead of liquid. The sudden changes in temperature and pressure—this is skin stuff. Newborns do not immediately feel hunger or the need for oral gratification, and people who practice natural childbirth understand this. What is the first thing that midwives do after a child is born? Even before the umbilical cord is cut, they place the baby immediately on mom's tummy or chest (both ruled by the Moon). Why? It's close to the womb, it's warm, the baby can hear the familiar heartbeat. What is the second thing that midwives do? They cover the baby with receiving blankets made of the softest material possible. Again, softness and reception are qualities of the Moon. All of this is attending to the touch needs of the infant. Only later, sometimes many hours later, does the baby actually need to eat.

Thus, the Moon-ruled newborn has a great need for touch, not just oral satisfaction. This is in complete agreement with astrological theory, for while the Moon rules the oral sign of Cancer, it is exalted in Taurus, the sign that rules touch and other physical senses.

The importance of touch is further recognized by obstetricians and midwives in one of the first tests they perform to make sure a newborn is "normal." In testing for the "grasp reflex," a finger is placed on the infant's

palm; the natural reflex response is that the infant automatically makes a fist and holds onto the finger. Interestingly, newborn infants can grasp, but they do not have the ability to release their hold. Their fingers must be pried open to get them to let go. (Astrologically, this reflects the typical "clinging" behavior of the Moon-ruled Crab, and to some degree, stubborn Taurus. Both signs tend to resist "letting go.") It is only later in the babies' development that they are physically capable of voluntarily opening the fist. At about the age of three months, babies are considered normal if they lose that "grasp reflex."

Being in Touch with Lunar Instincts

Astrologically, the Moon is also associated with instinctive responses and automatic reactions. After birth, and once the intimate bond of touch is established, the newborn seeks the breast with his mouth, an instinctual behavior called "rooting." Many people assume this is a direct response to hunger and the need for food, but the situation is not quite that simple. There are automatic movements—completely instinctive, unlearned behaviors—that the newborn makes to lead his mouth to the nipple. These innate movements are reflected in a second test that is done on newborns to see if they are "normal" and can respond to the rooting reflex. This is performed by stroking the infant across the cheek, from the nose and mouth towards the ear. Doing this should trigger the infant to turn his head in the direction of the stroking. The infant is rooting, or seeking with the nose and mouth, and literally "nosing out" (through touch) where the nipple is.

Most people, including many practitioners of modern medicine, assume that the baby is driven to seek the nipple by hunger. What is actually occurring is something even more basic and primitive; it is coming from the lowest, most instinctual area of the brain, and it has more to do with the other physical senses of smell and touch than it does with hunger messages from the stomach.

The mouth is not just an orifice for nourishment; it is a touch organ and a primary sensing organ of the young human. This fact explains a great deal about other infant behavior. For instance, as babies become more mobile and can move around to explore their world, they put things in their mouths. This is quite natural. They are touching with their mouths in order to find out information about the object. Once babies have learned about an object through mouth-touching, they then register the visual data associated with it. After repeated learning with the mouth, they begin to identify the object by sight alone. Eventually, their repository of mouth-to-sight associations becomes large enough that they no longer need to use the mouth and can just look at something to identify what it is. Because this is a completely natural, inborn method for babies to learn, it should not be discouraged. Grabbing something away from a baby and saying, "That's not yours!" or, "It's dirty!" will only delay their learning development, not to mention creating distorted associations that lead to touch-inhibition. If parents are concerned about sanitation, they should instead focus on making the environment baby-friendly and safe for exploration.

Instinctive lunar behaviors do not simply operate on their own. Just as the astrological Moon is reactive, these lunar instincts are triggered by external cues. In the case of a newborn, who is placed near his or her mother's breast, the external cue is touch, amplified by smell. The scent of colostrum, the first and most nutritional form of milk to exude from the breast, sends a message to the instinctual areas of the infant's brain. Led by the nose and the touch instincts, the mouth follows to the source. (Because the smell reaction is so vital to this process, another "first thing" that the midwife will do following birth is to clear the newborn's nasal passage.)

The Moon's Role in Human Survival

When they are born, babies do not feel the need to eat, rather, they are led to being fed through a sequence of triggered instincts. Thus, Mother Nature provides for the survival of babies, but only through a process of linking various instincts to contact with the mother. It should be obvious by now that every step of this process is ruled astrologically by the Moon—instincts, reaction, mouth, touch, breast, mother, food, stomach.

Sucking is another automatic, unlearned behavior response in newborns. But even the sucking instinct is triggered by touch and the rooting reflex; a baby will not start sucking until he or she first feels touch contact near his or her mouth. Some of these instinctive behaviors such as sucking are prepared for and practiced by the fetus while still in the womb.

The importance of touch and smell as triggers for instinct can be seen in the behavior of many mammals. (The term *mammal* itself is quite lunar; it is used to describe animals that are raised by suckling their mama's mammaries.) The mother mammal has an instinct to smell the newborn, which enables her to iden-

tify her offspring and later to distinguish them from others. Then, she sets to licking the newborn, usually all over its body. The purpose of this activity is not just to remove the vernix (birthing fluids), but to awaken the touch senses of the newborn and to trigger the instinct mechanisms like rooting for the breast.

While humans do not generally lick their babies, some women may have noticed the natural urge they have to stroke an infant. Behind every urge or instinct that exists, there's a reason. Mother Nature is not arbitrary. After all, if helpless human babies are going to survive, their instincts need to be triggered by mom, and that means that mom (or a female substitute) has got to have certain automatic urges inside her that will help trigger the infant. It is mom's stroking, touching, and petting that sets off the rooting reflex that leads to nourishment. The modern habit of owning house pets may thus preserve an evolutionary purpose, by keeping alive the instinct to pet and touch. This may also explain why so many childless adults own pets—they're an outlet for the natural touch urges that are necessary for the survival of our species.

In the act of breastfeeding, getting food is not the initiating drive. Gaining sustenance is simply an outcome of all the other instinctual activities of smelling, stroking, rooting, and sucking. Once the baby has found the breast and is nursing, then the milk tastes good, and it (almost incidentally) satisfies a vague feeling of hunger. After much repetition of this scenario, the association is made between the physical feeling of stomach hunger and the getting of food, so that gradually, the touch/smell/suck instincts are no longer needed to drive the operation, and the "hungry" stomach takes on a more active role. As the baby develops, more of the

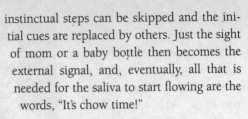

instinctual steps can be skipped and the initial cues are replaced by others. Just the sight of mom or a baby bottle then becomes the external signal, and, eventually, all that is needed for the saliva to start flowing are the words, "It's chow time!"

In Tune or Out of Phase

Of course, all of the above describes an ideal process that is more likely to occur among people born with harmonious Moon aspects. At any point along the way, in that ideal instinctual process designed by Nature, there are opportunities for a gap to occur, and this may be reflected in charts of people that have a "stressed" Moon. As the natural process unfolds, the interaction between the basic nature of the infant and the way the mother handles the responsibilities of child care becomes critical. If the mother is not in tune with her own lunar nature and she imposes an artificial feeding schedule that is unconnected to the infant's own needs, or if she responds inappropriately, problems may arise that will continue into adulthood.

Instinctual behavior patterns (healthy or otherwise) are established during the lunar period of infancy and early childhood, and they form the foundation for dealing with needs throughout the rest of life.

About the Author

Valerie Vaughan is a professional science research librarian, and a certified astrologer through National Center for Geocosmic Research (Level IV). She has published numerous books and articles on the scientific basis of astrology and the astrological roots of science.

Suggested Reading

Mothering Multiples: Breastfeeding & Caring for Twins or More by Karen Kerkhoff.

The Paradox of Natural Mothering by Christina Bobel.

Wise Woman Herbal for the Childbearing Year (Wise Woman Herbal Series, Book 1) by Susun S. Weed.

Birth Without Violence: The Book That Revolutionized the Way We Bring Our Children into the World by Frederick Leboyer.

Healing Emotions in Troubled Times

By David Pond

At the time of this writing, the terrorist attack on the United States has just occurred. The collective wound this event inflicted upon the soul of humanity is staggering. We feel emotionally wounded, and anticipating the consequences creates anxiety within us. Times of crisis, like this one, are particularly dramatic in our collective lives, but hard times periodically visit us in our individual lives as well. Our emotions take the brunt of the hit in difficult times, and astrologers look to the Moon in a birth chart, which represents our individual emotional responses to life, for ways to heal and cope.

The September 11, 2001, attack threw everyone's emotional nature out of whack. Issues of this magnitude need to be dealt with on many levels, but re-establishing a sense of well-being through a healthy connection with your emotional needs, as reflected by the Moon in your birth chart, should be a high priority. Helping the people in your life reconnect with their needs and emotions is a great way to care for those you love, too. For example, understanding your children's emotional needs, as reflected by their Moon sign, can give you clues as to how to help them heal.

I will go through each of the twelve Moon signs, outlining specific ways to help you reconnect and heal both yourself and others; then we will explore healing at the collective level.

At the Individual Level

The zodiac sign that your Moon is in points to the types of activities you can engage in to care for yourself in troubled times. Knowing the Moon sign for the significant people in your life will give you clues as to how to understand their emotional responses and needs, too.[1] If you can nurture the needs of the Moon in others, you can help them restore a sense of well-being. Consider your children's Moon signs and what you can do to help them express themselves, and return to healing and nurturing patterns in their lives. For all of us, returning to nurturing that which is simple and good in our lives goes a long way toward restoring our emotions, and the specific signs give clues about the important issues to attend to in times of crisis. The following information provides clues as to the direction to look.

Moon in Aries

In Aries, your Moon/emotional nature gives you a very strong fight-or-flight instinct in the face of a challenge, and most often you prefer to deal with challenges head on. If you support military solutions, you may feel called to join the action, doing what you can to support the effort. If you do not support military action, you may feel called to initiate movements for exploration of other alternatives. Either way, it is against your Aries nature to sit around and see what happens next. It can be frustrating for you when you feel blocked or unsure of what to do, so you need to take action to restore your sense of well-being. It is important to remember that your tendency is to be reactionary and impulsive. You can compensate for this by taking time, when you are not feeling reactionary, to give deep thought to how you handle emotional wounding. The deep thinking you do will come in handy when you need to back up your instincts with action.

---

1. You can obtain a natal chart, which will give you the Moon's sign at the time of your birth, by contacting Llewellyn at 1-877-NEWWRLD, or on the Internet from various sources including: www.patterns.com or www.astro.com.

You can expect the fiery temperament of Aries to display itself dramatically in others during times of crisis. But it is better that they rant and rave a bit as opposed to holding that sizzling energy inside. The emotional nature of an Aries is that of a warrior. They will rise to the challenge presented, and may display aggressive behavior. You'll want to give them room to vent their emotions, but it'll also be helpful to them if you help them think through any spontaneous plan of action that arises. If they say, "It's time to head for the hills," suggest that they join you in a rigorous hike; then engage them in discussion and let them talk it out. Aries needs action to feel at ease, and doing something will relax them more than doing nothing at all. Encourage them to focus their energy in ways that are consistent with their values.

Moon in Taurus

In Taurus, your Moon will feel threatened during a crisis, and your security alarms will be triggered. When you feel insecure, the ground beneath your feet seems to tremble. Don't judge yourself if you find yourself somewhat selfishly concerned with your own needs, though. It comes with the territory of Taurus. Two things can help you feel grounded again. First, return to the activities that comfort you and make you feel secure, such as stacking firewood, stocking your food storage, and replenishing emergency supplies. Gardening or tending to your piece of land can be quite grounding, too. A delicious meal, a walk, hugging the important people in your life, and beauty—wherever it can be found—will all nurture your Taurus Moon. Then, when you're back on solid ground and have gained perspective on the situation, donate to relief efforts as a way of coming out of yourself, helping others, and connecting with the bigger picture.

Those with a Taurus Moon do not adapt well to sudden changes, so expect them to be out of sorts until routines are re-established. Helping them get back to the daily routines that nurture their personal lives is the best way to care for them in times of crisis. It is also helpful to give them room to express their security issues. You don't need to fix them, just listen. Although slow to anger, when pushed to the extreme by trying circumstances, you might be surprised at the extent of their emotional response. This will die down as some sense of stability returns. Taurus needs comfort during a crisis, so massage their shoulders or prepare a warm bath for them. A well-prepared meal, including chocolates, and accompanied by their favorite music, can be very soothing, too. Taurus is soothed by creature comforts.

Moon in Gemini

In Gemini, your Moon is most often expressed by talking through a crisis. Your mind needs to be involved in the processing of your emotions. You are comforted by words—yours and others—that give you the distance you need from the actual emotions to put things into perspective. So, when a crisis hits, you are likely to get on the Internet, watch news shows, and research the angles you are interested in, all in order to satisfy your need to be totally informed about all the ins and outs of the situation. You could consider serving on a crisis line to talk with people about their concerns. It will be healing for you and helpful to others.

You can expect people who have the Moon in Gemini to respond to their emotional needs through their intellect and with words. If they become emotionally wounded during a crisis, they will need to do a great deal of communicating before they can feel settled again. They tend to feel off center and agitated when not informed, so give them space and time to pursue the news and information they need to feel comfortable again, and be willing to be a sounding board for the many and various tracks they will pursue with their minds. Expect your Moon in Gemini friends to start reviewing their options during a crisis. It doesn't mean they will act on all the ideas they come up with, but they need to be heard. But if they become obsessed with up-to-the-minute attention to current events and the news media, distract them with alternative forays into the world of ideas—movies, lectures, workshops, or deeper research into the material of current events—as they are useful distractions.

Moon in Cancer

In Cancer, your Moon awakens your concerns for personal and family security during a crisis. After you are sure all your people are safe, your concern may reach out to other groups of people for whom you feel attachment and loyalty—neighbors, community, and country. This Moon's influence imparts strong boundary lines with loyalty issues, and you'll likely find yourself feeling strongly protective and defensive of those you love. You are most affected by the stories of people whose lives have been directly touched by disaster. This can be quite healing for you, as is giving donations to the families in need. To heal yourself, return to what nurtures you most in your personal family life, and then extend this into the world by doing something to alleviate the suffering of victims.

You can expect others with the Moon in Cancer to draw on their personal relationships for their own emotional wellbeing, and you can expect them to be most needy from the onslaught of a crisis until their emotional balance is restored. Expect these individuals to take everything personally, and to have strong feelings concerning the tragedy. If they have strong emotional outbursts, try providing a shoulder to lean on. They don't need their emotions fixed, just to know that someone cares is healing. They will benefit by spending personal time with friends and family. You can also expect them to be very cautious, and not wanting to venture far from the family during times of crisis. Working on home and garden projects together, storing food, or doing other activities to fortify a sense of personal security would be helpful activities.

Moon in Leo

In Leo, your Moon feels royal, and you can expect pride to play an important role in how you handle a crisis. You rarely back down in a confrontation, and you'll stand by those you believe in. Because you like to win, your first response to conflict is to view it as competition. Leo is a very ethical sign, with a strong sense of right and wrong, thus when wronged, you like to make a dramatic display of putting the world right. After the initial sense of pride wears off, though, you will evaluate the situation with a strong intellect and try to find a creative way out of the conflict. To help you heal, you need to find creative projects and opportunities for fun and play. Because Leo rules the heart, keeping your aerobic activity up is important. You can be entertained, and also help those in need, by attending benefit concerts.

Those with the Moon in Leo seldom shrink in the face of conflict. You can expect pride, pompousness, and even arrogance, as their initial responses, but rarely will you see fear or cowardice. To help your Moon in Leo friends, remember Leo's three needs: to be the center of attention somewhere in their life; to be in heartfelt relationships; and to live a life born out of the heart. Focus on them as if all else in the world is just a backdrop, and get them out having some fun. It's heartbreaking to the rest of us when our Moon in Leo friends aren't smiling, so tickle their aura, acknowledge how important they are in your life, and above all—don't ignore them.

Moon in Virgo

In Virgo, your Moon first responds to a crisis by worrying. You know how you have a tendency to double-check the lock, even when you know that it is already locked? Well, you can expect this tenfold in a crisis, so go ahead and first check everything. You won't be at peace until you do. Later, when Virgo's service mode kicks in, you'll be able to shift your focus onto helping others. Know that your essential nature is service, and finding ways to be useful to others is the number one thing you can do for your own well-being. Your needs are simple and you are likely to pare your life down to bare essentials in times of crisis. Wherever your life seems out of control—simplify, simplify, simplify. And remember to do something for self-improvement on a daily basis, as this chases away the self-loathing you will feel if you let yourself go.

Your friends with the Moon in Virgo are likely to take an immediate dive at the onset of a crisis, but rebound quickly once they find a way to be useful. Virgo is an analytical sign, and these friends will need to analyze every aspect of the situation until they can feel centered. It would be helping them if you come up with some project with which you need help. When individuals with a Virgo Moon feel weakened, their critical nature can exert itself, and you will likely be called on to listen to what is wrong with our country, or the sorry state of the world. Remind them if they forget to tend to their dietary and health regime, or help out by preparing a simple, nutritious meal for them. Forget luxury or extravagance, though. Nothing offends the emotional nature of a person with the Moon in Virgo more than extravagance or wastefulness in times of crisis. Expect them to get quite frugal until they feel that their feet are firmly back on the ground.

Moon in Libra

In Libra, your Moon feels best when life is harmonious and everything feels balanced. So expect your emotional boat to rock during a crisis until you regain a sense of equanimity. Don't decide on a course of action until you feel balanced, and balanced decisions are born out of balanced thinking.

Libra, as an intellectual air sign, feels uncomfortable when pulled into strong emotions. It is not lack of sensitivity; rather, it is too much sensitivity that causes you to avoid anything unpleasant. Unfortunately for you, avoidance won't help. Know that everyone's life has its share of unpleasant moments, and avoiding that which is repugnant rarely sends it away. Fairness, justice, and honor are important to you, and you will settle on a course that you believe is honorable for everyone involved. You need to return to the beautiful and the refined to regain your equilibrium.

Your Moon in Libra friends will have to make intellectual sense of a crisis before they can begin to feel settled. Because Libra rules both peace and war, you can expect one of two responses from them. For some, the horrors of the situation are overwhelming, and they will feel tainted by the darkness until beauty and a life of refinement are restored. For others, peace cannot be felt within themselves until the score is settled. Justice must be served. Get them talking. It is good for them because words give them a comfortable distance from the raw emotions. Expect quite a bit of indecision until they have thoroughly explored both sides of the issues. Bring some refinements into their lives with a candle-lit dinner, flowers, or an elegant evening out for a cultural event are restorative activities suited to their temperament.

Moon in Scorpio

Your Scorpio Moon wants to take issues to a deep level and privately process the situation before you make your views publicly known. This is normal. In times of a crisis, you may find yourself going to a place within that other people believe is morbid. But you feel compelled to explore what might be going on beneath the surface. However, you can turn suspicious when threats are perceived, so explore the alternative press and any other resources that you can dig up to alleviate the feeling that someone is duping you. Scorpio is the one sign that has some understanding of the experience of death beyond grieving, and you can be particularly helpful to those who are struggling with death. Reconnect with the deep practices, such as *tonglen* (discussed at the end of this article) and yoga, which help to remove resistance and resentment, and will help you move the emotions through your body.

The phrase "Still waters run deep" describes the Moon in Scorpio temperament. So, frequently, you won't see all that is going on within people with the Moon in this sign. While many people believe it is healthy to talk about painful emotions, talking is not Scorpio's way. You can expect them to go into a deeply introspective phase in response to life's tragic events, but try not to ask them "What's wrong?" as doing so would imply they are somehow wrong in their behavior. Communicate with silent nods and knowing glances, and give your Scorpio friends and family space to explore their deep emotions, and you'll go a long way toward establishing the trust they need to heal themselves. If you are involved in an intimate sexual relationship with a Moon in Scorpio person, know that sex can be deeply healing and comforting for them. The suspicious side of their character and disgust for human darkness can be gently won over by drawing them into simple activities, such as a silent walk in nature, or a silent prayer vigil.

Moon in Sagittarius

If your Moon is in Sagittarius, you are enthusiastic and possess the ability to see things in a positive light. However, it is hard to put a positive spin on tragedy, and you can feel as if you might drown if you let the emotions in—but you won't. Although every instinct might be telling you to outrun the emotions and jump into action, it would be healing for you to put these instincts on hold, just for a moment, and enter into the true feelings of the tragedy. You won't stay down. Try to quell the drive to come up for air, and give you time to put a philosophical wrap on what is going on. If you don't stop and process the emotions, you will act them out in some fiery way. Your self-righteous side can emerge in a crisis, so do your Sagittarius homework: Explore and expand upon your existing beliefs. It would be helpful for you to study the religions and beliefs of all of the participants in the current crisis. You are at your best when you are questing outside of yourself, be it through travel, education, or philosophy. After the forced pause, get back on your path.

One thing is for certain: You will definitely know how your Moon in Sagittarius friends feel about the current situation. Good old-fashioned philosophical arguments are what people with the Moon in Sagittarius seem to need, and you won't find them shrinking from conflict either. The dark side of Sagittarius is expressed in a self-righteous, evangelical tirade about the nature of good and evil. Political types will likely launch into nationalism, religious types may take refuge in dogma of their church's teachings, and spiritual types will pray for higher truth to be revealed. Sagittarius needs freedom and mobility, so get them out in nature for a hike, or plan an adventure together to help restore their spirits.

Moon in Capricorn

If your Moon is in Capricorn, you feel most upset if issues in the world disrupt your productivity and security. You probably won't show your emotional concerns, but a crisis will impact you, too. Disruptions in your orderly life can make you irritable and quite stern with others. You see yourself as a provider, and it is best for you to get back to work and do something productive when upsets occur. You might feel good about fortifying your storage and emergency supplies. You'll want your cars tuned up and filled with gas—just in case. You are an organizer, so first get your world in order and then see what you can do to help organize in the community. You will take care of business, but don't forget to take care of your emotional needs, too.

Don't expect dramatic emotional expression from your Moon in Capricorn friends; they are very controlled and reserved with their emotions. Their steady expression masks the insecurity they go through in difficult times. When Capricorn's are thrown out of their work rhythm, they lose their sense of grounding. This Moon sign is task oriented, and in a crisis you will want to give them the space to get their world in order. Getting back to their routines will help a Capricorn more than anything else will. It is not just career, they need to tend to their personal chores and get things in their personal life running smoothly as well. Your Capricorn friends and family are not skilled at dropping this mask of competency, so if you are close enough to read the signs, realize that they need tender loving care and support, too. Don't tell them not to be so serious; this only makes matters worse. Better to side step their apparent gruffness and simply give them a hug.

Moon in Aquarius

If your Moon is in Aquarius, you won't find comfort in consensus beliefs; you need to come up with your independent view of the matter. Aquarius represents radical individuality, showing that you want to break free of the mainstream media and look into the alternative press and ultimately come up with your independent view of what is going on. Political activism is a good outlet for an Aquarius Moon, and you might benefit by aligning with groups of like-minded individuals to raise awareness for the cause you believe in. In the current crisis, civil liberties are being curtailed in the name of national security. This might affect you deeply. Getting on the Internet to research and send out your communiqués might be a way for you to get involved. Involvement in group rallies and demonstrations to support your beliefs can be rewarding, too. Friendships, whether political or personal, provide safe harbor and comfort for you.

Those with the Moon in this sign process their emotions through the mind. They can seem detached from the emotional feelings of the situation, but this is their way—pulling back from the personal to see the larger picture. Aquarius is the sign of the activist, so don't be surprised if they feel a need to get involved and let their voices be heard. Expect them to stand tall for human rights, both at home and abroad. If you are in a one-to-one relationship with someone whose Moon is in Aquarius, realize how important friendships are for him or her and give them some space to connect with their friends. Aquarius is not a consensus sign that just goes along with the media and general public-view. Expect them to offer a unique perspective on the situation. They will also question, badger, and provoke you to examine your beliefs to see where you have accepted conventional views without thinking it through for yourself. Joining them in public demonstrations that support causes you believe in can be a good way to connect with these friends and family members, and aid in their healing.

Moon in Pisces

If your Moon is in Pisces, no one is more compassionate for the suffering of others than you are. This sensitivity to collective emotions can be very confusing until you learn to separate your personal feelings from those of others. You will often fail to recognize the true source of the suffering you

might be going through, and this causes confusion. You are like a psychic, emotional sponge that absorbs everyone elses emotions as if they were your own. It is often cathartic to cry as a way of releasing the emotions, or you could try involving yourself in creative and spiritual activities as a great way to soothe the raw emotions that emerge in times of crisis. Practices such as tonglen or prayer vigils are excellent ways to address your emotional needs. Then, doing something to alleviate the suffering of others will help both you and them.

Where some signs can seem relatively unscathed by crisis that doesn't touch them directly, this is not true for those with the Moon in Pisces. It is important that you realize this when dealing with your friends who have this placement. They will feel the grief of a collective crisis and not be able to turn it off. Any attempts to rationally dissuade them from their emotionality will be futile. They can no more separate from their feelings than a harbor can isolate itself from the ocean. It is better to help them deal with their sensitivity than to expect them to toughen up. You might suggest lighting a candle and praying for those who are suffering, or doing volunteer work for any of the relief efforts, or simply sending money to the Red Cross. Realize that your Moon in Pisces friends' emotional well-being depends on doing something to alleviate suffering in the world.

At the Collective Level

This horrendous tragedy sent out an emotional shockwave, revealing a truth that has long existed on a subtler level: We all are emotionally interconnected. We feel the tragedy within ourselves as if it has happened to us. We are individual harbors in the same ocean of collective emotion. We each have our individual harbor of emotions. Now, picture waking up in the morning and seeing your little harbor polluted with litter. You diligently set about to clean it up and make yourself feel better, only to wake up the next morning to find it polluted again. You can do this day after day to no avail until you realize that the source is the ocean, and until you clean up the ocean your individual efforts to keep your personal harbor clean will always be futile. It is the same with our individual emotional harbors; they can't be free of pollution if the collective emotions of humankind are polluted. Thus, we learn that healing our personal emotional wounds is interdependent with tending and healing the emotional wounds of others.

Collective Emotions of Our Global Community

As we enter the twenty-first century, it is becoming more evident that many of our problems are global. We can't isolate ourselves from what is going on with the terrorist groups such as the al Queda, just as one nation can't isolate itself from what other nations are doing to the environment. We are all impacted by each other's actions. This reality calls for a radical revisioning of beliefs and attitudes about our global community. It is too late to decide if global community is a good idea—it has already happened. We tend to think of globalism as a political issue, but it needs to be looked at on other levels, including emotional.

It is time to take a serious look at religions, philosophies, and political beliefs, including astrology, for the ways that they promote separation. If we ever hope to live in peace, our collective beliefs need to evolve so that we can manage the interconnected reality we now live in.

Healing Emotional Wounds

In my forthcoming book from Llewellyn, *Western Seeker, Eastern Paths,* I present many practices from Eastern religions that can be helpful for Western seekers. The practice of tonglen, from Buddhism, is particularly helpful in wounding times. In many ways, tonglen is the inverse of the New Age technique of "breathing in the light, and breathing out the dark." Many of us practice this breathing technique before meditation, or to clear ourselves of tension. With tonglen, you actually breathe in the pain and suffering of others, and breathe out the light. You don't hold on to the pain that you breathe in, but imagine instead all of this emotion dissolving into *shunyata* (emptiness, a void). There is no place for the emotions to stick or become attached as they dissolve back into the oneness. Then on the out-breath, you send out the compassionate prayer, "May all beings be free of this and all suffering."

It can be helpful to picture yourself like a Hollywood storefront. Everything looks normal from the front, but behind you is just vast empty space. As you breathe the emotions you feel them pass through you into the void where they dissolve.

Practicing Tonglen

First, establish your intention of keeping an open heart. Then focus on your breath and become mindful of any emotion that is arising. As you breathe in, sink into the feelings and note their tone, quality, and temperament. Don't avoid any of the emotions; just experience them for what they are on the first half of your in-breath. On the second half of your in-breath, center your attention in shunyata and feel the emotions dissolve into the emptiness. As you breathe out, send out the compassionate prayer, "May all beings be free of this and all suffering."

After you have cleared your personal emotions—your emotional harbor—extend the process out into the ocean of collective emotions by imagining how many millions of people the world over must be going through similar suffering. Breathe it all in. Allow yourself to feel it all on the first half of the in-breath, and dissolve it all, for the world's sake, into shunyata. Complete the cycle with an out-breath and the compassionate prayer of all beings becoming free of suffering.

This is an amazing healing practice for your own emotions during wounding times, and it does help clean the ocean of our collective emotions. This general practice can be applied to specific situations, such as with individual families who have experienced loss and pain, or with an individual who is dying or troubled. Tonglen means exchanging yourself with another, and when someone is suffering you take it on, not to carry it yourself, but to dissolve it. It is a way of proactively dealing with this emotional interconnectedness that leads to healing for everyone involved.

About the Author

David Pond presents many of the ideas in this article in his recently published book, *The Art of Relationships* (ACS, 2000). His other published books include *Astrology & Relationships: Techniques for Harmonious Personal Connections* (Llewellyn, 2001), *Chakras for Beginners* (Llewellyn, 1999), and *The Metaphysical Handbook* (Reflecting Pond Publications, 1984), which he coauthored with his sister, Lucy. He is a contributing author in two of Llewellyn's *New World Astrology* series: *Exploring Consciousness in the Horoscope* and *Astrological Counseling*. David has a BA in education and a Master of Science degree in experimental metaphysics from Central Washington University. He is a national speaker, and has been a full-time practicing professional astrologer since 1976. He and his wife Laura frequently organize week-long retreats in exotic places to study astrology, practice yoga, and visit sacred sites. For astrological services, David can be reached through his website: www.reflectingpond.com.

2003 Lunation Cycle: New and Full Moons

By Leah Whiting

What can we learn from observing the New and Full Moon's? Astrologers believe that the Moon is intimately related to our emotions and feelings, so by looking at the birth chart of a New Moon, for example, we can gain important information to use in our daily lives. The birth chart symbolizes the promise an event or person holds.

At the New Moon, the Sun and Moon come together in one zodiac sign, and that sign along with placement of the ten planets holds clues about what we might expect to happen in the coming days. It is a time of new beginnings. On a personal level, you might feel an urge, or be inspired to do something new or different. Acting on instinct and impulse are typical responses to a New Moon. On a collective level—national or worldwide—we feel similar urges and impulses. Collectively, we tend to tune in and respond to the universe's "promise" as symbolized by the event chart. I don't believe that astrology is deterministic, however. We each have free will to respond or not to our inner urgings.

The Full Moon signals a time of completion. What was begun at a New Moon—and it doesn't necessarily have to be the previous New Moon—is complete and will be shown to us. The seed of a project that was planted has grown and produced results. The urge that prompted you to begin looking for a new residence has resulted in finding a home and signing a purchase agreement.

The Sun and Moon are in opposite signs—Cancer and Capricorn, Pisces and Virgo, for example—during a Full Moon. Symbolically, this represents tension. We might experience the tension reflected in the alignment of the Sun and Moon as pulling in opposite directions (polarization), but it can also "expose" a time to work toward balancing that which is out of balance. The Sun is shining on the Moon and the Moon is reflecting the Sun's light. Symbolically, then, Full Moons expose that which was begun in secret, and it is true that we often see things "come to light" during a Full Moon. Birthrates also rise around the time of a Full Moon.

January 2, 2003: New Moon at 3:23 pm EST

This Sun-Moon conjunction in Capricorn embraces the asteroid Chiron, named after the mythological centaur, who was a skilled hunter, warrior, and teacher. The Sun joined Chiron on January 1, which couldn't have been better timing for a celestial conversation to take place between the Sun, center of our universe, and the wise old magician-healer. Their "discourse"—that's what it would be in Capricorn, the sign that champions responsible actions, integrity, and security—would have been about healing the strife, and other ills (including environmental) here on planet Earth. When the Moon glided past Chiron, just two hours before joining with the Sun, she absorbed the emotional content of that recent conversation. She'll be reminding us about this conversation, and its importance, on a subtle level for the next few weeks.

A New Moon, like other things that are new, is the universe's way of reminding us of the appropriate time to start new initiatives that we would like to see grow and produce results. With the elements of earth and air prominent in this chart, our physical-material concerns and using the mind in constructive ways to achieve objectives—which will be given high priority—will seem to dominate our conversations and activities. In Capricorn, our concerns are apt to be around assuming new responsibilities and taking steps to improve or assure financial security for self and family. On a personal level, this might include the decision to marry or start a family; or deciding to join the 401(k) plan at your workplace. The influence of a New Moon can remain in effect for up to a month, but may be as short as a week, so don't languish with indecision for too long.

Mercury turned retrograde just prior to this New Moon conjunction, and will not turn direct until January 22. If you can, avoid signing important papers now. Activities undertaken at this time frequently must be redone at a later date.

If your birthday falls during the New Moon, March 31, April 1–2, October 4–6, or on July 3–5, you are more likely feel the impact of this New Moon more than others do.

January 18, 2003: Full Moon at 5:48 pm EST

The Sun is near the end of its journey through Capricorn as this Moon reaches fullness in Cancer. In Capricorn, the Sun represents the nearly universal drive to achieve success, to be financially secure, and to accomplish goals through organization and without emotional outbursts. But the Moon in Cancer suggests that we need to use sensitivity and empathy, and to try and center our emotions and actions around caring for others. This Full Moon is strongly representative of mother-caretaker (the Moon) and father-provider (the Sun). It is revealing how both love their family very much, but can want to go about things in very different ways. Both Capricorn and Cancer are traditional signs.

This Full Moon is exposing the struggle that exists within each of us as we try to balance career and family life, for example. It may also be shining a light on the expectations we have of our partners. You might experience a struggle about your role at home, at work, or in your relationships. What are you seeing in your life that needs adjustment? Where do you need to achieve more balance? Are your needs being met at your partner's expense, or vice versa? Expect emotions to feel intense during this Cancer Full Moon, but if you can be honest with yourself about your own emotional needs and the needs of others, you will benefit greatly.

The Moon is in an uncomfortable relationship with Uranus in this chart. Like two people standing apart, they can see each other, but they have no common ground for understanding. This translates into us feeling "edgy." But as the Moon reaches an opposition to Uranus on January 20, we will begin to feel our own purpose and objectives more clearly. When the opposition is complete, the Moon will be void-of-course for several hours, during which time we will have time to reflect and regroup our emotions.

Air and fire are the dominant elements here, so expect high energy and plenty of action to accompany thoughts and conversation.

You are apt to feel the affects of this Moon more than many others if your birthday falls on or near this date, or on April 17–19, October 20–22, or July 20–22.

February 1, 2003: New Moon at 5:48 pm EST

The Sun and Moon spent time with Neptune, the artist and dreamer, just hours before this New Aquarius Moon was born. Neptune has a special connection to the creative mind, and is considered to be very psychic and visionary. So pay attention to your own intuition, as the creative muse may tap you on the shoulder, or you may dream the answer to a perplexing problem. This Aquarius New Moon suggests that awareness will shift from the self to others. You'll remember that last month the universe gave us opportunities to take care of ourselves first. Well, now it's time to look outward and be more aware of others. Again, we have help, because this Sun-Moon conjunction represents the inspiration, vision, creativity, and idealism of both Neptune and Aquarius.

According to myth, Chiron (he was in attendance at the January 2 New Moon) was wounded by one of Hercules' poison arrows, and not even the healer could heal himself. But being an immortal, Chiron couldn't die either. Finally, he struck a bargain with Olympus. Zeus had decreed that Prometheus, a rebellious Titan who befriended humans, should be chained to a rock on a mountaintop, and that he could only be released if one of the immortal gods were to die and descend into Hades. Chiron walked willingly into the underworld and then demanded that Prometheus should be released. Prometheus, protector of mankind, was returned to Earth.

As you watch this New Moon be born, consider what you can do to protect others and ensure freedom for all of humankind. Ask the universe to reveal what you can do to help, and then catch those mental pictures or visions that flash into your awareness. They hold answers.

The elements of fire and air are still providing plenty of energy if you want to take action on creative thoughts that have been flying around like arrows. If you've been struck with an idea, let it germinate for a few days, think about how you can bring your thoughts to life, and then let loose and make it happen.

If your birthday falls on or near this date, or on May 2–4, August 3–5, or November 3–5, you may feel the effects of this New Moon more than others do.

February 16, 2003: Full Moon at 6:51 pm EST

This Full Moon in Leo is shining brightly—in the universe's closet! As most of us know, it's easy to abandon good intentions. We make great plans, maybe even build support to implement changes that we believe will help others. But then we get side-tracked, or lose interest. We don't necessarily turn our back on things, we just kind of "forget about them." Well, this Leo Full Moon is shouting, "Hey! Remember me?"

The Sun in Aquarius is one day from joining Uranus—a visit that is sure to inspire the desire for change, or breaking out of the mold. Uranus was discovered in 1781, during the American and French revolutions, and associations with this planet are of a rebellious nature—breaking with convention, pioneering new thought and actions, breaking barriers. You get the picture. This may be the universe's way of keeping us plugged in to the collective unconscious, and we need to take notice. Think back to the New Moon time. What inspiration did you receive? Have you followed through?

There is even more air in this chart than in the previous two (five planets and the North Node are in air signs), so mental activity and communications of all kinds are getting plenty of emphasis. In fact, there isn't much of the earth element to keep us grounded in reality or to carry ideas beyond the thought stage. The Moon goes void-of-course shortly after it reaches fullness, and then it moves into earthy Virgo, which may help. Another possibility is that you may find yourself working way too many hours because you think it is the right thing to do. Something that might help if you find yourself overdoing and overthinking, or if everyone is tired of hearing you talk, is to remember that the Full Moon emphasizes polarity, and the struggles we often engage in as we try to find balance in our lives.

If your birthday falls near this date, or on May 19–21, August 21–23, or November 20–22, you are more apt to feel the impact of this Full Moon than others will be.

March 2, 2003: New Moon at 9:35 pm EST

A Pisces Moon highlights emotions, sensitivity, and empathy for humanity. In January, we were reminded to take care of ourselves; and in February, we looked outward and became aware of others. But Aquarius uses the mind, not emotions, to see needs. Now we are being guided to use our imaginations, to dream, and to get in touch with spiritual beliefs and compassion (Pisces). Pisces is the most intuitive, sensitive sign in the zodiac, and this dark time of the Moon can be useful to get tuned into your own "gut feelings" and to see the real needs of those around us.

This is a highly creative Moon time, and staying aware of yourself—even while you're sensitive to others—is important. Let yourself daydream about some special project or the book you want to write. Try to remember your night dreams. Reflecting on them may provide you with important clues or answers to questions and concerns that you have. Be cautious in romance, if you find yourself attracted to someone new at this time. You may not be seeing the person or the situation clearly.

Personal values and beliefs are at the forefront for those who believe it is their business—politicians, religious leaders, and others who wish to exert control of the thoughts and actions of others—to establish standards we should all abide by. This doesn't apply to foreign powers only. The media is often the tool used to convey the message, but remember that people are behind the cameras, pens, and microphones. We are all—including our lawmakers and President Bush—susceptible to this influence.

Air and fire are still the prominent elements, and we'll probably see a lot of news coverage suggesting that change is in the air. It is. Uranus will have moved into Pisces by Full Moon time on March 18, initiating upsets and innovation in the realm of personal spirituality, public and private institutions, and pharmaceuticals, for example. Earth is almost nonexistent in this chart, so don't expect much to get done, though.

If your birthday is on or near this New Moon, or on June 2–4, September 4–6, or December 4–6, you may feel more affected by this Moon than many others will.

March 18, 2003: Full Moon at 5:35 am EST

This Full Moon in Virgo is exposing our need to clear away the confusion that may be finding an outlet in criticism of others and self-criticism. One Virgo quality is discernment—the ability to "sort the wheat from the chaff." This Full Moon highlights partnerships—personal and professional—service, and also health concerns. Take a step back and review the things you fill your days with. Maybe you're working too much, but neglecting your physical health. This earth element Moon along with Mars in Capricorn have a helpful suggestion for us. Mars represents action, and Capricorn represents setting goals. In this placement Mars is saying: "Get moving. Organize a routine, and stick to it." (Saturn, ruler of Capricorn, and structures and responsibilities, is influencing Mars, who is passing through Capricorn.) Stick with the decisions you make, and keep moving. Writing down your plan of action before you begin is one way to remind yourself of the direction you need to move in. Virgo is a practical sign, so don't bother with elaborate schemes, or with spending unnecessarily on sports gear. You only need a good pair of shoes and comfortable clothes. You might also consider doing some meditating (in honor of the Sun in Pisces, who has so graciously shown us the "light"). It would be beneficial to your mind as well as providing stress relief for your body.

Virgo and Pisces are both service-oriented signs. A Full Moon often points out disparities, and the disparity between what our head wants and how our heart feels is a common one. (The Moon moving into Libra before noon today will bring additional focus to partnerships this week.) During a Full Moon is a good time to let go of anything you no longer need or want in your life. An abundance of mutable (change, adaptation) energy—from Saturn, Mercury, the Sun, Uranus, Pluto, the Moon, and the Moon's nodes—accompanies this Full Moon. It's the universe's way of helping us let go and move on.

If you were born on March 17–19, June 17–19, September 19–21, or December 19–21, you are more likely to feel the effects of this Full Moon than many others do.

April 1, 2003: New Moon at 2:19 pm EST

Aries marks the beginning of the astrological year, and this New Moon in Aries represents a powerhouse of energetic and innovative ideas for us. There is such a strong Mars-type—blunt, impulsive, aggressive—imprint here, that caution is advised before speaking out or when decision making. Try to apply the rule of waiting twenty-four hours before taking action, which includes buying something. When your impulse or intuition is saying "No"—pay attention. Gut reactions are Moon related.

This Moon is supportive of taking calculated risks, and pioneering new ways. So harness this Aries-Mars energy and apply it toward positive outcomes. For example, if you're still resisting the need to let go of something or someone in your life, you might be getting strong signals from your inner-self about how you can end the old and begin anew—a great Aries theme.

The sign of Aries, and people born during this time, are frequently referred to as selfish and impulsive. It's true. They can be, and often are both of those things, or more. But that's not all bad. We should be concerned about ourselves and meeting our own needs, because only then can we begin to meet the needs of others. During this dark time of the Moon, try to find time to look inward. Perhaps you'll find the source of any anger that is burbling away inside of you. And then realize that you need to take care of yourself before you can nurture others. But nurturing—a Moon quality—implies caring for, not hurting either yourself or others. If nurturing yourself means finally signing up for college courses after putting it off for twenty years—DO IT!

This New Moon is accompanied by enough mutable (transforming) and cardinal (initiating) energy to bring about abundant changes. The element of fire gets things moving. It is also an agent of change. People might be more agreeable and adapt to changes at this time, too. And Mars, in earthy Capricorn, will help us to accomplish our desires.

If your birthday is on or near this date, or on July 2–4, October 3–5, or January 1–3, you are more apt to feel the effects of this New Moon.

April 16, 2003: Full Moon at 2:36 pm EST

The Sun is still in Aries at the birth of this Full Moon, but the Moon has moved to the sign opposite from Aries—Libra. This Libra Moon is showing us the need for balance, harmony, and partnership. It will illuminate our desires for beauty, creative outlets, and leisure activities. Mars (Aries' ruler) is currently in a very tight square aspect to both the Sun and the Moon. We may experience this as tension, or even conflict that demands resolution. If we choose to keep pulling away (Aries Sun) from the need to balance and harmonize (Libra Moon), life will go on, but the benefit of this Moon's teachings will be lost to us.

In its reflective light, we have time to evaluate where we are in relationship to ourselves and to others. Become aware of any desire you have to preserve peace at any cost because, as we know, that action will not help to achieve true balance. This Moontime also encourages us to make peace with the angry (Aries) part of ourselves.

The Moon goes void-of-course midafternoon today, making this an undesirable time to begin new projects or job-searches, buy a house, or conduct important business. But we can use the quiet time to work on personal issues that are in need of resolution, or to resolve conflicts with others and restore balance. Then, on Tuesday, the Sun will be attuned to Uranus in Pisces. That connection promises new insight and experiences that may help to break established routines. Try to be open to messages you may be getting through your intuition. It is possible to "see" what you are doing in relationships, and to understand intuitively.

Speaking of messages, Mercury will be retrograde from April 26 until May 20. You might experience a change in your thinking—understanding on a symbolic rather than in a concrete manner—during this time. The mind tends to work on a more subconscious level during Mercury retrograde periods, which may supply you with insights into problems or situations you want answers to.

You are more likely to feel the effects of this Full Moon if your birthday falls on or near this date, or on January 16–18, April 16–18, or July 20–22.

May 1, 2003: New Moon at 7:15 am EST

Taurus is a "laid-back" sign, but this New Moon in Taurus is showing its "bullish" disposition, which may be a carryover from the intense Aries Full Moon of two weeks ago. Add the challenging relationship of the Sun and Moon to Mars in Aquarius, and we have a bull ready to charge the red flag! The Sun and Moon in Taurus (a "fixed" sign) will resist change. In this chart, they act as a fulcrum, with Mars and Neptune weighing in on one side and Jupiter on the other. Let's imagine how this might look. Think of the Sun and Moon conjunction as your broad-shouldered, husky Taurus-type neighbor who really enjoys his peaceful yard, the smell of food cooking on the grill, the pleasant sounds of music, and the companionship of an attractive woman. Then, a young guy who belongs to a garage band and has hordes of friends, all looking for "a good time," moves in next door. To top it off, the Leo kid can't seem to stay in his own yard (Jupiter in Leo). A mature, intellectual-type (Aquarius) couple moved in on the other side. She's really spacey (Neptune). Mr. Aquarius is involved in causes (Mars), and he leaves campaign literature ("propaganda," according to Taurus) in neighborhood mailboxes.

The challenge here is to find a new way to live in the neighborhood—together. What would you do? One path through difficulties requires the willingness to see value in others—maybe to even incorporate a little of their differences within ourselves. Adapting isn't always easy, but doing so can create "buffer" zones. Astrologically, the buffer zone between Taurus and Aquarius is Pisces (acceptance and compassion), with a touch of Aries (selfishness and independence). The buffer zone between Taurus and Leo is Gemini (communication and sharing of ideas), with a touch of Cancer (caretaking and being the grown-up).

If your birthday falls on or near this New Moon, or on July 2–4, November 2–4, or January 30–February 1, you are more likely than others to feel the effects of this New Moon.

May 15, 2003: Full Moon at 10:36 pm EST

It's time to take stock of how we're doing—to dig down inside ourselves and see if what we have is really what we want—to bring it to full view. The Sun in Taurus is still focused on identity (emphasized in Aries) and physical comfort (emphasized in Taurus). But now the Moon, representing our emotions and feelings, has moved to Scorpio, an emotionally intense sign. As happens after most changes, we often feel a sense of loss, and this Scorpio Full Moon offers us time to see what lies in the past and also in the future so that we can regain perspective and balance. But there is a dichotomy here, because Scorpio is not good at "letting go"—the very thing the Moon is trying to show us. When feeling hurt, unenlightened Scorpios tend to seek revenge or isolate themselves. There is balance within each sign, however, and another of Scorpio's traits is finding that which is hidden. So, even if the search is painful, Scorpio will continue until the source of the feeling is found, often exposing our own fears and obsessions in the process.

Scorpio is also associated with power—the power exerted over self and the power others exert over you. There can be tremendous power struggles where Scorpio is involved. Pay attention to your intuition; find the source of your sense of loss, fear, obsessions, or your struggle for power. Scorpio and Taurus are fixed energy—resistant to change or loss—and both are extremely stubborn. Stubbornness can be turned into determination, though, and that determination can be used to finish projects and achieve objectives.

Again, the Moon goes void-of-course as this last aspect (conjunction) takes place in the sign of Scorpio. While not the time to begin new projects, this would be a good time for personal review. It is also a good time for transforming, in creative ways, the things that are no longer useful to you. That could mean repotting household plants, reassigning cupboard and closet space, polishing the silver, or cutting up old fabric to make quilts from next winter.

If your birthday falls on or near this Full Moon, or on February 12–14, May 14–16, or November 16–18, you are more likely to feel the effects of this Full Moon than others do.

May 30, 2003: Second New Moon at 11:20 pm EST

It's time to let loose, to have fun, to get together with old friends, and make new acquaintances! This New Moon in Gemini is definitely lightening the load and relieving us of the burdens we've been carrying around for a while. Remember our Taurus neighbor? Well, he has moved toward Gemini-like behavior, and now he's getting along much better with the neighbors on both sides of him, enjoying the exchange of ideas with the Aquarian couple (Ms. Neptune and Mr. Mars), and he sees the benefits of having some fun and staying in touch with his younger self, thanks to his young Leo neighbor.

We don't have to stay in the depths of intense emotional feelings. In fact, most of the time it's unhealthy to do so. Gemini represents superficial forays into a lot of different things. "Learn a little about a lot" might be one piece of advice we'd hear if this Moon could speak. Of course, the Moon doesn't speak—in a real voice—but intuition is within the Moon's realm. We "hear" a voice within that guides and directs us if we pay attention. We also have a well-laid-out curriculum for learning, courtesy of the universe, and all we have to do to benefit is show up and pay attention. As you may have noticed by now, the Full and New Moon cycle is systematically showing us how to proceed, showing us what is important, what must be accomplished before we can move on to the next level. There is great wisdom available to us; wisdom that recognizes the need for rest and play must balance out the need to work and grow.

We've got the green light to go ahead and make plans (no void-of-course Moon until late Sunday afternoon). Call your friends, write letters, take a road trip, pack a picnic and go to the park or beach, but above all, don't over analyze things.

If your birthday falls on or near this date, or on February 27–March 1, August 31–September 2, or December 1–3, you are more likely than others to feel the effects of this New Moon.

June 14, 2003: Full Moon at 6:16 am EST

Just in case we didn't get it in May, this Full Moon in Sagittarius carries a message from Pluto, the destroyer of illusion: You cannot refuse to change. Imagine a fiery force burning away the barrier constructed around our beliefs, our hidden feelings, our religions, and you have the Moon joined with Pluto in Sagittarius. It's unlikely that we will experience catastrophic change, like that which followed the destruction of the World Trade Center.[1] The change is more apt to occur quietly, as you see more accounts in the news of pedophiles operating in church settings, or about how some of the privileged elite in our society act without compassion toward the people with less status and no material wealth—the poor. You might be researching a subject for a class paper and become irate over some social or political injustice you uncover. Or, you may discover something simple, yet profound. For instance, you may see that you can spend less time at work by being more productive while you're there. That's Pluto acting with the Moon to peel away our illusions; to change what we see and how we feel. You're becoming aware of the bigger picture, and that's what Sagittarius is about.

This Moon also opposes Saturn—the teacher or authority—in Cancer, the sign that represents the home and family that we care for. With Saturn involved, we can expect the "lessons" to feel hard. You may feel lonely, isolated, as if no one else understands you. There is a strong potential here for you to get stuck looking only on the dark side of life. You may feel dissatisfied with your home or its occupants. Try to remember that moods change, and these feelings will pass in a few days. So be patient with others, and with yourself, until the mood lightens—and it always does.

This Moon may affect you more strongly than others if your birthday is on or near this date, or on March 9–11, September 11–13, or December 15–17.

1. Pluto's opposition to Saturn, and a Full Moon on September 2, 2001, in Pisces, ruled by Neptune, the king of delusion, are viewed as important planetary signatures for the events of September 11.

June 29, 2003: New Moon at 1:39 pm EST

The sign of Cancer, the Moon's "home" in the zodiac, is playing hostess not only to the Sun and Moon (conjoined), but to Saturn and Mercury, as well. And Venus, in the late degrees of Gemini, is close to joining those already mentioned. So, it isn't too much of a stretch to presume that sad feelings are lingering about. Cancer is well known for its tradition of hanging on—to everything. You probably know a few Sun sign Cancers whose homes are crammed full of doodads, clothes stored in boxes, and old pieces of furniture that will "come in handy someday." That's because they tend to hang on to things, as well as to emotions. Another thing that Cancer represents is the need to feel secure and safe. Change, as was called for with recent Full Moons, creates insecurity. One way to feel safer is to know what is going on outside of yourself. Cancer types observe, wait, and approach things indirectly (from the side, like a crab does) once they feel safe. And all the while this is going on, we're being bombarded with memories and unconscious responses to stimuli. It's hard! But a New Moon is about new opportunities and new beginnings. Again, we can look to the universe for assistance.

Mercury entered Cancer early this morning after spending two weeks in Gemini. Gemini, ruled by Mercury, symbolizes the intellect, communication, and new learning. In mythology, Mercury, also known as Hermes, carried messages back and forth between humans and the gods on Mt. Olympus. So, perhaps his timely arrival in Cancer is our cue that it's time to move out of our journey through dark feelings; to think, talk, write, add new learning, and to play. Try exploring other philosophies, read a serious book, or take a trip to some new and distant place to expose yourself to new ideas.

This chart contains a lot of the water element, which is associated with emotion. This does, however, tend to overemphasize emotions. And as with all instances of too much water and not enough earth, things (and people) have a tendency to flood. It will be hard to actually get things done for a while yet.

You're more likely to feel this Moon's effects if your birthday is on or near this date, or on March 28–30, September 30, October 1–2, or December 29–31.

July 13, 2003: Full Moon at 2:21 pm EST

Again, with perfect timing, the Full Moon in Capricorn is trying to bring our awareness to the need for balance. This Full Moon is acting as a spotlight to show us just how polarized we can become about some things. To help us find the time we need to consider our circumstances, this Full Moon coincides with a void-of-course period (time-out from acting on new plans and conducting new business), at a time when we have have traveled through half the year. It's a perfect position from which to look back and reflect on where we are in relation to where we wanted to be. Are you on the path you wanted to take when the year began? Detours can be okay, too, if they take us closer to our goals. But if you're not satisfied with what you see, this is the time to make a course correction.

Capricorn is about structure, rules and regulations, setting long-term goals and achieving them through hard work, striving to get ahead, and doing things alone, if need be. In fact, being alone is something Capricorns do well. But as with all Full Moons, the opposite sign (where the Sun is located) is equally emphasized. In this chart, the Sun is in the sign of Cancer. In scrutinizing our present position, we need to also look at what is going on in our relationships. What is your current attitude toward your significant other? Toward your kids? Your business partner? Your neighbor? Yourself? Is one area of your life being neglected and another overemphasized?

Mercury enters Leo today and, in his role as messenger, perhaps he is broadcasting back to us that it's time to lighten up, to have some fun, and to enjoy the rest of the summer before it's too late.

There are still a lot of planets in water signs, which means that emotions still rule the day. And with a shortage of earth, accomplishing goals may be difficult, so even if you've become aware that your house needs paint, this might not be the best time to start the job.

You will feel the impact of this Full Moon if your birthday is near this date, or on April 11–13, July 19–21, or January 11–13.

July 29, 2003: New Moon at 1:53 am EST

This New Moon in Leo initiates a time of celebration, joy, and new friendship—if you want to participate. Whether you have felt a desire to create something, to dance in your living room or on stage, or to play sand volleyball or with kids in the sandbox, the time is ripe to take a step toward turning those desires into reality. Leo represents the creative artist, whose function it is to create drama, dance, comedy, music, film, and jewelry—especially gold. And with Venus tagging along in close proximity to the Sun for the next couple of months, we can expect to receive added pleasure and confidence from our creativity or playful endeavors. This would also be a great time to entertain, so invite friends and family over and have a party! No need to say, "Be generous!" Leo is well-known for his generosity.

Venus symbolizes a positive and open giving and receiving of love. Love loves summer, and Venus loves being in love. So, this New Moon offers excellent timing and support if you feel ready to let your romantic inclinations move you toward a special someone. Pay attention to your inner desires, needs, and dreams; and be prepared to breathe life into them as you feel them amplifying and stretching out—beyond you—into the world.

The possibility exists, as shown in the chart above, that creating drama to get attention might be on a few minds. Frequently, this is done to direct attention away from your own feelings—feelings that you would just as soon not acknowledge. But that probably isn't the best outcome.

Again, the universe comes through, giving us an abundance of fire to energize any and all pursuits after fun, friendship, and celebrations. The energy is fixed, so people should be on time with their plans, although you might have some difficulty getting anyone to change their minds once a decision has been made.

You are more apt to feel the effects of this New Moon if your birthday is on or near this date, or on April 24–26, October 28–30, or January 25–27.

August 11, 2003: Full Moon at 11:48 pm EST

This Aquarius Full Moon all but guarantees that significant changes will reveal themselves, exposing to us what we were unaware of before. Whatever happens, it will definitely be out there in public view for everyone to see. Aquarius is associated with grand visions and ideas for the future, inventions, groups of people, and humanitarian works, among other things.

On Monday, the Moon meets Uranus, ruler of Aquarius and a strong agent for disrupting the status quo. Then on Tuesday (Mars' day), the Moon joins with Mars—symbol for action, flaring tempers, passion, courage, and daring. You get the picture. We can expect impulsive behaviors, quick mood changes, impatience with normal routines, and increased sensitivity to others as the Moon moves through the sign of Pisces this week. There is a catch here, though, and it's that while the Moon is out in full view, exposing our feelings, secrets, and desires, the Sun (representing our egos) is concerned with our own personal life and those closest to us. Events from the past, which continue to affect you, might surface, either through memory or another person.

As with other Full Moons, we have an opportunity to look at our relationships—those people we sometimes see as across from us rather than beside us—particularly at work and home. The Sun is marching through Leo, arm in arm with Venus and Jupiter, the two "benefactors" of the universe. These benefactors will lend a positive, upbeat, optimistic quality to our moods. It also becomes supereasy, however, to exaggerate our ability to fulfill promises made, so be careful about what you agree to do this week and next. All in all, watch for news of significant changes happening in your life, and in the world.

The elemental energy in this chart is more balanced, but the fixed—stubborn, sometimes rigid—energy still dominates. People won't be easily persuaded to change their opinions or minds, so you might consider putting such efforts off for a while. You are more likely to feel the effects of this Full Moon if your birthday is on or near this date, or on February 8–10, May 9–11, or November 11–13.

August 27, 2003: New Moon at 12:26 pm EST

This New Moon in Virgo coincides with Jupiter's move into that sign, as well as Uranus' move into the opposite sign of Pisces—all of which signal new beginnings. The Pisces-Virgo axis places emphasis on service in our daily lives to others. The Full Moon in July was bright with innovative ideas, humanitarian concerns, and a generous nature that may have exposed a desire within you to take some new action. Now we have, in this dark Moon time, the opportunity to let the world around us speak through our intuition. Be open to what you might hear. This New Moon time may feel difficult, causing you to overanalyze, turn critical, or overwork. All of these are negative traits of Virgo, and signals that you need to make some changes, or suffer the consequences.

Virgo is associated with health, too. If you need to improve your physical condition, use this time to develop an action plan that will really work for you, whether it's adding exercise to your daily routine, or changing something about your eating habits. The universe is supplying everything we need to get started in a direction that will be more beneficial.

If you feel like getting away (Uranus opposing Sun-Moon) from daily routines for a while, consider taking a class, or attending a seminar that is work related. If you feel the urge to get organized (Virgo), look around for a new project to apply yourself to. One of Virgo's strengths is discernment, determining what is valuable or important and what is not. Make your plan and, when the time is right, get moving on it.

We've been waiting for enough planets to move into the earth element to help us manifest all those dreams and ideas into reality, and they've arrived. We still have Mars in Pisces to keep us connected to the visions we had, but now we have the practical, get-down-to-business, earth element to help out. So bring those dreams down off the shelf, and get busy.

You will feel the effects of this Moon more if your birthday is on or near this date, or on February 23–25, May 25–27, or November 26–28.

September 10, 2003: Full Moon at 11:36 am EST

This Full Moon in Pisces brings our focus back to home and family, similar to the August 11 Full Moon. In August, the Moon was outside the home, looking back, permitting us time to reflect on things and people there. This month, the focus is inside the home, with the family, and we're looking at the work we do in the world. In this way the universe gives us opportunities to observe how or if we have balance in our lives. With the Sun in Virgo, we may find that we've been putting a lot of time in at work—maybe too much. And if we have gotten out of balance, the negative qualities of Virgo—overanalysis, criticism, overworking—and those of Pisces—daydreaming, fantasizing, denial, and abuse of drugs or alcohol—may be showing up. In addition, the Moon is in a tight square with Pluto, a relationship that can result in compulsive behavior and intensified emotions.

This Full Moon in the earth and water elements is giving us another opportunity to consider contrasts. We respond to the natural urge toward wholeness when we seek a partner whose character and qualities complement our own. But like complementary colors on a color wheel—red and green, blue and orange—the contrast between two opposite colors, and between two contrasting personalities, is optimal. How do you create balance? If you try to mix the two colors (or water and earth), you get mud. The same happens when two people try to mix their very opposite personalities, or when we try to mix home and work without the benefit of clear boundaries. Pisces (water) seeks to merge with all that is. Virgo (earth) seeks organization and order. We have enough earth now to contain water and minimize emotional flooding. When adequate boundaries are established people, careers, families—everything—can coexist with a minimum of emotional turmoil.

You are apt to feel the effects of this Full Moon more if your birthday is on or near this date, or on March 8–10, June 8–10, or December 9–11.

September 25, 2003: New Moon at 10:09 pm EST

Ruled by Venus, Libra is most interested in affairs of the heart, which includes partners, friends, and home. So romance that leads to commitment, and often to a home, takes on added importance with this New Moon. Being in love is a way to acquire emotional security to satisfy the emotional part of ourselves. Venus is just ahead of the Sun and Moon in this chart, so both of them will be paying her a visit very soon. Be prepared for anything—a new love interest, new interest in your home, yard, and gardens, a new wardrobe, or a desire to learn gourmet cooking.

Another quality of Libra is the desire to create balance, and one way to have balance is to keep the peace—sometimes, at any price. But the price may include denial of reality, or keeping secrets in an effort to avoid overreactions from certain people. The secret may be as simple as hiding new clothing purchases from your spouse. But secrets can extend deeper into relationships, too. If things are less than perfect at home, and one's attention strays to a new love interest, which may happen due to the desire to avoid conflict in an existing relationship or marriage, then the secrets that must be kept can be very destructive. Duplicity can evolve from one's desire to be liked.

Another of Libra's facets is the desire to be surrounded by beauty—beautiful art, possessions, homes, clothes, and people. During this New Moon would be a perfect time to get in touch with how you feel about what you have around you. Do you like it? Want to replace it? Give it a facelift? A new project could be calling to you.

You are more apt to feel the effects of this New Moon if your birthday is on or near this date, or on March 22–24, June 23–25, or December 23–25.

October 10, 2003: Full Moon at 2:27 am EST

What this Aries Full Moon may have to reveal to us is: where we stand in the desire to be free and independent versus the desire to be in relationships that necessitate taking someone else into consideration. With the Moon in Aries, we can expect impatience, angry outbursts, defensiveness, business, and, possibly, accidents to occur. In Aries, intuition will work through impulses, those gut feelings. It is always good to pay attention to these feelings because they often impart needed information to us. Dependency on anything is difficult for Aries, so we can expect issues around dependency to be highlighted in some way for us now. Aries frowns on weakness, and competitive behavior is often the result of feeling inadequate, so keep that in mind when you feel your thermostat rising.

This Full Moon in fire sign Aries is in a challenging relationship with Pluto, also in a fire sign. Expect already intense emotional responses to be amplifed. We will encounter people or situations that seem to only exacerbate the difficulties, but only because we can see the "issues" or "problems" in others much easier than we can see them in ourselves. At the same time, the Moon is squaring Saturn. This association will tend to intensify feelings of loneliness, or of being unloved. This, in turn, can cause problems in our relationships—because we look at others as being the source of the problem. Perhaps this would be a good time to remember the saying, "This too shall pass."

It is possible to experience separations under this aspect. The Full Moon may be revealing that something must come to an end, or go out of your life. When Pluto and Saturn are involved, it is best to just let go. If we don't, the lessons only get harder. You may experience an increased sensitivity and heightened sadness as part of the Saturn-Moon aspect, and this can lead to obsessive thinking. Are you beginning to see how many things—not just the Moon—travel in a circle?

You are more likely to feel the effects of this Full Moon if your birthday is on or near this date, or on April 5–7, July 8–10, or January 6–8.

October 25, 2003: New Moon at 7:50 am EST

If you find yourself in possession of information that you think would be better kept private, or if someone wants you to keep a secret, consider the consequences before you commit to any course of action. Secrets have a way of revealing themselves, and this New Moon in Scorpio is a symbol of that truth. Nothing stays hidden forever. Expect emotions to be intense in the coming days, and also for power struggles to develop. Another negative emotional response that is characteristic of this Moon sign is the desire to seek revenge. Resentment is an emotional habit, and not a very pleasant one. It's a way to hang on to the grief that may be inside of you. There are positive ways to use intense emotions, though. This is a very psychic sign, with a great capacity for compassion and empathy for others. Be compassionate with yourself, too, and use this New Moon time to start healing old emotional wounds. You will probably resist letting go—that's a Scorpio trait—but allow them to transmute into something else and pass through you.

Saturn turns retrograde in the sign of Cancer today, initiating a time when things may seem to slow down, not progress as we'd like them to, or when situations and emotions feel more melancholy.

You can also put intuition and the power of your emotions and self-will behind new enterprises. Imagine how much could be accomplished. Choose a worthy goal, and go about achieving it with a positive attitude.

You will have to depend on the power of emotions to keep things moving for the time being, though, because fire energy is in short supply, with only Pluto in the fire sign Sagittarius.

You are more likely to feel the effects of this New Moon if your birthday is on or near this date, or on April 21–23, July 24–26, or January 21–23.

November 8, 2003: Full Moon at 8:13 pm EST

This Full Moon in Taurus is opposing the Sun in Scorpio. Think back, and try to remember the thoughts you kept private and what your motivations were behind any reluctance to share possessions and resources with others. This New Moon may be trying to reveal to you the value—to yourself or to others—of those thoughts and the decisions that you might have made. The Moon will be opposing Venus from Gemini on Monday, giving you another opportunity to view your personal values, possessions, and so on. What are you seeing?

Taurus is associated with deep loyalty to friends and family, and a true appreciation for the finer things life has to offer—good food, wine, perfume, furnishings, art—that make us "feel good." It is the most sensual sign in the zodiac, bringing added enjoyment of taste, texture, aromas, sounds, and sights.

On a less-serious note, this would be a good weekend to invite friends over for dinner. It won't be difficult to please them if you just follow your intuition and satisfy your senses. Uranus turns direct today, which could introduce an element of surprise or unconventional fun into the evening or weekend.

The elements of air, fire, earth, and water are pretty well in balance now, meaning that inspired thoughts will be followed by actions, resulting in concrete outcomes; and emotional stability should follow. And while the energy is still predominately "fixed," meaning that you will very likely meet resistance to change, people's stubborn attitudes may be irritating, but progress can be made.

You are more likely to feel the effects of this Full Moon if your birthday is on or near this date, or on February 5–7, May 6–8, or July 8–11.

November 23, 2003: New Moon at 5:59 pm EST

Just in time for the season of thanksgiving and generosity, we have the New Moon in Sagittarius, with an abundance of fire energy to inspire and motivate us. If you have friends who were born during Sagittarius, you know how generous, benevolent, frank, good-humored, sociable, charitable, and freedom loving they can be. They can also be restless, philosophical (they just love to debate), and they tend to disappear from time to time on some grand adventure without so much as a farewell to you. This New Moon may motivate you to invite friends over, it may plant the seed of desire to take a long trip to someplace you've never been, or to take up a new course of study when the new year begins. You could also find yourself overworking and committing too much of your energy to too many different things. If you see this happening in your life, use your intuition and tune into yourself and ro determine just how much time and energy you really have to give away, because you'll want to still be going strong on New Year's Eve! It might be a good idea to minimize risk-taking or gambling at this time, too. Too much of a good thing can have negative results, too.

Pay attention to flashes of inspiration, hunches, or those certain feelings that come to you. What are they trying to tell you? Also, be aware of things that just "seem to happen" as if by chance. They're often synchronistic messages—arrows—to keep you on the right track.

You are more likely to feel the effects of this New Moon is your birthday is on or near this date, or on February 20–22, May 22–24, or August 24–26.

December 8, 2003: Full Moon at 3:37 pm EST

Don't have your holiday correspondence or communications done yet? This Gemini Full Moon, with its association to all forms of communication—talking, writing, faxing, computers, letters, phones, and paper—may be the perfect time for you to take care of business. Wit and good humor tend to accompany this sign, giving you an additional edge on the task. You'll also have plenty of motivation to get out there and do any errands that need to be done before the holidays. It would be a good idea to take care of business this week, because Mercury goes retrograde on December 17.

While the Moon in opposition to Pluto (in Sagittarius) can create intense emotional experiences and compulsive behaviors, Gemini does not like to experience emotions on a deep feeling level, preferring instead to keep things light. This could be experienced as a struggle, on a personal level, that causes mood fluctuations, or feelings could remain on a subconscious level until a later time, when the environment is more amenable to deep emotions and transformational urges.

Be on the lookout for feelings of jealousy, overpossessiveness, or the desire to control things or people, though, and try not to let them get out of hand. And, try not to succumb to urges to get into a heated philosophical debate that might manifest from the Sun/Pluto side-by-side partnership. Instead, apply that transformational energy to the repair of something that is broken, turning it into a useful object.

You are more likely to feel the effects of this Full Moon if your birthday is on or near this date, or on March 6–9, June 7–9, or September 8–10.

December 23, 2003: New Moon at 4:43 am EST

This is the last New Moon of the year, and it brings us back to Capricorn, the sign of the first New Moon of 2003. At this lunation, the Sun and New Moon are flanked by transformational Pluto in the sign of Sagittarius, and Mercury (the messenger) and Chiron (the healer), also in Capricorn. The entry of the Sun and Moon into Capricorn is likely to put a damper on spending through the end of the year, as a more restrictive feeling overtakes shoppers.

By the end of today the New Moon will be looking across at retrograde Saturn in Cancer, the Moon's home. If the Moon and Saturn could talk, Saturn would likely be heard giving instruction to the infant Moon about responsibilities, goals, and the importance of achieving. The Moon would, in turn, appeal to the softer side of Saturn, hoping to awaken the caretaker in the authority figure. This exchange could be mutually beneficial to child and parent, and, by extension, it could benefit both the home and work environments. Try to imagine how this same approach might be useful in your life and personal exchanges with others. Are you in a position of power or authority over others? And, if so, are you also taking care of those who work with and for you?

The earth element is plentiful in this chart, bringing in the energy to complete those things we might set out to accomplish.

You are more apt to feel the effects of this New Moon if your birthday is on or near this date, or March 20–22, June 21–23, or September 23–25.

In Conclusion

Astrology shows us that the planets and their aspects (relationships) to each other inform and instruct us through symbols, myth, and archetypes about what is important in life. We began the year thinking about responsible action, integrity, and security, with emphasis on personal concerns. Then, with the Full Moon on January 18, relationships were highlighted. Throughout the year, the focus alternated from the personal to others, from family to work, personal values to community values. We have been inspired to enhance first our own lives and then the lives of others.

Midyear, with the Moon in Capricorn once again, we were given the opportunity to look back on the previous six months and determine if we were going in the right direction, achieving those things we wanted to achieve in our lives.

After that, in late July, the emphasis turned to having fun!

All throughout the year we were guided and given inspiration. We were given times to reflect or to take action, and opportunities to look at ourselves and to gauge how we were doing. The cycle will begin again in January 2004, or, if you prefer, in March, with the arrival of the Sun in Aries.

There are many ways to interpret the symbolism of each New and Full Moon. But the best way to gain understanding of how lunar phases are represented in your life is to begin paying attention to the Moon's cycles and to note when things happen to you.

About the Author

Leah Whiting is a writer, and, believing that the vast amount of astrological knowledge cannot possibly be absorbed in one lifetime, she considers herself a student of astrology. It is, she says, the greatest teacher she's ever known. She lives in St. Paul, Minnesota, where she entertains herself with gardening and the art of Bonsai.

Note: All of the lunation charts for this article are cast for Washington, D.C., and use Eastern Standard Time. You will have to adjust for Daylight Saving Time between April 6 and October 26, 2003.

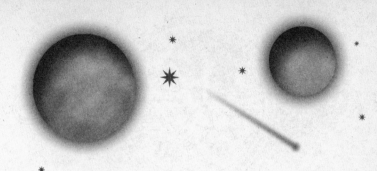

Leisure &
Recreation
Section

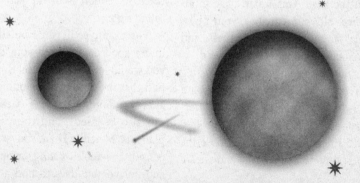

How To Choose the Best Dates for Leisure & Recreation Activities

Everyone is affected by the lunar cycle. Your lunar high occurs when the Moon is in your Sun sign, and your lunar low occurs when the Moon is in the sign opposite your Sun sign. The handy tables of favorable and unfavorable days on pages 34–57 give the lunar highs and lows for each Sun sign for every day of the year. This lunar cycle influences all your activities: your physical strength, mental alertness, and manual dexterity are all affected.

By combining the tables listing favorable and unfavorable dates and the lunar aspectarian with the information given in the list of astrological rulerships, you can choose the best time to begin many activities.

The best time to perform an activity is when its ruling planet is in favorable aspect to the Moon—that is, when its ruling planet is trine (T), sextile (X), or conjunct (C) the Moon in the lunar aspectarian, or when its ruling sign is marked *F* in the tables listing favorable and unfavorable days. Another option is when the Moon is in the activity's ruling sign.

For example, if you wanted to find a good day to train your dog, you would look under animals, and find that the sign corresponding to animal training is Virgo (Gemini can also be used), and the ruling planet is Mercury. Then, you would consult the tables listing favorable and unfavorable days to find a day when Mercury (the ruling planet) is trine, sextile, or conjunct (T, X, or C) the Moon; or when Gemini or Virgo (the ruling signs) are marked *F* in tables that indicate favorable and unfavorable days; or when the Moon is in Virgo or Gemini.

Animals and Hunting

Animal training: Virgo, Gemini; Mercury

Cats: Leo and Virgo; Venus

Dogs: Virgo; Mercury

Fish: Cancer and Pisces; Neptune or the Moon

Birds: Gemini; Mercury, Venus

Game animals: Sagittarius

Horses, trainers, riders: Sagittarius; Jupiter

Hunters: Sagittarius; Jupiter

Arts

Acting, actors: Leo or Pisces; Sun or Neptune

Art in general: Libra; Venus

Ballet: Neptune or Venus

Ceramics: Saturn

Crafts: Mercury or Venus

Dancing: Taurus or Pisces; Venus or Neptune

Drama: Venus or Neptune

Embroidery: Venus

Etching: Mars

Films, filmmaking: Leo or Aquarius; Neptune or Uranus

Literature: Mercury, Gemini

Music: Taurus or Libra; Venus or Neptune

Painting: Libra; Venus

Photography: Aquarius or Pisces; Neptune or Uranus

Printing: Gemini; Mercury

Theaters: Leo; Sun or Venus

Fishing

During the summer months the best time of the day to fish is from sunrise to three hours after, and from two hours before sunset until one hour after. Fish do not bite in cooler months until the air is warm, from noon to 3 pm. Warm, cloudy days are good. The most favorable winds are from the south and southwest. Easterly winds are unfavorable. The best days of the month for fishing are when the Moon changes quarters, especially if the change occurs on a day when the Moon is in a water sign (Cancer, Scorpio, Pisces). The best period in any month is the day after the Full Moon.

Friends

The need for friendship is greater when the Moon is in Aquarius or when Uranus aspects the Moon. Friendship prospers when Venus or Uranus is trine, sextile, or conjunct the Moon. The chance meeting of acquaintances and friends is facilitated by the Moon in Gemini.

Parties (Hosting or Attending)

The best time for parties is when the Moon is in Gemini, Leo, Libra, or Sagittarius with good aspects to Venus and Jupiter. There should be no aspects to Mars or Saturn.

Barbecues: Moon or Mars
Casinos: Venus, Sun, or Jupiter
Festivals: Venus
Parades: Jupiter or Venus

Sports

Acrobatics: Aries; Mars
Archery: Sagittarius; Jupiter,
Ball games in general: Venus
Baseball: Mars
Bicycling: Gemini; Mercury or Uranus
Boxing: Mars
Calisthenics: Mars, Neptune
Chess: Mercury, Mars
Competitive sports: Mars
Coordination: Mars
Deep-sea diving: Pisces; Neptune
Exercising: Sun
Football: Mars

Golf: Sagittarius, Aries, Libra; Mars or Jupiter
Horse racing: Sagittarius; Jupiter
Jogging: Gemini; Mercury
Physical vitality: Sun
Polo: Venus, Uranus, Jupiter, or Saturn
Racing (other than horse): Sun, Uranus
Ice skating: Neptune
Roller skating: Mercury
Sporting equipment: Sagittarius; Jupiter
Sports in general: Leo; Sun
Strategy: Saturn
Swimming: Pisces, Cancer; Neptune
Tennis: Mercury, Venus, Mars, or Uranus
Wrestling: Mars

Travel

Long trips which threaten to exhaust the traveler are best begun when the Sun is well aspected to the Moon and the date is favorable for the traveler. If traveling with others, good aspects from Venus are desirable. For enjoyment, aspects to Jupiter are preferable; for visiting, aspects to Mercury. To prevent accidents, avoid squares or oppositions to Mars, Saturn, Uranus, or Pluto.

For air travel, choose a day when the Moon is in Sagittarius or Gemini and well aspected to Mercury, Jupiter, or Uranus. Avoid adverse aspects of Mars, Saturn, or Uranus.

For automobile travels, choose a day when the Moon is in Gemini and making good aspects to Mercury.

For boating, the Moon should be in the water sign Cancer, or making easy aspects to Neptune.

Eat in restaurants when the Moon is in Cancer or Virgo, and making favorable aspects to Venus and Jupiter.

Hotels: Cancer, Venus
Motorcycle travel: Favorable aspects to Uranus
Parks: Leo; Sun
Picnics: Leo; Venus
Rail: Gemini; Mercury or Uranus

Writing

Write for pleasure or publication when the Moon is in Gemini; and Mercury should be direct, making favorable (T, X, or C) aspects to Uranus and Neptune to promote ingenuity.

2003 Hunting & Fishing Dates

January 6, 5:57 am - January 8, 4:15 pm	1st	Pisces
January 16, 2:56 am - January 18, 9:29 am	2nd	Cancer
January 24, 7:09 pm - January 26, 10:26 pm	3rd	Scorpio
February 2, 2:55 pm - February 5, 12:44 am	1st	Pisces
February 12, 12:19 pm - February 14, 7:04 pm	2nd	Cancer
February 21, 1:09 am - February 23, 3:46 am	3rd	Scorpio
February 23, 3:46 am - February 25, 8:11 am	3rd	Sagittarius
March 1, 10:26 pm - March 4, 8:30 am	4th	Pisces
March 11, 9:12 pm - March 14, 5:06 am	2nd	Cancer
March 20, 9:38 am - March 22, 10:33 am	3rd	Scorpio
March 22, 10:33 am - March 24, 1:48 pm	3rd	Sagittarius
March 29, 4:26 am - March 31, 3:04 pm	4th	Pisces
April 8, 4:36 am - April 10, 1:54 pm	1st	Cancer
April 16, 8:16 pm - April 18, 7:51 pm	3rd	Scorpio
April 18, 7:51 pm - April 20, 9:20 pm	3rd	Sagittarius
April 25, 10:02 am - April 27, 8:54 pm	4th	Pisces
May 5, 10:42 am - May 7, 8:46 pm	1st	Cancer
May 14, 7:14 am - May 16, 6:43 am	2nd	Scorpio
May 16, 6:43 am - May 18, 7:03 am	3rd	Sagittarius
May 22, 4:41 pm - May 25, 2:59 am	3rd	Pisces
June 1, 4:27 pm - June 4, 2:25 am	1st	Cancer
June 10, 4:39 pm - June 12, 5:12 pm	2nd	Scorpio
June 12, 5:12 pm - June 14, 5:38 pm	2nd	Sagittarius
June 19, 12:57 am - June 21, 10:06 am	3rd	Pisces
July 28, 10:52 pm - July 1, 8:13 am	4th	Cancer
July 7, 11:43 pm - July 10, 1:48 am	2nd	Scorpio
July 10, 1:48 am - July 12, 3:21 am	2nd	Sagittarius
July 16, 10:14 am - July 18, 6:20 pm	3rd	Pisces
July 18, 6:20 pm - July 21, 5:48 am	3rd	Aries

2003 Hunting & Fishing Dates

July 26, 6:23 am - July 28, 3:17 pm	4th	Cancer
August 4, 5:12 am - August 6, 8:11 am	1st	Scorpio
August 6, 8:11 am - August 8, 11:02 am	2nd	Sagittarius
August 12, 7:19 pm - August 15, 3:00 am	3rd	Pisces
August 15, 3:00 am - August 17, 1:52 pm	3rd	Aries
August 22, 2:44 pm - August 24, 11:48 pm	4th	Cancer
September 31, 11:00 am - September 2, 1:32 pm	1st	Scorpio
September 9, 3:07 am - September 11, 11:09 am	2nd	Pisces
September 11, 11:09 am - September 13, 9:50 pm	3rd	Aries
September 18, 11:07 pm - September 21, 9:02 am	4th	Cancer
September 27, 6:52 pm - September 29, 7:57 pm	1st	Scorpio
October 6, 9:20 am - October 8, 6:07 pm	2nd	Pisces
October 8, 6:07 pm - October 11, 5:05 am	2nd	Aries
October 16, 6:41 am - October 18, 5:41 pm	3rd	Cancer
October 25, 5:08 am - October 27, 4:55 am	4th	Scorpio
November 2, 2:52 pm - November 5, 12:02 am	2nd	Pisces
November 5, 12:02 am - November 7, 11:29 am	2nd	Aries
November 12, 1:10 pm - November 15, 12:48 am	3rd	Cancer
November 21, 4:24 pm - November 23, 4:02 pm	4th	Scorpio
December 29, 9:25 pm - December 2, 5:56 am	1st	Pisces
December 2, 5:56 am - December 4, 5:30 pm	2nd	Aries
December 9, 7:11 pm - December 12, 6:40 am	3rd	Cancer
December 19, 2:20 am - December 21, 3:16 am	4th	Scorpio
December 27, 6:10 am - December 29, 1:08 pm	1st	Pisces

Women's Relationships

By Sally Cragin

*E*veryone is a Moon, and has a dark side which he never shows to anybody.

Mark Twain

Some years back, a glittery career retrospective was held for Barbra Streisand. Among the cheerleaders was Shirley MacLaine, who shares Barbra's April 24 birthday. Amid the speeches, songs, and movie clips, MacLaine (who was born in 1934, seven years before Streisand) pointed out the earthy, material-minded Taurus tendencies they share: "She's very attracted to sensual specifics, notices perfume, and will know the name. She'll notice if someone has had a tooth capped ... she gets depressed when others don't live up to their brilliance." The presumption, of course, is that Streisand, and, by inference, MacLaine always live up to their brilliance. (This is demonstrable for both: The number of performers with Emmy, Grammy, Oscar, AND Tony awards on their mantelpieces is slender indeed.) Yet, these two women have never worked together, a fact that perhaps contributes to ongoing amity. Though, wouldn't they be fabulous in a remake of *Hush, Hush Sweet Charlotte*?

Shirley and Barbra—friends and countrywomen? Hardly newsworthy, but interesting from an astrological perspective. We can learn a surprising amount about who we are by looking at our platonic relationships. In my work as an astrologer, I always ask clients (they're overwhelmingly female) about their peers at work and play. And here's a general summary of what I hear: Fire sign women adore the FEELING of being in a group, even if they're mildly deluded about actually BEING in a group—especially among fellow fire signs; air sign women find fellow air or earth signs irresistible (that Libra/Taurus friendship axis is a classic), but they always welcome new personalities to cultivate; water sign women frequently suffer over loyalty issues (as in having too much), but they still cultivate pals in the fire or air sign realms; and earth sign women are often tremendously independent, but they appreciate the sensitivity of water sign buddies, whose passions are nonetheless eternally perplexing. Ah, but what does this have to do with the Moon?

The Moon in a woman's chart represents a complicated and delicate grouping of characteristics: everything from temperament to relationship to mother to affinities for friendship. Streisand has a diva-esque Leo Moon squaring her Sun (she doesn't mind friction in romance), while MacLaine has a more harmonious Virgo Moon trining her natal Sun (service IS work). Generally, if there's a pleasant relationship between the natal Moons, or between the Moon and Sun of two people, friendship is more likely, and it is apt to be deeper. Yet, as you can see with the closeness of the Leo and Virgo Moons, if people were born in adjacent signs, you can also find compatibility where you might not expect it.

Here's a non-Hollywood example of people drawn to be friends who share attributes. (I've changed names and significant places, but the charts are real!) For Lily and Anne, compatibility began in high school. Their Suns are square

(Gemini and Virgo), but their Moons are in sync (Gemini and Libra), so they share an air sign lunar temperament. Even so, Lily is a dark of the Moon type—intuitive and occasionally overcautious. Anne is a waxing crescent Moon type—adventurous and attracted to risk-taking.

"Eventually we became the best of friends," Lily explains. "We both had other friends, but I felt there was something special about Anne. I felt she thought the same about me. There was much to admire about Anne, she was, to my sheltered, impressionable eyes and ears, an extremely cosmopolitan, beautiful, sexy woman, with a great sense of style."

The friendship paused in their junior year, when Anne briefly left the area, but in their senior year the two were together again. "All was well the first semester when she came back," recalled Lilly. "Then over the holiday we had a terrible falling-out."

The two had been out partying, and Lily fell and hurt her ankle. Anne refused to drive her home in a snowstorm. "The next day, we had a heated, angry, hurtful exchange, the likes of which I have had few times in my life," says Lilly.

Eventually, Lilly called her folks to come get her. The estrangement lasted more than a year, although Lily initiated a rapprochement when both were freshmen at different colleges. "I went to visit her a couple of times, and she came to see me. We kept in sporadic touch over the next few years. But the friendship was never the same, no matter how much I wished it to be."

As time passed, Anne moved away from home, and lived, in fact, thousands of miles away in a number of exotic locations. She and Lily kept in touch, and Lily was initially quite flattered to be chosen to be a bridesmaid for her. But when she flew out for the wedding, she found she was one of nine other bridesmaids, all women important to Anne at different points in her life.

Rather than choose one or two friends, harmony-loving Anne (Moon in Libra) had refused to make the decision and asked everyone.

"During that wedding week, I found that although I admire the person she is, ultimately I am not quiet in my soul about this friendship," says Lily. "I feel the past and our disconnection quite frequently. That is somewhat troubling to me. I suspect she's always been in control of the relationship, and as a bit of a control freak myself, that's not comforting."

Sun sign astrology would suggest that the Gemini person is likely to be the capricious one, while the Virgo Sun would brood over slights and hurts. Yet, here we find the opposite occuring, though the signposts of trouble in this long relationship do clearly relate to Sun sign attributes. Here's Virgo Anne, taking a larger view of health issues by refusing to drive in dangerous snow. And Gemini Lily shows her airy flexibility by taking the lead in their reunions. And the fact that their Suns are square means that each is processing most stressful events at similar times. (A difficult square to Virgo is an opposition to Gemini, and so on, except for the 25 percent of the time when one has a square and the other is in orb.) Yet, despite differences there was a connection that has endured, and will probably continue to do so, albeit in diminishing force as each woman continues with her own life's agenda.

Waxing Moon folks can be tentative but earnest, especially if the Moon is in an earth or water sign. This is not a lunar phase that predisposes one to rush pell-mell into friendship. Air and fire sign Moon folks prefer hope to experience.

Full Moon folks (those born in the period between the gibbous Moon and several days after the peak of the Full Moon) welcome excitement, especially instant crises. These are the friends who can make a party happen with a box of Pringles, a paper plate, and a very, very high-quality sound system. People with earth or water sign Full Moons can throw themselves into friendship, but may tend to short-change romance. Fire or air sign people are especially likely to overlook inconsistencies in others. A flaw? Not always. A high threshold of tolerance is a positive boon to friendmaking. For these folks, a crowd can be more nourishing than being with one other person. Please be careful with Full Moon people. You may

find them adorable and self-deprecating, but they're always in danger of getting blinded and bruised if your character is more forceful.

Waning Moon folks can be skeptical in friendship, but what they actually do is to really want to believe. Grudges aren't comfortable for long, though, so waning Moon folks can move right along when they're ready. The willingness to cut losses is a positive side of this lunar phase. But the life lesson that must be learned is understanding when it's time to begin new relationships. You can't always be leaving without arriving somewhere else.

New Moon folks are remarkably sensitive and insightful to others. These are the people who can absorb spiritual energy, which isn't always healthy, but they make great confidantes. Their trouble comes with misplaced loyalty, or gullibility—their desire to act as if what they "want" to happen "is" happening is a defining trait.

Moon in Aries

These folks have high expectations for friendship, but no problem moving on when they're disappointed. In childhood, they might have found a friend who was a "trouble magnet." Yet Aries Moon people will surprise you with fearlessness, and they don't mind clearing the air when it seems no one else is doing anything practical.

Moon in Taurus

Loyalty counts—big time! So does acceptance at any cost. Criticize the behavior of these folks at your peril, though figure that they're impartial when it comes to you. Aren't you lucky! This is an interesting placement for someone who runs a store or who is a buyer, as Taurus influence is consumerism in capital letters.

Moon in Gemini

These folks enjoy a taste for excitement, perhaps more in terms of personal drama than excitement, like race cars. Conversation counts for a lot, and there's no shortage of gambits ("Did I ever tell you about the time I almost got a tattoo?"). Be careful about long-range plans with a Gemini Moon; they're more likely to say "Yes" to short-term dates.

Moon in Cancer

"Are you okay?" These folks worry about you and don't tell you. Treat them very carefully—they're pretty tough, but notably sensitive to how you treat them. If you've got Moon in Cancer, you've got to work very hard so you don't feel resentful about always being there for people who aren't necessarily there for you.

Moon in Leo

This placement can really change or minimize the effects of the Sun sign. The Moon in Leo type needs to know you're with the program, yet they don't need a lot of personal attention. This Moon sign is interested in "good times," and these folks are fabulous to shop with. Their downside is childishness in the form of pouting or grumbling.

Moon in Virgo

Virgo Moons are scrupulous in more than just emotional matters. Eat with a Moon in Virgo person and you'll never have to calculate an appropriate tip. (People think that Libra is overconcerned with fairness! Hah!) Watch for an attraction to folks who are very different temperamentally, and a fascination with how things work.

Moon in Libra

Friendship is especially meaningful, and there's often a gift that goes with it: hand-made presents, hand-drawn cards, and the like. The cynical may say that lip service sometimes gets paid to deep emotions, but Moon in Libra is also about processing emotions very, very quickly.

Moon in Scorpio

Passion? Plenty. Concealed? That's what they think. While not really needing friendship, they do appreciate teammates or cheerleaders. The Scorpio Moon person is remarkably self-sufficient. Skeptical, too, and dare I say a bit too brutally realistic. And unless there's heavy fire or air sign influence elsewhere, you will not know what these folks think about you.

Moon in Sagittarius

Sagittarius Moons often seek mentor-style friendships—either having one or being one. Sagittarius Moon friends can be surprisingly forgiving, and have a frequent bent for silliness. There's a real wild streak here, too. They'll always just "show up," but you have to call first.

Moon in Capricorn

This is a tough Moon to have in friendship, and my Capricorn Moon clients are sometimes quite baffled and angry when they get the runaround from peers. Capricorn Moon is about making plans, unless there's a heavy water or air influence in their chart. Do NOT trifle with these folks, and do try not to cancel plans.

Moon in Aquarius

When your friend develops a sudden interest in world religions, streamlining, and technology, or displays some new, unexpected mechanical aptitude, don't be surprised to find Moon in Aquarius. This is supposedly a "jealousy free" placement, but more often than not I've found the folks are surprised or appalled when they do feel jealousy in friendship issues. They'll joke about this, though.

Moon in Pisces

Incredibly lovable, people with this Moon placement can drive you completely around the bend with their inconsistency, and perhaps a little narcissism—that's unbelievably charmingly rendered, of course. If there's a lot of fire in their chart, there may be an inclination toward rash comments. Practice selective deafness.

About the Author

Sally Cragin writes "Moon Signs" for the *Boston Phoenix* newspaper group as "Symboline Dai." Her arts and lifestyle writing has appeared in numerous magazines and newspapers, including the *Boston Globe*, the *Village Voice*, and the *St. Louis Riverfront Times*. You can read Sally's forecasts by going to www.bostonphoenix.com and linking to "astrology."

Suggested Reading

The Sisterhood of the Traveling Pants by Ann Brashares.

The Friendships of Women by Dee Brestin.

The Woman Next Door by Barbara Delinsky.

It's a Chick Thing: Celebrating the Wild Side of Women's Friendship by Ame Mahler Beanland (Editor), et al.

Friendshifts: The Power of Friendship and How It Shapes Our Lives by Jan Yager.

The Moon: Your Travel Agent

By Bruce Scofield

In these times of complicated travel, when vacations cost a bundle and getting there and back could be a nightmare, astrology can make a difference in the quality of your trip experience. The branch of astrology called *electional* has long provided people with favorable times to begin a voyage or leave for an adventure. Before the age of insurance, ship captains would often consult astrologers regarding times to set sail. Today, astrologers are consulted regularly in regard to vacation and travel planning. Choosing a favorable time for a trip is not a simple matter, and a time-specific electional chart computed by an astrologer won't come cheap, but there are alternatives. For example, I've been doing a Sun sign report on this topic for Llewellyn's *Astrological Calendar* for many years now. Columns such as that one can give you an overview of what the year ahead may be like for travel or vacationing—and it may give warnings of unfavorable periods. Another approach is one you can try at home by yourself, using this copy of Llewellyn's *Moon Sign Book*. I'll show you how to do it, but remember that the techniques given shouldn't be considered a substitute for an electional chart calculated by a certified astrologer.

The time that you begin a trip, whether for business or pleasure, is a critical time. The conditions of your journey will be reflected in the astrological qualities of the moment you depart. Whether it's a fun trip or one full of aggravations will be shown by the moment it all starts. A certified astrologer will calculate an exact time to begin a trip. In most cases, this will be the time that you leave your home and set off with baggage in hand. Still, the quality of the day itself, regardless of time, is very important, and this you can handle yourself if you follow the simple instructions below.

Find the Moon Before You Decide

Before you make any decisions about your travel plans, be sure to know where the Moon is and what it is doing on the day of your departure. Armed with knowledge of the sign the Moon is in, the aspects it is making to other planets, and whether or not it is void-of-course, you can make informed decisions that could save you a lot of trouble, and possibly even money. If this conscious approach to traveling appeals to you, the next thing to do is to become familiar with the tables at the beginning of this *Moon Sign Book*. The first set of tables (Moon Tables) are on even-number pages beginning on page 34. They will show you the sign that the Moon is in for each day of the year. The Moon's sign will describe what kinds of activities and what kinds of trends you could reasonably expect to occur on a journey or vacation. For each month, a second set of tables (found on odd-numbered pages, beginning on page 35) will show you whether the Moon is making "favorable" or "unfavorable" aspects on any given day. As the Moon moves through the zodiac it makes alignments, called aspects, with the other planets. Some of these are stressful, others are harmonious. You can get more detailed information about the Moon's aspects from an "aspectarian" in an astrological ephemeris, or from Llewellyn's *Daily Planetary Guide*. The most important thing to keep in mind, however, is that you don't want to begin your travel on a day with unfavorable lunar aspects. You want your trip to start off on a good foot, so you want to start on a day with favorable lunar aspects.

The Moon void-of-course tables (pages 59–64) show you two things: the time of the last aspect the Moon makes to another planet before it changes signs, and the time that it enters the next sign of the zodiac. The difference between these two times is the period during which the Moon is considered "void-of-course." When you look for a date in these tables, you'll only find the days listed on which the Moon goes void-of-course, days that are not listed are days when the Moon is moving through a sign and still making aspects with other planets.

The void-of-course Moon is a condition that suggests a lack of direction, a general wandering off course from what was planned. This may be fine for a trip or vacation where you have no expectations, but it may be frustrating for a business trip or a trip with an itinerary. The void-of-course Moon can signify periods of time when it becomes difficult to stay on track. For example, a friend of mine once departed on a business trip when the Moon was void-of-course and reported that she had to change her room in the hotel three times, finding good food took up a lot of time, and she was ultimately unable to meet her objectives. I once left on a trip during a void-of-course Moon and found that I was unable to make any connections with the people I met along the way. However, in all other respects the trip was fine, but then I didn't have any specific goals in mind. In general, travel under a void-of-course Moon makes a trip less focused and often disappointing. Try to avoid it if you can. There is another side to the void-of-course Moon. It can signify periods of time that favor reaching closure or completion. Activities or projects that have been developing, or are still in process, are also appropriate for the void-of-course Moon. In general, it's a good time for having no game plan, for pursuing the intangible, as in spiritual work or meditation.

Choose the Day

The next step is to actually choose a day to begin your travel. Try to pick a day when the Moon is making favorable aspects to other planets and is not void-of-course. Once you've got a day picked out you're ready to consider the sign that the Moon is in. Here's where you will learn not only what to expect, but, more importantly, what activities or themes are appropriate for the trip. As you will see in the descriptions below, some types of activities are favored by certain signs while others are not.

Aries Travel Agent

If the Moon is in Aries on your departure date, you can expect an adventure. In fact, you should make sure that your trip will indeed be exciting. A boring week sitting in the Sun just won't do. The Aries Moon wants you to make things happen. It wants you to take some risks and try out some new things. Above all, it wants you to be active. Sports and athletics are great for a trip with an Aries Moon. Competitions of all kinds go favorably with this Moon, but don't expect that everyone will get along with each other all of the time. It's possible that the high energy of the Moon may be too much for some people so you should be sensitive to the needs of others. If you are getting the idea that the way to travel under an Aries Moon is to travel by yourself, you're getting the right idea. Aries is the sign of the soloist, the single player, and the first one there. Travel with an Aries Moon in that fashion and you'll do fine. But if you try to make an Aries Moon journey be peaceful and calm, or if you try to make getting along with others a priority, you will have your work cut out for yourself.

Taurus Travel Agent

When the Moon is in Taurus at departure, you can be sure that money will be an issue on the trip. For some this may mean shopping, and that's one activity that goes well under this Moon. Another is luxury. This is the Moon sign for luxuriating in paradise, for taking long periods for rest, and also for enjoying the best food and drink. The highlights of a Taurus Moon journey may turn out to be eating at that special restaurant, or strolling through a garden or a beautifully decorated building. But luxury and beauty cost money, so be prepared and take along an extra credit card. On the other hand, what you don't want to do on a journey with the Moon in Taurus is to get too adventurous. Taurus is the sign that wants you to have your feet firmly on the ground and your hands on the green—money, that is. A rugged, risky trip just won't work. I have some friends who embarked on a mountain climbing trip when the Moon was in Taurus. Nearly everything went wrong for them along the way. Things got even worse when they got sick and had to walk for miles to find a doctor. While it's true that Taurus rules the earth, and even mountains, the Moon in Taurus is only interested in "looking" at these landscape features—and, then, only when they are near to comforts and health facilities. Struggling up and down mountains is inappropriate for a Taurus Moon. The trip was a failure in many ways because the itinerary did not fit the horoscope.

Gemini Travel Agent

With the Moon in Gemini at a departure, one can expect that the trip will be a busy one with many things to do. These trips are usually multifaceted and filled with variety. You might notice that things will come in twos or threes, maybe even fours. Transportation arrangements will be an important theme. You may want to plan things carefully so as not to create any schedule problems. Driving is often the preferred mode of transportation under this Moon Road-trips are favored under this but, but this could also mean taxi, bus, and bicycle transportation. A trip that involves a lot of walking or riding is perfect for this Moon, but a trip that requires you to stay in one place would probably prove frustrating and disappointing. The Gemini Moon is symbolic of nervous energy that needs to be expressed in motion. Talks and discussions on a Gemini Moon trip will be frequent, possibly even excessive. Clever gadgets and technical matters may draw attention on this trip. Be ready to fix things by bringing some tools along—even if only a Swiss Army knife. (Please consider restrictions on luggage content when traveling by air.) Years ago, a friend and I left on a winter camping trip when the Moon was in Gemini. As we lay in our tents, drifting off to sleep, we were startled by the sounds of a large military helicopter. For the next hour this helicopter roared overhead, apparently using us as a pretend target. We later found out that it was the National Guard and they had indeed used heat-sensing technology to find our warm bodies in the cold woods. Needless to say, we were not amused, and my Gemini dog was deeply disturbed. The transportation theme and the technology theme of Gemini were well represented in this case.

Cancer Travel Agent

Like Taurus, travel with the Moon in Cancer is best when safety and securities are nearby. It's not a time for risk or adventure, but rather for seeking domestic security and getting yourself nurtured. What you want to do on a Cancer Moon trip is to put yourself in a safe and secure environment, perhaps in a comfortable dwelling, or maybe even a place from your past. Visiting parents and family members is the ideal activity on a trip with a Cancer Moon, but there are many other options. Traveling with the intention to dine at restaurants, or to sample the cuisine of a foreign country, is in keeping with the nature of the sign of Cancer. Spending time being nurtured by the hosts in a bed and breakfast is surely a Moon in Cancer kind of experience. The actual bed you sleep on may prove to be significant.

Remember that Cancer is the sign that seeks a return to the comfort of the womb, and after birth the best we can do is get in a good bed and maybe cuddle with someone. History and the preservation of antiquities, including old houses and museums, are Cancer-type concepts, and a trip that is dedicated to understanding and experiencing the past is exactly right for this lunar placement.

Leo Travel Agent

If the Moon is in Leo at your departure, you could reasonably expect to have fun, express your creativity, and possibly even experience a romantic encounter. Recreation is a key word for Leo and that's exactly what you should be doing on a trip that begins with the Moon in Leo. Cruising Manhattan after hours, playing cards in Las Vegas, and checking out the nightlife in Cancun are all ways to express this energy. For those who don't care for that much action, attending a concert, seeing a show, or even visiting an art gallery, amounts to the same thing. If you are an artist yourself, or if you want to be one, consider building the trip around a theme of creativity. Go somewhere to paint or photograph the landscape, be inspired and compose a tune, or travel to study under a master. Once on a camping trip to Arizona, which began under a Leo Moon, my friend and I camped at the base of Music Mountain (don't ignore the possible significance of things like names of places), which we climbed. I took many excellent photographs while we were there. Leo is the sign of self-expression, specifically where it enhances our self-esteem. More self-esteem means that others may be more attracted to us—and if there are members of the opposite sex nearby, a romance might be in the works. I know several people who have traveled under a Leo Moon and met someone special. In some cases it was only for the duration of the trip, in others the relationship continued. Don't forget that Leo is a fire sign, and fire signs take risks. When opportunity presents itself, Leo generally won't pass it up. But astrology is not fate, it's just a map. You will have to decide if you can handle the emotional fire of the Leo Moon.

Virgo Travel Agent

With a Virgo Moon at departure you will want to incorporate some work into your trip. This is not a Moon position that lends itself to simple rest and relaxation. Don't waste your money on a vacuous vacation—do something that will improve your mind and body. Learn how to make or fix something. Master a technique. Do something that heals you. Go to a spa and work on your wrinkles, and then work out in the gym. This is the perfect Moon sign for a spiritual retreat that involves a predictable daily schedule of meditation, healing, and meals of organic foods. Health and healing is often a theme under this Moon. I remember a trip to Mexico under a Virgo Moon where I was stung by wasps, hurt my back, and had a difficult time with allergies. For a week, I was asking the local people, *"¿Dónde está la farmacia?"* For many, travel under a Virgo Moon means attention to

schedule, that's why it's probably better to keep things simple. Bring a pocket planner if you're planning to do a lot because you will need it. Another theme under a Virgo Moon is that of repairs. Something will, no doubt, need to be fixed. So don't bring along things that can break, carry a tool box, have your AAA card handy, and don't push your car too hard. An ideal Virgo trip would be one in which you travel somewhere to learn how to fix things. So don't figure on a relaxing trip, but do what Virgo is about and figure that you could return a healthier and more knowledgeable person.

Libra Travel Agent

When the Moon is in Libra at a departure, it is the time to take a trip with a partner, or to meet a friend. Libra is one of the most social signs, and the last thing you want under its influence is to be alone. Solo travel is not recommended here unless your destination comes with plenty of social experience. I suppose that solo travel to a resort for singles might not be a bad idea, but for most people Libra travel means traveling with others. Another side of Libra has to do with comfort, decor, and the arts. It's not the best sign for roughing it, unless you happen to know that your campsite or cheap hotel is in a very beautiful environment. You're better off going to a classy, well-appointed inn, and taking in a concert or art show—along with your close friend or partner, of course. Libra is an air sign, and it values learning. Any kind of intellectual experience would be appropriate. Attending lectures and entering into group discussions, or even debates, are very much in line with the energies of this lunar position. Very often, significant friendships begin under the influence of the Libra Moon. I once began a trip under this Moon and met a man who is now one of my oldest friends. I attended a conference and offered him a ride home. The road trip back was full of engaging conversation and we have been friends ever since. One interesting sidelight to this trip is that we stopped off to take a look at a rock formation called "Balanced Rock."

Scorpio Travel Agent

Beginning a journey when the Moon is in Scorpio is an indication that the trip will be an intense or powerful one. Whether the travel arrangements turn out to be complex and deeply entangled with other people and their stuff, or the destinations themselves are mysterious and dark, you will know that you are on the path of the Scorpio Moon. Travel for healing and purification, or travel for investigative purposes are appropriate for this Moon position. On a trip to England, that began with the Moon in Scorpio, I visited Stonehenge and then the underground Roman-built baths of Bath. What you don't want to do is travel for petty, superficial reasons. If you do, something will likely happen to bring your trip to a different level. So start with the assumption that there is something to dig up on your trip, and you'll probably do fine. A major theme of the Scorpio Moon is entanglements with others. Chances are you will find yourself sharing space or money with others, and this may not always be easy. Make sure you know what the boundaries are before you agree to anything. The Scorpio Moon at departure could also indicate a trip that makes a powerful impact on you. This may be exactly what you want if you're of an adventurous disposition. Scorpio loves tight, dark spaces. The Flight of the Double Eagle II, a balloon trip around the world, was launched under a Scorpio Moon. The pilot spent his time in a very tight space high above the Earth, where it was difficult to breath. Another possible activity for the Scorpio Moon would be scuba diving or spelunking. But if these don't appeal to you, why not go to a hot springs and cover yourself with mud.

Sagittarius Travel Agent

Travel and Sagittarius are synonymous, and leaving under a Sagittarius Moon means you are opening yourself up for a real learning experience. Sagittarius is the most expansive of the fire signs, and it just loves to take risks and try new things. This is the Moon for outdoor adventures, for athletic activities, and for exploring remote, foreign places. On the day that

Columbus set sail to find the Orient, the Moon was in Sagittarius. What he found resulted in an expansion of travel and commerce. But his was no luxury trip. A Sagittarius Moon departure is probably better for budget travel and casual accommodations. As Sagittarius tends to cause things to increase and expand, trips taken to resorts under this Moon will often cost a bundle. So start low and you won't get too high. In fact, the only real detriments to a Sagittarius Moon trip are likely to be opulence and excess. Sagittarius is quick to see through meaningless displays and wants to cut to the chase. Unless you're a good gambler, or have unlimited funds, this may not be the wisest Moon placement for a gambling trip. Other themes of Sagittarius are religion and politics—what people believe. I once took a trip to Oaxaca and stayed in a former Catholic convent. During that trip I also learned about some of the political conflicts raging in Mexico. Be careful what you do if you begin your travel under a Sagittarius Moon, others may not understand your motives, and you could find yourself inadvertently breaking some local custom. Above all, the best thing you can do is plan to learn under this Moon.

Capricorn Travel Agent

The trip that begins under a Capricorn Moon is one that should accomplish something. If you don't have a goal, devise one. Make this trip a work trip, or it will make it that way itself. This Moon is not about meaningless fun, it's about getting to real things and making a difference. It's about respecting the rules and meeting the challenges, whether we're talking about a government meeting or climbing a mountain. Don't expect things to be comfortable, but you can expect them to be a challenge. Don't expect to spend a week in the Sun doing nothing. If you try this you might find that problems keep popping up. Every time you solve one thing, another arises. If this is the case, make the trip one in which you handle and solve problems. I once left for a trip to Virginia when the Moon was in Capricorn. My car broke down and I had to spend the night in the woods—in November! Fortunately, I was prepared and had a warm sleeping bag with me. Then I had to figure out how to get the car back to New Jersey. I also had to deal with the police at several points along the way. Authorities, like the police, come with a Capricorn Moon experience. The key under this Moon is to remain focused and disciplined. Don't fall asleep at the wheel, be prepared, and play by the rules. On a more positive note, travel under the Capricorn Moon is excellent for work and business. It will support you in being organized in dealings with lawyers, in negotiating with governments, and in interactions with authorities.

You will work during a trip under a Capricorn Moon, but you will also accomplish something.

Aquarius Travel Agent

Leaving on a journey under an Aquarius Moon can do wonders for your social life. If you are open to unusual and possibly awkward social circumstances, this Moon brings strange bedfellows together and encourages social unification under the banner of free-thinking. You can always expect to have some interesting conversations, and you can expect to meet some highly unusual people. I've left for astrology conferences under this Moon and have never been disappointed—there is quite a collection of characters in the field of astrology, as you might imagine. But all this potential social interaction is not necessarily the best for those seeking emotional contact. Aquarius is about freedom, ideas, and individuality. It's an energy for friendship, but not necessarily passion. It's perfect for conferences, workshops, gatherings, communal experiences, and one-of-a-kind happenings, though. I once took a solo backpacking trip under this Moon and found the experience wanting. I didn't meet a single person on the Appalachian Trail midweek in November (not that I really expected to), and yet I wanted to. I learned from this experience that solo travel under this Moon should be to a population center where the possibility for mixing is greatly increased. On another trip, taken when the Moon was in Aquarius, I connected with two of my friends who had never met. The three of us had a great time together, and so did our three dogs. The Aquarius Moon loves animals, and departures under this condition also go well with travel to places that offer contact with domesticated animals, like grandma's cats or the horses at a dude ranch.

Pisces Travel Agent

When leaving under a Pisces Moon, you may expect to feel the power of the larger world around you, whether this is nature itself or the religious customs of the natives. This Moon is about inspiration. If you climb the highest mountain you will be blown away by the view, or maybe even the wind. If you step into a museum or church, you will be moved to tears by the sheer beauty of the art, or even the building itself. If you engage in a conversation with someone close to you, the most profound communications may take place. Don't underestimate a Pisces Moon departure, it could mark a trip that changes your life in more ways than one. A friend of mine left under this Moon for a one-week trip. On his return he quit his job and left his wife. Another friend left under this Moon and returned inspired, rejuvenated, and ready to put his life on a firmer footing. Another feature of the Pisces Moon in a departure has to do with unfinished business and the need for completion. It is the right Moon to travel under if you want to bring things to some kind of closure, and it's the right Moon for feeling your way toward an agreement with others. The Pisces Moon is always aware of what's going on, but it's not necessarily rational. It works its magic in strange ways. Don't put limits on a trip under this Moon, just let it happen.

Final Note

Now that we've reviewed the general characteristics of each Moon sign, get out there and experience the world. Just remember that electional astrology is not about forcing your will on the world, its about consciously recognizing the influences of the moment and customizing your trip to fit the bill. ¡Bien Viaje!

About the Author

Bruce Scofield, C.A. NCGR, is a professional astrological consultant who works with clients in the United States and abroad. He has an M.A. in history and level four certification from NCGR. As a consulting astrologer, he specializes in both psychological astrology and electional astrology. His special interest is the astrology of ancient civilizations, especially those of the Maya and Aztecs. He is the author of thirteen books, numerous magazine and journal articles, and he serves on the faculty of Kepler College.

Suggested Reading

French Lessons: Adventures with Knife, Fork, and Corkscrew by Peter Mayle.

Shadows in the Sun: Travels to Landscapes of Spirit and Desire by Wade Davis.

Snow in the Kingdom: My Storm Years on Everest by Ed Webster.

Astrological Timing

By Maria K. Simms

It's been said that "Thoughts are things," and so they are, or certainly can be. Most of us know of instances where this seems to happen naturally. You hold a wish in your mind strongly, and work toward it, and the wish becomes reality, the thought becomes a "thing." You can do this quite deliberately by focusing the mind.

Familiar to nearly everyone are the words "As above, so below," which speak of the observed correspondence between the movements of the "signs" in the sky and what is happening on Earth below. When the quotation (attributed to the legendary Hermes Trismegistus) is limited to those four words, one could get the mistaken impression that what is above is causing what happens below. But, the quotation continues: "As within, so without." Ah! So, what is causing what? Are we on Earth only responding to our "fate" as read in the stars, or are we projecting on to the stars a collective tradition emerging from our minds? The fact is, we don't know. There is no proof that the phenomenon of "As above, so below" is anything more than what is implied in the final phrase of the Hermes adage: "As above, so below; as within so without; as the universe, so the soul." Correspondence? Synchronicity? If this is truth, then we, as individual souls, can be both cause and effect (response), and we have a very wide range of freedom of choice in which to operate.

So, you might think, what if the stars are depicting a "fate" we can't avoid? To that, I say, "So what?" You can't prove it, nor can you avoid choice. When you think something is going to happen, no matter how you respond to that thought, you are making a choice.

There is absolutely nothing in astrological tradition that has only one possible meaning. Indeed, every planet, every sign, every house, every aspect, every phase of the Moon—anything one can see in a chart—has the possibility of a wide range of correspondences with life, from that which you might consider "good" to that which you might fear as "bad." Each may have an observable generalized theme we can identify, but that theme can and does manifest in a variety of ways. Does it not then make sense to set your mind toward the "good" (most favorable or desired manifestation of a theme)? Will that always work? No, it won't, in large part because we are not in this world alone, and often the choices of others affect what happens to us, and there is little we can do about it except respond. Still, even in that, HOW we respond is a free and individual choice! Over that, each of us does have control. So, again, we can set our will and intent, as well as our hearts and soul, toward the "good"—the highest good we know. As within, so without—and the universe responds. As the universe, so the soul—one within spirit.

Now, in using astrology as a tool, we are dealing with one thing that is quite predictable. That is, the planets move in orderly orbital patterns that can be reliably calculated for future dates. We know the range of meanings we might attach to those positions is quite wide, but we also know of long-standing observations of general themes that we can interpret within our personal environmental context. When we are aware of those themes, we are essentially observing the cosmic flow or current. It tends to be easier to swim with a current than to fight against it. This is why, in setting your mind toward a specific intent, it is likely to be easier to act at a time that is "in the flow" and appropriate to your goal.

Electional astrology is the closest the art of astrology comes to magic. What may be lacking is the clarity that one is effectively choosing to cause a desired outcome, and also that the success of the effort involves the attitude and intent of all those who are directly party to the elected event. This is especially important, I believe, when the astrologer elects a time for someone else. If either the astrologer or the "someone else" operate from the assumption that the planets will cause the event to come out as hoped only because choosing exactly that "right" time has somehow outsmarted the universe, any effect is vastly weakened. No matter how beautifully a future chart for an event might be described in the astrology of that time, the astrologer has to take into account the individuals who are party to the event (and their birth charts). Those who enact the event (such as the new business owners, the bride and groom, the job applicant, etc.) must understand their own roles as co-creators of their future, both at the time of the event itself, and beyond. To most effectively use astrological timing, one needs the clear understanding of will, purpose, and intent, and also must be prepared to do the follow-up work that is necessary to fulfill the purpose that the elected event begins. And, one has to believe that the intended purpose can and will manifest into reality!

With awareness of the importance of your own role in focused intent and follow-through, choices you make have greater chance of success. Your repertoire for effective astrological timing can be expanded beyond this *Moon Sign Book* more easily than you think. My book, *A Time for Magick*, teaches the easiest types of astrological timing that can be utilized by beginners: planetary hours (the book includes easy look-up tables for these), and quick timing with an astrological calendar. The remainder of this article will show you, with a few specific examples, how to use such a calendar, like Llewellyn's *Astrological Calendar 2003*, as a companion to your *Moon Sign Book*.

Note this year's calendar shows the times of major planetary aspects on each day's square. Be sure to note the time zone for which times are calculated. If you live within Eastern Standard Time, you can use the times just as they are—except that during the period of summer, most locations will be on Daylight Savings Time, which this year is from April 6 to October 26. During that period of time, you must "spring forward" and add one hour to the standard time given on the calendar. If you live within Central Standard Time, subtract one hour; Mountain Standard Time, subtract two hours; Pacific Standard Time, subtract three hours.

Key Rules for Using the Calendar

Moon phase is shown in upper right of the date square. From New Moon until second quarter is the best time to take initiative and get things started. From second quarter to Full Moon, be decisive, take action on what's begun and move it forward, and build toward goals. At Full Moon, bring things to fruition. This is a good time to seek clarity and higher purpose by taking an honest look at others involved and if needed, seek

balance and refinement of purpose. Full
Moon is a powerful time. From Full
Moon to third quarter, present your ideas
and progress on projects. Demonstrate
and disseminate what you have learned.
And from third quarter to New Moon,
wind down and think beyond the
present. Evaluate and let go of that which
isn't working. Meditate on a possible next
project to begin at New Moon time.

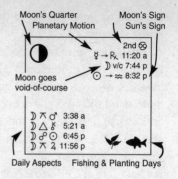

Moon Void-of-Course (v/c) is also shown in upper right of the date
square. In the example here, the time period begins with ☽ v/c 7:44 pm and
ends with ☽ → ≈ 8:32 pm (Moon entering a sign at a specific time).
During the v/c period, work effectively on things already begun as it is generally not a good time to begin new things. Work within normal routine; use
the time to think things over, or just relax. Avoid significant initiatives, major
purchases.

Mercury retrograde (☿ ℞) is shown at upper right corner of date
square. The retrograde period begins with ☿ ℞, and it ends with ☿ D. You
could highlight Mercury retrograde days with a yellow marker to remind
you it's a time of caution, with a reputation for communications problems
of all kinds. But, use common sense—communication can't stop. It just
may require some extra patience, and double-checking. This is a good
time for evaluation, revision, and reflection.

Planetary Aspects

In the lower left of each date square is a list of aspects along with times
they occur. The most important thing to know is: Action proceeds from
when the Moon enters a sign until it is void-of-course. The FINAL aspect
of the Moon within a sign (the one at exactly the same time as the the v/c
time) is highly important. It indicates the outcome of actions taken during
the sequence of aspects from the time Moon enters a sign to the one that
is the v/c aspect.

Only applying aspects count. This means that if the time you elect to
act is in the middle of a sequence of Moon aspects within a sign, the only
aspects that matter are those that occur after your chosen time to act and
before the v/c.

Conjunction (☌) is the strongest aspect. Whether this aspect is favorable or unfavorable depends on whether or not the planet the Moon conjuncts is appropriate or inappropriate to your purpose.

Sextile and Trine (✳, △) are generally favorable. They symbolize opportunity, smooth flow, and are preferred for final outcome aspect.

Square (□) symbolizes action, which may involve challenge. It's usually best to avoid a square as the final aspect, if possible, although challenges handled well can work to your advantage. If there are no squares in the sequence, there may not be enough action. But too much ease is not necessarily good either.

Opposition (☍) also symbolizes action. The challenge here is likely to represent the necessity to balance opposing forces, or to deal with issues of relationship compromise. Best avoided as final aspect.

Quincunx (⚻) is not used in traditional electional astrology, so note that it does not count for final aspect before going void-of-course. Its general meaning for those who use it: An adjustment needs to be made.

"Best avoided" does not mean *bad*, or don't ever choose this time. A challenging aspect as the final aspect can work okay, but judging the potential of this does call for a higher degree of expertise in how the planet combinations create meaning, and what correspondences each has to the matter being timed. This, however, is too much to cover in this short article.

Moon in Combination with Other Planets

The Moon sign shows the general mood of the day, and ideas for this are covered elsewhere in this book. Here are a few key words suggesting some general moods or themes for how the Moon in aspect with other planets might be expressed. A + sign indicates favorable potentials, while a – sign indicates challenging potentials.

Moon-Sun: + feeling good, in charge; – feeling conflicted. (For Moon-Sun square, see "Moon Phases" above; second and fourth quarter are squares with special meaning.)

Moon-Mercury: + talkative, sharp thinking, decisive; – scattered, distracted, indecisive.

Moon-Venus: + happy, graceful, sociable; – moody, irritable, on the fence, indecisive.

Moon-Mars: + energetic, assertive, direct, upbeat; – quarrelsome, confrontational.

Moon-Jupiter: + generous, jovial, upbeat; – indulgent, wasteful, dogmatic, arrogant.

Moon-Saturn: + self-controlled, practical, disciplined; – inhibited, nervous, pessimistic.

Moon-Uranus: + attentive, instinctive, sudden change; – overly stressed, erratic, detached.

Moon-Neptune: + inspired vision, imaginative; – spacey, deception or self-deception.

Moon-Pluto: + pursuit with zeal, intensity; – upsetting outburst, power struggle, skeptical.

Moon-Chiron: Chiron is not used in traditional electional astrology, so it is NOT considered for void-of-course Moon, or in this article.

Examples of Astrological Timing

Using Llewellyn's *Astrological Calendar 2003* as a reference, I'm going to discuss two ways to approach electing times. Either first decide what you want to do, and then look for a good time to do it; or scan the astrological calendar for generally favorable times, and then tailor the activity accordingly. I've done a little of both in selecting examples, and I've also mixed mundane actions with a few meditative acts. Meditation can be of great help in setting your mind to focus on a goal. Use the examples as guidelines for how to use the calendar. Please keep in mind that these are far from the only days for the actions suggested!

Example 1: It is January, and time to take off the pounds added during the holidays. When is the best date to start the diet? An obvious choice is the end of a waning Moon period. But, that's on January 1? I don't think so—that's still a holiday. Well, we can go into this a little more gradually. Looking at the next fourth quarter waning Moon, we find one during the last week of the month. For diet, self-control and discipline are defintely needed, so we would want to find a good Moon-Saturn aspect to help out. All the Saturn aspects seem challenging, but isn't this a challenge? Go for Tuesday the 28th. The Moon aspects Pluto for transformation, Venus for grace, Saturn for discipline and ends with a sextile to Uranus—the opportunity to change! Plan to start the diet Tuesday morning at sunrise, which is Mars hour on the day of Mars for action.

Example 2: On March 10, Uranus enters Pisces, after years in Aquarius, heralding a major shift in how people seek freedom, deal with change, and express individuality. New waves of idealism and compassion, spirituality and artistic expression are likely. March 11 we have a waxing half-Moon that begins second quarter, making this a time of decisive action to move forward. On the evening of March 11, with Moon trine Uranus, reach out for your own best expression of the Pisces theme, by participating in volunteer activity for a charity, by creating artistically, or by quietly meditating for insight.

Example 3: Let's project that in May you need to sign an important document, and have some choice of when to sign. First, we check for any Mercury retrograde period, and note that on April 26 Mercury goes retrograde. Scanning ahead, we see that Mercury is direct again on May 20. It would be best to wait for that, if you can. On May 21, the Sun enters Gemini. This day would be a good choice for your signing, but wait until after the Moon passes its aspect to Neptune. The remaining aspects up to the void-of-course favor action (Mars), power (Pluto), and stability (Saturn).

Example 4: In July, let's look for a time to plan for some success—a new job, promotion, or presentation, maybe. I'm inclined to scan past the holiday first week, to May 10. Why? The Moon is waxing and in Sagittarius, a fire sign, which is a very good sign for "speaking up." The Moon square Mars in the afternoon spurs action, the sextile to Neptune enhances vision, and the rest of the string is supportive, too. The final aspect before the Moon goes void-of-course is a trine to Jupiter on the morning of the May 11.

Example 5: August 28 begins another one of those dreaded Mercury retrogrades, and it is just a day past New Moon in Virgo. Feeling stuck? Well, don't be. Remember that the retrograde period is good for really thinking things through and revising them to your benefit. Pluto is direct (D) on that day, and the Moon conjunct Mercury is the final aspect before the Moon goes void-of-course. Thinking (Mercury) can be pretty clear for rechecking and revising. Think though your project step-by-step, and jot down notes as they come to you. When you come to something that you know you must do, underline the note. When you are finished, you will have a priority list. As you accomplish each thing, cross it off your list!

Example 6: It's September, and Mars has been retrograde since late July. Perhaps you've felt a slowdown in energy. When Mars turns direct on September 27 it will be a good time to revitalize. If that's not a good day for you, wait for Friday, just after the New Moon is born, with Moon sextile transformative Pluto, and the final aspect of the Moon a trine to upbeat

Uranus. A day like Friday is good for charging yourself up with a new burst of forward energy in any endeavor. Plan to do something very physically active that you enjoy in the evening. The charge will get you off and running in the weeks ahead. If you're alone, the moving meditation of dance to recorded drumming music—detailed in my book *A Time for Magick*—would be excellent.

Example 7: How about a romantic evening this month? Notice that on October 8 the Moon enters Aries early evening and Venus trines Uranus. That looks like a good night. October 9 suggests some difficulty early in the evening, but after the Moon passes Saturn, it looks like smooth sailing ahead. The Full Moon on Friday, October 10, includes a lovely Venus trine Mars, and the last aspect at the Moon void-of-course is a sextile to Uranus. Serendipity!

Example 8: In the season of nature's winding down toward winter's rest, it is traditional to give thanks and to honor the departed. Rituals of spiritual intent are transcendent, so I believe it matters not what day you pick—even astrological factors you might otherwise avoid are good. On Friday, November 14, the Moon in Cancer is void-of-course nearly all day. Take some time for quiet reflection, perhaps while walking or raking autumn leaves, strolling through a park or putting your garden to bed, or perhaps, in resting or meditating. Give thanks for the blessings in your life, including things of value you learned from those who've passed on (even if some of the lessons were hard ones.) As the Sun sets, light a candle of thanks to the departed and to Spirit, and let it burn all the way down (in a very safe location where you can monitor it—never leave a burning candle unattended).

Example 9: Winter Solstice, the longest night, is December 22, at 2:04 am EST. On Sunday, December 21, the Moon sextiles Neptune, and the successive aspects before Moon void-of-course—especially Mercury opposite Saturn—suggest an appropriate time for serious thinking that leads toward enlightened insight (final aspect is Moon sextile Uranus). There is a dark Moon on December 21, before the New Moon on the 23rd, an excellent time to release the past and prepare for the New Moon and a new season of waxing light. If you have a practical mundane matter that fits this theme, now is the time to take care of it. If this is not possible on this evening, prepare ritually to set your resolve. Get a pad and pen, and if you have a fireplace, begin by meditating before the fire. Reflect on feelings and concerns that you'd like to release from your life. Write them down. Then, write another list of positive resolves you could make moving forward. Ask spirit for assistance, knowing that the new light comes from within and will move outward to change your world. Burn the list of that which you would release, and as it burns feel the healing energy. Fold and keep your list of positive resolves and refer to it as needed.

About the Author

Maria Kay Simms has authored several astrology books, including *A Time for Magick* (Llewellyn, 2001). She has been an astrologer for twenty-seven years, and holds professional certification from the National Council for Geocosmic Research, Inc. (NCGR) and American Federation of Astrologers (AFA). She is currently the elected chair of NCGR.

Astrological Magic

By Christopher Warnock

The universe can be likened to a network of jewels, with each jewel, shining and beautiful, reflecting each of the other innumerable gems in the net. Each individual jewel, therefore, contains infinity.

The traditional astrologer uses this correspondence of all things to predict events. He or she looks to the cycles of the heavens, which foretell the cycles of events here on Earth.

The astrological magician takes this correspondence one step further. Not content to be the passive recipient of the messages of the stars, he or she seeks to affect and control the celestial influences.

How Does Astrological Magic Work?

For Renaissance astrologers and magicians, reality was composed of three basic levels, the Divine World of Ideas and Angels, the Celestial World of the stars and planets, and the Material World.

In the World of Ideas and Angels, things exist in a perfect, unchanging archetypal form. Because matter resists form and is subject to change, things in the Material World are born, grow, and die. The Celestial World is the essential intermediary between the Ideal and the Material realms. We should not think of the Ideal and Celestial Worlds as being in some other physical location from the Material World. All of the worlds interpenetrate and affect each other.

Thus, for example, in the Ideal World we have the perfect form of *justice*, where everyone receives exactly what they merit. In the Ideal World, justice is personified as the archangel Michael who carries the sword and scales of justice. Justice is embodied in the Celestial World in the constellation Libra and planet Jupiter, and in the Material World in just acts by just people, and sometimes, but not always, in courts of law, through judges and attorneys.

In Renaissance astrological magic, we focus on the Celestial World of the constellations of the zodiac and the planets. The zodiac provides a universal archetype and language for the creation and dissolution of all things in the Material World. For example, each sign of the zodiac is either active or passive, as well as being either fire (hot and dry), air (hot and wet), water (cold and wet), or earth (cold and dry). As the planets pass through the various signs of the zodiac, their basic energies and effects on the Earth are modulated by the nature of the sign they inhabit.

We can see this most clearly in the Sun's progression. As the Sun passes through each sign of the zodiac at a rate of one sign per month, so we, too, pass through the seasons, which correspond to the nature of the signs. Aries, for example, a spring sign, stimulates germination and growth.

Each planet embodies one or more of the divine ideas, which it then rules as the idea manifests itself in the Material World. These linked correspondences are known as the Great Chain of Being, and are the mechanism through which the astrological magician works his magic. A given chain can be quite complex with a long interlinked series of members, the higher members ruling those below. The Renaissance philosopher Marsilio Ficino gives the example of such a chain, beginning with the constellation Draco, the dragon, under whom is placed Saturn and sometimes Jupiter; then spirits who often take on serpent's form; then men of reptilian nature; then serpents (the animals); and below them, the snake-weed; then the stone draconite, which originates in the head of a dragon; and the stone commonly called serpentine.

The influence of higher upon lower members in a given chain can be seen either as an impersonal force, and is then termed *rays*, or it can be personified as spirits or angels. The Arabic philosopher Al-Kindi wrote that the stars give off their rays very strongly, but everything in existence also emits rays, binding together all parts of the cosmos. We should not analogize Al-Kindi's rays to adjust to electrical or magnetic rays; magical rays have a spiritual component as well. Like gravity, whose mechanism is yet unexplained by science, magical rays are capable of instantaneous action at a distance and are not limited by the speed of light or blocked by material objects.

The personified form of the rays of the stars are the various angels and spirits. The most important of these are the angels of the planetary spheres, such as Gabriel, who is the angel set over the Moon.

Thus, the power of the Divine Ideas, the highest level of reality, descends first to the Celestial World, and then through the mediation of the planets and the zodiac, it is scattered throughout the objects of the Material World. Jupiter, as mentioned, embodies the divine idea of justice, and so on Earth, Jupiter rules kings, leaders, judges, wealth, generosity, the colors sea-green or blue, the metal tin as well as gold, amethyst, sapphire and emerald, cloves, nutmeg, pomegranates, mint, daisies, and songs that are stately, but happy. We can see how many of these separate things have similarities, and by examining the various qualities of the things ruled by a planet we can refine our understanding of the nature of the planet and the Divine Idea or ideas it embodies.

Using Astrological Magic

If we wish to do astrological magic to influence Earthly affairs, we ascend back to the World of the Ideas and Angels. We decide which planet best embodies the *idea* we would like to manifest on Earth. For example, if we are pursuing a romantic relationship, we look to Venus, who embodies the divine idea of *love*. We then gather materials that are ruled by the planet and contain our selected idea or ideas. This not only includes plants, music, and metals, but also images, numbers, words, characters, and rituals. We then assemble our materials at a time when the appropriate planet is astrologically strong. We particularly like to use numbers, words, and images appropriate to the planets in our magic because these more abstract manifestations of the planetary energy have a closer connection to the Divine Ideas.

Astrological magic is therefore a multimedia process in which the beauty of images and pictures, precious metals and gems, music, incenses, and perfumes are combined at the appropriately auspicious moment to focus and capture our chosen astrological influences.

A Healing Talisman

To illustrate by example, several months ago a client sought my help with recovery from a back injury. Because of the nature of her injury, we felt that a talisman promoting growth would aid in the healing process. We looked to Mercury, the god of communications, eloquence, and thought, but also the ruler of the sign Virgo associated with growth and the harvest. Ficino says: "... if anyone looks for a special benefit from Mercury, he ought to locate him in Virgo ... and then make an image out of tin or silver; he should put on it the whole sign of Virgo and its character and the character of Mercury. And if you are going to use the first face of Virgo, add also the figure which has been observed in the first face."

The faces (or decans) are ten-degree divisions of the signs of zodiac. Our actual image from the talisman comes from *Picatrix*, an encyclopedic work of Arabic astrological magic: "And there ascends in the first face of Virgo a maiden girl covered in linen and wool, holding in her hand a pomegranate. And this is a face of planting, cultivation, germination of trees, collecting grapes and good vines. And this is its form."

The famous astrologer and mage Cornelius Agrippa says that the first face of Virgo: "signifieth getting of wealth, ordering of diet, plowing, sowing, and peopling."

The time I chose for the construction of the talisman was August 15, 2001, at 7:28 am EDT in Washington, D.C. At this time the first face of Virgo rises. Mercury the ruler of the Ascendant is conjunct the Ascendant and in the first face of Virgo. It is Wednesday, Mercury day, and it is the hour ruled by Mercury. In any election, we also like to see the Moon strong, as she conveys all influences from the superior spheres to us in the sublunary realm. Here she is in her sign, Cancer, and in the angular Tenth House. The Moon is applying to a sextile of Mercury, and the aspect is almost perfect (the Moon is in the same degree as Mercury).

At the chosen time, I prepared the paper talisman, using the picture of the girl holding a pomegranate, as shown above. I added the appropriate symbols of Mercury and Virgo to the picture of the girl and then placed the folded paper in an amulet holder on a necklace composed of moss agate, a stone ruled by Mercury. The client then wore the talisman daily, for as much time as possible. She reported immediate psychological relief and recovered quickly from the back injury.

While our traditional sources give us detailed instructions for creating talismans for specific aims, we can also rely on the basic nature of the planets to create an appropriate talisman for more general effects. For example, for overall good fortune, prosperity, honors, and dignities, we would look to Jupiter. For fame, power, and high position, the Sun. For love and marriage, Venus. For wealth, business success, memory, and eloquence, Mercury. For cheerfulness, safety in travel, wealth, and health, the Moon. Let me give some specific examples of talismans and times for their construction that you can make yourselves.

Let's use Venus and the Moon as two examples. Since Venus is the goddess of love, a Venus talisman would be appropriate to bring committed love into one's life, to stir up passion, or to attract a particular person. A Moon talisman would be useful for general good fortune. Agrippa says that a Moon talisman "renders the bearer thereof grateful, amiable, pleasant, cheerful, honored, removing all malice and ill will. It causeth security in a journey, increase of riches, and health of body."

Selecting a Time for Talisman-making

First, we pick appropriate times. If you simply use the times listed in this article, without adjusting for time zones, e.g. if the article says 8:00 am Eastern Time, use 8:00 am Central, Mountain, or Pacific time, and you will get a reasonable approximation of the appropriate time. You can use astrological software, or consult a traditional astrologer, if you would like to find the time at your location that has the identical astrological factors to those listed for each talisman.

For the Venus talisman, I observe that on March 29, 2003, at 9:54 am Eastern Standard Time at my location, Washington, D.C., Venus is highly dignified in her exaltation, triplicity, and term. She is precisely on the Midheaven, which is a very strong position. The Moon is conjunct Venus in the same degree of Pisces.

On April 3, 2003, at 4:28 am Eastern Standard Time at my location, Washington, D.C., Venus is dignified by exaltation and term. She is conjunct the Ascendant. The Moon, dignified by exaltation and triplicity, is making an applying sextile to Venus. Both of these times would be excellent for a Venus talisman.

For the Moon talisman, on both March 18, 2003, at 4:17 pm Eastern Standard Time and June 24, 2003, at 9:09 am Eastern Daylight Time at my location, Washington, D.C., the Moon is in exaltation in Taurus and conjunct the Midheaven. Both of these times would thus be excellent for the construction of a Moon talisman.

Planet Rulership and Exaltation

These examples illustrate some of the basic principles of astrological elections for talismans. We first wish to see that the selected planet is in a sign where it is strong, usually either the sign that it rules or the sign where it is exalted. Note that in traditional astrology we use the traditional rulerships and exaltations. Saturn rules Capricorn and Aquarius and is exalted in Libra, Jupiter rules Sagittarius and Pisces and is exalted in Cancer, Mars rules Scorpio and Aries and is exalted in Capricorn, the Sun rules Leo and is exalted in Aries, Venus rules Libra and Taurus and is exalted in Pisces, Mercury rules Virgo and Gemini and is exalted in Virgo, and the Moon rules Cancer and is exalted in Taurus.

After determining that our selected planet is in a sign where it has strength, we then place it in a house where it can manifest its effects. The best placements, as we can see from our examples, are on the Ascendant or the Midheaven, where the planet is either rising or culminating.

In any election, in addition to having our chosen planet strong and well placed, we look to the Moon. In Renaissance theory, as she was the closest planet to the Earth, and the fastest, she played an important role in conveying the celestial influences to the Material World. We would like to select a day when the Moon is making a favorable aspect to our chosen planet. In traditional astrology, the favorable aspects are the conjunction, sextile, and trine. Of course, if we are making a Moon talisman we cannot make the Moon apply to itself. In any talisman, we would also like to see the Moon strong and well placed. In our second Venus example, the Moon is well dignified by being in exaltation and triplicity.

So at our chosen time we create our talisman. Copper is the metal ruled by Venus, so it is an excellent material for a Venus talisman. The Moon rules the metal silver, so silver would be best for a Moon talisman. It is also possible to use paper for any talisman, as in the preceding Mercury talisman example. The metal talismans have a stronger effect and last longer, but the paper has the advantage of being less expensive. Since Venus rules the color white, for a paper talisman, you could use a pen with white ink or use white paper. The Moon is associated with the color green, so for a paper talisman, green ink or green paper would be appropriate.

At the chosen time, engrave or write the table of Venus or the table of the Moon (shown on page 225), as appropriate, on your talisman. Each of the planets has a table traditionally associated with it. These tables are known as magic squares because adding the numbers in a row horizontally, vertically, or diagonally produces the same result. You should also write on the talisman the aims (e.g., love, commitment) you wish to accomplish.

You could then incorporate the paper or metal plate with the appropriate table on it into a bracelet, necklace or other item of jewelry. Venus rules emeralds, sapphires, green jasper, lapis lazuli, and coral, so these would be appropriate stones to use for a Venus talisman. For a Moon talisman, we would use crystal, silver marcasite, pearls, and mother-of-pearl.

While making the talisman, it helps to burn incense and candles. For a love spell one would use pink or red candles. For the Moon we could use green candles, particularly if we sought to achieve prosperity. Venusian incense is sweet, so musk or rose incense would be appropriate. For the Moon we would use frankincense. You can also play Venusian music, which according to Marsilio Ficino is "voluptuous with wantonness and softness." Lunar music is moderate, neither too loud nor soft, and tends toward rhythmic change as does the Moon herself.

So make your Venus or Moon talisman as beautiful as possible, let the candles, incense, and music inspire you. Meditate on the goal you wish to achieve, visualizing the desired results, confident that they will be achieved. Wear the talisman next to your skin, and as frequently as possible until your goal is realized.

Another way to time the construction of astrological talismans is through the use of the planetary hours. Each day is ruled by one of the traditional planets: Sunday (the Sun), Monday (the Moon), Tuesday (Mars), Wednesday (Mercury), Thursday (Jupiter), Friday (Venus), and Saturday (Saturn). In English the names of Norse gods were substituted for some Roman gods in the days of the week, thus Tiw the Norse god of war gave his name to Tuesday; Thor, the god of thunder to Thursday; and Frigg, goddess of love to Friday.

Not only is each day ruled by a planet, but each hour is also ruled by a planet with the first hour of each day being ruled by the planet that rules the whole day. Planetary hours are not the same as our regular sixty-minute hours beginning at midnight. Instead, the planetary day starts at sunrise. To find out the length of a planetary hour, we find the sunrise and sunset times as well as the sunrise of the next day. We then take the time from sunrise to sunset and divide by twelve, and the time from sunset to sunrise of the next day and also divide by twelve. We can see that each planetary hour during the day will be different from each planetary hour during the night, and that the times of hours will vary between each day as the time of sunrise and sunset vary. The only time that these hours are equal are at the equinoxes when there are twelve hours of daylight and twelve hours of night.

Starting with the planet that rules the day, the hours follow in this order: Saturn, Jupiter, Mars, Sun, Venus, Mercury, Moon, and then repeat. Thus, the first hour of Sunday is ruled by the Sun, then Venus, Mercury, Moon, Saturn, Jupiter, Mars, and the eighth hour is again ruled by the Sun.

The easiest way to use the planetary hours is to construct a talisman on the appropriate day at dawn, which is always the day and the hour of the planet that rules that day. So, if we want to make a Moon talisman we make it Monday at dawn, a Venus talisman Friday at dawn, a Mercury talisman Wednesday at dawn, and so on. We can follow the same procedure I laid out earlier for materials, incense, candles, music, and meditation, so long as we use dawn of the appropriate day.

Because of the sympathy and harmony of all parts of the cosmos, the planetary energies are as much a part of us as they are "out there." By using Renaissance astrology to pick an appropriate time, and using appropriate materials—incense, music and meditation—we align the energy of the planets with our own internal energies. Thus, by returning, through the cosmos, to the ultimate source, the realm of Ideas and Angels, we can work the magic of our illustrious predecessors for blessings and benefits on Earth.

22	47	16	41	10	35	4
5	23	48	17	42	11	29
30	6	24	49	18	36	12
13	31	7	25	43	19	37
38	14	32	1	26	44	20
21	39	8	33	2	27	45
46	15	40	9	34	3	28

Table of Venus

37	78	29	70	21	62	13	54	5
6	38	79	30	71	22	63	14	46
47	7	39	80	31	72	23	55	15
16	48	8	40	81	32	64	24	56
57	17	49	9	41	73	33	65	25
26	58	18	50	1	42	74	34	66
67	27	59	10	51	2	43	75	35
36	68	19	60	11	52	3	44	76
77	28	69	20	61	12	53	4	45

Table of the Moon

About the Author

Christopher Warnock, Esq., practices as an attorney and traditional astrologer in Washington, D.C. He received an M.A. (Hons.) concentrating in Renaissance history from the University of St. Andrews (Scotland) and a J.D. from the University of Michigan. He has published in the *Horary Practitioner*, *Pathways*, the *Mountain Astrologer*, and Llewellyn's *Moon Sign Book 2002*. He was a faculty member at the 2002 United Astrology Conference in Orlando, Florida. His Renaissance Astrology website is located at http://www.renaissanceastrology.com.

Bibliography

Three Books of Occult Philosophy by Cornelius Agrippa
Three Books on Life by Marsilio Ficino
Christian Astrology by William Lilly
Picatrix, edited by David Pingree
Astrologie Restored by William Ramesey

37

Lunar Hot Spots: Keys to Overcoming Life's Obstacles

By Terry Lamb

The events that form the structure of our lives are as complex and varied as a Bosch painting. Even to the practiced astrologer, they can seem to arrive willy-nilly—before or after they should have. How can we make sense of the panoply of planetary energies that play out on the canvas of our lives?

One of the easiest ways to sort out what's happening with the planetary patterns is through lunar hot spots. Even though the other, slower-moving planetary bodies are where the action is coming from, the Moon carries planetary energies and brings on the heat of emotion to create movement—action—in our lives. By understanding lunar hot spots, we can anticipate times when we may experience more challenge than normal, or when we may be inclined to take an important action. Maybe you can identify with the stories that follow.

It had been a slow summer for sales, and David just hadn't brought in the money he needed to make ends meet. His little savings had gotten drained as the weeks went by. Then, from the end of July, it just seemed to be one thing after another. First, his car broke down and needed a transmission overhaul. As they were doing the work, the mechanics found a leak. David needed a water pump. Then his cat got sick and needed surgery. By the end of August, things had calmed down, but it was a month he wouldn't soon forget. "It seemed like every Wednesday something would hit me," he said. "I'd just figure out how to solve one problem when another would crop up."

Barbara was in a funk. She had broken up with her boyfriend at the end of November. Even though she cared for him, she had finally realized that he wasn't ready for the type of relationship she wanted. She seemed to manage her emotions okay most of the time, but it just seemed like every Tuesday was difficult for no apparent reason. However, by the time Christmas rolled around, Barbara was feeling considerably better.

The Moon in Our Daily Experience

The Moon is one of the two most important personality significators in our chart (the other is the Sun). The Moon rules facets of what we call the mind. (In fact, "Moon" and "mind" come from the same word root *měn* or *mōna*, as do "month," "menses," and "mental.") It has to do with the broad range of sensations that we call feelings derived from instincts, intuitions, sensations, moods, and longer-term emotional states. While the mind is not our intellect, it influences our intellect, because our feelings influence our interpretations of our intellectual understanding, resulting in our thoughts. (Thoughts = feelings + intellectual understanding.) We are taught that our feelings can cloud our mind, color our interpretations of events, but few of us realize just how seldom we have a thought clear of emotional content.

This is because of memory, another vital aspect of the Moon's role in our personality. The world is so full of stimuli, to which we can (and often must) respond, that we rely on our memory to make sense of it, to categorize the experiences we have in terms of priority: What requires my attention immediately? Is it dangerous or potentially enjoyable? What things can I ignore? We are constantly moving things into the background or foreground, depending on what we perceive around us.

As I sit here writing on my laptop, I am focused on the words that flow from the thoughts in my mind; the keys that I press are in the background—I'm not fully aware of them unless I strike the wrong one. When

I do hit a wrong key, this experience leaps into the foreground of my consciousness. I am relatively unconscious of the air conditioner humming in the background, and I have a vague sense of disquiet because my desktop computer has told me that it has encountered potential bad sectors and is doing an hours-long scan of each hard drive. All else around me is rated by my mind as "normal," but an unexpected sound could change that and divert my attention, influencing my thoughts and then my actions. This is the fabric of experience that arises from memory—that bundle of stored experiences that have been shaped and interpreted according to other, previous experiences, even going back to childhood, prenatal sensations, and previous lives. Say I had led a life away from machines, then the hum of an air conditioner might cause alarm and draw my attention away from my preferred task.

In short, if something is familiar, I put what I am sensing in a box with other similar occurrences. Associated with this box is a pattern of response, a strategy if you like, that is based on my interpretation of the previous similar episodes. This allows me to feel more secure and put the sensation on background status so that I can pay attention to stimuli that might be more unique, challenging, or necessary to my chosen task. I want to focus on the sentences forming in my head so that I can write.

Since memory and this sorting process are part of every moment and movement of our lives, even in sleep, the Moon is intrinsically involved in everything that we do. It is our own personal satellite dish, taking in every signal and directing it to the right channel. We then choose which channel to watch with our focusing mechanism (Mercury).

To keep our mind healthy, we need to take care to watch every channel periodically and unload any garbage that got stored there. This helps us to take clearer, more straightforward actions without hidden messages or unconscious self-sabotage.

Our ability to make sense of what we experience is influenced by our stored memories and how we interpret them. They also form the basis for our actions. We can train ourselves to make better, more conscious use of the influences of the Moon by observing our use of stored memories, formulae, and strategies.

Both David and Barbara could have chosen to interpret their experiences differently. Probably amidst the feelings they related were feelings like relief and openness. David could have thought, for instance, "Wow! At least the car didn't break down on the freeway or cause an accident. And now my car is more reliable." Barbara may have thought, "Now I can get on with my life and find a new partner who is better suited to me." Chances are they had these thoughts mixed in with the others, but they weren't the dominant ones.

By being able to stand back and look at their emotional states, David and Barbara may have been able to place some of their less-helpful sensations, like loss and fear, more in the background, while bringing the other sensations more to the foreground. This may have been helpful in reducing stress, finding ways to solve their crises, and just enjoying life. Detecting lunar hot spots can be a vital support in this process

Triggers and Motivators

There are two groups of planets in the zodiac, which for this purpose, we can call the *triggers* and the *motivators*. The triggers are the Moon, the Sun, Mercury, Venus, and Mars. The slow-moving planets track our motivations, operating in the background, because they stay at one degree for a long time and therefore present a longer-term, larger obstacle or issue that we must deal with over one to three years. The motivators are Jupiter, Saturn, Chiron, Uranus, Neptune, and Pluto.

Every motivating planet has four trigger points in the zodiac (at the conjunction, squares, and opposition). This means that the Moon assumes tremendous significance in our daily life. Since the Moon transits the entire zodiac once a month, it triggers every planet four times a month, or once a week. This equals fifty-two times a year (for each planetary combination)! The other triggers make contact to the motivators no more frequently than four times a year (unless retrograde). In this way, the Moon acts as a once-weekly trigger, moving us to take action on the longer-term issues and deeper motivations or bringing events to us. So, when a triggering planet touches a motivating planet, the background issue emerges.

It can produce a crisis in consciousness, a dilemma that we must deal with—a hot spot. This is what both Barbara and David experience. Little did David know that his chart had several placements being triggered by Uranus and Neptune, which were both in Aquarius at

the time of his breakdown. When the Sun went into Leo, opposing Aquarius, the contacts to his chart were stimulated, and they were ready for action. However, it was not until the Moon came along that these events were precipitated into his life.

The Moon, because of its importance in our moment-to-moment processing of stimuli in our environment, and because of the frequency of its contacts, is especially critical in how the story of our life unfolds, day by day. Just as the Moon is the primary planet associated with precipitation in weather, so too does it govern precipitation in our lives. So, how can we tell when the hot spots are? How can we tell when the Moon is likely to lead us into a cascade of feelings that we may experience as crisis?

Detecting Hot Spots

The first thing we have to do is to identify the critical patterns among the motivating planets. Sometimes these planets interact with each other, and sometimes they are relatively independent. When they act on their own—not tied in with another motivator—their interaction with the Moon and other triggers is not as powerful, although we can feel them if they are aspecting our natal planets.

However, when the motivating planets contact each other, they do so for a relatively long time, often a year or more. It is the challenging aspects (conjunctions, squares, and oppositions) that set the stage for crisis points and lunar hot spots. For instance, in the fall of 2002, Jupiter is interacting with Neptune by opposition, a pattern that will continue through the fall of 2003.

In 2003, Jupiter continues to oppose Neptune, then it shifts its force by the fall to oppose Uranus. So, one of the backdrops against which this year's dramatic events will be played out first is Jupiter-Neptune, then, quickly at the end of August, by Jupiter-Uranus.

When Jupiter and Neptune interact, they challenge us to put their energies together in some way. The closer they are to each other, the more closely in time the Moon will trigger them. The power of the lunar hot spots is that the Moon contacts each of them within minutes to hours of each other, and this generates psychological heat. We feel the energy of these planets hit our bodies, affecting our moods and attitudes. These in turn influence our actions and reactions. Every time that the Moon triggers these planets, the issues we associate with them will leap into the foreground.

Frequently, we have several challenging interactions happening at once. The more we have, the more lunar hot spots there are. Although Saturn and Pluto were opposing each other most powerfully in 2001–02, they are still exerting a mild influence on us in 2003. In April, Saturn will begin interacting with Chiron, and the hot spots will build toward the end of the year.

The prominence of the patterns varies, depending on the nature of the planets. The Saturn-Pluto opposition is unquestionably the most powerful of the ones we've named. Time will tell whether it will live up to its reputation as it loses steam. In addition, the extent to which it hits your chart will influence how strong any hot-spot pattern is for you.

When Will Lunar Hot Spots Occur?

Generally, the Moon triggers the same part of the heavens once every week on about the same day each time. Therefore, each outer-planetary pattern, such as the Jupiter-Neptune opposition, will be triggered once every week.

However, while it is true that we may feel something every week for a year, it is not true that every hit to Jupiter-Neptune produces an action-motivating or event-generating crisis point. It takes more than the Moon to do that. It is when other trigger planets are involved that the true lunar hot spots occur. The most powerful of these is the Sun. When the Sun enters a sign that conjoins, squares, or opposes Jupiter and Neptune, we get the "heat" of the hot spot. These signs are Taurus, Leo, Scorpio, and Aquarius (the fixed signs). For instance, when the Sun is in Leo in August 2003, it will conjoin Jupiter and oppose Neptune, creating general heat during the whole time that the Sun is in Leo. Every time the Moon conjoins, squares, or opposes any of these planets (Sun, Jupiter, Uranus), a lunar hot spot occurs, and our issue is suddenly brought to the foreground. We have to deal with it; it draws out attention, perhaps even becoming a crisis.

What this means is that, for a month four times each year, lunar hot spots form, creating a noticeable effect in our lives. When the other trigger planets interact with the motivators and the Moon, lesser hot spots will occur. However, since Mercury and Venus travel with the Sun, they often increase the heat at or near the same time as the Sun does. This will increase the intensity of the lunar hot spots. Other phenomena that can increase the intensity of lunar hot spots are retrogrades and eclipses. That is, if a trigger planet is retrograding or an eclipse occurs at the time of a lunar hot spot, the heat in greatly amplified.

The Lunar Hot Spots of 2002-03

Jupiter-Neptune

Jupiter is associated with the three E's: education, expansion, and enterprise. It is also linked to religion, especially the social, philosophical, and belief aspects. Neptune is tied to spirituality, imagination, and the unseen, as well as delusion, confusion, and insidious threats. It is also the realm of the collective unconscious, which links us to each other's mind through universal symbolism. When these two planets oppose each other, they can bring out religious or patriotic fervor, social idealism, or collective confusion, to name a few possibilities. They can pique the imagination in individuals, imbue a nation with religious zeal, or bring hidden threats to the surface. Often, people feel inspired under this aspect. Because both planets have in common the tendency to extremes or boundlessness, their interaction can bring out overreaction and polarization, often due to beliefs.

The potential for Jupiter-Neptune hot spots begins in September 2002, when Jupiter and Neptune first oppose each other. However, the first time that triggering planets come into contact with them is in October, when the Sun enters Scorpio on the 23rd, so this is where we will start. After April and May of 2003, the Jupiter-Neptune opposition falls apart, so there are no more hot spots.

October–November 2002

Sun in Scorpio, Moon in Leo	October 29
Sun in Scorpio, Moon in Scorpio (New Moon)	November 4
Sun in Scorpio, Moon in Aquarius	November 10
Sun in Scorpio, Moon in Taurus (Full Moon)	November 18

January–February 2003

Sun in Aquarius, Moon in Scorpio	January 25
Sun in Aquarius, Moon in Aquarius (New Moon)	February 1
Sun in Aquarius, Moon in Taurus	February 8
Sun in Aquarius, Moon in Leo (Full Moon)	February 15

April–May 2003

Sun in Taurus, Moon in Aquarius	April 23
Sun in Taurus, Moon in Taurus (New Moon)	May 1
Sun in Taurus, Moon in Leo	May 9
Sun in Taurus, Moon in Scorpio (Full Moon, lunar eclipse)	May 15

Jupiter-Uranus

Uranus has to do with the unexpected, the accidental, and the miraculous. It is our "cosmic purpose rudder," ensuring that we stay on course in fulfilling our life's path (or get as close as we can to it). It also represents challenges to the status quo, keeping us and the social systems around us responsive to the world as it is, vital and strong. When combined with Jupiter, there is often a spirit of invention and innovation in the air, but it can also represent sudden shifts in social realities, which may come from a broad range of sources, such as fashion trends, threats to safety, economic ups and downs, or innovations in society, science, and industry.

Jupiter and Uranus make a quick, one-pass opposition in September 2003, creating only one month of hot spots. However, this brief series could be very powerful.

August–September 2003

Sun in Virgo, Moon in Virgo (New Moon)	August 27
Sun in Virgo, Moon in Sagittarius	September 3
Sun in Virgo, Moon in Pisces (Full Moon)	September 10
Sun in Virgo, Moon in Gemini	September 17–18

Saturn-Pluto

Saturn has to do with the limiting influences of reality. On a personal level, this is society's rules and our responsibilities within them, as well as the structures and foundations of civilization. Through Saturn, we also experience our fears and limitations. When it is transiting, it often prompts a restructuring in areas it influences. Pluto represents deep transformation and influences on mass consciousness. When these two planets interact, we experience a profound restructuring that can bring about permanent change in society. This is especially true of the opposition. It is this planetary opposition that was the dominant influence at the time of the attacks on New York and Washington in September 2001. In our own psyche, we may feel how mass events affect us in ways that we can't control. Through these planets, we come to terms with what we can and can't control, and deal with our feelings of power, safety, and powerlessness.

Saturn-Pluto hot spots began in June 2001, with the hottest spots being in September and December 2001, and May–June of 2002. Because the energy of this planetary interaction is on the wane, these planets will be gentler with us than they were in 2001–02.

November–December 2002

Sun in Sagittarius, Moon in Virgo	November 28
Sun in Sagittarius, Moon in Sagittarius	
(New Moon, solar eclipse)	December 4–5
Sun in Sagittarius, Moon in Pisces	December 11
Sun in Sagittarius, Moon in Gemini	December 19

February–March 2003

Sun in Pisces, Moon in Sagittarius	February 24
Sun in Pisces, Moon in Pisces (New Moon)	March 3
Sun in Pisces, Moon in Gemini	March 10–11
Sun in Pisces, Moon in Virgo (Full Moon)	March 18

Saturn-Chiron

Chiron is popularly associated with wounding and healing, but it really has to do with subtle energies and our experience of them; wounding and healing are two things that give us such experiences. We can encounter Chiron through mystical experiences as well. When Saturn and Chiron interact, we may find out how the system we live in needs to be healed in order to be more supportive (healing) of life. Health practices may come under scrutiny. A particular disease may receive a lot of focus, or cures and palliatives for such a disease may be found. If you have planets in the cardinal signs, this planetary interaction will affect you by emphasizing your own experiences of subtle energies, possibly leading you into your own healing process.

In April, Saturn enters Cancer, approaching an opposition to Chiron. Their first contact is in October 2003, and their interaction will extend into 2004. The hot spots for these planets will be in the cardinal signs (Aries, Cancer, Libra, and Capricorn), and because they part widely after their first contact, there is only one set of hot spots in 2003.

September–October 2003

Sun in Libra, Moon in Libra (New Moon)	September 25
Sun in Libra, Moon in Capricorn	October 2
Sun in Libra, Moon in Aries (Full Moon)	October 9–10
Sun in Libra, Moon in Cancer	October 17

How to Use Lunar Hot Spots

So, how do you know if these lunar hot spots are important to you? First, these planets are global in influence, so we will all feel something, if not in our own lives, then in the lives of those around us. Then, the effects will be felt more acutely if your chart is actually touched by the planets.

You will be especially tuned in to Jupiter and Neptune if you have planets in the fixed signs: Taurus, Leo, Scorpio, or Aquarius. This is especially true if your planets are between 8 and 16 degrees. Jupiter-Uranus and Saturn-Pluto are affecting the mutable signs: Gemini, Virgo, Sagittarius, and Pisces; for Jupiter-Uranus, 0–1 degrees are hit, while Saturn-Pluto will be especially strong for those with planets from 17–29 degrees for the dates shown above. Saturn/Chiron will hit the cardinal signs (Aries, Cancer, Libra, Capricorn) from 6–17 degrees of these signs.

If you don't know what degrees, planets, or signs are involved in your chart, just pay attention. If you feel it when we hit a lunar hot spot, or something happens in your life, then you can bet that your chart is affected, and you can prepare by noting the hot spot dates in your planner and focusing on staying centered at those times. Then, no matter what happens, you'll be at your best.

Detecting Future Hot Spots

To detect future hot spots, you need an ephemeris or astrological software which will allow you to research the planets and their motion. Then, follow the steps below.

1. Look at the planets Jupiter, Saturn, Uranus, Chiron, Neptune, and Pluto. See how they are interacting with each other for the time frame you're investigating. Look for conjunctions, squares, and oppositions. For instance, in July 2003 Jupiter squares Pluto, and Saturn continues to oppose Chiron.
2. Find the critical months when the Sun is in the signs conjoining, squaring, or opposing these planets. For Jupiter and Pluto, this would be the mutable signs. For Saturn and Chiron, this would still be the cardinal signs.
3. Identify the days in each critical month when the Moon is conjoining, squaring, or opposing these planets, taking note of retrogrades and eclipses that may increase the intensity.

Making Use of Lunar Hot Spots

There are many ways to use astrology to see the rhythms of the universe in our lives. Understanding lunar hot spots is one of them. This technique will help us to anticipate when life may not go according to plan, either through our own actions or the events that occur around us, but they are not to be feared. They are simply times when our personal buttons are more likely to be pushed. Our Moon helps us cope with these times by giving us a storehouse of information through interpreted memories that we translate into strategies and formula for survival and success. However, if we react blindly, we may take mood- or fear-driven actions that may produce a less-than-desirable outcome. If we are able to observe and soften these responses, we can make the best of any situation, whatever it is. We can cut ourselves a little more slack when the Moon triggers critical events and respond with more attunement to create better outcomes.

About the Author

Terry Lamb, M.A., C.A., is a counselor, instructor, and healer, specializing in spiritually oriented growth through astrology and subtle-body healing. Fourth-level certified by the National Council for Geocosmic Research (NCGR), she is NCGR's treasurer and serves on their Board of Examiners. She is the author of *Born To Be Together: Love Relationships, Astrology, and the Soul*. Terry is published in magazines and on websites, including her own (www.flash.net/~tlamb). You can e-mail her at tlamb@flash.net.

Suggested Reading

The Gods of Change: Pain, Crisis and the Transits of Uranus, Neptune and Pluto (Arkana's Contemporary Astrology Series) by Howard Sasportas

Astrology for the Millions (Llewellyn's Classics of Astrology Library) by Grant Lewi

Time Out

By Lisa Finander

This article is dedicated to the memory of my beloved cat Sparky, who taught me the importance of taking time out from my intellectual gymnastics to enjoy the shared bliss of scratching him under his chin.

I hear a voice from a distant future; it seduces me from my daily life. I follow it willingly to escape a life I feel is lacking in splendor. There is joy and fun in this future. I can almost reach it, tomorrow, next week, or in five years, I'll be living it. I'm fantasizing about it now. I'm writing affirmations. It will be all that I want, jam-packed with fantastic prestige, money, relaxation. I'll be the envy of everyone. I'll have made it. I can tell everyone my story, the secret to my success, my life lived perfectly, every challenge mastered. I will be able to positively affirm my way out of every difficult situation and even prevent them. It is a good place to be, here in my imagination, safe and secure, especially on days when the Moon tugs on my emotions and I feel sad, disgusted, lethargic, and morose. In my daydreams, it is already here, but when I return to my daily reality, I'm so far from my future goals. Hours of my life have passed lost in this alluring call from the Moon and my emotional life. I feel let down by ordinary reality. There are so many things that have to happen first. I have to finish the daily tasks at hand. I have to have paid these bills. I have to live here. I have to have these people in my life and these people out of my life. Once this daunting, self-perpetuating list is completed, I'll have the time to live my dreams. And all those changes that would feel too scary to make right now will be easy in the future because I will face them as soon as I finish all the things on my list that keep me from realizing my future. Some days the simplest task is incredibly painful, so I find endless things to do to escape completing them.

TIME OUT.

Lunar Moon, emotions churning, changing. Can you love yourself through all of them?

Breathe in deeply.

Exhale slowly.

BUT … it is tomorrow, a year later, five years later. I said these same affirmations and had these same fantasies yesterday, last week, and last year. I'm still chasing that glorious future, full of promise, unblemished, and perfect. But … today is yesterday's future, and it is not enough. I don't feel like bragging or strutting, even though I have acquired many of the things that I said I needed to be happy. I take those achievements for granted now. Things I strove for, worked hard to obtain, and personal

 changes I made to become a better person, but I still fall short in my mind's eye. Something's missing. I don't possess all the jewels I believe society measures me by, so I blame society for my struggles; and my parents, my gender, and my feelings of my inadequacy. Now I hear the lure of the Moon enticing me to relive old memories of my past. I decide it's a worthy use of my time, since my "watertight" future hasn't arrived fast enough. I'll scrutinize my past for mistakes and find all the reasons I can't have or missed the chance to have the life I dream about.

BUT … today is tomorrows past, and I can't wait for the changes in my life the future will bring. I know; I'll plan for my future while I'm uncovering my past.

TIME OUT.

Lunar Moon, emotions churning, changing. Can you love yourself through all of them?

Breathe in deeply the totality of who you are.

Exhale slowly perfectionism.

BUT ... today is tomorrow's past, and I can't wait for the changes in my life the future will bring. I know; I'll plan for my future while I'm uncovering my past.

Life feels more stressful now. I have an imperfect past and an impossible future. It all feels like an incredible amount of work and pain. I'm trying to juggle my time between working toward my future and excavating repressed memories. I feel guilty if I spend too much time focusing on either one. I am convinced one will hold the key and unlock me from this vicious cycle. I'm trying to create a future in my mind strong enough to prevail over the pain of my past. I find that I have incredibly little time and energy left to focus on my daily experiences. Some days the smallest of tasks can become overwhelming and I will spend mountains of time trying to escape from it by doing anything else and convincing myself that it is important. Something within me will even defend this muddled existence to others. All the while, days, weeks, years of my life cycle by while I'm wishing for something other than what I have.

TIME OUT.

Lunar Moon, emotions churning, changing. Can you love yourself through all of them?

Breathe in deeply self-acceptance.

Exhale slowly self-hatred.

BUT ... what is it that I have? I am feeling everything but the moment. Why is it so hard to live here? Every now and then, my life will jolt me out of this disparaging cycle, reminding me that there is no past or future outside of my head and I need to return to the moment. The here and now is all I have with all its imperfections and uncertainties. It is not new, great teachers have been spreading this message for eons, but it is continually forgotten. I can't hold onto it. Incessantly, I seek it out in my journeys of self-improvement and spiritually, and incessantly this message evaporates as soon as I hear it. Like the cycles of the Moon, I instinctually return to the place where I started. My attempts at manipulating time have failed again. I can not lengthen pleasurable experiences and shorten difficult ones. But I can experience them differently, if I am truly present while they are happening.

During the time I was writing this article and intently practicing the art of living in the moment, my cat Sparky was diagnosed with cancer. In a span of three weeks, he went from diagnosis to death. I have experienced the death of other beloved pets before. It doesn't get any easier the more times I have experienced it, but I found I could be with him differently while he was dying. I struggled to stay in the moment and to focus on the fact that he was here with me now, and that I could still tell him how much I loved him. But ..., I was already missing him, grieving my loss and thinking about all the things that would no longer be. I couldn't stay in the present. My pain became larger and more distorted each time I attached it to experiences of the past and worries of the future. I wanted to run from the mounting anxiety. How many moments had I lost by avoiding the now? I hadn't escaped any pain. When I was able to stay in the present, I realized that there were many other feelings present along with the pain. There was joy, contentment, appreciation, and love. I only experienced pain, fear, and anger when I left the moment, and I wasn't really with Sparky at all. I missed moments with him that were wasted by losing my focus.

TIME OUT.

Lunar Moon, emotions churning, changing. Can you love yourself through all of them?

Breathe in deeply the inner knowing that you and your life are all they must be.

Exhale slowly the false belief that you and your life are fractured and incomplete.

BUT ... each morning when I awake leaving the hazy images of dream-time, there is a brief moment of confusion and uncertainty before I recall what day it is and what tasks are at hand. It is the time between past and future. It is present time. It is scary to live in the present, the uncharted path of the Moon. We create permanence in our minds by believing things will last forever and we will live forever. Maybe we are fearful that if we don't have our future lives mapped out, we will cease to exist. This unknown path of the moment deepens as I let go of my expectations and assumptions. If I can put down the struggle between work and play, right and wrong, past and future, I experience the sensation of just being versus judging the experience as good or bad. We are taught that we should do not be. It makes it hard to live life moment by moment without feeling shame for not doing something or accomplishing something. We long for these leisurely experiences and shield them from others. We falsely believe that they are few and are only enjoyed by others who are more successful than we are. How can we reassure ourselves emotionally to what the mind doesn't know? How can you find joy in the now? How can you feel fulfilled in doing something you don't like to do? How can you be happy now instead of projecting happiness into another time?

TIME OUT.

Lunar Moon, emotions churning, changing. Can you love yourself through all of them?

Breathe in deeply the cycles of life.

Exhale, slowly, resistance to change.

BUT … every moment holds an element of pleasure, pain, past, and future, it is all contained in the now. You need not look for it elsewhere or run from it. The wisdom of the Moon's cycles can be difficult to endure, when you're afraid, unaccustomed to, and degrading of her darkness. An emotion unexpressed or a moment unlived doesn't cease to exist, it is a burden we carry with us, adding it to the weight of our existence. Life is not as joyful when lived only in the archives of your mind. When you choose to focus yourself in the moment, you have allowed yourself the chance to experience your life differently. You now can experience each moment of life as it happens. Each emotion is felt and expressed not stored, abandoned, and reviled. Your senses are free to take in the current stimuli. These moments offer important clues to who and what you are. Maybe you will experience pain first, or fear, delight, awe, or reverence. The Moon expresses emotions in no particular order. Maybe it will be your most uncomfortable emotion first or your most enjoyable. They are all contained it the moment, and that is all any of us have and it is enough.

TIME OUT.

Lunar Moon, emotions churning, changing. Can you love yourself through all of them?

Breathe in deeply this moment.

Exhale out slowly this moment.

Blessed be.

Lunar Moon

The lack of Sun is dreary and hard to take.

I feel pain in my arms.

Disgust within my body.

Inactivity and tiredness.

Everywhere there are people struggling to survive.

Maybe I feel the weight of the collective.

Connected to everything?

Alone, feeling the loneliness of others?

Nothing but a container, a sieve for the world's sorrow?

Not very grand.

I would rather be superior, the chosen one, special,

filled with removed compassion.

Rather than suffering in the trenches.

I've suffered enough, done my time.

Life is difficult and I have no skills to master it.

I try to make wise words come through me.

I have nothing.

I come up dry.

I cry myself to sleep.

I tear myself down with nothing to build myself up with.

These are my good days of the month.

Perhaps I should fail and crawl back into her womb.

My mind is hopelessly dragged along through the quagmires of the psyche attempting to master her terrain so not to encounter these feelings again next month.

I am lost in her dark path.

A barren no-man's land.

She answers me.

Emotions, churning, changing.

Can you love yourself through all of them?

About the Author

Lisa Finander writes, teaches, and provides consultations for people in astrology, tarot, and dreamwork. She loves nature and animals. Currently, she is taking a course in evolutionary astrology. Lisa is grateful to Llewellyn for providing her with the opportunity to share her writings to a broader level. She lives in Minnesota with her loving husband Brian and their cats Jampers and Toby.

Suggested Reading

The Healing Power of Pets: Harnessing the Ability of Pets to Make and Keep People Happy and Healthy by Marty Becker, Danelle Morton.

Cold Noses at the Pearly Gates by Gary Kurz.

Angel Whiskers by Laurel E. Hunt (Editor).

Is Your Pet Psychic by Richard Webster.

Cosmic Construction

By Daniel B. Brawner

Home construction and repair are practical enterprises, requiring a no-nonsense approach. When you hit your thumb with a hammer, does it mean your Mercury is retrograde? Don't be silly! But if you hit your thumb eleven times in an hour during a New Moon, you're only getting what you deserve.

Any astrologically aware carpenter knows better than to start a construction project under a New Moon. To avoid accidents and losing a lot of tools, you should always wait at least until sunrise.

Roofing

In the spring, many a homeowner's fancy turns to roofing. Winter is hard on roofs. Ice dams build up in the gutters and tug on old brittle shingles. If your roof has three or more layers of shingles, it will probably be necessary to tear off all the shingles and start from scratch.

Reshingling your house is an adventure. Not only is it exciting to transform your lumpy, ragged, leaky roof into a nice new one, but there is always the exciting possibility that you might fall off. If you are not looking for sympathy from your spouse or neighbors, there are a couple of astrological tips to follow.

1. Do not attempt to shingle your roof when the Moon is waxing. You will find that your roof is already slick enough without any help from the Moon.
2. Avoid water signs. One of the defining characteristics of shingles is that they tend to repel water. Therefore, the absence of shingles allows water in. Or, to be more precise, not having shingles on your roof guarantees with mathematical certainty, that any celestial moisture in your time zone will pour down onto your naked roof like a funnel.

When several hundred gallons of rainwater enter your roof, you will see the irony of the name "drywall" as this thirsty, gypsum-based product slurps up moisture like terrycloth and collapses onto your swampy carpet.

At this point, the sign of Aquarius might come to mind. But remember that Aquarius is an air sign—a dry, mental sign—a good sign for roofing. But roofing under a water sign like Cancer, Scorpio, or Pisces is like a lightning rod to storm clouds.

Speaking of Pisces, if you find not only water coming through your bare roof but fish, too, you may have construction problems of biblical proportions and it is time to call in a professional. So, whatever you do, don't start a roofing project under a water sign. And while you're at it, you might also check your local weather forecast.

Building a Wall

At one time or another, every stalwart do-it-yourselfer decides to build a new wall. This is a thrilling but exacting enterprise. I recommend building a wall under the sign of Virgo, or at least having a Virgo lay out the project for you. Having an anal-retentive Virgo type actually assist on this kind of fussy and often frustrating project might not be advisable, considering there will be hammers, crowbars, and other blunt instruments within easy reach.

Virgo is an appropriate sign for a virginal project like a new wall. Virgo's tight, sexually repressed precision will help keep your wall straight and plumb and prevent it from leaning suggestively and inappropriately toward older, more experienced walls.

Also, Virgo's innocent optimism is a must for a first-time wall builder, whose motto is "What could go wrong?" If you suspected that your 2 x 4 inch wall frame should be constructed horizontally and nailed top and bottom BEFORE tilting up to a perfectly tight fit against the ceiling, you might start to see the value in living in a tent.

Building a wall can be a time-consuming job. Professional framers often use pneumatic nail guns to assemble walls quickly. Beginners will be amazed at how a nail gun allows them to make mistakes with blinding speed.

Painting

Painting is the do-it-your-selfer's project of choice. Homeowners bounce into Sears, buy $50 worth of latex paint, and have all they need to transform their dingy, hand-printed living room into a page out of *House Beautiful*.

It is advisable to paint under the sign of Libra, which invites balance and harmony. It is also advisable to use a thick sheet of polyurethane to cover your furniture and carpet, which are disaster magnets.

Libra is about equilibrium, and equilibrium is often about the attraction of opposites. There is order and chaos. There is beauty and ugliness. The one-inch square of plum that looked so sweet and tame on the color chart turns your dining room into a giant, throbbing eggplant. But under the influence of Libra, you can balance this eyesore with, say, large neutral curtains and lots of pictures.

Libra is also the sign of fairness. This is important to keep this in mind when using a roller. Paint falls on the just and the unjust alike. When your spouse catches you tracking sunshine-yellow paint over your terracotta patio tiles, remember that it's not about you.

If you feel a little Venus influence pulling your painting project toward the unusual, you might try faux antique painting. Using various techniques with sponges, rags, or other unlikely implements, you can make plain, modern walls look like they belong in a sixteenth-century Italian villa that is crumbling under the weight of generations of neglect. All your friends will envy you.

Construction can be daunting, especially for the beginner. But cosmic construction—hammering and sawing by the stars—should help give you the courage to begin.

About the Author

Daniel B. Brawner is an award-winning humor columnist and former housing contractor, living in Lisbon, Iowa. He is a member of Mystery Writers of America and has recently completed a New Age mystery novel. If you wish to inquire about jokes, construction, or murder, please write to the author in care of Llewellyn Worldwide, P.O. Box 64383, St. Paul, MN, 55164-0383, and we will forward your request.

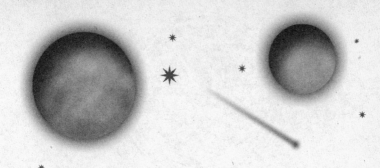

Business &
Legal
Section

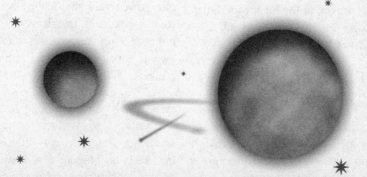

How To Choose the Best Dates for Business & Legal Activities

When starting a new business or any type of new venture, check to make sure that the Moon is in the first or second quarter. This will help it get off to a better start. If there is a deadlock, it will often be broken during the Full Moon. You should also check the aspects of the Moon to the planet that rules the type of venture with which you are becoming involved. Look for positive aspects to the planet that rules the activity in the lunar aspectarian (pages 34–57), and avoid any dates marked Q or O.

Planetary Business Rulerships

Listed below are the planets and the business activities that they rule. If you follow the guidelines given above and apply them to the occupations or activities listed for each planet, you should have excellent results in your new business ventures. Even if it is not a new venture, check the aspects to the ruler of the activity before making moves in your business.

Sun

Advertising, actors and actresses, administrators, executives, finance and financiers, foremen, furriers, gamblers, government and public offices, lawyers, politicians, presidents, prime ministers, princes, racing stable owners, stock brokers, and public relations.

Mercury

Accounting, ad writers, agents, animal trainers, attorneys, auditors, bee keepers, biographers, broadcasting technicians, brokerage, chemists, clerical workers, dieticians, disc jockeys, doctors, editors, employees (in general), inspectors, interpreters, librarians, linguists, mathematicians, medical technicians, opticians, opthamologists, orators, printers, proofreaders, public speakers, pupils, railroads, scholars, scientists, statisticians, tellers, teachers, ticket agents, ventriloquists, writers, publishing, communication, and mass media.

Venus

Amateurs, architects, art curators, artists, associates, bankers, beautician, cabinet makers, candy manufacturers, clothing designers, dancers, duets, fashion, gardeners, hairdressers, hat makers, hotel keepers, juries, limousines, marketing, marriage, motels, negotiators, patrons, music and musicians, poets, restaurants, securities, social functions, and wigmakers.

Mars

Agitators, armies and army officers, athletes, barbers, blacksmiths, bootleggers, butchers, carpenters, charitable institutions, chemists, claims, construction workers, defenders, dentists, embezzlers, fires and firemen, gun makers, locksmiths, lumberjacks, machinists, mechanics, manufacturing, metal workers, profiteers, surgeons, and wrestlers.

Jupiter

Advisors, ambassadors, archers, assessors, attorneys, auditors, brokers, censure, charitable institutions, claims and claimants, corporate law, counselors, doctors, embezzlers, financiers, heirs, horse men and horse trainers, jockeys, juries, judges, legislators, ministers, passports, pharmacists, preachers, professors, psychologists, public analysts, regimes, social clubs, researchers, senate and senators, sheriffs, ships and shipping, storekeepers, and self-improvement.

Saturn

Agriculturists, archeologists, architecture and architects, bailiffs, bankruptcy, buyers, carpenters, carpet layers, cattlemen, cemetery workers, civil engineers, chemists, contractors, debtors, elderly people, farms and farming, felons, funeral directors, gardeners, geologists, hardware manufacturers, historians, mathematicians, miners, misers, mortgages, morticians, organizers, papermaking, plumbers, real estate agents, repairperson, surveyors, tailors, wardens, and watchmakers.

Uranus

Aeronautics, astrologers, agitators, airplane mechanics and pilots, automobile manufactures, aviators, broadcasters, chiropractors, clock makers and repairers, computers, electricians, emancipators, fugitives, gasoline station owners, hydroelectric power, inventing and inventors, lecturing, magicians, photographers, radiology, sudden events, and technical writers.

Neptune

Actors and actresses, bartenders, blackmail, bribery, chemical engineers, con men, detectives, divers, druggists, embezzlers, glassware factories, impostors, investigators, magicians, naval men and officers, photographers, oceanographers, resorts, ships and shipping, travel by water, welfare, and wine merchants.

Pluto

Atomic energy, coroners, criminals, demolition, detectives, dictators, disasters, epidemics, gang leaders, global wars, gunmen, magicians, petroleum, racketeering, refuse workers, research, robbery and robbers, therapists, speculators, stockbrokers, and stool pigeons.

Business Activities
Advertising (in Print)

Write ads on a favorable Sun sign day while Mercury or Venus is conjunct, sextile, or trine the Moon. Hard aspects to Mars and Saturn should not occur after the time of your event. Ad campaigns are best when the Moon is well aspected in Gemini (to enhance communication) or Capricorn (to build business).

Advertising (Electronic)

The Moon should be conjunct, sextile, or trine Mercury or Uranus; and in the sign of Gemini, Capricorn, or Aquarius.

Business, Education

When you begin training, see that your lunar cycle is favorable that day and that the planet ruling your occupation is marked C or T.

Business, Opening

The Moon should be in Taurus, Virgo, or Capricorn, and in the first or second quarter. It should also be sextile or trine (X or T) Jupiter or Saturn.

Business, Starting

In starting a business of your own, see that the Moon is free of afflictions and that the planet ruling the business is marked C or T.

Buying

Buy during the third quarter, when the Moon is in Taurus for quality, or in a mutable sign (Gemini, Virgo, Sagittarius, or Pisces) for savings. Good aspects from Venus or the Sun are desirable. If you are buying for yourself, it is good if the day is favorable to your Sun sign.

Buying Clothing

See that the Moon is sextile or trine to the Sun during the first or second quarters. During Moon in Taurus, buying clothes will bring satisfaction. Do not buy clothing or jewelry when the Moon is in Scorpio or Aries. Buying clothes is best on a favorable day for your Sun sign and when Venus or Mercury is well aspected, but avoid aspects to Mars and Saturn.

Buying Furniture

Follow the rules for machinery and appliances but buy when the Moon is in Libra, too. Buy antiques when the Moon is in Cancer, Scorpio, or Capricorn.

Buying Machinery, Appliances, or Tools

Tools, machinery, and other implements should be bought on days when your lunar cycle is favorable and when Mars and Uranus are trine (T), sextile (X), or conjunct (C) the Moon. Any quarter of the Moon is suitable. When buying gas or electrical appliances, the Moon should be in Aquarius.

Buying Stocks

The Moon should be in Taurus or Capricorn, and should be sextile or trine (X or T) Jupiter and Saturn.

Collections

Try to make collections on days when your Sun is well aspected. Avoid days when Mars or Saturn are aspected. If possible, the Moon should be in a cardinal sign: Aries, Cancer, Libra, or Capricorn. It is more difficult to collect when the Moon is in Taurus or Scorpio.

Consultants, Working With

The Moon should be conjunct, sextile, or trine Mercury or Jupiter.

Contracts, Bid on

The Moon should be in the sign of Gemini or Capricorn, and either the Moon or Mercury should be conjunct, sextile, or trine (C, X, or T) Jupiter.

Copyrights/Patents, Apply for

The Moon should be conjunct, trine, or sextile Mercury or Jupiter.

Electronics, Buying

When buying electronics, choose a day when the Moon is in an air sign (Gemini, Libra, or Aquarius) and well aspected by Mercury and/or Uranus.

Electronics, Repair

The Moon should be sextile or trine Mars or Uranus in one of the following signs: Taurus, Leo, Scorpio, or Aquarius.

Legal Matters

A good aspect between the Moon and Jupiter is best for a favorable legal decision. To gain damages in a lawsuit, begin during the increase of the Moon. In seeking to avoid payment, set a court date when the Moon is decreasing. Good aspects between the Sun and Moon strengthens your chance of success. In divorce cases, a favorable Moon-Venus aspect is best. Moon in Cancer or Leo and well aspected by the Sun brings the best results in custody cases.

Loans

Moon in the first and second quarters favors the lender, in the third and fourth favors the borrower. Good aspects of Jupiter and Venus to the Moon are favorable to both, as is the Moon in Leo or Taurus.

Mailing

For best results, send mail on favorable days for your Sun sign. The Moon in Gemini is good, as are Virgo, Sagittarius, and Pisces.

Mining

Saturn rules mining. Begin work when Saturn is marked C, T, or X. Mine for gold when the Sun is marked C, T, or X. Mercury rules quicksilver, Venus rules copper, Jupiter rules tin, Saturn rules lead and coal, Uranus rules radioactive elements, Neptune rules oil, the Moon rules water. Mine for these items when the ruling planet is marked C, T, or X.

New Job, Beginning

Jupiter and Venus should be sextile, trine, or conjunct the Moon.

Photography, Radio, TV, Film, and Video

Neptune, Venus, and Mercury should be well aspected. The act of photographing does not depend on particular Moon phase, but Neptune rules photography, and Venus rules beauty in line, form, and color.

Promotions

Choose a day when your Sun sign is favorable. Mercury should be marked C, T, or X. Avoid days when Mars or Saturn is aspected.

Selling or Canvassing

Begin these activities during a favorable Sun sign day. Otherwise, sell on days when Jupiter, Mercury, or Mars is trine, sextile, or conjunct the Moon. Avoid days when Saturn is square or opposite the Moon.

Signing Papers

Sign contracts or agreements when the Moon is increasing in a fruitful sign, and on a day when Moon to Mercury aspects are operating. Avoid days when Mars, Saturn, or Neptune are square or opposite the Moon.

Staff, Fire

The Moon should be in the third or fourth quarter, but not full. There should be no squares (Q) to the Moon.

Staff, Hire

The Moon should be in the first or second quarter, and preferably in the sign of Gemini or Virgo. The Moon should be conjunct, trine, or sextile (C, T, or X) Mercury or Jupiter.

Travel

See the travel listing in the Leisure & Recreation section.

Writing

Writing for pleasure or publication is best done when the Moon is in Gemini. Mercury should be direct. Favorable aspects to Mercury, Uranus, and Neptune promote ingenuity.

Economic Forecasts
for the Year 2003

By Dorothy J. Kovach

The reasons why fortune smiles on one sector of the market while others go dry is determined not by Allen Greenspan and the Federal Reserve Board, but by the true masters of the universe: the Sun, the Moon, and the planets. It is the job of the business astrologer to direct clients to those areas that are ripe for the plucking, and to steer them away from those whose time has passed. Traditional business astrologers rely on strict rules to determine both current and historical trends. They differ from other astrologers in that they plot not only the course of individuals, but also the horoscopes of businesses and first trades, as well as using the methods of horary and elections to help their clients achieve optimum success in the financial markets. They determine future market trends by comparing historical and political charts against the backdrop of the present geocosmic conditions to determine whether it will be a year of bounty or a year of want.

Since the economic influence starts at the top and works downward, one of the main charts a business astrologer relies on is the annual administration chart, which is determined by the exact moment that the Sun returns to the place it was when the president was sworn in. The inauguration chart will point out where our government's focus, and thus much of the nation's resources, will be allocated in the coming year. With the planet of the greatest strength in President Bush's inauguration chart, placed in the Ninth House, we will continue to be spending much of our year being concerned with faraway places and religion, but not places we want to go to, or religions we want to join, because the planet is the chilly Saturn, diminishing our desire to be far from home.

It suggests stressful relationships with foreign nations, especially those who are strongly religious. It also indicates that our need for security will often border on paranoia in the year ahead. The part of the economy most affected is likely to be our lines of distribution and communications, that is, on our roads and highways and through our mail. All modes of travel will feel the crunch. This is an indication that tech stocks will not return to their former glory anytime soon, and that they are marked for trouble in the first quarter and third quarter.

Saturn-Pluto: The "No Place Like Home" Syndrome

The year begins with the same major astrological signature—Saturn opposing Pluto—that has been with us since the bombing of the World Trade Center, still in effect. We stand perched somewhere between precaution and paranoia, in a kind of bunker mentality, as we are reminded that the world is a very dangerous place after all. We do not know what tomorrow will bring. When we do not know what the future will bring, then we are less likely to spend. When the American people do not spend, markets go down. Until Saturn and Pluto finally get out of each other's grip, there will be little optimism in the markets. Since the opposition takes place in communications and travel signs (Gemini-Sagittarius) tourism and technology will continue to take the brunt of the beating. We should see some let-up for technology sector the spring of 2003, when Saturn leaves Gemini, but it will be longer for the airlines, as we face the reality that we really can die if we fly.

With all this, it is no wonder that Americans now prefer to relax in the relative safety and security of our own back yard. Since both Saturn and Pluto are the traditional and modern rulers of death, when these two are engaged, it is the astrological equivalent of Grim Reaper meets Darth Vader. As a result, Americans have become more restrained, more controlled, and certainly far more suspicious of others, as we enter the second year at war with an enemy who remains largely unknown.

Where there is uncertainty about the future, then the big bad bears enter the market place. Saturn and Pluto have taken the wind out of the market. The boom has gone bust. We need to adjust to a slower market with lowered expectations. A bear market is firmly in place on Wall Street. Traders beware, this means that the markets are also a much more risky place. Know the contents of your portfolio. Learn about the companies you are invested in. Do you have a balanced portfolio? Does it contain bonds? What percentage of it is in stocks? Are you heavily invested in tech stocks? These are some of the questions you should ask yourself or your broker. This market is far different than those of the 1980s–90s, and your portfolio should reflect this.

The great bull market of the 1990s is over. We all need to adjust to a chillier financial climate. During a bull market, three out of four stocks go up. A bear market is a much more ferocious animal. Nineteen out of twenty stocks go down in a bear market. It doesn't take a financial genius to see that the odds have changed against the investor, in a big way! You can lose your shirt! Interestingly enough, Saturn and Pluto were also opposed during the Great Depression.

Whether or not you own stocks, the market affects you because when it turns bearish, as we will continue to see, jobs are lost. Risk is a key word here, because as long as Saturn-Pluto stay enmeshed we will not be willing to take it. Venture capital dries up, which in turn creates a ripple effect, which eventually is felt in every segment of society. The result is a lowered stock market accompanied by higher unemployment. There will be tremendous competition in the tech industry. We will see computer makers leave the business or get eaten up by competitors, as a survival of the fittest mentality continues. All this benefits the consumer as computers and software become available at bargain prices.

Even "bad" planets can yield profits, though. W. D. Gann is still famous not because he made millions in the market, but because he made millions in spite of the market. By knowing the nature of the planets, we can begin to recognize trends and locate the opportunity within the downturn. For example, with Saturn and Pluto, we are dealing with the primal emotion of fearing the unknown. When people do not know what will happen there is the tendency to hoard for any eventuality. Therefore, those businesses associated with stocking up will do well. With this in mind, we can expect warehouse stores, like CostCo and Walmart, to do better than their department store cousins. Think cheap. In the 1930s it was Woolworth's. Discount chains are in a similar position now.

When we do not trust in the outside environment, we tend to stay home more. Therefore, those businesses that cater to our desire to crawl back under the covers are set to see opportunities for growth in 2003. (Entrepreneurs, stay alert.) During the first half of the year, we can expect growth in companies that deliver right to our doorstep. Some bright spots for the technology sector will include the new entertainment delivery systems, those companies that deliver movies to people online.

Since there is less trust in the outside world, we will be willing to pay for protection. Therefore, we can see growth in those businesses that sell protective gear, from gas masks to latex gloves. When we do not know, we seek to find out. By the same token, we can also expect to see the investigative and security businesses, especially those armed, increasing their rosters. We will also see an increase in those businesses that are in the business of, or manufacture of monitoring and surveillance equipment. Recognition technology may be another bright spot in a slowing economy. Since the thing that Saturn and Pluto have in common is that they are both killers in their own right, we can expect to see growth in those companies that deal in death and destruction, from undertakers to defense contractors. Pluto likes to "see through" things, so look for expansion in products from x-ray technology to night vision goggles. In this respect, a company worth watching is Rayovac, having the dual attributes of being both a manufacturer of night vision goggles and also a major supplier to the Pentagon.

Jupiter in Leo

When we look for positive signs in the economy, we always look to the planet Jupiter, because we can always count on those things that Jupiter touches to grow. We begin the year with Jupiter in the sign of Leo (the lion). This is going to be a good year for the highly placed—royalty. If we take the idea of royalty and apply it to the stock market, the blue chip stocks would be considered the royalty of the stock market. Wise investors know that economic down turns are opportunities for buying blue chips. We value our children more than ever before, and we can look to toy manufacturers and children oriented businesses. Leo has a great deal to do with having fun. We will see an increase of those businesses that help us forget our troubles. With this in mind, we will probably see a rebound in those beer and wine and the liquor industry in general.

Jupiter in Leo at Odds with Neptune in Aquarius

Jupiter has the Midas touch. It represents increase not only within the sign he is in, but he will also enlarge any planet he comes in contact with. As the year begins we will see Jupiter engaging Neptune. Neptune has to do with escaping the confines of reality, so anything that helps us leave the harsh realities that Saturn-Pluto have brought will do well in the first three quarters of 2003. Translating this to the market place: Neptune has influence over everything from pharmaceuticals to your local pub. As the threats from biological weapons increase, the drug sector as a whole, from aspirin to bioengineering companies, are in the right place at the right time. It is still not too late to invest in select pharmaceuticals, as the need for them promises to continue to rise in the first half of the year. Jupiter gives the magic touch not only to drugs, but stocks that took a beating in the 1990s, like tobacco and hard liquor. Expect them to make a come back as we seek to drown our senses about a downshifting economy.

Not all Jupiter contacts are good for the consumer, though. Neptune is also linked to oil and gasoline. A sad result of Jupiter's ability to enlarge is that the cost at the pump increases. Much like the Cadillac in the 1970s, our treasured SUVs may seem more like a dinosaur soon. We may see a run on gold, and with it, his sister silver. If you're thinking of investing in gold, make certain you study this market before entering it. Great fortunes have been lost in these commodities. One other unfortunate result of this combination is that it tends to stir up religious feelings. Since other factors agree, and there is a strong possibility of further violence in the Middle East, the Israeli government may see more instability in July and August, which could adversely affect the market's recovery.

Jupiter in Virgo: Separating Wheat from Chaff

By mid-September we should see the price of oil begin to drop off as Jupiter enters communications-oriented Virgo. We will also see some recovery in the shattered tech sector. However, we cannot expect too much out of this recovery because Jupiter does not have a great deal of strength in the sign of Virgo. He is crankier and less generous, operating much like Santa Claus on a diet. On the other hand, just having prices come down at the pump will help ease fears. Jupiter in Virgo, the sign of the wheat gatherer, is a sign of good harvest in an otherwise nervous business year.

Saturn in Cancer: Where Did All the Money Go?

Saturn forces us to streamline and do without. Heading as it does for the sector that has, along with our earnings, sobered, we now learn the lessons of thrift and savings our parents tried to teach us. Where Saturn goes, downturn follows. On June 4, Saturn makes its way into the sign of Cancer. We are a Cancer nation, therefore Saturn's sojourn here will be especially poignant for the United States, because when Saturn is in Cancer it hits the segment of our national chart that has to do with our collective income. We will feel it in our wallets. The second half of the year we will find ourselves working and earning less than we have in the past.

Cancer has to do with the home, so there is a direct link between the sign of Cancer and the real-estate market. With this in mind, we can expect to hear some bad news coming to the real-estate market. Saturn in Cancer is hard on cities. We will begin to see the end of the urban renaissance. City goods and services will begin to dwindle, and unemployment rise. As people begin to feel less secure in highly populated cities, seeking security for ourselves becomes a top priority. That this will benefit rural real estate is a logical conclusion, but it is worth noting that the "back to the land" movement of the 1960s–70s began when Saturn was last in Cancer. Business falters under Saturn in Cancer, but on top of that, Saturn enters the segment of our nation's chart that has to do with our collective income. September is crucial as transiting Saturn will conjoin the nation's Sun, and with it, a profound sorrow may prevail. Sadly, recent events have left us older and wiser than we were before. This is a very difficult time for the president. He will have to use the utmost care in all his decisions.

There are always opportunities if we know where to look for them. As the overextended and the unproductive go belly up, downturns mark tremendous buying opportunities. Saturn solidifies whatever it touches. Cancer rules fluids. This means achieving liquidity will be especially difficult—in financial speak, "Money will be tight." The wise will keep a higher percentage of their assets in cash before the Saturn ingress on June 3, putting them in a position to pick up bargains this fall.

Slow to No Recovery

Jupiter and Saturn control business cycles. Jupiter represents an optimistic market place full of money for expansion, known as a bull market. Saturn represents decline, contraction, less money for business, and dwindling profits, as epitomized by the bear market. As mentioned, Jupiter has less strength to expand when in Virgo. This means that Jupiter has less capacity to bring us out of the downturn we find ourselves in. On the bright side, however, Saturn also has less capacity to organize when he is in Cancer. Jupiter and Saturn are in signs that have little in common with their natures. This suggests stagnation will occur. Business will not really decline as much as in earlier years, but there just won't be a whole lot of growth out there. With Jupiter in the segment of the national chart that has to do with our homes, he will lend us some help in keeping real-estate prices from free fall. But he will not have enough strength to pull the market up from recession.

This combination should be good for businesses involved in scientific research because Jupiter will enhance our attention to details, while Saturn will keep emotions from getting in the way of fact. To find what branch of research might be enhanced, we might see if history can provide us with clues as to where to find a "silver lining" in a weak business climate. The last time that Jupiter was in Virgo, and Saturn was in Cancer, was the year 1885. In that year the link between fingerprinting and identification was established. If history is said to repeat itself, we might look for some break-throughs in the business of electronic identity recognition, such as bio-metric fingerprint scanners, or face and eye identification companies. As we can see, all the news need not be gloomy.

Uranus in Pisces: Getting in on the Bottom

Wouldn't you like to have the inside track on what was going to be the next "big" thing will be? Well, you can. On March 10, we will all be given a hint about where the fortunes will be made. The sign Uranus dictates where the next "craze" will be. In business, Uranus is linked to boom and bust cycles. When he first entered Aquarius in 1995, the Internet was used mostly by geeky types with more interest in equations than money. Those who saw the commercial value of the Internet early on made millions. Uranus will spend eight years in Pisces, and with a little bit of investiga-tion, we take a peek into future trends. We can expect there to be real opportunities in those things closely associated when the sign Uranus enters it. If we keep our eyes open, we will see glimpses of tomorrow today.

What Uranus in Aquarius did for technology, Uranus in Pisces is set to do for laboratories. Great discoveries will be made in the field of scientific research during the next eight years. Historically, wars have always brought medical breakthroughs. The war on terrorism promises to be no different. We don't usually think of Pisces as a warlike sign, but we should. Pisces has Mars as it's element ruler, and we can probably expect that the new discoveries will often spring from war related efforts. This indicates that breakthroughs will come from defense contractors. Since Pisces is a watery sign, we can expect to see the ocean provide us with much many new discoveries. In business, we might look for new uses for diving equipment such as decompression chambers.

Pisces has been linked to photography. As business travel continues to ebb, we can expect a rise in teleconferencing, not to mention telemedicine. We can expect to hear of major overhauls in the old photo giants. Companies like Kodak and Polaroid will continue to be hit hard unless they can change with the times. Pisces is also closely associated with chemistry. Little wonder that DuPont first made the list of the top Dow Jones Industrials during a Uranus in Pisces period, and the saying, "Better living through chemistry" was first popularized during the same time. On the downside, historically, Uranus' sojourn through Pisces has been linked to both the flu epidemic of 1919 and the great plague of Europe in the 1400s. This means that the threat of bioterrorism is real.

Simply put, illness is the darling of the pharmaceutical sector. Expect everything from aspirin to biotech stocks to go up. We will see some remarkable and often controversial discoveries. Bioengineering companies stand at the forefront of the revolution in medicine. Get ready to hear of names like Onyx, with its potential cancer treatment, and Abgenix, who is working with the Department of Defense on a possible antibody treatment of smallpox and ebola-like viruses, to join the better-known names, like Genentech and Chiron, at the forefront of the new medical discoveries. Biotech is not the drug sector on the rise, though. After a decade of decline, watch those old economy stalwarts, tobacco and hard liquor, make a comeback as hard times entice stiff remedies.

Since Pisces likes to operate behind the scenes, expect everything from companies that perform undercover work, private investigation firms, to x-ray technology, spy cameras, night vision goggles, air filtration and cleaning systems, to hazardous materials clean up specialists, to be the great white hope of the markets. And that neighborhood artist just around your corner could make you a fortune. Masters like Leonardo Da Vinci and Picasso have, historically, emerged during Uranus in Pisces periods. This is but a glimpse of the markets that stand to gain ground in an otherwise bearish climate.

Market Watch 2003

January

Study the market, but do not buy. We open January with Mercury retrograde. This is a signal to all to hold off signing any contracts until Mercury turns direct on January 23. Mars enters Sagittarius January 18. This could signal an upsurge in the war on terrorism, and a downturn in the markets for the rest of the month.

February

The price of gas rises and all commodities go up along with it, as Jupiter heads toward Neptune. This is a belt-trimming month with bad earnings news coming as Saturn sits on the previous eclipse degree for the duration. Stocks to watch: research and development stocks, and defense contractor stocks. Upsets are possible midmonth. Use care traveling between Valentine's Day and George Washington's birthday.

March

Like last month, this is a highly critical month. The market begins to recover after March 5, but events March 10–11 affect the market adversely. Markets turn downward on March 24, when Pluto turns retrograde. This spells trouble for business in general, but especially the travel sector.

April

Depressed at the beginning of the month and cautiously optimistic after April 21, this will be a month of swings for the market. Stocks to watch: oil, tobacco, and the old standards of the blue chips will outperform other stocks. As Jupiter makes his way toward Neptune, gas prices are up. When Mercury goes retrograde April 26–May 20, use care in signing any papers or contracts.

May

Investors seem to feel that tech stocks have gone as low as they will go, and we will see the best of tech start to look up. Biotech and pharmaceuticals will take a turn upward as will anything related to defense. From May 15 on, as Mars heads toward Neptune, drug stocks heat up.

June

An eclipse intensifies market activity in June. Markets are positive early in the month, but turn negative around the solstice as Saturn enters Cancer and conjoins the Sun. This does not bode well for summer trading. Expect bad news in housing starts.

July

The market slumps the first half of the month, following a Sun-Saturn conjunction June 24, and a Mercury-Saturn conjunction on June 30. The markets turn upward, culminating around July 25, as reports of better than expected new earnings start to come in. A lot is happening behind the scenes. Mars turns retrograde on the July 29 in Pisces.

August

We begin to see the price of oil and gas go down, and with it an upwards directing market with defense contractors leading the way. Action increases at the end of the month in the over-the-counter market as some positive news comes in. Get important business completed by August 28, when Mercury will retrograde.

September

This is a crucial month. Business slows as Saturn edges closer to the U.S. Sun in Cancer. Expect the unexpected. Do not sign on the dotted line until after September 20, when Mercury is direct again. Markets are volatile across the board. We're likely to see potential trouble, especially from gas and or shipping all month, which may bring markets down, especially between September 24–27.

October

Trading is still hazardous in all sectors. Communications could feel the heat, and not in a positive way. The market takes a real dive between the October 10–20. Bad news from leading economic indicators do not look good, especially around October 25, as Saturn stations. The market slumps.

November

Market regains some ground early in the month as traders look for bargains. Losses are possible in technology on November 8, when Uranus goes direct. Watch for great intensity and potential dangerous doings in the market, especially from November 16 through the Thanksgiving holiday. The defense industry stands to gain. Much is being done in secret. All economic indicators turn negative as the holiday season gets underway and people stay home.

December

Markets continue to slump all month as bears come out in a big way to all indexes. If there is a bright spot, it will be in the defense industry, as Jupiter squares Pluto all month. Try to get your shopping done before December 17, when a retrograde Mercury will tend to make purchases somehow useless or redundant.

About the Author

Dorothy J. Kovach is a practicing astrologer, writer, and timing expert, based in northern California. She acts as a consultant to both businesses and persons interested in finding the best time to initiate projects for successful outcomes, such as launching new businesses, stock and other purchases, surgery, weddings, etc. Beyond her interest in finances, she is also interested in astrology's effect on world situations. She is the owner and comoderator for an Internet group-study of traditional events. She utilizes both Western and Eastern methods in her work and can be contacted through her website: www.worldastrology.net.

Your Lunar Guide to Career and Reward

By Leeda Alleyn Pacotti

With economic volatility, stock market corrections, and curtailed spending, wage earners and business persons are befuddled by constantly changing dynamics. Besieged with an endless litany of financial do's and don'ts, we must plan and prosper, marshaling precious inner resources to gain a career foothold, rise the promotional ladder, and fret over retirement.

Creating a sound economic standing is wise, but the platitudes of financial advisors, uttered as though one size fits all, or as a cookbook process, ignore the talent, inclination, and motive power we bring to bear in our pursuits as productive members of society. Charting a course for a satisfying career through economic upheaval takes objective self-appraisal and self-acceptance to know our strengths and limitations. We must apply creative imagination and inner conviction to map a career plan, which enhances natural qualities and provides curiosity and growth, yet gives a strong sense of accomplishment.

Not all of us will be the head of a corporation, and many are not geared to manual labor. Some prefer the isolation of a laboratory or workshop. Still others want a constant supply of publicity or socialization. But, in the end, we need solid financial prospects that fulfill our desires for reward and our duties to support loved ones.

Astrology offers a wealth of information about your best career prospects and likely financial portrait. The Moon, in particular, indicates the foundation of your career aims, the strata of your professional placement, the flow of your economic outlook, and the environment of your golden years. Whether you are beginning your career, considering a new one, contemplating business ownership, or planning for retirement, you deserve the benefit of this important lunar influence.

The Moon As Your Career Barometer

Quick in its orbit, the Moon constantly changes, casting directives throughout the chart. Ruling the Fourth House, the lunar orb asserts deep motive power, demanding that psychological needs be met, no matter what we accomplish through other areas of the horoscope. The Moon interplays with the opposing Tenth House of career, compelling career pursuits that answer the requirements of nurturing. Consequently, if you have a job or profession inimical to your deep-seated feelings, you will be continually impelled to seek a fulfilling career.

Despite worldly pressure to rise to the heights, the Moon indicates your best career strata, befitting your psychological needs. We do well when we feel secure in what we are doing. The natal Moon tells whether your security resides in being the "indispensable" employee, who sticks with the same employer for twenty years, or in being an entrepreneur with start-ups every three years. In a general way, your natal Moon also indicates lifelong financial conditions, their stability, and the retention of earnings.

A valued precept of astrology is that the Fourth House, the house naturally ruled by the Moon, deals with "end of the matter" matters. In modern terms, this "end" suggests the years at the close of life, or retirement. Drawing upon this meaning, the Moon resolves your need for security, surrendered during long years of work and economic turbulence, foreshadowing the likely conditions of your retirement.

Your Framework for Economic Stability

The following lunar portraits assess your prospects and challenges, delineated by the Moon's placement in house or sign. Review them, as you make career and economic plans or changes. Bear in mind that the economics of your early life, the obligations of family in your adult life, and your resolve to attain your highest desires can substantially alter these guidelines.

Moon in Aries or First House

The fire of Aries gives energy, high spirits, and independence to the person with an Aries Moon or Moon in the First House. When your enthusiasm is aroused, you move through ideas quickly, with flashes of genius. However, your mind and body move too swiftly to do more than pass on these brilliant gems for someone else to implement. You enjoy risk and uncertainty, satisfying your ambition to make your name in an original way. You do best out in front, pushing forward and gaining recognition.

Aries has affinity with sharp instruments, fire, iron, and steel. Being skillful as well as quick, you shine in careers requiring strategy and precision, such as a military commander, surgeon, medical doctor, dentist, barber, or butcher. The fire of Aries suggests chemistry and cooking. Physical labor, steelwork, ironwork, or smithing may satisfy your mechanical skills and need for activity. Labor organizing brings the prominence you desire.

Expect to make your name early in life. Although you are ambitious, business ownership is not your best prospect, because your impulsiveness and general passion tend to arouse conflict among employees and business associates. Unless you commerce in Aries type businesses, expect disrepute to hamper, even eliminate, business prospects.

You receive honors and recognitions. However, competitors and rivals cast aspersions on your name and success, causing economic highs and lows. Learn careful spending and saving, when finances are good, to see you through lean periods and to help you remain solvent after retirement.

During retirement, you probably won't have a permanent home. Financial situations late in life may force you to sell it, or land and community disputes push you out. Insure your possessions and holdings against loss from fire. Despite careful planning, you may find yourself roving, traveling, or living temporarily in several households.

Moon in Taurus or Second House

Earthy Taurus is conservative and materially acquisitive. You have confidence and high self-esteem, exhibited as extraordinary patience, deliberation, and methodology. You pace your energies, appearing reserved and somewhat aloof. This pacing, however, is the basis for your renowned persistence. Generally, you feel a sense of fate about your endeavors.

Earthy Taurus loves pleasure and adornment, and occupations involving women and their needs. Combining both appeal and ornament, consider employments or professions as a manufacturer of women's apparel and accessories, perfumer, embroiderer, fashion designer, draper, or upholsterer. Taurus appreciates round, feminine lines and promotes them through occupations of pastry chef and confectioner, or enhances them in the vocations of personal servant, dresser, or costumer. From the element of earth, you do well as a florist or landscape designer.

Your success comes slowly, but endures. Good friends boost your career or introduce you to better circumstances. Expect to rise and remain at an economic level considerably higher than your early life. Because you understand conservative spending expands a modest income, your natural frugality pays off. The adage "A well-paid servant is better than a bankrupt master" is not lost on you. Your long-term investments provide a continuing yield.

Rewards in your retirement are ample, comfortable, and serene. Pick any domestic circumstance that makes you happy. Friends and family members, who are emotionally harmonious and genuinely interested in your well-being, frequent your later years.

Moon in Gemini or Third House

Gemini confers a keen intellect, geared to refined thought and possibility thinking. Your experiences, like your thoughts, benefit from a diversity of people and circumstances. Your excellent memory is a file box, stuffed with colorful details. Ponderous thinking and petty behaviors, however, depress your nervous system. Socially, you excel, using politeness, courtesy, and an engagingly bright smile.

Because of your breadth of observation and phenomenal recall, consider careers as a journalist, novelist, science teacher, or writer, especially science fiction. Getting the message to others is important; try delivery person, messenger, postal worker, or printer.

Your career is satisfying, although short on opportunities for public recognition or prominence. Among your peers, you are well respected. One of them recommends you for some position of distinction, but you serve without attracting special attention. The environment of your career reflects your efforts, more than the influence of others. Fortunately, your enjoyment of variety offsets extravagant financial rewards.

Even in retirement, your mind remains sharp, which serves you well, because you need to document everything important. Read deeds, investment disclosures, pension papers, and wills very carefully. Be alert to sharp-witted people who appeal to your intellect but are likely to attempt a swindle. If you need funds late in life, consider contracts or employments which keep you in contact with young people, with whom you have a mental rapport.

Moon in Cancer or Fourth House

Cancer promotes romantic and sensitive ideas, expressed as sentimentality and sympathy. As you encounter the shifting emotions of others, your sensitivities make you impressionable and changeable. The Moon rules Cancer, helping you accept change and movement. This variety of persons and conditions brings a wealth of understanding and an uncanny ability to read people. Expect pronounced experiences or circumstances in your career.

Cancer's sociability attracts professions with plentiful public interaction, such as a facilitator, interpreter, or negotiator. Specifically, consider careers as an agent, broker, detective, fisherman, inspector, or steward. Cancer careers emphasize mother's needs, such as dairy, daycare, midwifery, and obstetrics.

Your career goes through phases, moving you through jobs and locations. What positions you attain don't have innate prominence. However, when you promote yourself, you are well received and remembered. Any prominence comes early during a specific career venture or phase.

In retirement, expect changes and fluctuations. You won't live in one residence, instead staying at the homes of relatives or children for intervals throughout the year. Interestingly, the changes you encounter reinforce your understanding of occult principles. If you didn't study these subjects before, you find time now. Never believe you are sponging off relatives; you prefer to live with them, because you love them. At the end of your life, you leave them not only a legacy of wisdom, but also an inheritance.

Moon in Leo or Fifth House

Leo gives determination and practicality, with a strong will to attain goals. Like Aries, you are ambitious, but you stay silent and reserved. You attract many people, who promote your success. The aims and ideas of others don't sway you, and you remain persistent and faithful to your pursuits. "Conscientious" and "loyal" are words others use to describe you. For you, silence is truly golden.

Leo seems aloof, but is discreet and careful with information. Others recognize your objectivity in assessing people, situations, and solutions, which makes you a natural for authority, governance, and organization. You do well in executive, governmental, and scientific careers, as a businessperson, corporate executive, or mayor. Leo understands gold, excelling as a goldsmith or jeweler.

Expect continuing success throughout your career, owing to your diligence and persistence. You do well financially, because you look for new incomes and maintain revenues with continuing returns. Leo wants the best and finds it, which pays off in business. Others trust you, and you gain contracts and income well into your retirement.

Through retirement, Leo basks in the sun. Others seek you out, and you can expect contact with powerful people or have their assistance. All your ventures come to a satisfactory conclusion. Condominium or townhouse luxury appeals to your regal senses, and you can well afford it. Expect to head up more than one important political or philanthropic fund-raiser.

Moon in Virgo or Sixth House

Virgo supplies method, offsetting its tendency to nervousness. Activities or pastimes with repetitions or recurring organization reinforce your need for order. Strongly analytical, you choose events and situations to fit the mold of your ideas and observations, rather than disarraying your thoughts with exceptions. You feel responsible for others and go out of your way to assist them, although extending yourself stretches the limits of your nervous energy.

Virgo benefits from habitual processes and the safety of the method. Look for employments with recurring responsibilities by the week, month, or year. Consider positions of bookkeeper, bookseller, cashier, secretary, or shop manager. Because Virgo safeguards, you do well as an accountant, health administrator, interpreter, nurse, occupational therapist, or physical therapist.

The reticent nature of Virgo doesn't bring fame or fortune. However, you are careful with money and know to prepare for the future. Your salvation comes from abundant, commonplace occupations, in which you excel. Owing to your reliability, you are frequently the most valued employee. Although your income is not extravagant, it is steady. Forgo creating a lasting estate for generations to come, and let your accumulations produce a healthy nest egg to prevent worries over day-to-day living.

Your retirement is a well-deserved reward after years of diligent service. Because income is limited, consider an assisted-living community or a senior commune, where everyone shares daily responsibilities. Whatever your preferred arrangement, read the fine print or have a lawyer review contracts. Earthy Virgo benefits from pastoral settings and country life, which prolong your years.

Moon in Libra or Seventh House

Libra gives a noble mind, refined thoughts, and honorable intentions. Politeness and courtesy are your companions. Considering your direct and diligent thinking, you have no need for ambiguities. Your ambitions are mental, and your theoretical pursuits benefit from your objective, dispassionate appraisals. In appearance and speech, you make an excellent presentation, getting your ideas across to others.

You are the true professional, involved with service, rather than showy possessions. Your adventures into physical reality consist of outlining your ideas on paper for interpretation. Your cerebral bent prepares you for careers such as arbitrator, architect, composer, designer, executive manager, lawyer, lyricist, musician, orator, or politician.

Libra produces extraordinary magnetism. Early on, a well or highly placed mentor sees the best possibilities in you. This person offers introductions and opens doors that help you rise, almost without your effort. Actually, your work is exceptional, which augments your recognition and success.

Retirement is your fond reward. You spent your energies well and accomplished your goals. Even if you did nothing monumental, you recognize your original thoughts in others' subsequent ideas. You set money aside for your elder years and find your circumstances are very good. You live better after retirement than before, and certainly better than when you were very young.

Moon in Scorpio or Eighth House

Scorpio produces extremes and mystery, with a dark side, suppressed and unspoken. Your emotions run so deep you have trouble understanding them, let alone explaining them. Others don't know your goals, despite your usually visible career choice. Your public image has nothing to do with who you are on the inside. One thing is certain: your career must be profitable, to forestall brooding and self-recrimination.

Your career is camouflage, letting you blend in, preventing unwanted attention. You do well as a middle-management executive, government contractor, or merchant. Careers that plumb the depths, such as archaeology, mining, natural gas and oil drilling, appeal to your sense of the hidden. Nuclear science, outer space, and television or video engineering let you apply intense examination.

Scorpio makes up for life's disappointments by immersing in work and business. Ever astute to hidden agendas, you find financial opportunities and lucrative contracts well before these are public, and you maneuver to be johnny-on-the-spot with your services. Consequently, your income grows and continues well beyond retirement age.

Scorpio likes time alone, and this remains true in your retirement. You have no illusions about needing family in your declining years. More than likely, you outlived everyone who was important to you. As for immediate family, your work strained those relationships, and none of you desire togetherness. Consider living your retirement years in an isolated place, such as a small island or developing country.

Moon in Sagittarius or Ninth House

Sagittarius confers genius, independence, and keen intellect. Not lost in thought, you possess ardor, enthusiasm, and passion, best expressed through adventure and sport. Some accuse you of ignoring humanity's needs; but, when it comes to feelings, you are helpful and sympathetic. You tend to idiosyncrasy, placing importance on the meld of lofty ideas with pragmatic experience. Sagittarius rules the "golden mean" and seeks a bridge between dreams and earthly life.

Your pursuit of ideologies, philosophies, and theologies makes you comfortable as an author, educator, judge, physician, religious leader, financial representative, or legal theorist. Drawn to physical activity, you combine mental and physical talents as an athletic agent or scout.

Interestingly, Sagittarius doesn't bring fame or prominence, but an eventful career, crowded with momentous experiences and unusual people. Sagittarian generosity causes you to believe there is another pot of gold at the end of another rainbow. Consequently, you release money easily; so expect to go through lean times.

The youthful exuberance of Sagittarius makes later years your very best. Surprisingly, you do better in your native country, rather than living abroad or traveling for success. Gain comes from domestic necessities, such as starting a business to help others of your generation. If you do so, you are more prosperous each year, securing an excellent financial status, permitting that one last show of generosity through inheritance.

Moon in Capricorn or Tenth House

Powerful Capricorn gives practical ambition and material advancement. You are systematic and cautious with your energies, expending them carefully through organization and diplomacy. Your financial abilities are well-known, and your advice is sought. You prefer the tangible acquisitions of money and land, as opposed to credit cards and deeds. Earth-driven, you persevere to your goal through common sense, developed from self-protection and self-preservation. However, your decidedly progressive attitude gives you independence and a sense of pioneering.

The earth element is prominent in your professions, where you apply yourself as an agriculturalist, agronomist, chemist, horticulturist, or scientist. Your sense of protection lets you excel in alarm systems, security, or night work. Capricorn is the sign of business, and you need to be your own boss.

Capricorn creates genius through necessity and restriction. You assess your possibilities early in your career, using timing and effect to bring recognition. Your income will have highs and lows, so learn to save for the lean times.

Your retirement is seclusion, a welcome relief after so many years of dealing with the public and machinations of business. Whatever your finances, avoid fears of loss, to safeguard against miserliness and pessimism. Capricorn confers long life and outlives its beneficiaries. Consider establishing a foundation to perpetuate the work to which you dedicated your life.

Moon in Aquarius or Eleventh House

Aquarius is dignified, noble, and refined. You appreciate civility and order, carrying yourself with aristocratic bearing. Many of your novel, inventive ideas have their basis in conservative values and preferences for orthodoxy. You want to know, rather than establish, your place in the social scheme, giving you freedom to investigate ideas and possibilities. Aquarius tends to preservation, principally of shared beliefs. Although you are extremely literate, your ideas build from archetypal thinking, which you find difficult to verbalize.

Your concerns for social order fit you for civil service to enforce laws, or as a legislator to develop regulations. Your sense of order is satisfied by careers of electrical engineer, electrician, electronics technician, or inventor. Not one to shirk your grand social view, you express it through tactile arts, such as painting and sculpture, which saves you from mundane, explanatory conversations.

As a perpetual tinkerer, you are interested in new developments. You know the mind doesn't grow old, and you expect to continue working. Invention brings a new item or process, which earns you a name and royalties. Aquarius needs age to develop calm concentration, which delays your best work until mid-years.

In retirement, you earn the well-deserved title "eccentric." You prefer solitude and are a real curmudgeon when interrupted. Others, especially younger adults, misread your conduct. Consider donations to a foundation, endowment, or nonprofit program to show you do have your community's concerns at heart.

Moon in Pisces or Twelfth House

Pisces creates an impressionable nature, affected by influences of surrounding emotions. Feeling out of sync, you are formal and careful in social interactions. Emotional interplays continually sway your thinking, making you capricious and fanciful. Mastering the emotional turbulence, you express an incredible sympathy and high empathy, using the arts as an outlet for emotional accumulations.

Sympathetic Pisces increases your ability to listen and desire to heal others' woes. You do well as a bartender, nonprofit coordinator, psychological counselor, or social worker. Piscean duality prepares you for an additional career in acting, singing, poetry, or watercolor, for which you display an exceptional genius.

Your career has no high profile; Pisces prefers to serve others. Nonetheless, an obscure career shines from the interjection of your personal sympathies. Your finances rise and fall. Unless you were born into money, you are unlikely to be wealthy. If you inherit, you tend to give your inheritance to those less fortunate.

Involved with other people and ethereal realms, Pisces forgets to plan for the future. You know it will come, but you don't see yourself old or unable to work. You sap your energies to the end, needing someone to give you the care you've given to others. That someone will be there. In later years, you encounter parapsychological phenomenon, which enters through the electromagnetism of your residential environment. If you become uncomfortable, you will need to move.

About the Author

Leeda Alleyn Pacotti practices as a naturopathic physician, nutritional counselor, and master herbalist. In keeping with the precept to "do no harm," she incorporates specialized diagnostics of dream language, health astrology, observations from Chinese medicine, and the resurrected science of personology. Of late, her investigations have extended into neural and brain dysfunctions, particularly ADHD and the emotional signals of physical illness.

Suggested Reading:

The Art of Synthesis by Alan Leo.
The Key to Your Own Nativity by Alan Leo.
"Sepharial": The Manual of Astrology (W. Foulsham & Co., Ltd).

Astrology Looks at a Changing World

By Alice DeVille

A strology is a unique and diversified tool that helps explain personal information about you and patterns that emerge in your life, but nothing is cast in stone. Every person born has the right to choose the various paths. Astrology does not order you around or dictate how you ought to behave. Instead it offers insight into your physical, emotional, mental, and spiritual makeup. This branch of astrology is called natal astrology because it covers what the planets say about you from birth until the time you leave the Earth plane.

Several other schools of astrology exist besides natal, including one called mundane, that studies the history of nations and world conditions —countries, leaders, industries, economies, and wars. Happenings around the globe are fodder for the practitioners of this branch of astrology. A compatible arm of the craft, called event astrology, tracks outbreaks, riots, earthquakes, mass murders, and cataclysmic shifts that disrupt everyday life. These practitioners are at work studying all the aspects when wars break out, dams burst, the underdog wins an election, or accidents occur that affect many lives. Certain astrologers claim to predict these circumstances based on their study of the planets, eclipses, and fixed stars; most see the trends in hindsight and piece their findings together after an incident occurs. Events like these are front-page news and grab headliner billing in the media. There is no escaping the blitz of information or the emotional drain it has on your psyche. When you find yourself confronted by far-reaching events that occur suddenly, you focus attention exclusively to that particular incident. Then you begin to absorb the shock and witness the shift of circumstances. In the blink of an eye your personal worldview meets an irresistible force of global magnitude. Such an event is the focus of this article.

To tell a story about how the world you knew to be your reality changed in one day is no easy undertaking. You may wake up on that fateful day with a feeling in your stomach that leaves you uneasy, yet make no connection to the current state of affairs. Perhaps that inner "knowing" of yours has a way of alerting you that transformation is in the wind, and until it occurs you feel as if your very core is on alert. Or, you can be totally at peace, feeling no anxiety one minute, and find your world in chaos the next.

Each of you has a different definition of what that world means. For some it has to do with people you love, where you live, whom you play with, familiar places, your favorite food, and the joy you carry around in your hearts. Others define reality as the way you do business, how you get where you want to go, and how secure you feel about living in the land of the free: the United States of America. You, no doubt, have internalized a solid picture of your life and appreciate the comfort and dependability of your routines. It's not that you have a blind spot to the possibility of change; it's just that you hope to have a hand in the outcome.

Your personal astrology chart contains information about your natal planets in twelve different departments of life called houses. In truth, conditions seldom stay in a holding pattern in each area of your life simultaneously. The basic patterns are subject to change when transiting planets (planets in their orbit) influence natal planets. Sometimes the change is mild and pleasant, but when harsh aspects hit a planet, your life undergoes a drastic transformation and you are left bewildered, shocked, and pained. You need time to catch your breath and figure out how your world has rearranged itself.

Each and every one of us experienced such a change on September 11, 2001. On that beautiful late summer morning, New York City's World Trade Center, hit by two highjacked planes, collapsed, and the whole world witnessed via live television news broadcasts the destruction of life and a treasured landscape. Where were you? Can you ever forget the devastation of that moment and the subsequent scenes that filled the tube as plane number three crashed into the Pentagon in Arlington, Virginia, and a fourth plane plowed into the pristine acres surrounding New Baltimore, Pennsylvania?

Astrological Insight

Mundane and events astrologers use their expertise to study the planets for evidence of global change. Although they have access to data that helps them pinpoint areas of high focus around the world, the matter of putting it all together is not easy. A combination of information about specific countries (nations have astrological charts based on when they came into existence, charters were signed, names changed, or new governments took over) and leaders' birth data puts them on alert as they watch current planetary trends unfold. Their lectures, classes, or writing often highlight emerging planetary patterns and allude to the intensity of upcoming events and the effect on world figures. Just like you, astrologers are caught off guard when dire events occur, and often they can't readily grasp the impact of the emerging astrological conditions. They grab their notes and consult an ephemeris (manual or software directory that lists the planets' daily positions by sign and degree) to see what current placements influenced the drastic change, and zero in on the scope of the interference. If they weren't expecting the actual event, but had a clue that something big was coming down the pike, they look at all the variables and hone in on the planets they suspect of triggering the events. You can be sure they realize that a pivotal event will become the hot new astrological topic for years to come and they want to share their insights. Astrologers realize that mundane events extend a global hand toward all of humanity and perceive that after the storm unleashes its most violent wave comes a new dimension and reckoning. That has certainly been the case regarding the terrorist attacks that occurred on September 11, 2001.

Very few individuals in the astrological community actually narrowed down the attacks by Osama bin Laden's handpicked crew to that infamous day, but many saw the astrological conditions unfolding. I salute those who linked this fateful day to a disaster similar to Pearl Harbor. I was not one who knew the actual day or the horrific extent of events that would occur. My astrology-based suspicions, aided by my gift of intuition, were that our powerful country would emerge on the world stage under very unusual circumstances with Saturn and Pluto opposing each other in the United States chart's First and Seventh Houses.[1] I doubt that much could have been done to prevent the attacks even though many of us were studying the astrological aspects. All the systems of detection and internal watchdog agencies seemed to fail in the art of surveillance and suppression of dissidents. Intelligence forces missed out on coordinating critical information and connecting the puzzle pieces. Perhaps world history needed to be written so that people on the planet could rediscover their purpose, evaluate complacency, and find new resources for healing.

I do not consider myself a practitioner of predictive astrology, in fact, I have turned down interviews by reporters over the years that I knew were looking for sensational tidbits. As I have worked with a number of individuals, including the prominent in my practice, my first concern is their privacy and the agreement we have that assures them of client/consultant confidentiality. However, I identify strongly with the flow of activity triggered by transiting planets and understand the trends and how they influence my clients' actions.

During the nine months preceding the hijackings, I made several references to national safety, terrorist threats (including hijacked planes), biological warfare, the president's chart, and the U.S. chart, being the high focus of attention by enemies. In a workshop the Sunday before Election Day 2000, I related that election night would be a fiasco due to the planetary lineup that included Mercury, the Moon, and Mars. I indicated we would go to bed without knowing the outcome. I also conduct an annual seminar in December and outline the global and individual trends for the year ahead. The agenda includes topics of interest, such as world themes, finances, politics, entertainment figures, and the outlook for each Sun sign. I track eclipse patterns by solar houses so that clients have a clue

---

1. I use the Gemini rising chart for July 4, 1776. However, the exact birth time of our nation is unknown, and several other natal charts are in use by astrologers.

   More on the astrology: I also felt the Cancer-Capricorn eclipses in the nation's Second and Eighth Houses of money would influence new spending bills, our country's debt load, the stock market as a whole, and redefine the options for employment in government and the nation as a whole.

about which department of life will be most affected by eclipse activity in the year ahead. That is my strongest contribution to what others call predictive astrology. I like to say it is the astrology of choice because I believe the chart is a guide and you have options for facilitating the outcomes.

In December 2000, the date of my workshop fell before the final result of the 2000 election was known. Rather than turn the event into a political fiasco, if I tipped my hand (strong Republicans and Democrats were present, including future political appointees), I chose to cover the chart of Vice-President-to-be Dick Cheney in the political segment. Only the astrologically astute caught on to my hint. My advice to attendees was to keep this man's chart handy because we would be learning a lot about how he does business and his health in the months ahead. I also asked the group to pray for the incoming president, and indicated the winner would be the loser as critical events would claim his attention day and night shortly after the eclipses in the summer of 2001. How true it all came to be.

A client of mine from Colorado related that I told him shortly after George W. Bush emerged as the president that our country could go to war the latter half of the year. You can be sure he contacted me in September after the attacks on our nation. A number of similar revelations occurred during monthly workshops that further pointed to the role of Congress and the intensity in the astrology charts of the Cancer Sun sign president; the Aries Sun sign Secretary of State Colin Powell; National Security Advisor Condoleezza Rice, with her cadre of Scorpio planets receiving harsh aspects from the transits of Uranus and Neptune; and Defense Secretary Donald Rumsfeld, another Cancer with critical ties to the U.S. chart.

In the summer of 2001, I began to see an Arab man in my meditation routine. I knew this figure was a clue to something that would affect my life, but as I usually do, I just wait for events to unfold knowing the pieces will fit together. The Monday before the terrorist hijackings (September 10), a client phoned to ask me whether she ought to drive her own car to New York City that weekend or book a rental. She was concerned about whether her ten-year-old vehicle could withstand the trip. After consulting the ephemeris and her natal chart transits, I told her I didn't feel there was anything wrong with her car, but I advised her to have it serviced anyway. I told her I did see another type of problem involving mass transportation in New York City, and that it would somehow influence her trip. Too close for comfort? Read on. My client, the owner of an insurance agency, also knew that I was flying out of town the very next day via Dulles Airport and she wanted to catch me before I left. Later on we would have some very interesting chats.

My theory is that several planets had a hand in the unfolding horror, but I was particularly drawn to the behavior of transiting Neptune right before the attack at the time of the September Full Moon in Pisces on September 2. I also looked at transiting Mercury[2] and the degree caught my eye, because whenever this degree appears in the charts of my clients by progression or transit, some aspect of that client's life undergoes a drastic change.

Personal History

Before we delve into my September 11 flight details, a bit of background information about me may help you. I am deeply tied to all the sites you watched on the twenty-four-hour-a-day broadcasts that followed the incidents or that you read about in the news. I live outside of Washington, D.C., approximately ten miles from Washington-Dulles Airport, the departure point of the American Airlines plane that hit the Pentagon. I worked right across the street from the Washington Monument for eleven of the fifteen years I was based in Washington, D.C., enjoying a variety of government positions, including that of a change agent or internal consultant. The remaining years I worked in Arlington, Virginia, close to the Pentagon and not very far from Reagan National Airport in Alexandria, Virginia.

I was born in suburban Philadelphia on July 3. My family moved to picturesque New Baltimore in western Pennsylvania for a year when I was eight years old. The closest large airport is located in Pittsburgh. I still have cousins living in the general area. The three Pennsylvania locations that made the news throughout the stressful ordeal were New Baltimore, Windber (birthplace of my parents), and Somerset County, the jurisdiction housing both Windber and New Baltimore. These are places that bring tears to my eyes and fond remembrance of happy family celebrations and relatives who have passed on. Every Fourth of July while I was growing up my family made the trek across the state from suburban Philadelphia to the area, past the Gettysburg Battlefield, resplendent with our nation's flags, banners, and bunting, and the decorated graves of fallen soldiers who lost their lives in the service of their country. The news blurbs further

---

2. Dane Rudhyar, a renowned humanistic astrologer, gives this interpretation to the esoteric degree Mercury was transiting: "The dawn of a new day reveals everthing changed."

mentioned Bedford, Pennsylvania, the exit closest to these locations from the Pennsylvania Turnpike. Little did I know on the morning of September 11, that before long I would be driving past these very locations that never fail to stir the memories of my soul.

Vacation Bound

In 2001, all of my travel prior to September 11 had involved business trips. I had a little free time on my calendar and was ready for a short get-away to recharge my batteries. (I have Capricorn rising, with Saturn and Mercury in the Sixth House of everyday habits and routines. All are indicators of a tendency to be a workaholic.) When my Florida-based Pisces sister suggested in late August that we meet in Las Vegas for a three-day reunion (she already planned to be there with a friend), I booked a flight that would take me first to Denver, then on to Las Vegas. Travel aspects were good for me, yet something did not feel right to me as departure time approached. The Sunday before our trip I wrapped up after a seminar and phoned my younger son in San Francisco (the destination city of United Flight 93, which crashed into the Somerset County area) to give him my flight information. I told him that I am usually very upbeat and excited when I am traveling and was looking forward to seeing my sister, but something seemed very different about this trip. I thought perhaps it was because I had never been to Las Vegas and had little interest in gambling. I mentioned I had scheduled a side trip to tour Hoover Dam to get away from the smoke in the casinos. With his gregarious Aquarian personality he assured me that I would have a good time and encouraged me to enjoy the reunion.

Late the next evening, while I was packing (hours after the New York City–bound client had phoned), my oldest son (Sun sign Libra) called and asked me to phone him when I landed in Denver on the morning of September 11. I told him I needed to catch a connecting flight that didn't have much wiggle room. But he insisted that I call from my cell phone, and then he went on to request that I phone him immediately when I landed on the ground in Las Vegas. I knew he was picking up on something (he has the Moon intuitively placed in the Ninth House and has psychic Neptune sextile Pluto and the Ascendant in the Third House), especially since he had never made such a request before this time. He also has strong ties to the World Trade Center, since it was the national headquarters of his investment firm and he had just been there for a week of management training. Ironically, I have a third child, a daughter, who lived at the time in Los Angeles, the intended arrival city of three of the four hijacked planes. Can you imagine what my family was going through while I was in the air oblivious to the violence taking place in eastern sky space?

Unprecedented Journey

The morning of September 11 proved to be a glorious. As I headed to Dulles Airport, the sky was blue and cloudless, with no hint of approaching autumn. School buses made the rounds picking up children on street corners. I commented to the taxi driver on the unusually light volume of rush-hour traffic, and on the few passengers who lined up at curbside check-in.

I arrived at the airport ninety minutes before departure on my United Airlines flight scheduled to take off at 9:05 am for Denver. Security was a breeze. Boarding began on time. In fact, everything seemed too easy. Ten minutes before departure the captain announced that twenty more passengers would board the half-full cabin and he wanted them seated quickly so the plane could take off. Boarding took all of five minutes and the plane actually started moving away from the gate at 9:00 am. My mind was whirling and my self-talk marveled that for the first time in three years I was on a United Airlines flight that was actually leaving on time.

I sat in an aisle seat noting that another woman about my age occupied the window seat. We made brief small talk and settled into the reading material we had chosen for the flight. Before this day would end, we would become friends, and I would discover that she was born not far from New Baltimore, Pennsylvania. Coincidence? I don't think so. A little more than half an hour later the captain signaled the flight attendants to begin serving breakfast. They no sooner served a few passengers in first class, then the captain asked them and everyone else to take their seats. He said the following: "The good news is that you are safe; the bad news is that you are not going to Denver. This flight is heading for Pittsburgh. We have been asked to abort this flight due to a national emergency. Keep your seatbelts fastened and do not use your cell phones or the in-flight telephones." Passengers received no other information from airline personnel about the nature of the emergency for as long as we remained on the plane.

A hush came over the already quiet cabin; then people began talking to one another wondering what had happened. A surreal quality hung in the air. I knew it was bad, very bad, yet I felt physically safe. What I am about to tell you is absolutely true.[3] When my seatmate asked what I thought had happened I told her the captain's message suggested either our country had gone to war, someone had been assassinated, or a plane had been taken hostage. I knew in my sinking heart of hearts that I was right, and all of it proved to be true in the end.

Soon the captain signaled the flight attendants to serve breakfast but within a few minutes he told them to take their seats again as we were going to prepare for our landing in Pittsburgh. Once again he came on the system and told us we were not going to land in Pittsburgh because "there were too many planes," and we would head for Indianapolis, Indiana, instead. (Although we did not know it at the time, the last of the downed planes had crashed southwest of Pittsburgh Airport in New Baltimore and we would have been unable to pass by that airspace due to the endangered conditions.)

As we headed for our target destination, the captain once again gave the go-ahead for breakfast and just as quickly canceled again. The tension grew with the uncertainty of information. Even when we received direction to prepare for our landing in Indianapolis, the plane kept circling the airport because no landing strip was open. With air traffic halted, nationwide availability was restricted. Then we finally landed and parked on a remote strip, which would be our interim refuge from the airspace chaos for a few hours, and awaited further instructions.

The captain gave us permission to use the lavatories, and everyone jumped up and grabbed their cell phones. He told us we would have to wait for clearance to a gate, but because so many planes had landed in this modest-sized airport, the wait time would be considerable. Every plane would be searched and inspected and no baggage would be released. Once again he gave permission to serve the now overnuked breakfast.

While some of the famished travelers munched on shriveled bagels, several passengers called the rental car agencies at the airport looking for vehicles to get away from their unplanned stop. Since at least forty other unscheduled planes had landed in Indianapolis, cars were in short supply. Rumors were flying that airports were targets of these mad bombers.

---

3. In hindsight, I feel that retrograde Neptune (chaos, confusion, mixed signals) and the void-of-course Moon leaving transportation-related Gemini were two of the major players in what unfolded during this flight.

Although cell phones appeared in just about every hand, few passengers could get through to anyone on the East Coast because the airwaves were jammed. Bits and pieces of the horror began trickling in to passengers. Hijackings! Bombings! Hostages! The World Trade Center! The Pentagon! Somerset County! Passengers could not really put these horrific pictures together. Travelers attempted to call colleagues but no one was answering phones. Washington, D.C., government employees had been evacuated. Reports came in of massive traffic jams and collapsing buildings. I wondered what type of monster we had on our hands.

I have sixty-five names programmed into my cell phone, and I was unable to get through to anyone on either the East or West Coast. My index finger was on automatic pilot hitting the redial button hundreds of times. At last I got through to my San Francisco son's voice mail and left an emotional message requesting him to let everyone know I was safe. I'm sure I didn't sound convincing, yet I knew I was physically stable. I found myself getting an all too big picture of the tragedy. My seatmate turned to me for reassurance that we were going to be okay, and that I would stay with her. I eked out words of comfort and agreed to stay close. We chatted, exchanged critical information just in case, and kept phoning our loved ones. I knew from all my work in self-help psychology that we were in shock. A stream of information came in and I told her I was afraid of contamination from the debris and anthrax! Yes, anthrax! Now where did that come from? We did not hear that term for a few weeks after the crashes, yet I said it! Right now I just wanted to be home in familiar surroundings and to hear a cherished voice.

Early in the afternoon (still on the plane), I managed to get through to my wonderful daughter-in-law, and she is the one who finally filled me in on the details of the morning. I cannot describe the anxiety I felt for the next several days, when I found myself stranded at the Indianapolis Airport Holiday Inn. I remained planted in front of the TV set and glued to my cell phone, waiting for release from this temporary bondage and grieving with the rest of the nation. While I saw much caring, comforting, and sharing among the stranded travelers in the next few days, I related to Dorothy in the *Wizard of Oz*, who woke up from her dream saying, "There's no place like home." How I wished I could take the Yellow Brick Road back to Virginia!

After three days it became apparent that no planes would be heading to the Washington, D.C., airports. I was booked and rebooked on several flights that never took off. My seatmate, who had a hotel room next door to mine, and I drove a rental car back to Virginia. Our long ride took us through Indiana and Ohio to the Pennsylvania Turnpike, right past the scene of the New Baltimore crash. An aura of awe was in the air. Tribute flags and flowers appeared everywhere and tears filled my eyes, reminding me of a hero of mine who would have celebrated his birthday that week if he were still alive—my father. I felt the presence of this special guide, a man who served his country during World War II as one of the court stenographers at the Nuremberg Trials, and knew I was safe.

You can be sure I hugged my home when I opened that welcoming front door. I felt sick for a few days, and had to release all that anxiety and fear. I had little recovery time, though. The trip was really a catalyst to help me understand the changing dimension of my life path. As a transition consultant, my contract work with the federal government took on a new life, but that is another story. See the companion article on catalysts for career change in Llewellyn's *2003 Sun Sign Book* for details.

The Planets Influence on That Fateful Day

Neptune and Mercury in harsh aspect to Jupiter in the World Trade Center Attack chart represent trouble in long-distance transportation that could stem from interference by foreigners and their devious machinations. The time of this chart calculated for the initial attack is 8:45 AM EDT, New York City. The Third House (transportation and public grief) of the attack chart is badly afflicted, with Pluto in Sagittarius opposing Saturn in Gemini in the Ninth House of long-distance travel and religious fanatics. Also in the Third are: Chiron (Wounded Healer) in Sagittarius opposing the fading Moon in Gemini in the Ninth, Mars in the Third House(crashes, accidents, fire, wars) in Capricorn conjunct (occupying the same or close to the same degree) the Moon's South Node (fated or karmic conditions) and Ceres (the universal mother caring for the wounded) opposes the Gemini Moon, as well as the Moon's North Node (current direction; reward and recognition from Allah for carrying out a daring suicide mission), and Jupiter in Cancer (masses of lives affected) in the Ninth House, suggesting that conditions are out of control on the ground as well as in the air.

Remember my earlier reference to watching the Full Moon Chart of September 2, 2001, cast for 4:43 pm EDT, Washington, D.C.? A loaded Twelfth House (Chiron, Mars, Moon's South Node) suggests secret enemies at work plotting violent deeds. Opposite that stellium (lineup of three or more planets) are the Moon's North Node, Jupiter, and Part of Fortune in the Sixth House of health and welfare, meaning those subversive acts are going to jeopardize the lives of masses of people. Retrograde Neptune in the First House opposes Venus in Leo in the Seventh, suggesting the presence of deceptive and insecure alliances. That same Neptune has been hugging the door of President Bush's natal Seventh House ever since his election, dropping clues about the slippery nature of his open enemies. Perhaps that is why military intelligence could not figure out where bin Laden was hiding. (At my fall 2001 workshops I stated that he had left Afghanistan in disguise and simply wouldn't set himself up as bait for the armed forces.) Mercury in the same Full Moon chart at revealing 3 degrees of Libra is ready to cross into the Ninth House of distant travel and foreign soil, hinting that revolutionary warfare tactics (airplanes becoming live bombs) are in the making.

Finally, Saturn in Gemini opposed Pluto in Sagittarius while simultaneously squaring (aspect of high tension) the Sun in Virgo and the Moon in Pisces, creating a Grand Cross in the heavens that affected the security, economy, foundation, and human resources of our country. There's no doubt in my mind the critical Full Moon chart set the stage for a day the twenty-first-century world will forever remember—September 11, 2001. Let's fly the flag for all our heroes.

About the Author

Alice DeVille, an internationally known astrologer and writer, has a busy consulting practice in northern Virginia. Her specialties include relationships, career and change management, government affairs, real estate, and business advice. She has developed and presented nearly 100 workshops and seminars related to astrological, metaphysical, motivational, and business themes. Alice also writes astrology articles for Star IQ.com website. The only birthday present she ever asked for was an American flag, and she enjoys Fourth of July celebrations.

Recommended Reading

Civilization Under Attack, edited by Stephanie J. Clement.

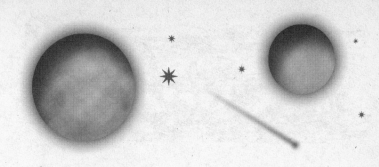

Farm,
Garden,
& Weather
Section

How To Choose the Best Dates for Farm and Animal Activities

Animals and Breeding

Animals are easiest to handle when the Moon is in Taurus, Cancer, Libra, or Pisces, but try to avoid the Full Moon. Buy large animals when the Moon is in Sagittarius or Pisces, and making favorable aspects to Jupiter and Mercury. Buy animals smaller than sheep when the Moon is in Virgo with favorable aspects to Mercury or Venus. Neuter or spay animals in Sagittarius, Capricorn, or Pisces. Slaughter for food in the first three days after the Full Moon in any sign except Leo.

To encourage healthy births, eggs should be set and animals mated so births occur when the Moon is increasing in Taurus, Cancer, Pisces, or Libra. Those born during a semi-fruitful sign (Taurus and Capricorn) will produce leaner meat. Libra yields beautiful animals for showing

and racing. To determine the best date to mate animals or set eggs, subtract the number of days given for incubation or gestation from the fruitful dates given in the following tables. For example, cats and dogs are mated sixty-three days previous to the desired birth date. See tables on page 326.

Garden Activities

Cultivating

Cultivate when the Moon is in a barren sign and waning, ideally the fourth quarter in Aries, Gemini, Leo, Virgo, or Aquarius. Third quarter in the sign of Sagittarius will also work.

Cutting Timber

Cut timber during the third or fourth quarter in Taurus, Gemini, Virgo, or Capricorn—especially during the month of August. Look for favorable aspects to Mars.

Fertilize and Composting

Fertilize when the Moon is in a fruitful sign (Cancer, Scorpio, Pisces). Organic fertilizers are best when the Moon is waning, chemical fertilizers when the Moon is waxing. Start compost when the Moon is in the fourth quarter in a water sign.

Grafting

Graft during the first or second quarter Capricorn, Cancer, or Scorpio.

Harvesting Crops

Harvest root crops when the Moon is in a dry sign (Aries, Leo, Sagittarius, Gemini, or Aquarius) and waning. Harvest grain for storage just after Full Moon, avoiding water signs (Cancer, Scorpio, Pisces). Harvest in the third and fourth quarters in dry signs. Dry in the third quarter in fire signs.

Irrigation

Irrigate when the Moon is in Cancer, Scorpio, or Pisces.

Lawn Mowing

Mow in the first and second quarters (waxing phase) to increase growth and lushness, and in the third and fourth quarters (waning phase) to decrease growth.

Picking Mushrooms

Gather mushrooms at the Full Moon.

Planting

For complete instructions on planting by the Moon, see Gardening by the Moon on page 302, A Guide to Planting on page 309, Gardening Dates on pages 315–322, and the Companion Planting Guide on page 327–329.

Pruning

Prune during the waning phase (third and fourth quarters) in Scorpio to retard growth and to promote better fruit, and in Capricorn to promote better healing.

Spraying and Weeding

Destroy pests and weeds during the fourth quarter when the Moon is in Leo or Aquarius, and making favorable aspects to Pluto. Weed during a waning Moon in a barren sign. For the best days to kill weeds and pests, see pages 324–325.

Weather

For complete weather forecasts for your zone for this year, see page 331.

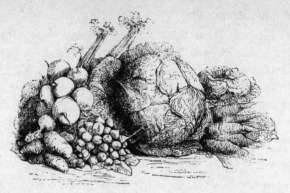

GARDENING BY THE MOON

Today, people often reject the notion of Moon gardening. The usual nonbeliever is not a scientist but the city dweller who has never had any real contact with nature and no experience of natural rhythms.

Camille Flammarian, the French astronomer, testifies to Moon planting: "Cucumbers increase at Full Moon, as well as radishes, turnips, leeks, lilies, horseradish, and saffron; onions, on the contrary, are much larger and better nourished during the decline and old age of the Moon than at its increase, during its youth and fullness, which is the reason the Egyptians abstained from onions, on account of their antipathy to the Moon. Herbs gathered while the Moon increases are of great efficiency. If the vines are trimmed at night when the Moon is in the sign of the Lion, Sagittarius, the Scorpion, or the Bull, it will save them from field rats, moles, snails, flies, and other animals."

Dr. Clark Timmins is one of the few modern scientists to have conducted tests in Moon planting. Following is a summary of his experiments:

Beets: When sown with the Moon in Scorpio, the germination rate was 71 percent; when sown in Sagittarius, the germination rate was 58 percent.

Scotch marigold: When sown with the Moon in Cancer, the germination rate was 90 percent; when sown in Leo, the rate was 32 percent.

Carrots: When sown with the Moon in Scorpio, the germination rate was 64 percent; when sown in Sagittarius, the germination rate was 47 percent.

Tomatoes: When sown with the Moon in Cancer, the germination rate was 90 percent; but when sown with the Moon in Leo, the germination rate was 58 percent.

Two things should be emphasized. First, remember that this is only a summary of the results of the experiments; the experiments themselves were conducted in a scientific manner to eliminate any variation in soil, temperature, moisture, and so on, so that only the Moon sign is varied. Second, note that these astonishing results were obtained without regard to the phase of the Moon—the other factor we use in Moon planting, and which presumably would have increased the differential in germination rates.

Further experiments by Dr. Timmins involved transplanting Cancer- and Leo-planted tomato seedlings while the Moon was increasing and in Cancer. The result was 100 percent survival. When transplanting was done with the Moon decreasing and in Sagittarius, there was 0 percent survival. The results of Dr. Timmins' tests show that the Cancer-planted tomatoes had blossoms twelve days earlier than those planted under Leo; the Cancer-planted tomatoes had an average height of twenty inches at that time compare to fifteen inches for the Leo-planted; the first ripe tomatoes were gathered from the Cancer plantings eleven days ahead of the Leo plantings; and a count of the hanging fruit and its size and weight shows an advantage to the Cancer plants over the Leo plants of 45 percent.

Dr. Timmins also observed that there have been similar tests that did not indicate results favorable to the Moon planting theory. As a scientist, he asked why one set of experiments indicated a positive verification of Moon planting, and others did not. He checked these other tests and found that the experimenters had not followed the geocentric system for determining the Moon sign positions, but the heliocentric. When the times used in these other tests were converted to the geocentric system, the dates chosen often were found to be in barren, rather than fertile, signs. Without going into a technical explanation, it is sufficient to point out that geocentric and heliocentric positions often vary by as much as four days. This is a large enough differential to place the Moon in Cancer, for example, in the heliocentric system, and at the same time in Leo by the geocentric system.

Most almanacs and calendars show the Moon's signs heliocentrically—and thus incorrectly for Moon planting—while the *Moon*

Sign Book is calculated correctly for planting purposes, using the geocentric system. Some readers are confused because the *Moon Sign Book* talks about first, second, third, and fourth quarters, while some almanacs refer to these same divisions as New Moon, first quarter, Full Moon, and fourth quarter. Thus the almanacs say first quarter when the *Moon Sign Book* says second quarter.

There is nothing complicated about using astrology in agriculture and horticulture in order to increase both pleasure and profit, but there is one very important rule that is often neglected—use common sense! Of course this is one rule that should be remembered in every activity we undertake, but in the case of gardening and farming by the Moon if it is not possible to use the best dates for planting or harvesting, we must select the next best and just try to do the best we can.

This brings up the matter of the other factors to consider in your gardening work. The dates we give as best for a certain activity apply to the entire country (with slight time correction), but in your section of the country you may be buried under three feet of snow on a date we say is good to plant your flowers. So we have factors of weather, season, temperature and moisture variations, soil conditions, your own available time and opportunity, and so forth. Some astrologers like to think it is all a matter of science, but gardening is also an art. In art, you develop an instinctive identification with your work and influence it with your feelings and wishes.

The *Moon Sign Book* gives you the place of the Moon for every day of the year so that you can select the best times once you have become familiar with the rules and practices of lunar agriculture. We give you specific, easy-to-follow directions so that you can get right down to work.

We give you the best dates for planting, and also for various related activities, including cultivation, fertilizing, harvesting, irrigation, and getting rid of weeds and pests. But we cannot tell you exactly when it's good to plant. Many of these rules were learned by observation and experience; as the body of experience grew we could see various patterns emerging that allowed us to make judgments about new things. That's what you should do, too. After you have worked with lunar agriculture for a while and have gained a working knowledge, you will probably begin to try new things—and we hope you will share your experiments and findings with us. That's how the science grows.

Here's an example of what we mean. Years ago, Llewellyn George suggested that we try to combine our bits of knowledge about what to expect in planting under each of the Moon signs in order to gain benefit from several lunar factors in one plant. From this came our rule for developing "thoroughbred seed." To develop thoroughbred seed, save the seed for three successive years from plants grown by the correct Moon sign and phase. You can plant in the first quarter phase and in the sign of Cancer for fruitfulness; the second year, plant seeds from the first year plants in Libra for beauty; and in the third year, plant the seeds from the second year plants in Taurus to produce hardiness. In a similar manner you can combine the fruitfulness of Cancer, the good root growth of Pisces, and the sturdiness and good vine growth of Scorpio. And don't forget the characteristics of Capricorn: hardy like Taurus, but drier and perhaps more resistant to drought and disease.

Unlike common almanacs, we consider both the Moon's phase and the Moon's sign in making our calculations for the proper timing of our work. It is perhaps a little easier to understand this if we remind you that we are all living in the center of a vast electromagnetic field that is the Earth and its environment in space. Everything that occurs within this electromagnetic field has an effect on everything else within the field. The Moon and the Sun are the most important of the factors affecting the life of the Earth, and it is their relative positions to the Earth that we project for each day of the year.

Many people claim that not only do they achieve larger crops gardening by the Moon, but that their fruits and vegetables are much tastier. A number of organic gardeners have also become lunar gardeners using the natural rhythm of life forces that we experience through the relative movements of the Sun and Moon. We provide a few basic rules and then give you day-by-day guidance for your gardening work. You will be able to choose the best dates to meet your own needs and opportunities.

Planting by the Moon's Phases

During the increasing or waxing light—from New Moon to Full Moon—plant annuals that produce their yield above the ground. An annual is a plant that completes its entire life cycle within one growing season and has to be seeded each year. During the decreasing or waning light—from Full Moon to New Moon—plant biennials, perennials, and bulb and root plants. Biennials include crops that are planted one season to winter over and produce crops the next, such as winter wheat. Perennials and bulb and root plants include all plants that grow from the same root each year.

A simpler, less-accurate rule is to plant crops that produce above the ground during the waxing Moon, and to plant crops that produce below the ground during the waning Moon. Thus the old adage "Plant potatoes during the dark of the Moon." Llewellyn George's system divided the lunar month into quarters. The first two from New Moon to Full Moon are the first and second quarters, and the last two from Full Moon to New Moon the third and fourth quarters. Using these divisions, we can increase our accuracy in timing our efforts to coincide with natural forces.

First Quarter

Plant annuals producing their yield above the ground, which are generally of the leafy kind that produce their seed outside the fruit. Some examples are asparagus, broccoli, Brussels sprouts, cabbage, cauliflower, celery, cress, endive, kohlrabi, lettuce, parsley, and spinach. Cucumbers are an exception, as they do best in the first quarter rather than the second, even though the seeds are inside the fruit. Also plant cereals and grains.

Second Quarter

Plant annuals producing their yield above the ground, which are generally of the viney kind that produce their seed inside the fruit. Some

examples include beans, eggplant, melons, peas, peppers, pumpkins, squash, tomatoes, etc. These are not hard-and-fast divisions. If you can't plant during the first quarter, plant during the second, and vice versa. There are many plants that seem to do equally well planted in either quarter, such as watermelon, hay, and cereals and grains.

Third Quarter

Plant biennials, perennials, and bulb and root plants. Also plant trees, shrubs, berries, beets, carrots, onions, parsnips, peanuts, potatoes, radishes, rhubarb, rutabagas, strawberries, turnips, winter wheat, grapes, etc.

Fourth Quarter

This is the best time to cultivate, turn sod, pull weeds, and destroy pests of all kinds, especially when the Moon is in the barren signs of Aries, Leo, Virgo, Gemini, Aquarius, and Sagittarius.

Moon in Aries

Barren, dry, fiery, and masculine sign used for destroying noxious weeds.

Moon in Taurus

Productive, moist, earthy, and feminine sign used for planting many crops when hardiness is important, particularly root crops. Also used for lettuce, cabbage, and similar leafy vegetables.

Moon in Gemini

Barren and dry, airy and masculine sign used for destroying noxious growths, weeds, and pests, and for cultivation.

Moon in Cancer

Fruitful, moist, feminine sign used extensively for planting and irrigation.

Moon in Leo

Barren, dry, fiery, masculine sign used only for killing weeds or for cultivation.

Moon in Virgo

Barren, moist, earthy, and feminine sign used for cultivation and destroying weeds and pests.

Moon in Libra

Semi-fruitful, moist, and airy, this sign is used for planting many crops, and producing good pulp growth and roots. A very good sign for flowers and vines. Also used for seeding hay, corn fodder, and the like.

Moon in Scorpio

Very fruitful and moist, watery and feminine. Nearly as productive as Cancer; used for the same purposes. Especially good for vine growth and sturdiness.

Moon in Sagittarius

Barren and dry, fiery and masculine. Used for planting onions, seeding hay, and for cultivation.

Moon in Capricorn

Productive and dry, earthy and feminine. Used for planting potatoes and other tubers.

Moon in Aquarius

Barren, dry, airy, and masculine sign used for cultivation and destroying noxious growths and pests.

Moon in Pisces

Very fruitful, moist, watery, and feminine sign especially good for root growth.

A Guide to Planting

Using Phase & Sign Rulerships

Plant	Phase/Quarter	Sign
Annuals	1st or 2nd	
Apple tree	2nd or 3rd	Cancer, Pisces, Taurus, Virgo
Artichoke	1st	Cancer, Pisces
Asparagus	1st	Cancer, Scorpio, Pisces
Aster	1st or 2nd	Virgo, Libra
Barley	1st or 2nd	Cancer, Pisces, Libra, Capricorn, Virgo
Beans (bush & pole)	2nd	Cancer, Taurus, Pisces, Libra
Beans (kidney, white, & navy)	1st or 2nd	Cancer, Pisces
Beech tree	2nd or 3rd	Virgo, Taurus
Beet	3rd	Cancer, Capricorn, Pisces, Libra
Biennials	3rd or 4th	
Broccoli	1st	Cancer, Pisces, Libra, Scorpio
Brussels sprout	1st	Cancer, Scorpio, Pisces, Libra
Buckwheat	1st or 2nd	Capricorn
Bulbs	3rd	Cancer, Scorpio, Pisces
Bulbs for seed	2nd or 3rd	
Cabbage	1st	Cancer, Scorpio, Pisces, Libra, Taurus

Plant	Phase/Quarter	Sign
Cactus		Taurus, Capricorn
Canes (raspberry, blackberry and gooseberry)	2nd	Cancer, Scorpio, Pisces
Cantaloupe	1st or 2nd	Cancer, Scorpio, Pisces, Libra, Taurus
Carrot	3rd	Taurus, Cancer, Scorpio, Pisces, Libra
Cauliflower	1st	Cancer, Scorpio, Pisces, Libra
Celeriac	3rd	Cancer, Scorpio, Pisces
Celery	1st	Cancer, Scorpio, Pisces
Cereals	1st or 2nd	Cancer, Scorpio, Pisces, Libra
Chard	1st or 2nd	Cancer, Scorpio, Pisces
Chicory	2nd, 3rd	Cancer, Scorpio, Pisces
Chrysanthemum	1st or 2nd	Virgo
Clover	1st or 2nd	Cancer, Scorpio, Pisces
Corn	1st	Cancer, Scorpio, Pisces
Corn for fodder	1st or 2nd	Libra
Coryopsis	2nd or 3rd	Libra
Cosmo	2nd or 3rd	Libra
Cress	1st	Cancer, Scorpio, Pisces
Crocus	1st or 2nd	Virgo
Cucumber	1st	Cancer, Scorpio, Pisces

Plant	Phase/Quarter	Sign
Daffodils	1st or 2nd	Libra, Virgo
Dahlias	1st or 2nd	Libra, Virgo
Deciduous tree	2nd or 3rd	Cancer, Scorpio, Pisces, Virgo, Taurus
Eggplant	2nd	Cancer, Scorpio, Pisces, Libra
Endive	1st	Cancer, Scorpio, Pisces, Libra
Flowers	1st	Libra, Cancer, Pisces, Virgo, Scorpio, Taurus
Garlic	3rd	Libra, Taurus, Pisces
Gladiola	1st or 2nd	Libra, Virgo
Gourd	1st or 2nd	Cancer, Scorpio, Pisces, Libra
Grape	2nd or 3rd	Cancer, Scorpio, Pisces, Virgo
Hay	1st or 2nd	Cancer, Scorpio, Pisces, Libra, Taurus
Herbs	1st or 2nd	Cancer, Scorpio, Pisces
Honeysuckle	1st or 2nd	Scorpio, Virgo
Hops	1st or 2nd	Scorpio, Libra
Horseradish	1st or 2nd	Cancer, Scorpio, Pisces
House plants	1st	Libra, Cancer, Scorpio, Pisces
Hyacinth	3rd	Cancer, Scorpio, Pisces
Iris	1st or 2nd	Cancer, Virgo
Kohlrabi	1st or 2nd	Cancer, Scorpio, Pisces, Libra

Plant	Phase/Quarter	Sign
Leek	1st or 2nd	Cancer, Pisces
Lettuce	1st	Cancer, Scorpio, Pisces, Libra, Taurus
Lily	1st or 2nd	Cancer, Scorpio, Pisces
Maple tree	2nd or 3rd	Virgo, Taurus, Cancer, Pisces
Melon	2nd	Cancer, Scorpio, Pisces
Moon vine	1st or 2nd	Virgo
Morning glory	1st or 2nd	Cancer, Scorpio, Pisces, Virgo
Oak Tree	2nd or 3rd	Virgo, Taurus, Cancer, Pisces
Oats	1st or 2nd	Cancer, Scorpio, Pisces, Libra
Okra	1st	Cancer, Scorpio, Pisces, Libra
Onion seed	2nd	Scorpio, Cancer, Sagittarius
Onion set	3rd or 4th	Libra, Taurus, Pisces, Cancer
Pansies	1st or 2nd	Cancer, Scorpio, Pisces
Parsley	1st	Cancer, Scorpio, Pisces, Libra
Parsnip	3rd	Taurus, Capricorn, Cancer, Scorpio, Capricorn
Peach tree	2nd or 3rd	Taurus, Libra, Virgo, Cancer
Peanut	3rd	Cancer, Scorpio, Pisces
Pear tree	2nd or 3rd	Taurus, Libra, Virgo, Cancer
Pea	2nd	Cancer, Scorpio, Pisces, Libra

Plant	Phase/Quarter	Sign
Peony	1st or 2nd	Virgo
Pepper	2nd	Cancer, Pisces, Scorpio
Perennials	3rd	
Petunias	1st or 2nd	Libra, Virgo
Plum tree	2nd or 3rd	Taurus, Virgo, Cancer, Pisces
Poppy	1st or 2nd	Virgo
Portulaca	1st or 2nd	Virgo
Potato	3rd	Cancer, Scorpio, Taurus, Libra, Capricorn
Privet	1st or 2nd	Taurus, Libra
Pumpkin	2nd	Cancer, Scorpio, Pisces, Libra
Quince	1st or 2nd	Capricorn
Radish	3rd	Cancer, Libra, Taurus, Pisces, Capricorn
Rhubarb	3rd	Cancer, Pisces
Rice	1st or 2nd	Scorpio
Rose	1st or 2nd	Cancer, Virgo
Rutabaga	3rd	Cancer, Scorpio, Pisces, Taurus
Saffron	1st or 2nd	Cancer, Scorpio, Pisces
Sage	3rd	Cancer, Scorpio, Pisces
Salsify	1st or 2nd	Cancer, Scorpio, Pisces

Plant	Phase/Quarter	Sign
Shallot	2nd	Scorpio
Spinach	1st	Cancer, Scorpio, Pisces
Squash	2nd	Cancer, Scorpio, Pisces, Libra
Strawberry	3rd	Cancer, Scorpio, Pisces
String bean	1st or 2nd	Taurus
Sunflower	1st or 2nd	Libra, Cancer
Sweet Pea	1st or 2nd	
Tomato	2nd	Cancer, Scorpio, Pisces, Capricorn
Shade tree	3rd	Taurus, Capricorn
Ornamental tree	2nd	Libra, Taurus
Trumpet vine	1st or 2nd	Cancer, Scorpio, Pisces
Tubers for seed	3rd	Cancer, Scorpio, Pisces, Libra
Tulip	1st or 2nd	Libra, Virgo
Turnip	3rd	Cancer, Scorpio, Pisces, Taurus, Capricorn, Libra
Valerian	1st or 2nd	Virgo, Gemini
Watermelon	1st or 2nd	Cancer, Scorpio, Pisces, Libra
Wheat	1st or 2nd	Cancer, Scorpio, Pisces, Libra

2003 Gardening Dates

Dates	Qtr.	Sign	Activity
Jan. 1, 6:42 pm- Jan. 2, 3:23 pm	4th	Capricorn	Plant potatoes and tubers. Trim to retard growth.
Jan. 2, 3:23 pm- Jan. 3, 10:56 pm	1st	Capricorn	Graft or bud plants. Trim to increase.
Jan. 6, 5:57 am- Jan. 8, 4:15 pm	1st	Pisces	Plant grains, leafy annuals. Fertilize (chemical). Graft or bud plants. Irrigate. Trim to increase growth.
Jan. 11, 4:48 am- Jan. 13, 5:08 pm	2nd	Taurus	Plant annuals for hardiness. Trim to increase growth.
Jan. 16, 2:56 am- Jan. 18, 5:48 am	2nd	Cancer	Plant grains, leafy annuals. Fertilize (chemical). Graft or bud plants. Irrigate. Trim to increase growth.
Jan. 18, 5:48 am- Jan. 18, 9:29 am	3rd	Cancer	Plant biennials, perennials, bulbs, and roots. Prune. Irrigate. Fertilize (organic).
Jan. 18, 9:29 am- Jan. 20, 1:32 pm	3rd	Leo	Cultivate. Destroy weeds and pests. Harvest fruits and root crops for food. Trim to retard growth.
Jan. 20, 1:32 pm- Jan. 22, 4:23 pm	3rd	Virgo	Cultivate, especially medicinal plants. Destroy weeds and pests. Trim to retard growth.
Jan. 24, 7:09 pm- Jan. 25, 3:33 am	3rd	Scorpio	Plant biennials, perennials, bulbs, and roots. Prune. Irrigate. Fertilize (organic).
Jan. 25, 3:33 am- Jan. 26, 10:26 pm	4th	Scorpio	Plant biennials, perennials, bulbs, and roots. Prune. Irrigate. Fertilize (organic).
Jan. 26, 10:26 pm- Jan. 29, 2:30 am	4th	Sagittarius	Cultivate. Destroy weeds and pests. Harvest fruits and root crops for food. Trim to retard growth.
Jan. 29, 2:30 am- Jan. 31, 7:44 am	4th	Capricorn	Plant potatoes and tubers. Trim to retard growth.
Jan. 31, 7:44 am- Feb. 1, 5:48 am	4th	Aquarius	Cultivate. Destroy weeds and pests. Harvest fruits and root crops for food. Trim to retard growth.
Feb. 2, 2:55 pm- Feb. 5, 12:44 am	1st	Pisces	Plant grains, leafy annuals. Fertilize (chemical). Graft or bud plants. Irrigate. Trim to increase growth.
Feb. 7, 12:59 pm- Feb. 9, 6:11 am	1st	Taurus	Plant annuals for hardiness. Trim to increase growth.
Feb. 9, 6:11 am- Feb 10, 1:45 am	2nd	Taurus	Plant annuals for hardiness. Trim to increase growth.
Feb. 12, 12:19 pm- Feb. 14, 7:04 pm	2nd	Cancer	Plant grains, leafy annuals. Fertilize (chemical). Graft or bud plants. Irrigate. Trim to increase growth.
Feb. 16, 6:51 pm- Feb. 16, 10:22 pm	3rd	Leo	Cultivate. Destroy weeds and pests. Harvest fruits and root crops for food. Trim to retard growth.

2003 Gardening Dates

Dates	Qtr.	Sign	Activity
Feb. 16, 10:22 pm- Feb. 18, 11:48 pm	3rd	Virgo	Cultivate, especially medicinal plants. Destroy weeds and pests. Trim to retard growth.
Feb. 21, 1:09 am- Feb. 23, 3:46 am	3rd	Scorpio	Plant biennials, perennials, bulbs, and roots. Prune. Irrigate. Fertilize (organic).
Feb. 23, 3:46 am- Feb. 23, 11:46 am	3rd	Sagittarius	Cultivate. Destroy weeds and pests. Harvest fruits and root crops for food. Trim to retard growth.
Feb. 23, 11:46 am- Feb. 25, 8:11 am	4th	Sagittarius	Cultivate. Destroy weeds and pests. Harvest fruits and root crops for food. Trim to retard growth.
Feb. 25, 8:11 am- Feb. 27, 2:24 pm	4th	Capricorn	Plant potatoes and tubers. Trim to retard growth.
Feb. 27, 2:24 pm- Mar. 1, 10:26 pm	4th	Aquarius	Cultivate. Destroy weeds and pests. Harvest fruits and root crops for food. Trim to retard growth.
Mar. 1, 10:26 pm- Mar. 2, 9:35 pm	4th	Pisces	Plant biennials, perennials, bulbs, and roots. Prune. Irrigate. Fertilize (organic).
Mar. 2, 9:35 pm- Mar. 4, 8:30 am	1st	Pisces	Plant grains, leafy annuals. Fertilize (chemical). Graft or bud plants. Irrigate. Trim to increase growth.
Mar. 6, 8:36 pm- Mar. 9, 9:38 am	1st	Taurus	Plant annuals for hardiness. Trim to increase growth.
Mar. 11, 9:12 pm- Mar. 14, 5:06 am	2nd	Cancer	Plant grains, leafy annuals. Fertilize (chemical). Graft or bud plants. Irrigate. Trim to increase growth.
Mar. 18, 5:35 am- Mar. 18, 9:43 am	3rd	Virgo	Cultivate, especially medicinal plants. Destroy weeds and pests. Trim to retard growth.
Mar. 20, 9:38 am- Mar. 22, 10:33 am	3rd	Scorpio	Plant biennials, perennials, bulbs, and roots. Prune. Irrigate. Fertilize (organic).
Mar. 22, 10:33 am- Mar. 24, 1:48 pm	3rd	Sagittarius	Cultivate. Destroy weeds and pests. Harvest fruits and root crops for food. Trim to retard growth.
Mar. 24, 1:48 pm- Mar. 24, 8:51 pm	3rd	Capricorn	Plant potatoes and tubers. Trim to retard growth.
Mar. 24, 8:51 pm- Mar. 26, 7:51 pm	4th	Capricorn	Plant potatoes and tubers. Trim to retard growth.
Mar. 26, 7:51 pm- Mar. 29, 4:26 am	4th	Aquarius	Cultivate. Destroy weeds and pests. Harvest fruits and root crops for food. Trim to retard growth.
Mar. 29, 4:26 am- Mar. 31, 3:04 pm	4th	Pisces	Plant biennials, perennials, bulbs, and roots. Prune. Irrigate. Fertilize (organic).
Mar. 31, 3:04 pm- Apr. 1, 2:19 pm	4th	Aries	Cultivate. Destroy weeds and pests. Harvest fruits and root crops for food. Trim to retard growth.

2003 Gardening Dates

Dates	Qtr.	Sign	Activity
Apr. 3, 3:20 am- Apr. 5, 4:24 pm	1st	Taurus	Plant annuals for hardiness. Trim to increase growth.
Apr. 8, 4:36 am- Apr. 9, 6:40 pm	1st	Cancer	Plant grains, leafy annuals. Fertilize (chemical). Graft or bud plants. Irrigate. Trim to increase growth.
Apr. 9, 6:40 pm- Apr. 10, 1:54 pm	2nd	Cancer	Plant grains, leafy annuals. Fertilize (chemical). Graft or bud plants. Irrigate. Trim to increase growth.
Apr. 14, 8:42 pm- Apr. 16, 2:36 pm	2nd	Libra	Plant annuals for fragrance and beauty. Trim to increase growth.
Apr. 16, 8:16 pm- Apr. 18, 7:51 pm	3rd	Scorpio	Plant biennials, perennials, bulbs, and roots. Prune. Irrigate. Fertilize (organic).
Apr. 18, 7:51 pm- Apr. 20, 9:20 pm	3rd	Sagittarius	Cultivate. Destroy weeds and pests. Harvest fruits and root crops for food. Trim to retard growth.
Apr. 20, 9:20 pm- Apr. 23, 1:58 am	3rd	Capricorn	Plant potatoes and tubers. Trim to retard growth.
Apr. 23, 1:58 am- Apr. 23, 7:18 am	3rd	Aquarius	Cultivate. Destroy weeds and pests. Harvest fruits and root crops for food. Trim to retard growth.
Apr. 23, 7:18 am- Apr. 25, 10:02 am	4th	Aquarius	Cultivate. Destroy weeds and pests. Harvest fruits and root crops for food. Trim to retard growth.
Apr. 25, 10:02 am- Apr. 27, 8:54 pm	4th	Pisces	Plant biennials, perennials, bulbs, and roots. Prune. Irrigate. Fertilize (organic).
Apr. 27, 8:54 pm- Apr. 30, 9:26 am	4th	Aries	Cultivate. Destroy weeds and pests. Harvest fruits and root crops for food. Trim to retard growth.
Apr. 30, 9:26 am- May 1, 7:15 am	4th	Taurus	Plant potatoes and tubers. Trim to retard growth.
May 1, 7:15 am- May 2, 10:27 pm	1st	Taurus	Plant annuals for hardiness. Trim to increase growth.
May 5, 10:42 am- May 7, 8:46 pm	1st	Cancer	Plant grains, leafy annuals. Fertilize (chemical). Graft or bud plants. Irrigate. Trim to increase growth.
May 12, 6:42 am- May 14, 7:14 am	2nd	Libra	Plant annuals for fragrance and beauty. Trim to increase growth.
May 14, 7:14 am- May 15, 10:36 pm	2nd	Scorpio	Plant grains, leafy annuals. Fertilize (chemical). Graft or bud plants. Irrigate. Trim to increase growth.
May 15, 10:36 pm- May 16, 6:43 am	3rd	Scorpio	Plant biennials, perennials, bulbs and roots. Prune. Irrigate. Fertilize (organic).
May 16, 6:43 am- May 18, 7:03 am	3rd	Sagittarius	Cultivate. Destroy weeds and pests. Harvest fruits and root crops for food. Trim to retard growth.
May 18, 7:03 am- May 20, 10:01 am	3rd	Capricorn	Plant potatoes and tubers. Trim to retard growth.

2003 Gardening Dates

Dates	Qtr.	Sign	Activity
May 20, 10:01 am– May 22, 4:41 pm	3rd	Aquarius	Cultivate. Destroy weeds and pests. Harvest fruits and root crops for food. Trim to retard growth.
May 22, 4:41 pm– May 22, 7:31 pm	3rd	Pisces	Plant biennials, perennials, bulbs, and roots. Prune. Irrigate. Fertilize (organic).
May 22, 7:31 pm– May 25, 2:59 am	4th	Pisces	Plant biennials, perennials, bulbs and roots. Prune. Irrigate. Fertilize (organic).
May 25, 2:59 am– May 27, 3:32 pm	4th	Aries	Cultivate. Destroy weeds and pests. Harvest fruits and root crops for food. Trim to retard growth.
May 27, 3:32 pm– May 30, 4:32 am	4th	Taurus	Plant potatoes and tubers. Trim to retard growth.
May 30, 4:32 am– May 30, 11:20 pm	4th	Gemini	Cultivate. Destroy weeds and pests. Harvest fruits and root crops for food. Trim to retard growth.
Jun. 1, 4:27 pm– Jun. 4, 2:25 am	1st	Cancer	Plant grains, leafy annuals. Fertilize (chemical). Graft or bud plants. Irrigate. Trim to increase growth.
Jun. 8, 2:30 pm– Jun. 10, 4:39 pm	2nd	Libra	Plant annuals for fragrance and beauty. Trim to increase growth.
Jun. 10, 4:39 pm– Jun. 12, 5:12 pm	2nd	Scorpio	Plant grains, leafy annuals. Fertilize (chemical). Graft or bud plants. Irrigate. Trim to increase growth.
Jun. 14, 5:38 pm– Jun. 16, 7:41 pm	3rd	Capricorn	Plant potatoes and tubers. Trim to retard growth.
Jun. 16, 7:41 pm– Jun. 19, 12:57 am	3rd	Aquarius	Cultivate. Destroy weeds and pests. Harvest fruits and root crops for food. Trim to retard growth.
Jun. 19, 12:57 am– Jun. 21, 9:45 am	3rd	Pisces	Plant biennials, perennials, bulbs and roots. Prune. Irrigate. Fertilize (organic).
Jun. 21, 9:45 am– Jun. 21, 10:06 am	4th	Pisces	Plant biennials, perennials, bulbs, and roots. Prune. Irrigate. Fertilize (organic).
Jun. 21, 10:06 am– Jun. 23, 10:15 pm	4th	Aries	Cultivate. Destroy weeds and pests. Harvest fruits and root crops for food. Trim to retard growth.
Jun. 23, 10:15 pm– Jun. 26, 11:13 am	4th	Taurus	Plant potatoes and tubers. Trim to retard growth.
Jun. 26, 11:13 am– Jun. 28, 10:52 pm	4th	Gemini	Cultivate. Destroy weeds and pests. Harvest fruits and root crops for food. Trim to retard growth.
Jun. 28, 10:52 pm– Jun. 29, 1:39 pm	4th	Cancer	Plant biennials, perennials, bulbs, and roots. Prune. Irrigate. Fertilize (organic).
Jun. 29, 1:39 pm– Jul. 1, 8:13 am	1st	Cancer	Plant grains, leafy annuals. Fertilize (chemical). Graft or bud plants. Irrigate. Trim to increase growth.
Jul. 5, 8:20 pm– Jul. 6, 9:32 pm	1st	Libra	Plant annuals for fragrance and beauty. Trim to increase growth.

2003 Gardening Dates

Dates	Qtr.	Sign	Activity
Jul. 6, 9:32 pm- Jul. 7, 11:43 pm	2nd	Libra	Plant annuals for fragrance and beauty. Trim to increase growth.
Jul. 7, 11:43 pm- Jul. 10, 1:48 am	2nd	Scorpio	Plant grains, leafy annuals. Fertilize (chemical). Graft or bud plants. Irrigate. Trim to increase growth.
Jul. 12, 3:21 am- Jul. 13, 2:21 pm	2nd	Capricorn	Graft or bud plants. Trim to increase growth.
Jul. 13, 2:21 pm- Jul. 14, 5:38 am	3rd	Capricorn	Plant potatoes and tubers. Trim to retard growth.
Jul. 14, 5:38 am- Jul. 16, 10:14 am	3rd	Aquarius	Cultivate. Destroy weeds and pests. Harvest fruits and root crops for food. Trim to retard growth.
Jul. 16, 10:14 am- Jul. 18, 6:20 pm	3rd	Pisces	Plant biennials, perennials, bulbs, and roots. Prune. Irrigate. Fertilize (organic).
Jul. 18, 6:20 pm- Jul. 21, 2:01 am	3rd	Aries	Cultivate. Destroy weeds and pests. Harvest fruits and root crops for food. Trim to retard growth.
Jul. 21, 2:01 am- Jul. 21, 5:48 am	4th	Aries	Cultivate. Destroy weeds and pests. Harvest fruits and root crops for food. Trim to retard growth.
Jul. 21, 5:48 am- Jul. 23, 6:42 pm	4th	Taurus	Plant potatoes and tubers. Trim to retard growth.
Jul. 23, 6:42 pm- Jul. 26, 6:23 am	4th	Gemini	Cultivate. Destroy weeds and pests. Harvest fruits and root crops for food. Trim to retard growth.
Jul. 26, 6:23 am- Jul. 28, 3:17 am	4th	Cancer	Plant biennials, perennials, bulbs, and roots. Prune. Irrigate. Fertilize (organic).
Jul. 28, 3:17 pm- Jul. 29, 1:53 am	4th	Leo	Cultivate. Destroy weeds and pests. Harvest fruits and root crops for food. Trim to retard growth.
Aug. 2, 1:48 am- Aug. 4, 5:12 am	1st	Libra	Plant annuals for fragrance and beauty. Trim to increase growth.
Aug. 4, 5:12 am- Aug. 5, 2:28 am	1st	Scorpio	Plant grains, leafy annuals. Fertilize (chemical). Graft or bud plants. Irrigate. Trim to increase growth.
Aug. 5, 2:28 am- Aug. 6, 8:11 am	2nd	Scorpio	Plant grains, leafy annuals. Fertilize (chemical). Graft or bud plants. Irrigate. Trim to increase growth.
Aug. 8, 11:02 am- Aug. 10, 2:23 pm	2nd	Capricorn	Graft or bud plants. Trim to increase growth.
Aug. 12, 7:19 pm- Aug. 15, 3:00 am	3rd	Pisces	Plant biennials, perennials, bulbs, and roots. Prune. Irrigate. Fertilize (organic).
Aug. 15, 3:00 am- Aug. 17, 1:52 pm	3rd	Aries	Cultivate. Destroy weeds and pests. Harvest fruits and root crops for food. Trim to retard growth.

2003 Gardening Dates

Dates	Qtr.	Sign	Activity
Aug. 17, 1:52 pm- Aug. 19, 7:48 pm	3rd	Taurus	Plant potatoes and tubers. Trim to retard growth.
Aug. 19, 7:48 pm- Aug. 20, 2:41 am	4th	Taurus	Plant potatoes and tubers. Trim to retard growth.
Aug. 20, 2:41 am- Aug. 22, 2:44 pm	4th	Gemini	Cultivate. Destroy weeds and pests. Harvest fruits and root crops for food. Trim to retard growth.
Aug. 22, 2:44 pm- Aug. 24, 11:48 pm	4th	Cancer	Plant biennials, perennials, bulbs, and roots. Prune. Irrigate. Fertilize (organic).
Aug. 24, 11:48 pm- Aug. 27, 5:27 am	4th	Leo	Cultivate. Destroy weeds and pests. Harvest fruits and root crops for food. Trim to retard growth.
Aug. 27, 5:27 am- Aug. 27, 12:26 pm	4th	Virgo	Cultivate, especially medicinal plants. Destroy weeds and pests. Trim to retard growth.
Aug. 29, 8:41 am- Aug. 31, 11:00 am	1st	Libra	Plant annuals for fragrance and beauty. Trim to increase growth.
Aug. 31, 11:00 am- Sep. 2, 1:32 pm	1st	Scorpio	Plant grains, leafy annuals. Fertilize (chemical). Graft or bud plants. Irrigate. Trim to increase growth.
Sep. 4, 4:51 pm- Sep. 6, 9:15 pm	2nd	Capricorn	Graft or bud plants. Trim to increase growth.
Sep. 9, 3:07 am- Sep. 10, 11:36 am	2nd	Pisces	Plant grains, leafy annuals. Fertilize (chemical). Graft or bud plants. Irrigate. Trim to increase growth.
Sep. 10, 11:36 am- Sep. 11, 11:09 am	3rd	Pisces	Plant biennials, perennials, bulbs, and roots. Prune. Irrigate. Fertilize (organic).
Sep. 11, 11:09 am- Sep. 13, 9:50 pm	3rd	Aries	Cultivate. Destroy weeds and pests. Harvest fruits and root crops for food. Trim to retard growth.
Sep. 13, 9:50 pm- Sep. 16, 10:32 am	3rd	Taurus	Plant potatoes and tubers. Trim to retard growth.
Sep. 16, 10:32 am- Sep. 18, 2:03 pm	3rd	Gemini	Cultivate. Destroy weeds and pests. Harvest fruits and root crops for food. Trim to retard growth.
Sep. 18, 2:03 pm- Sep. 18, 11:07 pm	4th	Gemini	Cultivate. Destroy weeds and pests. Harvest fruits and root crops for food. Trim to retard growth.
Sep. 18, 11:07 pm- Sep. 21, 9:02 am	4th	Cancer	Plant biennials, perennials, bulbs and roots. Prune. Irrigate. Fertilize (organic).
Sep. 21, 9:02 am- Sep. 23, 3:04 pm	4th	Leo	Cultivate. Destroy weeds and pests. Harvest fruits and root crops for food. Trim to retard growth.
Sep. 23, 3:04 pm- Sep. 25, 5:49 pm	4th	Virgo	Cultivate, especially medicinal plants. Destroy weeds and pests. Trim to retard growth.

2003 Gardening Dates

Dates	Qtr.	Sign	Activity
Sep. 25, 10:09 pm- Sep. 27, 6:52 pm	1st	Libra	Plant annuals for fragrance and beauty. Trim to increase growth.
Sep. 27, 6:52 pm- Sep. 29, 7:57 pm	1st	Scorpio	Plant grains, leafy annuals. Fertilize (chemical). Graft or bud plants. Irrigate. Trim to increase growth.
Oct. 1, 10:21 pm- Oct. 2, 2:09 pm	1st	Capricorn	Graft or bud plants. Trim to increase growth.
Oct. 2, 2:09 pm- Oct. 4, 2:45 am	2nd	Capricorn	Graft or bud plants. Trim to increase growth.
Oct. 6, 9:20 am- Oct. 8, 6:07 pm	2nd	Pisces	Plant grains, leafy annuals. Fertilize (chemical). Graft or bud plants. Irrigate. Trim to increase growth.
Oct. 10, 2:27 am- Oct. 11, 5:05 am	3rd	Aries	Cultivate. Destroy weeds and pests. Harvest fruits and root crops for food. Trim to retard growth.
Oct. 11, 5:05 am- Oct. 13, 5:45 pm	3rd	Taurus	Plant potatoes and tubers. Trim to retard growth.
Oct. 13, 5:45 pm- Oct. 16, 6:41 am	3rd	Gemini	Cultivate. Destroy weeds and pests. Harvest fruits and root crops for food. Trim to retard growth.
Oct. 16, 6:41 am- Oct. 18, 7:31 am	3rd	Cancer	Plant biennials, perennials, bulbs, and roots. Prune. Irrigate. Fertilize (organic).
Oct. 18, 5:41 pm- Oct. 20, 1:01 am	4th	Leo	Cultivate. Destroy weeds and pests. Harvest fruits and root crops for food. Trim to retard growth.
Oct. 21, 1:01 am- Oct. 23, 4:27 am	4th	Virgo	Cultivate, especially medicinal plants. Destroy weeds and pests. Trim to retard growth.
Oct. 25, 5:08 am- Oct. 25, 7:50 pm	4th	Scorpio	Plant biennials, perennials, bulbs, and roots. Prune. Irrigate. Fertilize (organic).
Oct. 25, 7:50 pm- Oct. 27, 4:55 am	1st	Scorpio	Plant grains, leafy annuals. Fertilize (chemical). Graft or bud plants. Irrigate. Trim to increase growth.
Oct. 29, 5:37 am- Oct. 31, 8:41 am	1st	Capricorn	Graft or bud plants. Trim to increase growth.
Nov. 2, 2:52 pm- Nov. 5, 12:02 am	2nd	Pisces	Plant grains, leafy annuals. Fertilize (chemical). Graft or bud plants. Irrigate. Trim to increase growth.
Nov. 7, 11:29 am- Nov. 8, 8:13 pm	2nd	Taurus	Plant annuals for hardiness. Trim to increase growth.
Nov. 8, 8:13 pm- Nov. 10, 12:14 am	3rd	Taurus	Plant potatoes and tubers. Trim to retard growth.
Nov. 10, 12:14 am- Nov. 12, 1:10 pm	3rd	Gemini	Cultivate. Destroy weeds and pests. Harvest fruits and root crops for food. Trim to retard growth.
Nov. 12, 1:10 pm- Nov. 15, 12:48 am	3rd	Cancer	Plant biennials, perennials, bulbs, and roots. Prune. Irrigate. Fertilize (organic).

2003 Gardening Dates

Dates	Qtr.	Sign	Activity
Nov. 15, 12:48 am- Nov. 16, 11:15 pm	3rd	Leo	Cultivate. Destroy weeds and pests. Harvest fruits and root crops for food. Trim to retard growth.
Nov. 16, 11:15 pm- Nov. 17, 9:36 am	4th	Leo	Cultivate. Destroy weeds and pests. Harvest fruits and root crops for food. Trim to retard growth.
Nov. 17, 9:36 am- Nov. 19, 2:42 pm	4th	Virgo	Cultivate, especially medicinal plants. Destroy weeds and pests. Trim to retard growth.
Nov. 21, 4:24 pm- Nov. 23, 4:02 pm	4th	Scorpio	Plant biennials, perennials, bulbs, and roots. Prune. Irrigate. Fertilize (organic).
Nov. 23, 4:02 pm- Nov. 23, 5:59 pm	4th	Sagittarius	Cultivate. Destroy weeds and pests. Harvest fruits and root crops for food. Trim to retard growth.
Nov. 25, 3:31 pm- Nov. 27, 4:48 pm	1st	Capricorn	Graft or bud plants. Trim to increase growth.
Nov. 29, 9:25 pm- Nov. 30, 12:16 pm	1st	Pisces	Plant grains, leafy annuals. Fertilize (chemical). Graft or bud plants. Irrigate. Trim to increase growth.
Nov. 30, 12:16 pm- Dec. 2, 5:56 am	2nd	Pisces	Plant grains, leafy annuals. Fertilize (chemical). Graft or bud plants. Irrigate. Trim to increase growth.
Dec. 4, 5:30 pm- Dec. 7, 6:26 am	2nd	Taurus	Plant annuals for hardiness. Trim to increase growth.
Dec. 8, 3:37 pm- Dec. 9, 7:11 pm	3rd	Gemini	Cultivate. Destroy weeds and pests. Harvest fruits and root crops for food. Trim to retard growth.
Dec. 9, 7:11 pm- Dec. 12, 6:40 am	3rd	Cancer	Plant biennials, perennials, bulbs, and roots. Prune. Irrigate. Fertilize (organic).
Dec. 12, 6:40 am- Dec. 14, 4:07 pm	3rd	Leo	Cultivate. Destroy weeds and pests. Harvest fruits and root crops for food. Trim to retard growth.
Dec. 14, 4:07 pm- Dec. 16, 12:42 pm	3rd	Virgo	Cultivate, especially medicinal plants. Destroy weeds and pests. Trim to retard growth.
Dec. 16, 12:42 pm- Dec. 16, 10:46 pm	4th	Virgo	Cultivate, especially medicinal plants. Destroy weeds and pests. Trim to retard growth.
Dec. 19, 2:20 am- Dec. 21, 3:16 am	4th	Scorpio	Plant biennials, perennials, bulbs and roots. Prune. Irrigate. Fertilize (organic).
Dec. 21, 3:16 am- Dec. 23, 2:55 am	4th	Sagittarius	Cultivate. Destroy weeds and pests. Harvest fruits and root crops for food. Trim to retard growth.
Dec. 23, 2:55 am- Dec. 23, 4:43 am	4th	Capricorn	Plant potatoes and tubers. Trim to retard growth.
Dec. 23, 4:43 am- Dec. 25, 3:13 am	1st	Capricorn	Graft or bud plants. Trim to increase growth.
Dec. 27, 6:10 am- Dec. 29, 1:08 pm	1st	Pisces	Plant grains, leafy annuals. Fertilize (chemical). Graft or bud plants. Irrigate. Trim to increase growth.

2003 Dates to Destroy Weeds and Pests

Jan. 18	9:29 am	Jan. 20	1:32 pm	Leo	3rd
Jan. 20	1:32 pm	Jan. 22	4:23 pm	Virgo	3rd
Jan. 26	10:26 pm	Jan. 29	2:30 am	Sagittarius	4th
Jan. 31	7:44 am	Feb. 1	5:48 am	Aquarius	4th
Feb. 16	6:51 pm	Feb. 16	10:22 pm	Leo	3rd
Feb. 16	10:22 pm	Feb. 18	11:48 pm	Virgo	3rd
Feb. 23	3:46 am	Feb. 23	11:46 am	Sagittarius	3rd
Feb. 23	11:46 am	Feb. 25	8:11 am	Sagittarius	4th
Feb. 27	2:24 pm	Mar. 1	10:26 pm	Aquarius	4th
Mar. 18	5:35 am	Mar. 18	9:43 am	Virgo	3rd
Mar. 22	10:33 am	Mar. 24	1:48 pm	Sagittarius	3rd
Mar. 26	7:51 pm	Mar. 29	4:26 am	Aquarius	4th
Mar. 31	3:04 pm	Apr. 1	2:19 pm	Aries	4th
Apr. 18	7:51 pm	Apr. 20	9:20 pm	Sagittarius	3rd
Apr. 23	1:58 am	Apr. 23	7:18 am	Aquarius	3rd
Apr. 23	7:18 am	Apr. 25	10:02 am	Aquarius	4th
Apr. 27	8:54 pm	Apr. 30	9:26 am	Aries	4th
May 16	6:43 am	May 18	7:03 am	Sagittarius	3rd
May 20	10:01 am	May 22	4:41 pm	Aquarius	3rd
May 25	2:59 am	May 27	3:32 pm	Aries	4th
May 30	4:32 am	May 30	11:20 pm	Gemini	4th
Jun. 14	6:16 am	Jun. 14	5:38 pm	Sagittarius	3rd
Jun. 16	7:41 pm	Jun. 19	12:57 am	Aquarius	3rd
Jun. 21	10:06 am	Jun. 23	10:15 pm	Aries	4th
Jun. 26	11:13 am	Jun. 28	10:52 pm	Gemini	4th
Jul. 14	5:38 am	Jul. 16	10:14 am	Aquarius	3rd
Jul. 18	6:20 pm	Jul. 21	2:01 am	Aries	3rd

2003 Dates to Destroy Weeds and Pests

Jul. 21	2:01 am	Jul. 21	5:48 am	Aries	4th
Jul. 23	6:42 pm	Jul. 26	6:23 am	Gemini	4th
Jul. 28	3:17 pm	Jul. 29	1:53 am	Leo	4th
Aug. 11	11:48 pm	Aug. 12	7:19 pm	Aquarius	3rd
Aug. 15	3:00 am	Aug. 17	1:52 pm	Aries	3rd
Aug. 20	2:41 am	Aug. 22	2:44 pm	Gemini	4th
Aug. 24	11:48 pm	Aug. 27	5:27 am	Leo	4th
Aug. 27	5:27 am	Aug. 27	12:26 pm	Virgo	4th
Sep. 11	11:09 am	Sep. 13	9:50 pm	Aries	3rd
Sep. 16	10:32 am	Sep. 18	2:03 pm	Gemini	3rd
Sep. 18	2:03 pm	Sep. 18	11:07 pm	Gemini	4th
Sep. 21	9:02 am	Sep. 23	3:04 pm	Leo	4th
Sep. 23	3:04 pm	Sep. 25	5:49 pm	Virgo	4th
Oct. 10	2:27 am	Oct. 11	5:05 am	Aries	3rd
Oct. 13	5:45 pm	Oct. 16	6:41 am	Gemini	3rd
Oct. 18	5:41 pm	Oct. 21	1:01 am	Leo	4th
Oct. 21	1:01 am	Oct. 23	4:27 am	Virgo	4th
Nov. 10	12:14 am	Nov. 12	1:10 pm	Gemini	3rd
Nov. 15	12:48 am	Nov. 16	11:15 pm	Leo	3rd
Nov. 16	11:15 pm	Nov. 17	9:36 am	Leo	4th
Nov. 17	9:36 am	Nov. 19	2:42 pm	Virgo	4th
Nov. 23	4:02 pm	Nov. 23	5:59 pm	Sagittarius	4th
Dec. 8	3:37 pm	Dec. 9	7:11 pm	Gemini	3rd
Dec. 12	6:40 am	Dec. 14	4:07 pm	Leo	3rd
Dec. 14	4:07 pm	Dec. 16	12:42 pm	Virgo	3rd
Dec. 16	12:42 pm	Dec. 16	10:46 pm	Virgo	4th
Dec. 21	3:16 am	Dec. 23	2:55 am	Sagittarius	4th

2003 Egg Setting Dates

Dates to be Born	Sign	Qtr.	Set Eggs
Jan. 6 5:57 am-Jan. 8 4:15 pm	Pisces	1st	Dec. 16
Jan. 11 4:48 am-Jan. 13 5:08 pm	Taurus	2nd	Dec. 21
Jan. 16 2:56 am-Jan. 18 5:48 am	Cancer	2nd	Dec. 26
Feb. 2 2:55 pm-Feb. 5 12:44 am	Pisces	1st	Jan. 12
Feb. 7 12:59 pm-Feb. 9 6:11 am	Taurus	1st	Jan. 17
Feb. 12 12:19 pm-Feb. 14 7:04 pm	Cancer	2nd	Jan 22
Mar. 2 9:35 pm-Mar. 4 8:30 am	Pisces	1st	Feb. 9
Mar. 6 8:36 pm-Mar. 9 9:38 am	Taurus	1st	Feb. 13
Mar. 11 9:12 pm-Mar. 14 5:06 am	Cancer	2nd	Feb. 18
Apr. 3 3:20 am-Apr. 5 4:24 pm	Taurus	1st	Mar. 13
Apr. 8 4:36 am-Apr. 9 6:40 pm	Cancer	1st	Mar. 18
Apr. 14 8:42 pm-Apr. 16 2:36 pm	Libra	2nd	Mar. 24
May 1 7:15 am-May 2 10:27 pm	Taurus	1st	Apr. 10
May 5 10:42 am-May 7 8:46 pm	Cancer	1st	Apr. 14
May 12 6:42 am-May 14 7:14 am	Libra	2nd	Apr. 21
Jun. 1 4:27 pm-Jun. 4 2:25 am	Cancer	1st	May 11
Jun. 8 2:30 pm-Jun. 10 4:39 pm	Libra	2nd	May 18
Jun. 29 1:39 pm-Jul. 1 8:13 am	Cancer	1st	Jun. 8
Jul. 5 8:20 pm-Jul. 6 9:32 pm	Libra	1st	Jun. 14
Aug. 2 1:48 am-Aug. 4 5:12 am	Libra	1st	Jul. 12
Aug. 29 8:41 am-Aug. 31 11:00 am	Libra	1st	Aug. 8
Sep. 9 3:07 am-Sep. 10 11:36 am	Pisces	2nd	Aug. 19
Sep. 25 10:09 pm-Sep. 27 6:52 pm	Libra	1st	Sep. 4
Oct. 6 9:20 am-Oct. 8 6:07 pm	Pisces	2nd	Sep. 15
Nov. 2 2:52 pm-Nov. 5 12:02 am	Pisces	2nd	Oct. 12
Nov. 7 11:29 am-Nov. 8 8:13 pm	Taurus	2nd	Oct. 17
Nov. 29 9:25 pm-Nov. 30 12:16 pm	Pisces	1st	Nov. 8
Dec. 4 5:30 pm-Dec. 7 6:26 am	Taurus	2nd	Nov. 13
Dec. 27 6:10 am-Dec. 29 1:08 pm	Pisces	1st	Dec. 6

Companion Planting Guide

Plant Helpers and Hinderers

Plant	Helped By	Hindered By
Asparagus	Tomato, parsley, basil	
Bean	Carrot, cucumber, cabbage, beet, corn	Onion,
Bush bean	Cucumber, cabbage, strawberry	Fennel, onion
Beet	Onion, cabbage, lettuce	Pale bean
Cabbage	Beet, potato, onion, celery	Strawberry, tomato
Carrot	Pea, lettuce, chive, radish, leek, onion	Dill
Celery	Leek, bush bean	
Chive	Bean	
Corn	Potato, bean, pea, melon, squash, pumpkin, cucumber	
Cucumber	Bean, cabbage, radish, sunflower, lettuce	Potato, herbs
Eggplant	Bean	
Lettuce	Strawberry, carrot	
Melon	Morning glory	
Onion, leek	Beet, chamomile, carrot, lettuce	Pea, bean
Garlic	Summer savory	
Pea	Radish, carrot, corn cumumber, bean, turnip	Onion
Potato	Bean, corn, pea, cabbage, hemp, cucumber	Sunflower

Plant	Helped By	Hindered By
Radish	Pea, Lettuce, Nasturtium, Cucumbers	Hyssop
Spinach	Strawberry	
Squash, Pumpkin	Nasturtium, Corn	Potatoes
Tomatoes	Asparagus, Parsley, Chives, Onions, Carrot, Marigold, Nasturtium	Dill, Cabbage, Fennel
Turnip	Pea, Bean	

Plant Companions and Uses

Plant	Companions and Uses
Anise	Coriander
Basil	Tomato; dislikes rue; repels flies and mosquitos
Borage	Tomato and squash
Buttercup	Clover; hinders delphinium, peony, monkshood, columbine
Chamomile	Helps peppermint, wheat, onions, and cabbage; large amounts destructive
Catnip	Repels flea beetles
Chervil	Radish
Chives	Carrot; prone to apple scab and powdery mildew
Coriander	Hinders seed formation in fennel
Cosmos	Repels corn earworms
Dill	Cabbage; hinders carrot and tomato
Fennel	Disliked by all garden plants
Garlic	Aids vetch and roses; hinders peas and beans
Hemp	Beneficial as a neighbor to most plants
Horseradish	Repels potato bugs

Plant	Companions and Uses
Horsetail	Makes fungicide spray
Hyssop	Attracts cabbage fly away from cabbages; harmful to radishes
Lovage	Improves hardiness and flavor of neighbor plants
Marigold	Pest repellent; use against Mexican bean beetles and nematodes
Mint	Repels ants, flea beetles and cabbage worm butterflies
Morning glory	Corn; helps melon germination
Nasturtium	Cabbage, cucumbers; deters aphids, squash bugs, and pumpkin beetles
Nettle	Increase oil content in neighbors
Parsley	Tomatoes, asparagus
Purslane	Good ground cover
Rosemary	Repels cabbage moths, bean beetles, and carrot flies
Sage	Repels cabbage moths and carrot flies
Savory	Deters bean beetles
Sunflower	Hinders potatoes; improves soil
Tansy	Deters Japanese beetles, striped cucumber beetles, and squash bugs
Thyme	Repels cabbage worms
Yarrow	Increases essential oils of neighbors

2003 Weather Forecast

By Kris Brandt Riske

P eople relied on astrology to forecast weather for thousands of years. They were able to predict drought, floods, and temperature variations through interpreting planetary alignments. In recent years there has been a renewed interest in astrometeorology, the ancient branch of astrology that focuses on weather forecasting. Unlike meteorology, which at best can forecast weather trends a week in advance, astrometeorology is limitless. A weather forecast can be composed for any date—tomorrow, next week, or a thousand years in the future. Astrometeorology reveals seasonal and weekly weather trends based on the cardinal ingresses (Summer and Winter Solstices, and Spring and Fall Equinoxes) and the four monthly quarterly lunar phases in combination with the transiting planets. According to astrometeorolgy, each planet governs certain weather phenomena. When certain planets are aligned with other planets, weather—precipitation, cloudy or clear skies, tornados, hurricanes, and other weather conditions—is generated.

Sun and Moon

The Sun governs the constitution of the weather and, like the Moon, it serves as a trigger for other planetary configurations that results in weather events. When the Sun is prominent in a cardinal ingress or lunar phase chart, the area is often warm and sunny. The Moon can bring or withhold moisture, depending upon its sign placement.

Mercury

Mercury is also a triggering planet, but its main influence is wind direction and velocity. In its stationary periods, Mercury reflects high winds, and its influence is always prominent in major weather events, such as hurricanes and tornados, when it tends to lower the temperature.

Venus

Venus governs moisture, clouds, and humidity. It brings warming trends that produce sunny, pleasant weather if in positive aspect to other planets. In some signs—Libra, Virgo, Gemini, Sagittarius—Venus is drier. It is at its wettest when placed in Cancer, Scorpio, Pisces, or Taurus.

Mars

Mars is associated with heat, drought, and wind and can raise the temperature to record-setting levels when in a fire sign (Aries, Leo, Sagittarius). Mars also provides the spark that generates thunderstorms and is prominent in tornado and hurricane configurations.

Jupiter

Jupiter, a fair weather planet, tends toward higher temperatures when in Aries, Leo, or Sagittarius. It is associated with high-pressure systems and is a contributing factor at times to dryness. Storms are often amplified by Jupiter.

Saturn

Saturn is associated with low-pressure systems, cloudy to overcast skies, and excessive precipitation. Temperatures drop when Saturn is involved. Major winter storms always have a strong Saturn influence, as do storms that produce a slow, steady downpour for hours or days.

Uranus

Like Jupiter, Uranus indicates high-pressure systems. It reflects descending cold air and, when prominent, is responsible for a jet stream that extends far south. Uranus can bring drought in winter, and it is involved in thunderstorms, tornados and hurricanes.

Neptune

Neptune is the wettest planet. It signals low-pressure systems and is dominant when hurricanes are in the forecast. When Neptune is strongly placed, flood danger is high. It's often associated with winter thaws.

Temperatures, humidity, and cloudiness increase where Neptune influences weather.

Pluto

Pluto is associated with weather extremes, as well as unseasonably warm temperatures and drought. It reflects the high winds involved in major hurricanes, storms, and tornados.

SEASONAL FORECASTS

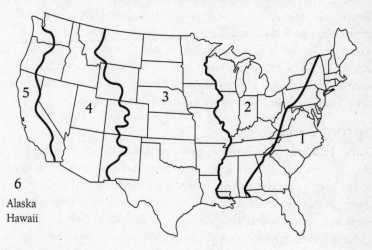

Winter 2003

Zone 1: Winter storms deliver snow—abundant at times—in the northeast, creating high flood potential in low-lying areas. Be alert to unseasonably warm conditions; some signal moisture-laden southerly winds. Precipitation in the mid-Atlantic states ranges from normal to above, with heaviest downfalls occurring on the coast and in the Carolinas. Temperatures fluctuate under cloudy skies, but are generally seasonal. Conditions are mostly seasonal in the Southeast, but warmer, drier weather prevails inland.

Zone 2: Moisture levels throughout the zone range from dry to seasonal. Some areas see major winter storms, and the northeast receives abundant precipitation. Central areas are cloudy, cold, and at times frigid, with northern air dipping far south. Western areas are more seasonal, with some dryness.

Zone 3: Wind and above normal temperatures contribute to dryness and drought potential in the eastern Plains. Similar conditions influence the central and western Plains, but temperatures are more seasonal. Southern areas see more clouds and precipitation; and wind is a factor in Texas, Colorado, and New Mexico. Overcast skies and major storms with strong winds are the norm in Montana and the foothills, where temperatures are below normal.

Zone 4: Storms, overcast skies, and temperatures ranging from above to below normal are the dominant weather pattern in the west. Northern areas of the zone experience more precipitation than areas to the south, and are cooler than the desert Southwest. Wind is a factor in Washington, Oregon, Montana, and Idaho.

Zone 5: The West Coast experiences mostly seasonal weather. Periods of damp, cold rain alternate with warm, dry, sunny days, especially in California, where wind and higher temperatures prevail.

Zone 6: Overall winter conditions in Alaska are very wet, cold, and stormy. Flood potential in coastal areas is high during periods of above-normal temperatures. Hawaii also sees abundant moisture under overcast skies, but with below normal temperatures. Both states are windy.

Spring 2003

Zone 1: Winds prevail in the northern half of the zone, while cloudy skies dominate in central and southern areas. Temperatures are seasonal to above, and very warm and dry to the north in late April.

Zone 2: Western areas of the zone are warm and sunny, with higher temperatures south. Overall conditions are dry with drought potential. Central and eastern sections are cooler and more humid; the east sees more precipitation and storm potential.

Zone 3: Temperatures range from normal to above in the northwest and mountains, where conditions are dry overall with drought potential; major storms bring some precipitation. The western Plains see precipitation, temperatures from normal to above, and mostly sunny, windy, skies. In the central Plains, precipitation is normal to below and mostly sunny to partly cloudy. Cloudy skies are more prevalent to the south, along with warmer temperatures. The northern tier of states is cooler. Tornado potential is low because of a lack of moisture-laden storms. The eastern Plains are warm and sunny.

Zone 4: Temperatures throughout the zone vary from above to below normal. Dryness and drought potential are prevalent in some areas, while others see cloudy skies and windy storms.

Zone 5: Temperatures are unseasonably warm and dry throughout the zone with high winds in the southern deserts that increase drought potential.

Zone 6: Although cooler and cloudy in April, overall conditions in

Hawaii are unseasonably wet and warm with significant precipitation and wind in May. Central and eastern portions of Alaska see abundant precipitation; temperatures are seasonal to cool with fog in coastal areas. A warming trend in May signals thawing and flood potential.

Summer 2003

Zone 1: Conditions are mostly seasonal to cool, dry, and sunny. Southern areas see more cloudiness and chance of precipitation.

Zone 2: Generally, temperatures are seasonal to above; cool to the east. Precipitation potential is highest east and west, an area that sees scattered thunderstorms and tornado warnings.

Zone 3: The western Plains see cloudy, wet weather with a high probability of tornados and storms with high winds. The northwest portion of the zone is drier, as are the Plains, which see little precipitation until later in the season, when rising temperatures lead to an increase in moisture and cloudiness.

Zone 4: Chances of precipitation are higher in the deserts, where humidity rises, bringing an active monsoon season, and in the eastern mountains, where cloudy, wet conditions are the result of major storms with high winds. Other areas of the zone are dry with drought potential.

Zone 5: Temperatures are normal to above with varied humidity. Although precipitation is heavy at times, dryness prevails. Coastal areas, where conditions are windy and major storm potential is high, see the best chance of precipitation. Drier south.

Zone 6: Hawaii is wet, humid, cloudy, and cooler, with significant precipitation. Alaska is cloudy and cool. Storms bring high levels of precipitation to the east and central, while moisture levels are more seasonal in the western portion of the state.

Autumn 2003

Zone 1: Fair, cool, dry weather prevails in the northeast, and areas to the south are warm and humid with precipitation seasonal to below.

Zone 2: Overall, conditions are warm and dry, but potential exists for periodic major storms in western and central areas of the zone. Wind dominates the autumn season, and clouds are variable. Humidity rises to the east, where the chance of precipitation is higher.

Zone 3: Cool temperatures in the northwest; stormy, cool in the Rockies and western Plains. Warm, humid, and variable cloudiness on the Plains, while wind and cloudiness increases storm potential to the east.

Zone 4: Precipitation and cool temperatures are the norm throughout the zone, but eastern areas see cooler temperatures and more storms. Cloudy skies prevail to the south and east.

Zone 5: Northern areas are cool and cloudy with increased precipitation; drier, warmer conditions prevail to the south. Wind is a factor throughout the zone.

Zone 6: Hawaii is warm, humid, and wet, as cloudy, overcast skies deliver significant precipitation, followed by cooler temperatures. Similar weather dominates in Alaska, where precipitation is heaviest in central areas of the state. Temperatures are seasonal to above in most areas, but cooler in the midsection because of storms.

Monthly Forecasts

January 1–9

Zone 1: Weather is seasonal throughout northern and central areas, and windy in the mid-Atlantic states. Stormy conditions lower temperatures to the south, with possible freeze warnings in Florida.

Zone 2: Brilliant skies form a backdrop to warm dry weather in the western part of the zone, with a chance of showers on the Gulf. Areas to the east are colder and overcast, with precipitation.

Zone 3: The northwest is stormy, cloudy, and windy. In the Plains, seasonal to below-normal temperatures and variable cloudiness prevail. Eastern states are cloudy, with locally heavy precipitation.

Zone 4: Weather is cloudy, windy, and cool with precipitation. The Rockies see significant snowfall and falling temperatures.

Zone 5: Wind, variable cloudiness and seasonal temperatures dominate, with precipitation and fog to the north. Southern California sees high winds, with warmer temperatures later in the week and a chance for precipitation.

Zone 6: Hawaii is warm and windy, with clear to partly cloudy skies and brief showers. Temperatures are seasonal to above in Alaska, along with gusty winds in central portions of the state.

January 10–17

Zone 1: New England is partly cloudy and seasonal, with winds picking up by week's end as a front moves through the area. Precipitation is heavy northeast and in the mid-Atlantic states, where prime storm conditions could prompt an off-season tornado. The southeast is partly cloudy and windy, with a chance of showers under seasonal to cool temperatures.

Zone 2: Western portions of the zone are cloudy to overcast with precipitation, some locally heavy, later in the week. Temperatures are seasonal midzone, cooler to the east. Wind and partly cloudy skies signal a chance for precipitation.

Zone 3: Winds blow into Montana and western Plains, cooling temperatures under variably cloudy skies that bring precipitation. The Plains see calmer, more seasonal to cool weather, with a chance for moisture. Areas to the east are cloudy and damp, with a chance for snow and rain midweek.

Zone 4: Wind and clouds, with a chance for precipitation, cool but otherwise pleasant temperatures to the east. Weather to the north and west is seasonal, but colder in the mountains with a chance for moisture. Winds increase later in the week.

Zone 5: Weather is mild with precipitation to the north. Southern California is cooler, with variable cloudiness, precipitation, and fog in coastal areas. A warming trend follows.

Zone 6: Eastern portions of Hawaii are warm and mild with showers, but an approaching front cools temperatures. Winds prevail to the west. Western Alaska is cold. Weather is seasonal to the east until a front moves through the area bringing precipitation, increasing winds and falling temperatures.

January 18–24

Zone 1: Seasonal temperatures in the northeast contrast with cooler areas to the south, primarily due to cloudiness. Precipitation is scattered.

Zone 2: Western and central areas are windy, cloudy, and damp. Eastern portions of the zone are drier, cool, and partly cloudy to cloudy.

Zone 3: Montana could see precipitation at week's end, but conditions are generally dry. In the western Plains, temperatures dip with overcast skies and scattered precipitation. The central and eastern Plains are sunny to partly cloudy and cool to the north, with a better chance for precipitation midzone.

Zone 4: The desert is warm and dry in contrast. Temperatures are seasonal to chilly to the north, and wind prevails. Some areas see abundant rain as a front moves eastward through the area by week's end.

Zone 5: Northern areas are windy and mostly fair and cool as precipitation moves away from the coast and travels inland, bringing increasing cloudiness. Southern areas are windy and cool.

Zone 6: Hawaii is mostly fair under a warming trend, but with scattered showers. Seasonal conditions are the norm in Alaska, except to the east where cloudy skies signal moisture.

January 25–31

Zone 1: The northeast is cold, windy, and mostly fair, but areas south are under overcast skies and see significant precipitation.

Zone 2: The western part of the zone is windy and damp; cooler to the north with scattered precipitation. Other areas are overcast, and conditions are ripe for a major storm with excess precipitation.

Zone 3: The northwest part of the zone sees cloudy skies, cooler temperatures and precipitation. The western plains and mountains are cold, windy, and stormy, as are the central and eastern Plains as a front moves east.

Zone 4: Overcast skies yield abundant precipitation in the west as a major snowfall blankets the area. Eastern areas of the zone are seasonal with increasing cloudiness as stormy conditions move into the area.

Zone 5: Partly cloudy to cloudy skies accompany precipitation, and some areas see significant downfall, particularly to the south and inland. Temperatures range from seasonal to above.

Zone 6: Hawaii is seasonal with scattered showers. Eastern Alaska is windy and cool, and the west is warmer with fog and precipitation later in the week.

February 1–8

Zone 1: Wind, clouds, and precipitation are the zone's main conditions, with the heaviest downfall in the mid-Atlantic region, where skies are overcast and flood potential is high. Temperatures are seasonal to above.

Zone 2: Variable cloudiness and cool throughout the zone, with scattered precipitation in middle and eastern sections. Western states are windy.

Zone 3: The northwest is seasonal and dry, while the central Plains are windy and clear with rising temperatures that lead to thawing. Clouds are variable in the western Plains.

Zone 4: Eastern areas are seasonal and dry with rising temperatures. Clouds blanket the west, where precipitation, some locally heavy, is the norm.

Zone 5: Wind is the dominant weather factor in northern areas, where temperatures are seasonal to cool. California is cool under overcast skies with some locally heavy precipitation, especially inland. Expect fog in coastal areas.

Zone 6: Hawaii is warm with scattered showers. Alaska is windy, cold, and clear to partly cloudy with warmer temperatures to the west.

February 9–15

Zone 1: Temperatures drop following stormy weather in the windy northern areas. Seasonal to cool temperatures and scattered precipitation with variable cloudiness to the south.

Zone 2: Conditions are favorable for precipitation throughout the zone, as is the potential for abundant moisture in western areas, where skies are overcast. Variable cloudiness with precipitation will prevail to the east; where temperatures are seasonal to above.

Zone 3: Temperatures are seasonal in the northwest; wind and partly cloudy skies dominate the foothills. The Plains are fair, windy, and dry, but the eastern Plains see some precipitation as the week progresses.

Zone 4: The zone is mostly dry and clear with precipitation in the windy west at the end of the week.

Zone 5: Showers, some locally heavy, are prevalent inland and to the south. Temperatures are seasonal to above.

Zone 6: Temperatures are mixed in Hawaii. Expect cool in the east, warm in the west with rain later in the week. Eastern and central Alaska is chilled by a front that moves across the state, bringing precipitation and wind.

February 16–22

Zone 1: Cold, overcast skies signal stormy conditions in New England and the northeastern states. Weather to the south is milder, with some precipitation and high humidity.

Zone 2: Precipitation accompanied by cold northerly winds produces snow, sleet, and freezing rain, with the coldest temperatures to the west.

Zone 3: Increasing cloudiness and wind signal an approaching low-pressure system that brings abundant precipitation to the mountains and western areas. Clouds build in the Plains, where conditions are cold and damp as the storm continues its eastward path. The eastern Plains are very cold.

Zone 4: A storm moves out of the northwest and through the zone, bringing a low-pressure system with precipitation, buffeting winds, and falling temperatures.

Zone 5: The West Coast is cool, dry, and windy; variable cloudiness primarily to the north.

Zone 6: Winds pick up in Hawaii under variable clouds, particularly in the eastern islands, which see showers and cloudbursts. Central Alaska is stormy, with high winds, overcast, and cold as a front moves eastward.

February 23–28

Zone 1: Cold temperatures over much of the stormy East Coast. Out-of-season tornados are possible in the mid-Atlantic states. Areas to the south are cloudy and wet.

Zone 2: Warmer temperatures result in a thaw and precipitation that raises river and stream levels in the Mississippi Valley. Flood danger is high throughout western areas of the zone as a cold front moves east. Cool, overcast conditions with precipitation prevail to the east.

Zone 3: Expect precipitation and cooler temperatures in western Plains by week's end, while central Plains are mostly cool and dry with scattered precipitation. Cloudy and warmer to the south and east where flood danger is high.

Zone 4: Precipitation, which is heaviest in the Rockies, and cloudy to partly cloudy skies are prevalent throughout the zone as a front moves across the area, bringing cooler temperatures. Areas to the south are mostly fair and warm, with some scattered precipitation.

Zone 5: Temperatures are seasonal to above with patchy fog; winds pick up inland and to the south, where skies are partly cloudy to cloudy with cooler temperatures and showers.

Zone 6: Hawaii is warm, mild, and partly cloudy with scattered showers. Heavy precipitation in central Alaska moves east as a front crosses the state. Temperatures are seasonal to above; fog develops along the coast.

March 1–10

Zone 1: The northeast and mid-Atlantic states are seasonal to cool and cloudy, with snow, rain, and sleet—some heavy. Farther south, conditions are seasonal and cloudy with showers.

Zone 2: Dry, cold weather dominates the zone; skies are partly cloudy in the central region. Precipitation centers east, where temperatures are cold.

Zone 3: Northwest winds blow across the zone, bringing precipitation and colder temperatures to the northwest and western Plains. Areas to the east are partly cloudy to fair and cool.

Zone 4: Windy conditions prevail as a storm approaches from the west, bringing cloudy skies, precipitation and cooler temperatures. Moisture is significant in the western portions of the zone.

Zone 5: Precipitation, overcast skies, and much cooler temperatures prevail inland and south as a storm front moves through the zone.

Zone 6: Hawaii is seasonal with showers and then warmer. Alaska is windy, cool, and cloudy, with precipitation—some locally heavy—in central and eastern areas. Eastern Alaska is cold and stormy with high winds.

March 11–17

Zone 1: Wind contributes to cool temperatures throughout the zone. Areas to the south see increasing cloudiness and precipitation.

Zone 2: Temperatures are seasonal to warm, and humidity rises as clouds increase, bringing precipitation to western and central areas of the zone. Eastern areas are seasonal to cool, with wind and variable cloudiness.

Zone 3: Weather is pleasant to the northwest, becoming cooler and windy later in the week. Mountain areas and the western Plains are overcast, cold, and stormy. Precipitation moves into the central Plains, bringing cooler temperatures, while eastern parts of the zone are warmer and drier with variable cloudiness.

Zone 4: Scattered precipitation and wind cover the western areas of the zone, with lower temperatures in the mountains. The front moves east, bringing cooler conditions later in the week. Areas to the south are warm and dry.

Zone 5: Temperatures are seasonal to cool under the influence of a cold wave accompanied by variable cloudiness and wind. Southern areas are warmer and mostly fair.

Zone 6: Hawaii is windy with increasing clouds, cooler temperatures and precipitation. Western Alaska is warmer and drier than areas to the cloudy east, where abundant precipitation increases flood potential.

March 18–23

Zone 1: Wind prevails in the northeast and mid-Atlantic states under cool, overcast skies, signaling an approaching storm. The southeast is fair and seasonal with a chance of precipitation. Florida sees scattered thunderstorms.

Zone 2: Temperatures are seasonal to above in western areas. Although mostly dry, there is a chance of precipitation later in the week. Look for higher precipitation to the east, along with warm temperatures.

Zone 3: The northwest, mountains, and foothills are windy as a front moves through the area, bringing cloudy skies and precipitation. Temperatures are seasonal to cool. The central Plains are windy, warm, and sunny to partly cloudy until a front brings precipitation and cooler temperatures to the area.

Zone 4: Sunny, windy, and normal to above temperatures throughout the area. Thawing in the mountains increases flood risk. Temperatures are seasonal to the south, increasing at week's end after clouds and precipitation dissipate.

Zone 5: Seasonal and temperate across the zone; areas to the north are windy with a chance of showers; southern areas are windy, warm, and partly cloudy with a chance for showers.

Zone 6: Hawaii has precipitation to the east, while conditions to the west are warmer, drier, and partly cloudy. Temperatures are seasonal in Alaska, with scattered precipitation and fog in southern coastal areas.

Week of March 24–31

Zone 1: Northern and central areas are fair and cool, with heavy precipitation later in the week. Warm and windy conditions prevail to the south, where sunny to partly cloudy skies signal generally fair weather.

Zone 2: Western areas are partly cloudy and cool. Colder temperatures prevail to the east, where conditions are fair, breezy, and sunny to partly cloudy. Southern areas are warmer and mostly dry.

Zone 3: Western areas are very windy and unseasonably warm until a front moves into the mountains, foothills, and western Plains, bringing scattered thunderstorms and cooler temperatures. Heat rises in the central Plains by week's end, when weather is fair and dry.

Zone 4: Temperatures are seasonal to above in the east and hot in the desert, with gusty winds, cloudy skies, and scattered showers. Areas to the west are windy with a chance for precipitation.

Zone 5: Cool inland with a chance of precipitation and warmer on the coast with fog. Skies are partly cloudy to cloudy.

Zone 6: Windy, showers, thunderstorms, and cooler in Hawaii. Western and central areas of Alaska receive precipitation, some heavy, under an advancing cold front. Eastern areas are drier and cold later in the week.

April 1–8

Zone 1: Northern skies are fair to partly cloudy and breezy, with rising temperatures there and in the mid-Atlantic states. Southern areas get showers and thunderstorms, some locally heavy with tornado potential.

Zone 2: A front approaches from the west, bringing showers and thunderstorms, some locally heavy. Tornado potential is high in western areas of the zone. Temperatures are seasonal to above throughout the zone. Humidity rises in central and eastern areas, which also see precipitation and the possibility of flooding.

Zone 3: Warm temperatures in the west are gradually replaced by high winds as an advancing front moves into the central Plains, generating cloudy skies, precipitation, and tornado potential.

Zone 4; Rising temperatures signal dryness sand sunny skies—especially in desert areas. Humidity rises in some areas.

Zone 5: Northern areas are cool and cloudy to overcast with precipitation and fog. Southern portions of the zone are warm and dry, especially inland.

Zone 6; Hawaii is breezy and partly cloudy, with little precipitation; temperatures gradually warm. Winds accelerate in central and eastern Alaska as a storm front moves through the area after delivering abundant moisture to western areas, where flood potential is high. Fog is prevalent in coastal areas.

April 9–15

Zone 1: Seasonal conditions in the northeast, with a chance of showers. Areas to the south are hot with variable cloudiness, showers, and thunderstorms that could spawn tornados.

Zone 2: Temperatures and humidity rise, sparking showers and thunderstorms with high tornado potential, followed by cooler air.

Zone 3: Overcast skies, windy with precipitation northwest. Dry, windy, seasonal temperatures, and more cloudiness on the Plains and to the south.

Zone 4: The desert is hot and above normal temperatures exist throughout the zone until a windy storm front moves across the area, bringing cloudy skies and abundant precipitation.

Zone 5: The zone is warm and dry with rising temperatures as the week progresses. The southern deserts are hot, but with precipitation in coastal areas.

Zone 6: Hawaii is windy, partly cloudy to cloudy, warm and humid, with increased wetness midweek. A windy front with locally heavy precipitation moves through central and eastern Alaska under cloudy skies. Temperatures are seasonal to warm, with fog in coastal areas.

April 16–22

Zone 1: Heat and humidity rise to the north, and southern areas see a warming trend throughout the week.

Zone 2: Western areas are partly cloudy and warm, with a chance for showers. Thunderstorms build to the east, with rising temperatures, as the week progresses.

Zone 3: Dryness and above normal temperatures prevail to the west. The foothills and western and northern Plains are cloudy with precipitation as a front moves through the area and into the central and eastern Plains. Southern areas are variably cloudy and warm with scattered showers and thunderstorms.

Zone 4: Above normal temperatures and dryness dominate western areas of the zone, with some cloudiness to the north. The desert is hot and dry, but the east is more temperate.

Zone 5: Weather to the north is seasonal with fog and a chance of precipitation. Temperatures rise to the south, where dryness prevails.

Zone 6: Hawaii is warm and mild with showers and thunderstorms. In Alaska, precipitation centers east under stormy, overcast skies and cool temperatures.

April 23–30

Zone 1: The northeast is warm, windy, and partly cloudy with a chance of precipitation. Areas south are windy and warm with scattered thunderstorms; the southeast is hot and very humid with locally heavy precipitation.

Zone 2: Thunderstorms build to the west midweek as heat and humidity rise. Central and eastern areas are humid, but not as warm because of some cloudiness and scattered thunderstorms.

Zone 3: Much of the zone is seasonal, fair, dry, and windy. The Plains are warmer, especially to the east.

Zone 4: Mostly fair and seasonal, northern areas see precipitation late in the week. Southern portions of the zone are dry and fair.

Zone 5: Although mostly fair and warm, scattered showers and fog are possible throughout the zone. Southern areas are very windy.

Zone 6: Hawaii is warm and mostly dry, with scattered showers. Alaska is seasonal to warm, dry, and fair; the midsection receives precipitation.

May 1–8

Zone 1: Maine is cool, and much of the northeast has a chance for showers. Scattered thunderstorms prevail in the mid-Atlantic states, and the southeast is windy and seasonal with showers later in the week.

Zone 2: High heat and humidity produce severe thunderstorms with tornado potential in western and central areas. Temperatures are cooler to the east, where it is windy and receiving scattered showers.

Zone 3: Windy, dry weather dominates the zone. Temperatures are seasonal to above. Severe thunderstorms develop in the eastern Plains.

Zone 4: Breezy, dry weather prevails throughout the zone, along with temperatures that range from normal to above.

Zone 5: Conditions are seasonal but windy, with temperatures ranging from normal to above in northern portions of the zone. Fair and seasonal weather follows showers and some fogginess to the south.

Zone 6: Hawaii is warm, dry, and fair. Alaska is mostly dry and seasonal, but temperatures rise midstate, as does the chance for precipitation.

May 9–14

Zone 1: The northeast is cool with showers, while areas to the south are hot and mostly dry under fair to partly cloudy skies; there's a chance for showers in the southeast.

Zone 2: Threat of tornadoes and severe thunderstorms in western areas of the zone. Heat prevails throughout much of the zone. The east has scattered showers.

Zone 3: Showers and seasonal temperatures in the northwest and western Plains, which are hot and dry. Severe thunderstorms and tornado warnings to the east.

Zone 4: Seasonal temperatures prevail; northern and mountainous regions are windy with scattered showers.

Zone 5: Weather is warm and seasonal with some humidity and fog; areas south are windy and dry.

Zone 6: Although humid, Hawaii is mostly dry, fair, sunny, and warm. Temperatures rise in Alaska, where weather is generally fair.

May 15–21

Zone 1: Cloudy skies bring showers to much of the zone; the southeast is drier and warmer. Winds bring lower temperatures in the northeast.

Zone 2: Most of the zone is hot and dry, with increasing cloudiness and showers to the east.

Zone 3: Overcast skies bring precipitation to the northwest and mountains, where temperatures are seasonal to above. The Plains are hot and dry, but muggy with scattered thunderstorms.

Zone 4: Seasonal and fair in mountains areas; cloudy to overcast conditions, heat and humid with thunderstorms prevail east and south.

Zone 5: Conditions in northern areas are seasonal but windy, as a front moves through the area. A chance for showers exist to the south, where temperatures are warmer, as they are inland throughout most of the zone.

Zone 6: Hot and humid in Hawaii, with a chance for cloudbursts later in the week. Southern areas of Alaska are warm and windy; northern areas are cool; clouds and locally heavy precipitation prevail midstate.

May 22–31

Zone 1: The northeast is windy, wet, and overcast, as are the mid-Atlantic states. Temperatures rise to the south, and the southeast is drier, but with a chance for showers.

Zone 2: Weather is seasonal to cool throughout much of the zone; warmer east with showers. Thunderstorms are likely to the west at week's end.

Zone 3: The west is dry with above normal temperatures, changing to showers and thunderstorms later in the week. The Plains are cooler, mostly dry, and partly cloudy, except for eastern areas, where thunderstorms could generate tornadoes.

Zone 4: As a front moves through the area, abundant precipitation could produce flash floods in the mountains and to the west. Eastern areas are hot and humid, with showers later in the week.

Zone 5: Skies are variably cloudy with showers to the south and inland, where temperatures are warmer. The remainder of the zone is seasonal and partly cloudy.

Zone 6: Increasing clouds in Hawaii could result in scattered showers, but the state is mostly warm and dry, although humid. Western Alaska is cool under an eastward moving front that brings precipitation; warmer, drier weather prevails to the east.

June 1–6

Zone 1: Heat generates scattered thunderstorms throughout much of the zone, with the most severe occurring in the southeast. Tornadoes are possible.

Zone 2: Heat and humidity rise; showers and thunderstorms develop throughout the zone.

Zone 3: Northwest is sunny with increasing temperatures; mountains and western Plains are partly cloudy and slightly cooler. In the Plains, temperatures and humidity are above normal. There is little precipitation except to the east, where severe thunderstorms with tornado potential develop.

Zone 4: Dryness and above normal temperatures rule. Temperatures to the east and south rise as the week progresses.

Zone 5: Above normal temperatures and dryness prevail throughout the zone, which is mostly sunny. Southern areas see some cloudiness.

Zone 6: Seasonal to cool weather is the norm in Hawaii. Cool weather dominates all but western areas of Alaska, where conditions are fair and warm; showers center to the east.

June 7–13

Zone 1: The northeast and southeast are warm and humid with showers and scattered thunderstorms. Other areas are mostly dry and hot.

Zone 2: Wind and dryness accompany seasonal to above temperatures. Scattered precipitation and variable cloudiness cover the east.

Zone 3: The northwest is cloudy with scattered showers, and the Plains are hot, windy and humid with scattered thunderstorms.

Zone 4: Temperatures are above normal, and skies are variably cloudy, especially in the mountains. Showers are scattered, but some are locally heavy.

Zone 5: Sunny, hot weather prevails, with some cloudiness to the south.

Zone 6: Hawaii is breezy and warm with a chance of precipitation. Central and eastern Alaska are very windy as a storm front moves through the state.

June 14–20

Zone 1: The northeast is overcast, humid, and receiving scattered showers. Muggy weather prevails in the mid-Atlantic states, and areas to the south and inland are hot and dry.

Zone 2: Conditions are humid and seasonal to cool in all but the east, where there are scattered showers.

Zone 3: The northwest and western Plains are mostly hot and dry with some cloudiness and a chance of showers. Severe thunderstorms with high tornado potential develop in the Plains, followed by cooler temperatures.

Zone 4: Showers and thunderstorms, some heavy, center north and in the mountains. Temperatures are seasonal to above in the desert, which is dry with scattered clouds.

Zone 5: Northern areas see showers, thunderstorms, and variably cloudy skies. Rising temperatures are seasonal to above throughout the zone.

Zone 6: Skies are variably cloudy and temperatures are seasonal in Hawaii, with a chance of showers. Seasonal conditions prevail in Alaska, except for midstate, where it is warmer.

June 21–28

Zone 1: Weather is seasonal to the south, and hot with scattered thunderstorms to the north.

Zone 2: Heat prevails throughout most of the zone, but conditions to the east are more seasonal. Western and central areas are muggy; thunderstorms, some severe, carry with tornado potential and significant downfall.

Zone 3: The northwest and western Plains are seasonal and dry, turning warm and windy later in the week. Scattered thunderstorms, some severe with tornado potential, build in the Plains, which are hot under variably cloudy skies.

Zone 4: Heat to the north and in the mountains sparks thunderstorms with high winds. Seasonal temps, but dry with winds picking up midweek in south.

Zone 5: Northern areas are partly cloudy to cloudy and cool with a chance of precipitation later in the week. Warmer, mostly fair but humid conditions prevail to the south.

Zone 6: Hawaii is warm to the west, cool to the east with thunderstorms and high winds. A major storm in central Alaska moves eastward; warm to west.

June 29–30

Zone 1: Mostly partly cloudy and dry, temperatures are seasonal to above throughout the zone.

Zone 2: Scattered thunderstorms and heat prevail in all but eastern portions of the zone, where weather is cooler.

Zone 3: The northwest is hot and windy with scattered showers, and the Rockies and western Plains receive significant precipitation. The Plains are hot with scattered thunderstorms.

Zone 4: Scattered showers to the north and in the mountains provide some relief from the heat. Humidity rises to the south, and eastern areas see precipitation, which is heavy in some areas.

Zone 5: Temperatures rise, especially to the south; overall conditions are dry and windy.

Zone 6: Hawaii is hot, humid, and partly cloudy to cloudy, with showers. Much of Alaska is wet, especially western portions of the state.

July 1–6

Zone 1: Seasonal temperatures and partly cloudy skies prevail. The zone has little chance for precipitation.

Zone 2: Western areas are hot and humid, but lack precipitation. Cooler weather prevails to the east.

Zone 3: The northwest is hot and dry with a chance of showers early in the week. Overcast skies bring significant rain, and possible snow in the mountains and western Plains; falling temperatures follow. The central Plains are hot with scattered thunderstorms, some severe with high winds.

Zone 4: Northern areas are mostly hot and dry. Southern and eastern areas are windy and wet, followed by cooler temperatures.

Zone 5: Although skies are partly cloudy, heat and dryness could result in drought conditions.

Zone 6: Hawaii is windy; heat and humidity produce significant precipitation. Rising temperatures bring fog and scattered showers to Alaska.

July 7–12

Zone 1: The northeast is seasonal and humid. Rising heat and humidity to the south generate scattered thunderstorms.

Zone 2: Seasonal weather prevails, with showers and thunderstorms in western and central areas of the zone; temperatures warmer to the east.

Zone 3: Western areas of the zone are windy, warm, and cloudy; it's cooler in the mountains. The Plains are temperate with increasing cloudiness, showers, and cooler temperatures. Precipitation is more prevalent to the north, where some is heavy.

Zone 4: Northern areas are warm and dry; the desert is hot with variable cloudiness and humidity; higher elevations to the east are cooler.

Zone 5: Weather is hot, dry, and windy, with a chance for showers early in the week.

Zone 6: Hawaii is breezy, humid, and warm. Showers, some heavy, bring cooler weather to central and eastern Alaska; western areas remain warmer and foggy.

July 13–20

Zone 1: Heat and humidity are normal, except for northern New England, where scattered thunderstorms bring cooler temps. The southeast is very hot and dry.

Zone 2: Heat and humidity prevail throughout the zone. Tornado warnings accompany severe thunderstorms in eastern and central areas. Abundant rain increases flood potential.

Zone 3: Temperatures are higher west, more seasonal east. The Plains are windy, hot, dry, and partly cloudy.

Zone 4: Warm, seasonal, and generally dry, with a chance for isolated showers throughout most of the zone. Desert heat soars.

Zone 5: Northern areas are overcast and cool with showers from a low pressure system. Southern and inland portions of the zone are warmer.

Zone 6: Hawaii is hot, dry, and partly cloudy. Alaska is much the same, with highest temperatures in the east and more temperate conditions to the west, where thunderstorms bring high winds.

July 21–28

Zone 1: New England is cool and cloudy with showers. Other areas of the zone are warm and dry, and heat increases south with some cloudiness as scattered thunderstorms develop.

Zone 2: Windy, hot, and muggy, with much of the zone seeing scattered showers and thunderstorms, some with heavy rain. The east is drier, but increasing winds later in the week bring a chance of thunderstorms.

Zone 3: Western areas are warm and wet; the Plains are mostly hot, dry, and sunny with scattered clouds.

Zone 4: Mountain showers move eastward; the desert is hot and windy. Variable cloudiness covers the zone.

Zone 5: Northern areas are overcast, damp, and foggy, but temperatures rise and winds pick up the end of the week as a front moves through the area. Warmer conditions prevail inland and to the south, which is sunny.

Zone 6: Hawaii is partly cloudy, windy, and hot; rain later in the week. Alaska temps are seasonal, but windy as a front moves across the state. Precipitation is locally heavy to the east later in the week.

July 29–31

Zone 1: Northern coastal areas are cloudy and cool, with warmer temperatures inland and to the south. The mid-Atlantic states experience severe thunderstorms with tornado warnings, and conditions are ripe for a hurricane to move up the coast from Florida to Maine.

Zone 2: Western areas are hot, and eastern portions of the zone have scattered thunderstorms and possible hurricane activity.

Zone 3: Thunderstorms cool temperatures in western portions of the zone, and the Plains are partly cloudy under an approaching front. Heat and humidity rise in the central and eastern Plains.

Zone 4: Thermometers rise throughout the zone, producing afternoon thunderstorms to the east.

Zone 5: Seasonal temperatures shift to cooler and windy, with precipitation north. Southern areas are seasonal and partly cloudy.

Zone 6: Hawaii is partly cloudy to sunny, windy, and warm with scattered showers. Temperatures rise throughout much of Alaska, except for the east. Wind increases midstate, with a chance for precipitation.

August 1–4

Zone 1: Mid-Atlantic and northern states are more windy and cooler than areas to the south. Storms with very high winds, possibly hurricane velocity, move to the north, targeting the northeast and New England.

Zone 2: Western areas are hot and dry, and central portions are partly cloudy and hot, with a cooling trend at week's end.

Zone 3: Heavy rain, scattered thunderstorms in central and eastern sections under cloudy skies and rising humidity. Temperatures are normal to above.

Zone 4: Mostly seasonal conditions prevail, with wind and a chance of showers east and south.

Zone 5: The zone has a chance of showers and is mostly seasonal. Southern areas are windy.

Zone 6: Hawaii is warm and seasonal with showers at week's end. Weather in Alaska is warm and windy—especially west—later in the week, when increasing clouds signal an approaching front; precipitation cools temperatures.

August 4–11

Zone 1: The northeast is seasonal with scattered showers; areas to the south are hot, humid, windy, and dry.

Zone 2: Central and eastern areas are windy as a front moves through the area, causing severe thunderstorms with hail and tornado potential, followed by cooler temperatures. Western areas of the zone are warmer.

Zone 3: The northwest and mountains see showers and thunderstorms, some heavy. Heat in the Plains generates clouds and scattered thunderstorms. The western Plains are hot and dry as the week ends.

Zone 4: Cloudy skies, showers, thunderstorms, and seasonal to above temperatures prevail. Monsoon rains in the desert could cause flash flooding.

Zone 5: Northern portions of the zone are windy with temperatures seasonal to above normal, except for cooler coastal areas. Drier weather prevails to the south and inland.

Zone 6: Scattered showers accompany warm and seasonal weather in Hawaii. Alaska is warmer west, cooler east, before showers cool western and central areas.

August 12–18

Zone 1: Throughout the zone, heat and humidity produce showers and thunderstorms. Some areas see significant downfall.

Zone 2: Wind, heat, and humidity prevail throughout the zone, which has scattered showers and thunderstorms, especially to the east, where clouds are more prevalent.

Zone 3: Northern areas are cloudy and cool, with precipitation. The Plains are windy with scattered thunderstorms and seasonal temperatures. Rising heat and humidity prevail to the east.

Zone 4: Much of the zone is cloudy and cool with showers and thunderstorms. Heat and humidity prevail to the south.

Zone 5: Northern areas are sunny to partly cloudy and pleasant. Weather is warm to the south, with a chance of showers.

Zone 6: Hawaii is mostly sunny and seasonal with scattered showers. In Alaska, temperatures are seasonal to above and fair from midstate to the east; the west is cooler, with a chance for precipitation.

August 19–26

Zone 1: Heat and humidity generate thunderstorms throughout the zone, bringing significant rainfall to some areas and severe storms in southern areas.

Zone 2: Western areas are cloudy, warm, and humid. Central portions of the zone are hot, and wind increases to the east.

Zone 3: The northwest and western Plains are cloudy and windy as showers and severe thunderstorms arrive, bringing cooler temperatures; snow could fall in the mountains. The central and eastern Plains also experience severe thunderstorms, high winds, and cooler weather as the storm front moves to the east.

Zone 4: Much of the zone is wet under cloudy skies. High winds accompany desert monsoon storms.

Zone 5: Showers, cloudy skies, cool temperatures, and fog prevail to the north, while southern areas are warm and partly cloudy.

Zone 6: Hawaii is mostly seasonal and humid, with scattered showers. Central and eastern Alaska are cloudy and wet, and western areas are cooler and drier.

August 27–31

Zone 1: Weather is cool and windy in the northeast. Areas to the south are cloudy and humid with showers.

Zone 2: Western areas are hot, dry, and windy; thunderstorms with heavy precipitation bring cooler temperatures to central and eastern portions of the zone.

Zone 3: Weather is warm in the northwest, and dry and hot in the Plains. The mountains and western Plains are cloudy and windy with precipitation; some areas see excess moisture with flash flood potential.

Zone 4: Sunny skies and normal to above temperatures prevail throughout the zone.

Zone 5: Northern areas are seasonal to warm and windy with a chance of showers. Southern areas are very windy and cooler.

Zone 6: Temperatures are seasonal to above in Hawaii, with partly cloudy skies and variable winds. Central Alaska is warm and dry; eastern areas are cooler and windy.

September 1–2

Zone 1: The northeast is damp with scattered showers, while areas to the south are warm, humid, and windy, with scattered precipitation.

Zone 2: Much of the zone is cool and windy, but areas to the west are warmer. Precipitation, some locally heavy, brings moisture to midzone states and a chance of showers to the east.

Zone 3: Some precipitation and wind from a front moving through the mountains and foothills and into the Plains; cooler temperatures follow.

Zone 4: With the exception of showers to the east, weather is seasonal and dry.

Zone 5: Southern areas are sunny, windy, and seasonal, with showers inland. Northern portions of the zone are warm, windy and partly cloudy, with a chance of showers.

Zone 6: Hawaii is warm and seasonal. Western Alaska is warm; cooler and windy conditions, with a chance for precipitation, prevail to the east.

September 3–9

Zone 1: Overcast skies signal precipitation and cooler temperatures in the northeast, while areas to the south are hot. The coast is cooler, with thunderstorms.

Zone 2: Western areas are hot, dry, and windy, with a chance of showers at week's end. Central and eastern portions of the zone are humid, with scattered showers and thunderstorms as temperatures rise.

Zone 3: The northwest is hot, but cooler after thunderstorms. Although mostly dry and hot, variable clouds and scattered showers develop in the Plains. The central Plains are hot and humid.

Zone 4: Skies clear and temperatures fall after precipitation in northern and mountain areas. Heat generates thunderstorms, some severe with abundant precipitation to the east and south.

Zone 5: Scattered showers give way to a warming trend to the north. Southern areas of the zone are windy with variable clouds and scattered showers.

Zone 6: Hawaii is warm and sunny to partly cloudy with scattered showers. Alaska is warm and dry west, and cooler with precipitation east as a slow moving front advances from the west.

September 10–17

Zone 1: The northeast is stormy with high winds, hail, and cool temperatures. In the mid-Atlantic states, conditions are cloudy, windy, cool, and wet, and the southeast is humid with scattered showers.

Zone 2: Cloudy skies and thunderstorms with tornado potential dominate central portions of the zone; Gulf states could experience a hurricane or tropical storm. Western areas are warm; eastern areas are cooler.

Zone 3: Heavy precipitation with flash flood potential in the mountains and foothills moves into the western Plains. The central Plains are windy and dry, and temperatures in much of the zone are above normal.

Zone 4: The zone is windy and mostly dry, with a chance for scattered showers.

Zone 5: Temperatures are seasonal, and variable clouds bring coastal showers that move inland.

Zone 6: Hawaii is warm and humid with showers; temperatures rise by week's end. A storm front in western Alaska generates high winds that move across much of the state, bringing cooler temperatures.

September 18–25

Zone 1: Temperatures are sunny and seasonal to warm in the northeast, with a chance of showers. The south is hot and dry.

Zone 2: Western areas are hot, humid, and windy, with increasing cloudiness, rain, and cooler temperatures at week's end. The midsection is hot, sunny, and dry; it's windy and a little cooler to the east.

Zone 3: The northwest is warm and sunny to partly cloudy with scattered showers. Variable clouds in the central and eastern Plains result in scattered showers, but cloudiness increases at week's end as humidity rises, bringing soaking rain and cooler temperatures.

Zone 4: Mostly warm, dry, and windy throughout the zone. Southern areas are hot and humid with scattered showers.

Zone 5: Weather to the north is mostly sunny, but cool with scattered showers; temperatures warm at week's end. Southern areas are warm and cloudy, but cooler after precipitation.

Zone 6: Temperatures are seasonal to above in Hawaii under breezy, sunny skies. Although mostly seasonal, western Alaska is cool, cloudy, and windy; eastern areas are warmer with precipitation and fog.

September 25–30

Zone 1: Weather is cool and mostly fair, with a chance of showers in the northeast. To the south, temperatures are seasonal to above prior to severe thunderstorms with tornado potential.

Zone 2: Warm, dry conditions prevail, with rising temperatures later in the week.

Zone 3: The northwest is cool prior to a warming trend, and temperatures rise in the western Plains, which are dry and windy. Central areas of the zone are warm and humid with precipitation.

Zone 4: Northern areas are fair and warm; areas to the east and south are windy and dry with temperatures seasonal to above.

Zone 5: Winds, cool temperatures, and coastal cloudiness and precipitation dominate northern regions of the zone, but temperatures rise at week's end. Southern areas are warm and sunny to partly cloudy.

Zone 6: Hawaii is warm and windy with a chance of precipitation at week's end, followed by higher temperatures. Central Alaska is windy, and most of the state has seasonal weather; areas to the east are cooler.

October 1–9

Zone 1: The northeast is seasonal, while central and southern areas receive precipitation—some heavy—with accompanying humidity and dampness.

Zone 2: Western areas are temperate until week's end, when cooler temperatures increase frost potential. Middle and eastern sections of the zone are fair to partly cloudy and windy, also with frost potential.

Zone 3: The mountains are cloudy and wet, and the Plains are fair, warm, and dry, but with a chance for precipitation. The eastern Plains are cool with frost potential at week's end.

Zone 4: Conditions are seasonal, dry, and fair to the north, where winds increase later in the week. Cloudy skies signal precipitation to the east, some heavy. Areas to the south are warm.

Zone 5: Northern coastal areas are cloudy and windy with showers and fog under a low-pressure system. Areas to the south are warm, windy, and cloudy with a chance of precipitation.

Zone 6: Variable clouds produce a chance for precipitation in Hawaii, which is warm and breezy. Alaska is warmer west, cooler east, where cloudy skies bring precipitation, followed by clearing from a cold front moving through the area.

October 10–17

Zone 1: Northern sections of the zone are chilly and dry, and the mid-Atlantic states are cloudy, cool, and wet. Wind and humidity prevail to the south.

Zone 2: Cloudy and cool, western areas see heavy precipitation, and central and eastern portions of the zone are windy, cool, and damp.

Zone 3: Conditions are fair and seasonal west, and the central and eastern Plains are cloudy and wet. Eastern areas receive more precipitation—some abundant—followed by a warming trend.

Zone 4: Thermometers dip as increasing clouds signal precipitation throughout much of the zone, followed by a gradual warming trend.

Zone 5: Northern areas are windy, fair, and warm. Increasing clouds generate showers to the south, along with wind and cooler temperatures.

Zone 6: Hawaii is seasonal with scattered showers under partly cloudy skies. In Alaska, temperatures are seasonal west, and cool central and east, as a storm front moves through the region.

October 18–24

Zone 1: The northeast is cold; areas to the south are cool with abundant precipitation.

Zone 2: Chilly temperatures bring frost, and cloudy skies signal precipitation across most of the zone.

Zone 3: A cold front moves across the zone, bringing cooler temperatures, frost, and precipitation, especially in the eastern Plains. The northwest is fair to partly cloudy and cool.

Zone 4: Mostly fair weather with scattered showers prevails to the north and west. Cloudy skies in eastern and southern areas generate rain and snow—some heavy—and damp, chilly temperatures.

Zone 5: Northern coastal areas are cool with precipitation. Drier, warmer weather prevails inland and to the south.

Zone 6: Except for western areas, which are cool with showers, Hawaii is warm, seasonal, and partly cloudy. Alaska is cold and stormy midstate, cool west, and warmer east, as a cold front pushes eastward.

October 25–31

Zone 1: The northeast is seasonal and windy with precipitation that extends into the mid-Atlantic states and areas south, bringing snow, sleet, and freezing rain.

Zone 2: Cool and damp under variable clouds, and becoming colder, precipitation is heavier midzone as a front moves to the east.

Zone 3: The northwest is fair and cool, and western areas of the zone see precipitation from a weather pattern that moves across the Plains, bringing considerable moisture to some areas.

Zone 4: The north is variably cloudy, cool, and windy. Southern areas are warmer and partly cloudy.

Zone 5: Mostly overcast and cool; scattered showers and fog.

Zone 6: Hawaii is warm, humid, and partly cloudy. In Alaska, temperatures are seasonal to above under partly cloudy skies with some fog; western areas are windy.

November 1–8

Zone 1: Wind cools temperatures in the northeast, which is damp with coastal fog. Areas to the south are warmer.

Zone 2: Temperatures are seasonal to above, with precipitation to the west later in the week. Eastern areas are mostly fair.

Zone 3: The northwest and mountains are windy and seasonal with a chance of precipitation. The western and central Plains are seasonal and dry. Eastern areas are cooler with cold nights, increasing clouds and precipitation.

Zone 4: Mostly seasonal to cool and dry, eastern portions of the zone are warmer and windy with a chance of precipitation under variably cloudy skies, followed by cooler temperatures.

Zone 5: Skies are fair to partly cloudy with coastal fog and seasonal to cool temperatures. Areas inland and to the south are warmer and drier.

Zone 6: Temperatures are seasonal to above in Hawaii, with abundant rain. Alaska, windy and cool with precipitation—some heavy—in central and eastern areas, as a low-pressure system dominates much of the state.

November 9–16

Zone 1: Wind is the featured theme throughout the zone. The northeast is cloudy and cool, and severe storms in the southeast produce heavy precipitation.

Zone 2: Most of the zone is stormy, with abundant precipitation to the east, along with high winds and falling temperatures.

Zone 3: A storm front moves out of the northwest and into the Plains, replacing fair skies with overcast skies and lower temperatures that dip into the south.

Zone 4: Cloudy skies bring precipitation—some heavy—to much of the zone, followed by clear and colder weather.

Zone 5: Temperatures are seasonal to cool under windy, variably cloudy skies that generate some precipitation north. Conditions are warmer south, fair to partly cloudy and breezy, with a chance of showers.

Zone 6: Hawaii is fair and seasonal. Alaska is seasonal, but warmer west and cooler east.

November 17–23

Zone 1: Cold and cloudy conditions throughout the zone bring excessive precipitation to southern areas, which are windy and damp.

Zone 2: Precipitation—some abundant—is the norm throughout much of the zone, which is cloudy and cold.

Zone 3: The northwest is cloudy, cool, and wet, with some locally heavy rain. A storm front, with high winds, continues to move east through the Plains, reaching eastern areas by the end of the week.

Zone 4: Wind signals cooler temperatures and precipitation from a front moving through the zone. Eastern areas see heavy precipitation; the mountains are cold and stormy.

Zone 5: Northern areas are cool with variable clouds and fog. Dryness and warmer temperatures prevail inland and to the south.

Zone 6: Temperatures are seasonal to above in Hawaii, with variable clouds and a chance for showers. Alaska is seasonal to the west, while the east stays dry and cool with cloudy skies and only scattered precipitation.

November 24–30

Zone 1: The northeast is seasonal, and the mid-Atlantic states are cloudy, windy, and cold, with precipitation heaviest to the south.

Zone 2: Cloudy skies and wind in the west signal precipitation, which extends into the midsection and east. Temperatures are seasonal to cool.

Zone 3: The northwest, west, and northern Plains are cool, windy, and stormy. Areas to the south are warmer, overcast, with precipitation—some heavy.

Zone 4: The zone is seasonal to cool, windy, and variably cloudy with precipitation.

Zone 5: Most of the zone is overcast and cold with precipitation, which is abundant to the north.

Zone 6: Hawaii is cloudy and windy; Alaska receives precipitation, some heavy, central and east, with dry, warm conditions to the west.

December 1–8

Zone 1: The northeast is cool and windy with variable clouds. Southern areas are overcast, with precipitation and seasonal temperatures.

Zone 2: Mostly cold, cloudy, and wet throughout the zone, temperatures are coldest to the west. Some areas see abundant snow.

Zone 3: Mountain areas receive heavy snowfall as a storm moves in from the northwest and continues into the Plains, which are cloudy and cold. Heaviest precipitation in the Plains centers east, with coldest temperatures to the north and east.

Zone 4: Cool, windy weather with precipitation moves west to east, bringing much cooler temperatures and abundant moisture to the area.

Zone 5: Northern coastal areas are cool with fog and precipitation moving inland as winds increase. To the south, weather is cloudy, cool, and windy with showers.

Zone 6: Hawaii is warm, humid, and windy with showers. High winds in central and eastern Alaska signal a cold wave. Western portions of the state are warmer, with variable clouds and precipitation.

December 9–15

Zone 1: Mostly seasonal to warm, much of the zone is cloudy with thunderstorms in the mid-Atlantic states. The southeast is windy and fair.

Zone 2: The zone is generally seasonal, but windy with precipitation west at week's end. Temperatures are warmer to the south, cooler to the east.

Zone 3: The mountains and western Plains are windy, cloudy, and wet prior to cooler temperatures. Mostly pleasant, seasonal weather in the Plains changes to scattered precipitation, wind, and cooler temperatures.

Zone 4: Mostly seasonal but dry, some areas of the zone are cool and windy with increasing cloudiness.

Zone 5: Temperatures are seasonal to above under partly cloudy, windy skies. Coastal areas see fog.

Zone 6: Cloudy skies bring showers to Hawaii, where temperatures are mostly seasonal. Alaska is windy, cloudy, and cooler after precipitation.

December 16-22

Zone 1: Cloudy to overcast skies and high winds bring cooler temperatures and precipitation to the northeast. Areas to the south are warmer, but windy.

Zone 2: Weather is seasonal, with fair to partly cloudy skies north and west. Central and eastern areas of the zone are windy and cooler with a chance for precipitation.

Zone 3: Although generally dry with seasonal temperatures, gradually increasing cloudiness brings precipitation and cooler air to the central Plains. Areas to the south are drier, warm, and breezy.

Zone 4: Northern and western areas are cloudy, with precipitation, followed by falling temperatures. The desert is dry and unseasonably warm.

Zone 5: Much of the zone is unseasonably warm and windy. Partly cloudy to cloudy skies inland and to the south yield precipitation.

Zone 6: Temperatures in Hawaii are seasonal to above under partly cloudy skies. Central Alaska is windy with precipitation, followed by cooler temperatures; other areas of the state are seasonal.

December 23-31

Zone 1: Cold, cloudy, and wet, with the heaviest precipitation in the mid-Atlantic states. Southern areas clear at week's end, bringing warmer temperatures. Thermometers remain low to the north, however.

Zone 2: The zone is cold and cloudy as a moisture-laden storm moves in from the west. A slight warming trend arrives at week's end, but skies remain cloudy.

Zone 3: A storm front moves through the western part of the zone into the Plains, bringing cold air and abundant precipitation to the mountains and western Plains. Frigid temperatures in the Plains dip far south.

Zone 4: Much of the zone sees precipitation, with the heaviest centered east and south early in the week. The west sees abundant moisture at the end of the week as a storm front moves in from the northwest, cooling temperatures.

Zone 5: Mostly seasonal and fair to partly cloudy throughout the zone, colder temperatures and cloudy skies bring precipitation at week's end.

Zone 6: Fair and windy with temperatures in Hawaii above seasonal highs, but cooling at the end of the week. Central and eastern Alaska are stormy and receive significant precipitation; western areas are cooler at week's end.

About the Author

Kris Brandt Riske is an astrologer and author who serves on the National Council for Geocosmic Research Board of Directors and holds professional certification from the American Federation of Astrologers (PMAFA). She has a master's degree in journalism. The author of *Astrometeorology: Planetary Power in Weather Forecasting*, Kris also writes for AMI astrological publications and allpets.com, and has had numerous articles published in popular astrology magazines. Kris is an avid auto racing fan. Although NASCAR is her favorite and she'd rather be a driver than a spectator, she also has a pole-side seat at the Indianapolis 500 each May. An avid gardener, Kris recently transformed her yard into a flowering Arizona garden, complete with a fountain and two brick patios.

Saving Seeds for Garden Success

By Penny Kelly

Until you've tried it, you're likely to underestimate the huge difference that saving your own seeds can make in your garden plants. I discovered this difference by accident, when my spring lettuces bolted during hot July weather, and I was too busy to cut them down and remove them to the compost pile. The next spring I found a whole row of self-sown lettuces coming up where last year's lettuces had stood. I couldn't help noticing the good health, color, and sturdy structure of the volunteer lettuce compared to the frail, pale plants in the greenhouse. As the lettuces went to seed that year, I watched their tall, weedy-looking flowers open, and once fertilized, lose their petals. What was left was a small, dry, pot-bellied receptacle that had been at the base of the flower. I carefully opened this with my fingernail, and discovered a cache of seeds—Mother Nature's treasure! I collected about three dozen of these small pods, and put them in a jar to store over the winter. The next spring I began opening the pods to plant some early lettuce. Not all of the seedpods had been dry, and their seeds were destroyed by mildew. My first seed collecting lesson was: Be sure the seeds are dry before putting them into an airtight, glass container.

As I opened the pods and dumped out their precious cargo, I noticed some of the seeds were white and some were brown, and I realized I had

 not paid any attention to the fact that there had been at least six different lettuce varieties growing in the row from which I'd harvested seeds. My second lesson was: Mark the plants from which I seeds are to be saved.

When planting my saved seeds in flats, I wasn't sure they would come up so I planted two or three seeds in each cellpak of the flat, thinking that I would avoid ending up with a half-empty flat. Then, after planting the saved seeds, I decided maybe I wouldn't have enough lettuce, so I found some of the seed left in the packages that I had originally purchased and planted them in a second flat. When finished, I marked the first flat as "Lily Hill Farm seeds," and the second flat as "commercial seeds," I watered them all, and left them to germinate. Three days later, the seeds I had collected and saved were sprouted and growing! It took seven days for the commercially grown seed to come up. Germination among the saved seeds was at least 90 percent, with two and sometimes three plants coming up in each cell. Now I had the unhappy task of snipping off one or two young lettuces from each group, leaving one for transplanting. I realized I had wasted a lot of seed by double and triple planting. Lesson three was: Count on the seeds coming up.

Although both sets of flats had the same care, the same Sun and watering, it was obvious from the start that the seeds I saved were going to outperform the commercially grown seeds hands down! Two weeks after planting, the saved seeds were twice the size of the commercial seeds. They were ready to transplant at three weeks, while the commercial seeds weren't ready for five weeks. For the entire growing season, the saved seeds outpaced the store-bought seeds. The lettuce from the homegrown seeds was bigger, more colorful, much sturdier in its structure, and was the last to bolt when hot weather came. It put out more flowers, the seed-pods were bigger, and the seeds inside were fat and healthy looking. This experience changed my entire view of gardening as well as my gardening practices. It was as though a door had opened to a new world. I became acutely aware of the intelligence and adaptability of plants, and began to see my garden as a place where families of young mother-plants were raising seed-children that would be completely familiar with the environment of my garden. The plants were assuming that their seeds would drop into the soil around them, not be transported in small packages across the country to other gardens where unfamiliar and perhaps incompatible conditions reigned. These young mothers were creating a legacy of understanding in their seeds as to what the soil structure in my garden was, what kinds of nutrition they could expect to find there, what shortages of chemistry they might have to make up for, the pests and diseases they might encounter, what to expect in terms of daytime high temperatures and nighttime lows, how much rain fell and in what patterns. The result was seeds that were familiar with the environment. They didn't have to waste a lot of time putting together adaptive strategies.

This year, expand your own awareness of nature by collecting seeds from some of your favorite vegetables. Start by tying a piece of colored fabric or twine on the plant you want to collect seeds from. If you have several varieties of one vegetable and want seeds from each, use a color-coded system of ties that won't fade in the Sun. Don't trust yourself to remember which plant has which color tag! Write down your coding system in a garden notebook. One year I put heavy cardboard tags on my chosen plants and wrote the name of the variety on the tag. Between the rain and the Sun, the name faded completely and I was left guessing. If you put a stick in the ground to mark your chosen plant, be aware that a child or the garden tiller will think nothing of moving it. And if the plant falls over while a neighboring plant is still standing, you can become confused as to which plant you wanted to collect from. Again, make sure the seeds are dry before you put them away!

One year, I tried putting "mostly" dry seeds into envelopes instead of jars, thinking that because they would have better access to air they would dry out the rest of the way and be okay. It didn't work. When I went to get them out for early spring planting I found half the envelopes all mucky and stuck together. The moisture from the seeds caused mildew in the pods and the envelopes. Another year, after all the seeds were dry, I put them in envelopes, wrote the name on each, and put them in a box in the basement, where it was cool and dry. A mouse thrived happily in the box, unnoticed by anyone, eating all the seeds and building a snuggly nest out of the paper from the envelopes. I had to start my seed collecting from scratch the next year. Tin boxes or glass jars for storage are pretty important to me now.

Tomatoes, green beans, squash, melons, okra, cucumber, eggplant, zucchini, and peppers all produce seeds inside the vegetable itself. Select a few of each vegetables and leave them on the vine until they are overripe to ensure the seeds are fully developed. If you pick a young vegetable, the seeds will be thin, flat, and undeveloped—great for eating but not planting. Once you pick the vegetable, open it, scoop the seeds into a sieve or colander (with small holes), then rinse away the remaining vegetable pulp. Allow the seeds to dry thoroughly on pieces of waxed paper, put them into envelopes or jars, label, and store them. Potatoes are seeds, too, so after digging let them dry, brush the dirt off, and put them in a cool, dark place until spring. They'll start to sprout about the time they need to go in the ground. Let corn dry on the cob, then remove the kernels and store them in a jar. Radishes, broccoli, cauliflower, lettuce, and other greens go to seed the same season they are planted. Shortly after a radish becomes too tough and woody to eat, it sends up tall, branching stalks on which the flowers and seedpods form. When the plant begins to dry out, pick the pods, dry and store them. You can break them open to get the three or four radish seeds out, or plant the entire pod and watch the radishes come up. You can't do this with lettuce very well because there are too many seeds in a pod, they all come up at once in one spot, and choke each other's growth.

If you want to collect seeds from carrots, parsley, cabbage, and beets, which are biennials, plant them off to the edge of the garden in a section that you can leave undisturbed over the winter. Don't harvest them all, and keep them weeded and mulched with a little straw or leaves. The following spring, pull back the mulch once the ground warms. (If you pull it back too soon, your local rabbits and deer will discover the tops of these delicacies and have a spring feast.) The beets and carrots left in the ground from last year will proceed to send up weedy-looking tops that flower, dry, and turn to seeds. The beet seeds look like they have been literally glued to the sides of the stems. Just pick the stems, dry them, and strip the beet seeds off. The carrots will look like Queen Anne's Lace, and so will the parsley. The parsley seeds will look like commercial parsley seeds—bald, curved, and sort of striped. Carrot seeds that form on the flower heads look like tiny brushes or burrs. The cabbage, like any brassica, puts out a long, thin seedpod with round, dark-brown seeds inside.

Of all the things I have learned in my years of gardening, I would have to say that collecting and saving seeds is in the top three practices. Until I began the practice of seed collecting, I didn't understand that there was a gap in my connection with nature, nor did I realize how powerful the effect would be once I filled that gap. It brought me to an awareness of how shattered Mother Nature has been, and how disruptive our habits are. Too often we grow things only for their flowers, or their seeds, wood, or oils in places where they will look good, regardless of whether it is a good place for the plant. Not that we haven't always grown some things in these ways, for we have. In the last fifty years, however, there has been a subtle shift in our attitudes characterized by the sense that appearance or product are the main reasons for growing anything.

Today seed-collecting it is one of my little passions. I used to buy seeds and bedding plants every year. Depending on the size of our vegetable garden and how many flower gardens I thought I needed, the bill for these purchases usually fell between $200 and $400 each year. Now the amount is minimal, maybe $50, while the health and quality of our garden produce is extraordinary.

About the Author

Penny Kelly's bio is on page 91.

Suggested Reading

Seed Sowing and Saving: Step-By-Step Techniques for Collecting and Growing More Than 100 Vegetables, Flowers, and Herbs by Carole B. Turner.

The Real Dirt on Earth Signs

By Maggie Anderson

Planting guides tell us that water and earth signs are the most "fruitful" of the four elements (earth, air, water, and fire) of the zodiac. Old farmers and others experienced in planting by the phases of the Moon suggest we sow when Luna is in a water sign—Cancer, Scorpio, or Pisces—or an earth sign—Taurus, Virgo, or Capricorn. Planting during these times is said to assure sturdy, disease-resistant plants and a bountiful harvest. Evidently agriculture and astrology have a working partnership, because we can produce 600-pound pumpkins if we really want to.

However, it appears that earth signs are not as popular with astrologers and almanac writers as water signs. Gardening guides propose that we first mark our planting calendars for the dates when the Moon is in a water sign. It's hinted that we should consider the Moon in earth signs only as secondary planting days. They tell us it's okay to sow during an earthy Moon, but only of we have a good reason—like an emergency!

For instance, we may plant while the Moon is in Capricorn if our potato sets have sprouted and are frightening the children. If we've unwisely offered to host a garden walk, it's acceptable to transplant flowering plants while the Moon is in Taurus on the morning of the big event. But poor Moon in Virgo must be our very last choice. We can use her as a plant date only if we've missed all the others while giving birth to quintuplets and it's a week past Memorial Day.

When fertility kudos are passed out in the almanacs, earth signs definitely take second place. This is curious because, with the exception of weeds that sprout from cement sidewalks, most growing things require a combination of dirt and moisture to thrive. They also need the tender loving care of green-thumbed Taurus, Virgo, and Capricorn types, because it's these folks who willingly weed and feed while other signs of the zodiac cruise or snooze.

Being an earth sign, I've tried for many years to discover why a Moon in Taurus, Virgo, or Capricorn should not be the very first choice for planting. The roots of this prejudice are planted in layers of misunderstandings, which can and should be uncovered. To help speed the process along, I'll share my favorite theories on discrimination against Moon in earth signs.

Theory One: Earth Generates Envy

The opposite is true for the element of earth. Growing mediums that pass for dirt seem to have been distributed around our homes at random by anonymous soil spirits out for their own amusement. Some gardeners inherit rich, black soil, while others are challenged by dirt so laden with rocks, clay, or pulverized limestone that they feel singled out by the universe for unfair treatment. Gardeners take this very personally. It's difficult for even the most spiritually advanced among us not to be envious of a pile of light, loamy earth lying just over the fence.

Since the quality of earth varies so widely, it can pit neighbor against neighbor. I once had a yard with so much clay that lawn darts bounced off of it and Creeping Charlie refused to procreate. In contrast, my next-door neighbor's lawn was lush and her garden so bountiful that she kept me supplied with fresh produce all summer. Even though she was generous, my fondness for this woman diminished as the growing season wore on. So, earth creates envy and divides people.

Theory Two: Earth Breeds Boastful Pride

In spite of their hardships, people who grow their own veggies, flowers, and herbs take great pride in overcoming adversity. Those who buy salad-in-a-bag never face the intellectual challenge of proper soil management. Nongardeners pay real money to work out at health clubs instead of building muscle the natural way: tilling, shoveling, hoeing, and raking dirt. Gardeners are smart, tough, cheap, and proud of it.

So, while dirt-challenged humans whine about their soil conditions, there's a competitive quality to these complaints. Put two gardeners together and they immediately begin a game of "My dirt is worse than your dirt." The goal is to prove your soil is unimaginably infertile and infinitely more difficult to work with than the other person's dirt, but that you have prevailed and produced a truly magnificent garden with your superior green thumb. So, earth divides humans with boastful pride.

Theory Three: Earth is Lots of Work

Another reason earth element Moons are given second place as a planting option is that dirt requires so much more work than water (or so they say). A gas-powered tiller bucks like a cross-eyed mule. Gardeners who have their own television shows make tilling look easy, but we all know Arnold Schwarzenegger pulverized the dirt clumps off camera before the film started rolling. The belief is that tilling a twenty-by-fifty-foot garden bed requires more energy than Arnold expended conquering the world.

This is because one tilling is never enough. The first time we work our garden soil in the spring, squirrels wait on the sidelines. They rush in and bury their stash of black walnuts when we take a coffee break. The nuts sprout over night, along with last year's dill seed, and all must be rooted out and raked down. The next day it will rain hard enough to pack the earth back down and the whole thing must be tilled a second time.

Theory Four: Earth is Complicated

Earth varies widely. Even if you rid it of a rock, you still have to worry about its chemical composition, and growing plants will leach soil nutrients, and these minerals must be continually replaced. Gardeners must regularly apply composted manure or balanced fertilizer from a bag.

Some people make their own dirt. Seasoned composters—those devoted gardeners who know how to cook a pile of leaf mold into perfect humus— have a real edge in soil management. (Even Martha Stewart rolls her own compost bin, so it must be a snap.) It's true that you can buy sterilized dirt in plastic bags at the discount store but, if the word gets out, you will never be asked to appear on *The Victory Garden*. Composting is in!

On the Other Hand: Water Builds Community

Water element Moons have an edge over earth because H_2O is such a simple element. It's always the same, whether delivered via a lovely spring rain or a rusty watering can. Just the fact that it's wet counts. And when it comes to water for our gardens, we're all in a similar position. Ogden Nash said it best, "Rain falleth alike on the just and the unjust fella." Where water is concerned, the Lord of Water Distribution pours water on neighbors with equal intensity. He doesn't play favorites.

Also, whether there's too much or too little of it, water brings people together. Thousands volunteer to fill sandbags during floods, helping perfect strangers defend their homes against rising water. Should there be a water shortage, whole nations come together and pray for an end to the drought. Water brings out the best in humans. It helps to build community and, therefore, it has an edge in our subconscious minds over earth.

So, there are indeed a few good reasons why gardening guides prefer water sign Moons over earth sign Moons. Water is simple, easy to administer, and it's a real relationship builder. Earth is always complicated, lots of work, and causes division between gardeners. Still, earthy Moons must be good for something more than planting potatoes. Perhaps astrology can help us discover their true cosmic function.

Just Give Earth a Chance

The next time you look at your gardening calendar, consider planting while the Moon is in one of the earth signs. Do this deliberately and there will be benefits. You'll notice that it hardly ever rains when the Moon is in Taurus, Virgo, or Capricorn. You will not have to transplant seedlings while standing ankle-deep in mud as you did in the past with the Moon in Cancer. This will improve your gardening morale.

As your morale improves, so will your confidence. You will be more willing to learn from your own gardening experience. Plants really want to grow no matter when you tuck them in the ground so you can't fail completely. If you plant while the Moon's in an earth sign, you may just have the best garden ever. If so, take great pride in your accomplishment. Hope and pray that the neighbors are very envious of your tomatoes.

The Moon in Taurus

Astrologically speaking, the Moon is "exalted" in Taurus. She's as happy there as the queen mother, and just as bountiful with her blessings. Venus, the planet of beauty and fragrance, rules Taurus, giving a Taurus Moon an affinity with flowering plants. However, Taurus is one of the fixed signs of the zodiac and not easily budged. Be sure you are crazy about the flowers you plant during a Taurus Moon because, once established, they'll be there for your lifetime.

When the Moon is waxing (increasing) in Taurus, plant flower seeds or seedlings. The annuals will self-seed the following year and perennials will multiply fast even if you would rather they didn't. While the Moon is full or decreasing in Taurus, plant bulbs, flowering shrubs, and trees. The roots will send themselves deep and produce magnificent blooms year after year. An increasing Taurus Moon is perfect for planting any vegetable that forms a flower. Bees find these very seductive and a good crop is ensured.

The Moon in Virgo

Of the six female signs that astrologers and almanac writers consider "fruitful," Virgo comes in dead last. Mercury, the planet of mind and intellect, rules Virgo, and she's the very best record-keeper in the cosmos. While the Moon is transiting Virgo, take an objective look at your garden. What is working? Where are the surprises? Does that Heritage variety tomato taste good, or is there a reason why its popularity waned? How many horseradish roots can you really grate in one year? The Moon in Virgo will help you make rational decisions about future gardens.

Virgo is also reputed to be the perfectionist of the zodiac. Her Moon may not produce the quantity of a prolific Moon in a water sign, but you can expect real quality from this virginal maiden. She will do her best to gift you with at least one absolutely perfect vegetable or flower. Gardeners who hope to win a blue ribbon at the county fair should try planting while the Moon is in Virgo. Of course, you'll still have to prune, fertilize, stake, and mulch. Virgo is infinitely fussy, but she knows anything worthwhile takes effort.

Moon in Capricorn

Capricorn is one of the cardinal or "start-up" signs of the zodiac. She must always have a major project in the works. Saturn, the planet of form, structure, and limitations, rules it so Capricorn likes to stay in control. When the Moon transits this sign, it's the perfect time to build raised beds or install fences and trellises. Lay paths or dig out a formal herb garden when the Moon's in Capricorn. Any work you do to keep your plants restrained and in good order will be highly effective.

Seasoned gardeners swear by the Capricorn Moon for planting vegetables that have been the daily fare of peasants for centuries, especially the winter "keepers." Try sowing turnip, parsnip, onion, beet, and carrot seed when the Moon is full or decreasing in this sign. While the Moon is increasing in Capricorn, plant hard winter squash. Properly stored in your root cellar, these vegetables will be edible until the first spring thaw.

About the Author

Maggie Anderson, has been a professional astrologer for twenty-five years. She holds a master's degree in marital and family therapy from Northern Illinois University, DeKalb, Illinois. In addition to her work as a therapist, she's a writer, teacher, and avid gardener. Maggie was a staff writer for AstroNet and her work has been featured on StarIQ and Sowell Review. Her weekly column, *HumorScopes,* received national syndication. Maggie specializes in relationships and all affairs of the heart. She lives in Mount Vernon, Iowa. You can view her website at www.astromaggi.com and contact her at astromaggi@aol.com.

How Dad Learned About Planting by the Moon

By Maria K. Simms

My father didn't accept what others told him without investigating for himself—not even the widely popular wisdom of *The Old Farmer's Almanac*. He wasn't an astrologer, but I remember, with fondness, when Dad discovered that maybe planting by the Moon really did work.

We lived in a very small town in rural Illinois while I was growing up. We weren't farmers, but our house in the town was on a double lot, and my parents always had a big garden. The soil was rich, and the vegetables that came out of that garden in season were so delicious that one could happily make an entire meal from them.

Mom and Dad used organic gardening methods without ever calling it that, at least that I can remember. They always had a compost bed and constantly added to it. And Mom always planted a row of marigolds around the vegetables because she said they kept the pests away.

One year, Dad decided to put planting according to Moon signs to a very stringent test. He carefully planted one row of vegetable seed during the time that was considered "favorable." Right next to that row, he planted a row of the same vegetable seed under conditions that were, as much as possible, identical—except that for this row, he chose a day to plant was "unfavorable." He carefully tended both rows just the same, and observed them carefully. His conclusion: There was no doubt that the vegetables planted at the "right" time were healthier and yielded bigger and tastier vegetables!

I've always remembered what my dad told me about his experiment. After that, he always consulted the Moon sign for the best days to plant.

My experience, so far, has been with flowers rather than vegetables. I love to garden—it is so peaceful, satisfying, and restorative to work with the earth—especially when one spends so much time working with a computer, as I do. I have many beautiful flowers and shrubs around my home—something for color in every season. You can bet that I always check for the Moon sign for times to plant, and I strongly recommend that you do the same!

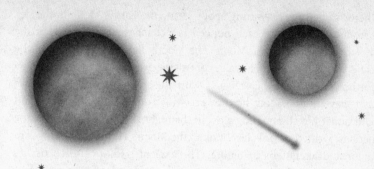

Gloria Star's
Personal
Lunar
Forecasts
for 2003

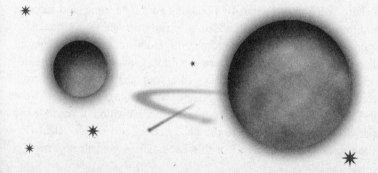

There's something reassuring about seeing the Earth's Moon in the sky. From childhood, we each noticed her changes and marveled at the many faces reflected by the Moon. The Moon's light is a reflection of the Sun's fiery splendor, and her cycles control the ever-changing ebb and flow of Earth's oceanic tides. Fascinated with the mystery of the Moon, we humans have mused about her power, written songs about her light, and danced under her shimmering glow in the night sky. Since the time of the Sumerians, written records have linked the Moon's cycles with changes in behavior and alterations in nature. The ancient traditions teach us "As above, so below." This premise—one of the basic tenets of astrology—brings the heavens down to a personal realm. In astrology, the Moon comes to life as a significant drive behind your emotional nature and the way you express your feelings and needs.

Your horoscope is not actually the column you read in the morning newspaper. In reality, the horoscope is the picture of your personal astrological chart based upon precise mathematical calculations. An astrologer charts the positions of the Moon, Sun, and planets based upon the exact time and place of your birth. This detailed picture—your natal horoscope—symbolizes the complex levels of energy that make up your whole being. Your basic needs, drives, and self-expression are symbolized by the Sun, Moon, and planets in your astrological chart. Astrologers call these bodies the energies in the horoscope. You probably know about your Sun: It describes the ways you express your ego and your drive to be recognized—something easy to see and even easier to show to others. Your Moon tells a more intimate story: It symbolizes your subconscious nature. The Moon represents a more internalized quality than the energy of the Sun. You feel your Moon.

To determine the zodiac degree of the Moon in your personal astrological chart, you'll need to start by obtaining your date, time, and place of birth. From that information, an astrologer can calculate your Moon's sign and position in your horoscope. Since the Moon moves into a different zodiac sign every couple of days, you can understand why an accurate calculation is necessary. You can also order your chart calculations from directly Llewellyn Chart Services by using the "Astrological Services Order Form" in the back of this book. To find an approximation of your Moon's zodiac degree and sign, refer to the handy tables and simple calculation method described on page 65 of this book. These guidelines provide a close estimate of your Moon's sign. However, if you want a more precise placement of your Moon, you'll need a copy of your astrological chart.

Okay, now that's done, where do you go next? Even if you are not familiar with the vocabulary of astrology, you are already intimately acquainted with the energy of your Moon. Take a moment to tune in to your feelings—what's going on inside. That's your connection to the energy of your Moon. Imagine that your Moon is an ultrasensitive recording device—constantly collecting, storing, and assimilating everything you experience and feel. At its essence, the Moon is your databank. The messages in your databank constantly replay themselves in the form of your reactions and attitudes, and most of them operate automatically. You can add more information at any time, and you can also make alterations. However, since you hold these impressions at a very deep level it's not always easy to change or erase an old internal message, even when you want to. Your habits are also part of this very "message system," stored through the experience of your lunar energy.

That's the core of your Moon energy, and knowing about your Moon's zodiac sign gives you insights about your inner strengths. Your Moon sign illustrates what makes you feel secure—and it also shows where you feel most susceptible. Your lunar energy shapes your thought patterns, and the Moon is the storehouse of your emotions. The Moon stimulates your underlying emotional nature. Of course, you have some familiarity with your Sun sign, but each planet and the Moon are in specific signs in your astrological chart, too. The characteristics of your Moon sign show how you absorb your impressions about your life experiences. Your Moon sign describes your emotional filter—it shows the kinds of feelings and attitudes that can penetrate your subconscious mind.

It's your Moon that drives your needs when it comes to feathering your nest. The astrological sign and placement of the Moon in your chart point to the best way to build a sense of home—right down to the type of environment that helps you relax into a true feeling of inner peace. You can explore the meaning of your Moon sign to help you tap into the best ways to assure that you create a personal environment that provides for your unique needs. Once you're in the flow with your Moon, you carry your sense of home into every life situation. In other words, you feel right at home with yourself and with the world.

Not only does your Moon sign describe how you tap into your "feeling" nature, it also shows how you reach out to nurture and support anyone or anything. Whether you're male or female, your Moon indicates your style of "mothering." Psychologically, your Moon portrays your archetypal feminine and represents your relationship with your mother, with women, and with the feminine part of your own psyche. Your Sun, on the other hand, represents the archetypal male quality, and illustrates your connection to men, father, and the masculine elements of your inner self. Your Moon's sign illustrates the qualities you seek through the psychological feminine archetype.

Let's peel away yet another layer. Beneath the psychological qualities of your Moon rests the cradle of your soul. At this level, your Moon contains all that you have been, and therefore influences all that you can become. Shining forth from deep within your eyes, the light of your Moon reflects the innermost soulful part yourself. It makes sense that your soul's needs would influence your most dominate emotional tendencies and needs. Your Moon is the part of you that has flown to the pinnacle of ecstasy and here you also remember the true emptiness of despair. Your capacity for contentment increases when you strive to fulfill the needs defined by your Moon's sign. Essentially, you will feel most satisfied when you embrace your Moon.

Use this section of the *Moon Sign Book* to explore the basic planetary cycles during the year 2003 that will influence you at an emotional level. I'll describe the planetary transits to your Moon that will stimulate change and also show you where you'll find challenges. You'll discover that some of the cycles will help you reshape your life, while others stimulate a desire to delve into the mystery of yourself. Astrology can show you the cycles, but you are the one who determines the outcome through your responses. Open to your needs. Listen to your inner voice, and be attentive to signals that tell you when it's time to change, or time to hold fast. Ultimately, this awareness and sense of fulfillment will sustain your sense of security and safety in a rapidly changing world.

Aries Moon

As long as you're moving along, life is good. Your Aries Moon loves to take the reins, and you have no patience with people or situations that seem to be stuck. For you, life is about stepping up to the plate and meeting challenges head-on. Joy fills your soul when you can let your pioneering spirit take charge. There are all sorts of things that meet the bill, but the spice of your life is just right when your creativity has plenty of room to develop. That's when your passion and zest for life itself is unmatched, and it shows through that fiery sparkle in your eyes and kick in your step.

You're at your best at the beginning of a new project, in the throes of fresh romance, or when you initiate change. Living "in the moment" is much more to your liking than getting stuck in the past. Even if other parts of your personality seem to impel you to settle into a routine, you'll feel best if you alter it from time to time. You may be the hero in a crisis, since your eagerness to rush in and face a challenge is always on alert status. In life or at work, you might enjoy competitive or crisis situations like emergency rescue, sports, crisis intervention, or counseling, or military service. Emotionally, a part of you may always seem eager, and it's this quality that can be equally endearing and frustrating for others, and for you. Boredom can be your ultimate nemesis, and sometimes when life is running smoothly, you might be tempted to rock the boat just to remind yourself you're still alive. While this flirtation with disaster keeps you happy, it can spawn havoc in your relationships. Your need to take risks can stimulate insecurity from others who may seek consistency or comfort.

At home, you need room to play—no matter how old you are. You'll appreciate a personal environment that invites laughter and love, and may welcome a chance to entertain.

The Year at a Glance for Aries Moon

Optimism comes easily as the year gets underway. Jupiter's contact to your Aries Moon can be emotionally uplifting, but more important, this connection adds enthusiasm to whatever you do. Some of the ideas you've never had a chance to explore may manifest into real life opportunities, and it's up to you to decide whether or not they fit into your "master plan."

From January through August, Jupiter travels in territory friendly to your Moon, and continues to stimulate your desire to expand your base of operations. Saturn's energy brings focus to your top priorities, and with these two cycles working harmoniously, you'll feel more secure. From June through the remainder of the year, you may need to scale back on your desires in favor of handling your top-drawer responsibilities. After June, Saturn's cycle tests your capacity to make choices that work toward your highest needs instead of simply following a path without the awareness of why you're doing it.

This year, as Uranus changes signs in the spring and moves into Pisces, the spiritual implications of our scientific and technological advances become even more noteworthy. This seven-year cycle helps you develop a more profound connection with your intuitive mind, accompanied by a few challenges to what you tend to think of as "rational thinking."

If your Moon is 0–9 degrees Aries, it's important that you pace yourself. From January through May, Jupiter and Neptune's cycles help you crystallize your ideas and better fulfill your needs. Practice mindfulness, since a lack of focus can result in missed opportunities or a diminished self-confidence. You can afford to take greater risks early in the year, but once Saturn moves into a tense square contact to your Moon in June, your responsibilities grow. Conscientious focus helps you cope with a heavier emotional load. Whether it's increased family responsibilities, or that you need to spend more time taking care of yourself, you're definitely ready to let go of anything that falls into the category of "unnecessary."

If your Moon is 10–19 degrees Aries, your creativity and imagination work harmoniously to help you fulfill your security needs. Pluto's cycle stimulates your desire to renovate or move. This may be your year to build your dream home or to make a commitment to a relationship that's part of the foundation of your life. It may be necessary to take a few risks or to try something out of the ordinary in order to make significant progress—but that's right up your alley, isn't it.

If your Moon is 20–29 degrees Aries, it's time to cultivate your talents to the max and to take bold steps that serve to mark a major change in your life focus. The cycle of Uranus in contact with your Moon supports innovation throughout the year, and Jupiter's cycle opens opportunities well into the summer. Creative changes at home may also be in the offing, so grab some paint swatches and get busy with your remodeling plans. Of course, this could also mean additions to your family, so make room.

January

You may feel that you're just going through the motions during the New Moon on the 2nd. Part of the problem stems from the difference between what you need and what others demand from you. Dig deeper to uncover the real source of your discontent, and consciously make an effort to express feelings of love and tenderness after the 7th, when close relationships shed light on more positive options. Just in time for the Full Moon on the 18th, Mars sends you off and running in directions that spark your confidence. Bold career moves may be in order, but it's your personal life that transforms into a more satisfying experience from the 20th–29th. Feather your nest with comforts, colors, and accessories you love, since expressing your personal tastes adds a delightful quality to the mix. Travel can also give you reasons to smile, so plan to add a few frequent flyer miles to your portfolio after Mercury turns direct on the 22nd.

February

Confidence shines through your actions, and an opportunity to present your ideas or showcase your talents opens new pathways from the 1st to 7th. While conservative types may argue with your logic, you can sway even the most hardline objections by putting a fresh spin on things during the Full Moon on the 16th. (This can be effective at home and at work.) Your passions lead the way from the 1st to 16th, with imaginative innovation providing just the right avenue for you to turn around a situation that's been on the fence. You're ready to know who's in and who's out, and if "they" can't decide, you may fly the coop for greener pastures. Reach out to friends who enjoy your vivacity, since you can mutually benefit from joining forces to get things done. Concentrate on completing projects close so home, since you'll enjoy seeing the results of your hard work.

March

Knee-jerk reactions get you into trouble, but you may decide to jump into hot water anyway. It's the irritation from Mars to your Moon that's creating that itch to act, and the results can require major damage control. To determine whether you're part of the solution or the problem, watch reactions and gauge your intensity accordingly. Overly idealistic people can be irritating from the 3rd to 12th, since your eagerness to reach a resolution can block your capacity for what seems to be too much compassion. Adjustments during the Full Moon on the 18th help heal hurts, and after the Vernal Equinox on the 20th, telling it like it is works to your advantage. You'll still need to watch your temper, but may find better ways to channel your anger. It is strong energy, and you just need a constructive direction for it.

April

Red alert! With the Aries New Moon on the 1st, you're more connected to what you truly feel. This can be a wondrous thing if you're happy, but if discontent rules your emotions, you'd better give some folks a heads-up. Think of it this way: You simply cannot sit on your feelings, and you need to open up to avoid an internal explosion. Artistic projects and finesse may have to wait. This is the time to clean out closets and attics, or to fix things (or situations) that have withered in disrepair waiting for your attention. Progress is most promising through the 5th. You may have to let someone else take the lead during the Full Moon on the 16th, even if you disagree with the choice or direction. It's your turn to take the lead after the 21st, when a more assertive approach works to your advantage.

May

Loving, honest, heartfelt expressions can flow through your life, and you're eager to make room for them. It's easier to show how you feel than it is to talk about it, and gifts of love have a powerful impact from the 1st to 16th while Venus travels through Aries' territory. Decorating and home repair work best in planning stages, however, since Mercury's retrograde can throw a wrench in the works until the 20th, and the Moon's eclipse on the 16th can bring more problems to the surface. Consult experts when necessary, but use the time before the solar eclipse on the 31st to repair a rift in a relationship, or clarify problems with your finances. Then, you'll be ready for a fresh start coupled with a different attitude thanks to a clear path that opens just as the Sun's eclipse opens to a new dawn.

June

A flexible attitude is the key to getting through June, and even if someone else is pushing for a solid commitment, you may be reluctant to agree unless there's room for change. Of course, every contract does not come with an escape clause, and that's why you feel a bit nervous—especially where money is concerned. Saturn moves into Cancer's watery realms on the 3rd, and what once seemed like a solid foundation in your life may now be slipping away. Study the competition from the sidelines until the 12th, when you can refine your strategy by getting to know your rival. The game's afoot during the Full Moon on the 14th, but there are new rules. After the 22nd, you may discover a more fascinating option where romance is concerned, but watch out—it could be a decoy designed to test how you truly feel about an old love.

July

Before you complain about that rain on your parade, think about how you truly feel. At least it's an excuse not to be on display when you'd rather be away from prying eyes. Although you prefer a sunny attitude, there are times to turn inward, and your need to express sentiments of compassion or sadness may overwhelm your desire to joke around. Just before the Full Moon on the 13th, there's a shift in your focus. It's easier to let someone else into your personal space, and a gathering of friends can be just the ticket to cast your blues away. Or, maybe you'd prefer time with a special somebody, including your desire to trek off into places yet undiscovered. The New Moon on the 29th is just the right time to let go, indulge your ever-eager inner child, and reclaim your joy once more.

August

Changes at home make a huge difference in your peace of mind, and this is an excellent time to remodel, redecorate, or move. At the least, study the feng shui of your personal space, and do what's necessary to open the flow of energy, love, and abundance into your life. Subtle alterations may surprise you, although you'll be in the mood for a bold touch here and there. And your love life is simply—ooh, la, la, my dear. Venus and Jupiter join forces in their trek through Leo, and your passions are definitely riding high. Health issues can be worrisome, but by the time the Full Moon arrives on the 12th, you can feel a resurgence of vitality. There's still work to do, and a change in your diet and daily routine can go a long way toward helping you feel better. A little extra lovin' won't hurt anything, either.

September

Mars continues its retrograde track, and you may feel that you're just not accomplishing anything worthwhile. You like a direct approach, and all the negotiations and analytical research seem like a waste of time. While Mercury retrogrades (through the 20th), offer a helping hand to your friends, who may be overdoing it in the worry department, by planning a healthy diversion—you'll enjoy it, too. Finally, progress is on the horizon with the New Moon on the 26th and Mars turning direct again. There's just one problem: Cooperation is required, and that usually means you have to give over the reins for a while. Run the race in your mind, while someone else is in the driver's seat. Your turn comes soon enough.

October

If you're thinking there's a little déjà vu going on, you're probably right. You have returned to emotional territory already covered, but now, you're armed with information and experience. It's like having a map of your subconscious pathways. Old habits you've attempted to abandon are easier to release now, since you have little patience with anything that's going to slow you down. The Aries Full Moon on the 10th can be a test of your resolve, since it's time to let go of the past and to move confidently and responsibly forward. Cooperative agreement with others—even your competitors—makes all the difference. It's time to acknowledge who's on the other side of the fence, and to draw workable boundaries that allow for your differences. Still, there's a bit of deception in the air during the New Moon on the 25th, so if it's important, iron out details you're willing to support. Otherwise, continue negotiations when there's more clarity.

November

Tensions building through the time of the total lunar eclipse on the 8th can be the result of circumstances you simply cannot control. Part of the problem is a lack of certainty about the best way to resolve property or financial disputes. It's tempting to overestimate the value of some things because of their emotional investment, but what is significant is the way you determine whether or not you feel right about your decision. Destructive action is definitely not the answer. Take another look at your options after the 13th, when identifying the ideals you have in common can lead to a happy conclusion. Then, during the solar eclipse on the 23rd, open your heart and mind to a new vision. It's time for you to experience nurturance on spiritual, emotional, and physical levels—truly a period of thanksgiving. Still, power plays can emerge, so keep your radar on alert.

December

There's nothing worse than awkward silence with the lights on, and since your foot may be in your mouth, you could be the central focus of attention. Ack! Part of the problem arises when you jump to conclusions, or act without determining someone else's comfort zone. Personal relationships are tested against the backdrop of your needs. If you're emotionally invested in something that does not fit, you'll feel it big time during the Full Moon on the 8th. Fortunately, you're in a good space to make alterations, or to reach some type of closure. Once Mars enters Aries on the 16th, you'll feel eager to move along. For the remainder of the month, when you take the initiative, things happen. The best results arise when you listen to the voice of experience before you take the first step.

Taurus Moon

At the core of your being, you're solid as a rock. Your Taurus Moon reflects an inner quality of endurance and stability, enhancing your ability to create a reliable emotional foundation. You're drawn to natural beauty, and yearn to experience timeless love. Others can feel your earthy sensuality when they walk into your comfortable home, when you serve a hearty meal, or if you offer one of your prized hugs that grounds and protects at the same time.

Although you love to share your abundance with others, you never like to waste anything. For that reason, you consciously reach out only when you've determined that it's safe (or when you feel you can afford it). Your conservative nature can be a blessing, since once you feel you are ready to make a commitment to an idea, a goal, or a relationship, you're there for the long haul. You go out of your way to determine what's real and what's not, and sometimes block an opportunity to experience something new until you feel certain of it. Of course, some actions require a leap of faith, and tests that require such a bold level of trust can be difficult. You are much more comfortable building on the foundations under your feet. Letting go of anyone or anything can hurt because you may feel that you are losing part of yourself.

Your stubborn streak may be legendary. What they may not realize is how much you value the experience of the tried and true. Your patience is a positive offshoot of this same quality, and comes in quite handy during the times you're the one holding things together during a crisis. Nurturing beauty is a big part of your life, and when you develop your artistic sensibilities, you feel alive and complete. Whether it's in the garden, at a potter's wheel, singing in the choir, preparing dinner, pulling together the perfect costume for your child's school play—you are an artist at heart. Just remember that when it's time to give your loved ones room to follow their own paths your love goes with them. After all, love itself knows no bounds.

The Year at a Glance for Taurus Moon

After a bumpy start, 2003 settles into a productive and rewarding year. The trouble plaguing you is nothing new, since for the past few years you've felt the uncertainty of uninvited change—and you've coped pretty nicely. Now, there's something to feel good about! Jupiter and Saturn move into a positive zone of support and opportunity, and you'll fee that you have time to cultivate the ideas and nurture the projects that mean the most to you.

It's time to get in touch with the way you feel, since the Moon's North Node begins its cycle in Taurus this year. Your underlying feelings can hide from your conscious mind, but you'll be able to see some of your deeper motivations if you take the time to look. Be especially attentive to the ways you are taking care of your emotional needs during the lunar eclipses on May 15 and November 8.

For the first half of 2003, you may still feel you're barely making ends meet in some ways, since the demands on your emotional energy can be exacting. When Saturn heads into Cancer's comfort zone in June, you will feel the shift and see evidence of new growth. For the next two years you'll feel a greater sense of emotional stability.

The key to feeling you have more control over your destiny starts when you cooperate with the temptations from Jupiter's cycle from January through August. Traveling in Leo's zone until August 27, Jupiter provides ample opportunities to overextend yourself. Watch your promises, since more may be required than you assume. Since Jupiter will be in a tense contact to your Moon, it's easier to gain weight when you overindulge in the dietary department. Once Jupiter heads into Virgo's territory, you'll feel that your judgment and decisions fit with your needs more easily. From September through December, your self-confidence rests in an excellent place, too.

If your Moon is 0–9 degrees Taurus, you have the most positive support from the cycles of Jupiter and Saturn this year. Plus, from April through September, you're feeling a stimulus from Uranus to make creative changes in your life. A move, expansion of your family, or expansive changes in your home can be especially rewarding from September through December. This is an excellent year to change some outworn habits, too!

You may feel more uncertain of yourself if your Moon is 10–15 degrees Taurus. Neptune's friction comes in the form of an emotional smoke-screen. You may see only what you want to see when it comes to relationships, and for that reason, others can more readily take advantage of you. The trap of denial is most powerful during this cycle, although this is an excellent time to let go of the past. Concentrate on forgiveness, but try to keep your emotional boundaries in a safe zone.

If your Moon is 16–20 degrees Taurus, you're challenged to make some major adjustments while Pluto travels in a quincunx to your Moon this year. It's a good time to renovate—physically and emotionally. You're also strongly affected by the Moon's eclipses in May and November, when family crisis or other change can have a more significant impact.

Although you may feel somewhat unsettled this year if your Moon is 21–29 degrees Taurus, the changes are not likely to be a total surprise. You're completing a cycle of Uranus in a frustrating square to your Moon, and there's some relief from the rollercoaster ride of change during the months from March through September. Consider this the perfect year to get rid of the stuff that's cluttering your life. Your impulse is to feel more emotionally free, and resisting that need brings the most unsettled feeling of all.

All Taurus Moon individuals will find 2003 to be a productive, more energetic, year—particularly during the last half of the year. This is the time to make repairs, heighten your physical activity level, or take a more active stance in your family or community.

January

Confrontations may undermine your security, but your common sense arms you with workable options during the New Moon on the 2nd. It's time to tear down your defensiveness and get to the core of what's bothering you in your personal relationships. If you feel too vulnerable, consider work with a counselor to help you mediate a relationship dispute or explore your issues. The last thing you need now is to feel that you're stuck in a rut. Even though Mercury retrogrades until the 22nd, take advantage of this time to look at old issues or unresolved conflicts. At home, repairs can be a ridiculous problem, but you may have to deal with them anyway. Reasonable progress and workable solutions emerge during the Full Moon on the 18th. Watch for hidden expenses after the 23rd, when previously obtained written estimates can save you a small fortune.

February

Love's healing energy soothes rough edges in your close relationships, although you may still be irritated by habits or attitudes from others that are not exactly your cup of tea. Call it a test of priorities. Confusing signals during the New Moon on the 1st can leave you feeling that you've been left holding the bag while everybody else gets off the hook. An open conversation clears the air, but you may not be satisfied until you see a more even distribution of responsibility. Part of the problem rests in the lap of empty promises, so investigate before you decide to trust an agreement. Family matters can be complicated, and near the time of the Full Moon on the 16th you may be in for surprising news. Fortunately, you have the capacity to take in the whole story before you respond, since a knee-jerk reaction would be likely to work against your best interests.

March

Despite a few misunderstandings, it's a productive month. Gather your supporters together during the New Moon on the 3rd to explore the best ways to initiate a project. Whether it's at home or at work, you're eager to see signs that your efforts make a difference. Teamwork definitely plays a positive role, and from the 4th–20th amazing progress is possible. Uranus moves into the realm of Pisces on the 10th, beginning a seven-year cycle during which your own creative impulses and expressions can be easier to accomplish. March and April are good times to float a few ideas just to see the response—but take care not to give away the most valuable elements. (It's just a test balloon.) Make room for romance the weekend of the 29th. You'll adore the results!

April

Your no-nonsense approach to problem-solving is in demand, but you might prefer to focus your energy and effort on a pet project close to home. The song of your heart needs to be heard, and whether it's through sharing your talents or devoting more energy to an intimate relationship, you're ready to bare your true feelings. Expectations can be a problem from the 9th–13th, when clarification of agreements can keep your life on a more even keel. It's not a time to leave anything hanging. With Mercury transiting through Taurus from April 5 to June 13, you'll find it easier to talk about your feelings. But you have to be careful to avoid getting in a rut. It's a great time to write, even if you're only in a dialog with yourself through your journal entries. Watch for the possibility that a small tiff could lead to a major rift after the 21st. Keep those lines of communication open.

May

Knowing what to say and when may be an art form. Old issues seem to turn up like a bad penny, when Mercury is retrograde in Taurus until the 20th. While this might be helpful when you're talking with a therapist, you may be frustrated that things take too long in the "outside world." The Taurus New Moon on the 1st is an excellent time to take an inventory of your needs, and to target what you feel is most significant. Love certainly takes a front seat after the 16th, when Venus moves into Taurus and sweetens your appetite for romance. The lunar eclipse on the 16th brings your issues back into focus, just in time to take a look at your progress. The problem is that the view is a bit hazy, since you may desire one thing, while you need something (or someone) else entirely! It's the old problem of not being able to have your cake and eat it, too. Drat!

June

If you're counting on consistency, you may be disappointed this month. It comes in small measure. From the 1st through the Full Moon on the 14th you'll have some success when you focus on your top priorities. Of course, you're good at those determinations, even when others try to distract you with their personal dramas. It's just that kind of disruption that puts the lumps in your gravy from the 12th to 22nd. While the surprises may have a pleasant ring, you don't like changing your plans or your routine, but after the initial shock wears off, you may be quite pleased with the news. Your emotions enter a smoother course during the New Moon on the 29th, when you may feel you're back in charge of things that matter most.

July

A move, remodel, or redecoration of your home space can be just what the doctor ordered to cure your discontent. At the least, consider utilizing the ancient art of feng shui to redirect the flow of energy through your home and office. The results can be more immediate from the 1st to 12th, although you might, at first, resist some of the changes suggested. Give it a try before the Full Moon on the 13th—since you're eager to feel that life is flowing good things your way. Love grows, too, from the 4th to 28th, and promises made now are likely to stick. All you have to do is determine what you want, since manifesting what you desire is much easier that it's been for a long time. Start with something small. Overdoing your wish list can cost you in the long run. Someone else's needs may come first during the New Moon on the 29th, so keep that in mind when they cut in line.

August

Despite the grandstanding you're required to witness, there's plenty to enjoy during August. You have the good sense to focus on what matters most, and until the Full Moon on the 12th your most valuable efforts may take place behind the scenes. This is your time to plan, review details, and work on infrastructure. That includes your health, since overindulging in habits that are not good for you will leave you feeling the worse for wear. The cycles shift after the 23rd, and practical matters take top priority once again. Pull out unfinished plans, or take a second look at an abandoned project to determine if you're still interested. Fulfilling your dreams is more than a whim after Jupiter begins its cycle in Virgo on the 27th, accompanied by a New Moon cycle. It's finally your turn to put your energy into the things you've always wanted to accomplish.

September

With fewer disruptions and more opportunities to concentrate on what you want, you may feel like you're at a marvelous feast! Despite two retrogrades—Mercury (through the 20th) and Mars (through the 26th)—progress seems to continue. The setbacks give you a chance to do troubleshooting, and you may also have an opportunity to redeem yourself in matters of the heart. An old emotional wound may come to the surface on the 5th–6th, and by exploring the issue and letting go of the pain you'll be ready to move forward and enjoy the fruits of the Full Moon on the 10th. Cooperative efforts work nicely until the 15th, when a different agenda alters your priorities. Stay below the radar screen if you're working on personal issues. You'll be in no mood for anybody else to interfere.

October

Put the finishing touch on a home project early in the month. You may have a different set of priorities after the Full Moon on the 10th. Venus enters Scorpio, an opposition to your Moon sign, marking a time when your deepest personal urges emerge from the shadow of your subconscious. Creative endeavors can be gratifying now, but you might prefer to turn your attention to your love life. The same-old-same old just will not do, so take advantage of the passionate energy emerging during the New

Moon on the 25th and try something completely different! Attending a party might be fun, but you may not want to host, since you'll definitely prefer to enjoy the fun instead of the "work."

November

The big cosmic event for you is the total lunar eclipse in Taurus on the 8th. Think of this as a completion cycle of sorts, since it marks the perfect time to let go of the things you don't need in your life anymore. Such soulful clearing can leave you feeling empty in some ways—but it's a good kind of empty. This is the emptiness that invites you to fill your heart with what you truly need. Some parts of these changes feel a bit awkward, since you may be in territory you've never explored, or that you've been afraid to explore with much effort. The tricky thing is what you do with the old resentment emerging from others before and during the Sun's eclipse on the 23rd. It's simply a reaction to the fact that you have decided to say "No" when it counts!

December

An easy pace helps you maintain a smooth course until the 21st. You're eager to share tender moments with the ones you love, and you may enjoy time away from the hustle and bustle—even if only a few hours emerge here and there. Petty arguments are likely during the Full Moon on the 8th, but you can be objective and not get too involved unless the dispute means something to you. After Mercury turns retrograde on the 17th you'll prefer to stay close to home. Have others come to visit you. It's the New Moon on the 23rd that ushers in a more fun-filled time, and despite a few irritations, you'll enjoy sharing the bounty of the year during your Yuletide celebrations.

Gemini Moon

Your busy mind never seems to stop. There's so much to see and experience—and you definitely don't want to miss anything! Change itself can be delectable for you, and your need for independence may drive you to make changes just to keep life interesting. Your Gemini Moon feeds on a diet of perpetual variety. When you're on a journey from place to place, writing in your journal, in a class exploring great ideas, reading a wonderful book or engaged in stimulating conversation—you simply feel more alive. Most attracted to people and situations that challenge your mind, your soul is nourished when you make connections, or when you can be instrumental in bringing the right people together at the right time.

You have a knack for seeing the directions that open up in the midst of change, and in a crisis, you can extract the logical alternatives that lead to fresh solutions. You spot the trends that are part of social transition. Objectivity is your forte; humor, your life-long companion. Your downfall is your tendency to be distracted from your priorities—something you can remedy by developing mindfulness. It's just that you are a good juggler, even if you do sometimes overuse this talent!

Only when you honor your need to express yourself freely can you let go and allow yourself to develop an intimate connection in a relationship. It helps, too, when you share similar levels of enthusiasm and curiosity. However, you can feel uncomfortable in emotionally charged situations, since emotion and logic are not always compatible. Much like Spock on *Star Trek,* you frequently try to make sense out of feelings, and more often than not, it's just not possible. You're a natural when it comes to dealing with kids, since, in your heart-of-hearts, you'll always feel like a child. You love the thrill of innocent steps into the unknown, and giggle at the prospect of outwitting those who symbolize status quo. For you, home can be just about anywhere. But to feel safe, certain, and settled, you must embrace the joy that comes from linking your mind and soul to higher principles and the wisdom of the ages.

The Year at a Glance for Gemini Moon

After the past couple of years of self-examination, you're probably ready to examine something else! You've experienced some definite trials while Saturn's traveled in tandem with your Gemini Moon, although you may feel a keen sense of direction and focus as a result. This is the year to expand your foundation and to experience positive acknowledgment for your accomplishments.

The solar eclipses for 2003 are indicators that you can move beyond old habits and attitudes, and that you may finally feel ready to speak your mind when it counts the most. It's critical that you are attentive to the effects of your choices and actions, otherwise you can leave a trail of unfinished business behind you as you travel toward new horizons.

Jupiter's cycle in the sign Leo works harmoniously with your Moon through the end of August. This influence is quite helpful if you move or remodel, but it's also highly beneficial when it comes to self-improvement. Replace destructive habits and attitudes with confidence-inducing changes, and you'll see amazing benefits in your life. Saturn completes its long cycle in Gemini on June 3, and with this change, you'll feel lighter and less restrained. It's important to remember the lessons you've learned since 2000, because those experiences will shape your emotional foundations for a long time to come.

The very slow cycles of Uranus, Neptune, and Pluto will be most noticeable during the years these planets make a more exact contact to the degree of your Moon. These cycles require that you make an effort to understand and experience your inner self. If your Moon is 0–4 degrees Gemini, this is a transition year for you. Under the stimulus of Uranus in a high-friction square aspect to your Moon, you'll feel a desire to break away. Call it a kind of personal revolution. Use this time to free yourself from the situations and attitudes that inhibit your true needs. The key is to make these changes without destroying your foundations in the process!

If your Moon is 5–9 degrees Gemini, you have room to breathe during 2003. It's a great year to take inventory of your needs. From June through December, Saturn's cycle supports your ability to take significant steps that help you move further toward a sense of personal fulfillment.

You're feeling creatively inspired and a deepening sense of compassion if your Moon is from 9–15 degrees Gemini, as Neptune's transit opens the way for you to reach into the space of higher consciousness. From artistic expression to charitable outreach, you're feeling drawn to the spiritual. You'll make the most significant progress after October, when Saturn's cycle helps you stick with your priorities.

If your Moon is from 16–21 degrees Gemini, you're experiencing deep emotional transformation while Pluto transits in opposition to your Moon during 2003. You may decide that a move is necessary, but at the very least, big changes occur at home. It's quite possible that your family structure will be significantly altered. Health issues can be troublesome, but this cycle makes it easier to let go of habits that could undermine your health and happiness.

Your responsibilities dictate the structure of your life, and this year you can feel that you have more than your share of responsibility if your Moon is from 22–29 degrees Gemini. Saturn and Uranus are both making contact to your Moon, continuing cycles that began late last year. Saturn's conjunction to your Moon ends in June, but the effects of your commitments will last much longer. The stimulus of Uranus continues throughout the year, and helps you identify situations that you need to eliminate, and also sheds light on fresh possibilities.

January

The grass may only appear to be greener across the fence, but it's tempting to jump over just to find out for sure! It may just be that you feel stuck— or bored—and desperation could drive you to make choices you'll later regret. That emotional itch you can't quite scratch is most irritating from the 1st to 18th, and then you can go to extremes. The cycles of Venus and Mars stir your desires, but Saturn's caution reminds you that there can be consequences. Drat! Yes, there is a positive direction for the passionate needs welling in your soul, and it's all about eliminating the clutter of the unfinished. Once you start, you'll realize that there's more "stuff" than you thought, and that it's blocking your capacity to see the golden treasurers just under your feet. After the 21st, you'll start to feel more hopeful, and relationships are more interesting, too.

February

You're feeling quite lively during the New Moon on the 1st, and the inspiration to make headway on a pet project, or in a cherished relationship, stirs your creativity. Competition may be unavoidable, but it's how you handle the situation that makes all the difference. While some power plays can put you in the middle of chaos, others try your patience and may lead you to believe that you have few options—if any. The most trying period—just around the time of the Full Moon on the 16th—can tax your capacity to be cooperative when it counts most. It's also highly possible that you'll be involved in mediation of disputes between others, and in that situation your objectivity can be extremely valuable—even if family is involved.

March

The winds of Venus blow harmony and romance into your life, cooling the tensions you've felt for the past couple of months. Repairs at home may still get on your nerves, but at least the reason for the disruption makes sense. The problems arise when you have to deal with someone whose emotions seem to be block understanding. It's a test of that premise that emotions defy logic—just in case you've missed it n the past! This circumstance escalates during the Full Moon on the 18th, and somebody may try to drag you into his or her drama. (Unless you get a mask and a shield, refuse the offer.) Communication improves after the 22nd, but be on the alert for mixed signals from the 28th through 31st. Some people are just more trouble than they're worth!

April

It's a mixed bag for you this month. The New Moon on the 1st ushers in increased optimism, but there may be more empty promises than you like to hear. The overtures have their merit, and you're seeing evidence that you've made an impression. it's just that you still have to deal with somebody else's agenda overriding yours. You may have obligations to satisfy, and may have to wait a while longer before you feel that you've paid your debt (emotionally speaking) in an existing commitment. Reflect on your own leftover feelings of resentment or hurt during the Full Moon on the 16th. You're ready to open to fresh possibilities, but first you may need to let go of the pain. A trip or time away from the daily grind improves your perspective after the 21st.

May

The direct approach works best right now. Anything else is likely to create confusion. If you're heart's aching to tell someone how you feel, take the initiative. Set the stage with your favorite things, or go to your most enjoyable place—where you can let down your guard and just enjoy being together. It's time to find out where you stand, and that starts when you reflect on what's in your heart. Then, love can't help but show in your words and actions. The lunar eclipse on the 16th marks a time to turn away from old patterns that have not worked for you in the past. You may feel that you need to retreat for a little while, but if you have evidence that you can take the next step, then use the second half of the month to regroup. The Gemini solar eclipse (and New Moon) on the 31st is a time of rebirth, and you'll want to share the renewed "you" with the people who matter most.

June

Relationships move into the driver's seat, although there are a few bumps that test your resolve. It is through your connections to others that you open to fresh creative inspiration after the 10th, and with the Sun, Mercury, and Venus feeding energy to your Moon, you may be more willing to trust your feelings. It's also time to beautify your home, and after the 12th, you may be filled with all sorts of creative ideas about the best way to improve your personal space. If you're considering a move, be sure that the circumstances in your life will support the commitment required before you sign any contracts or call the moving van. Family conflicts can arise from out of the blue after the 18th, and that could change your mind and your plans.

July

Minimize your social activities from the 4th to 13th, since obligations at home can take more time than you anticipate. Plus, for the next five months, Mars cycles in an irritating square contact to your Moon sign, symbolizing a period of general unrest and a tendency to feel unnecessarily agitated. If you remind yourself that your fuse is a bit short, it will help. You'll feel an emotional uplift after the Full Moon on the 13th, when you'll be more inclined to share ideas and talk about your feelings. A desire to reach out and express yourself can stimulate you to add a unique touch to your home space or take more risks with the more creative elements of your job. Headway in a close relationship may also require that you risk letting go of your old responses or reactions, and during the New Moon on the 29th your first priority will be playful interaction.

August

It's all about give and take. Any situation that's too one-sided is likely to backfire. Your usual objectivity lends an understanding to those who need clarification, and those caught in the midst of conflict may seek out your mediation skills. (Whether they'll listen or not is another story.) A little romance near and during the Full Moon on the 12th may be in order, but it's also a great time to invite friends to dinner, share your favorite entertainment, or add finishing touches to your most promising project. Fortune smiles from the 13th–22nd, when Venus and Jupiter join forces to open the way for you to fulfill your needs and desires. By the time the New Moon rolls around on the 27th, practical matters take the top slot, and you may feel that you're buried until a mound of details. Call in a Virgo to help.

September

Dissatisfaction seems to hang in the air like a heavy fog; it's the result of unfulfilled expectations. You are not immune to getting stuck on either end of the spectrum. You could be the victim of somebody else's disappointment, or may feel crestfallen yourself. Mars and Jupiter are in a face-off, adding fuel to a tendency to overreact. If you're drawn into conflicts near the Full Moon on the 10th that are not yours to resolve, you could end up looking like the bad guy! Gentle support from Venus enters the picture on the 15th, aiding peace making, and bringing more comfort to your day-to-day activities. However, you may not see signs of progress until the New Moon on the 26th.

October

Frustration with an unfinished "work in progress" may continue to be a central element of the daily grind. Even though some will resist, you're eager to break a stalemate, and just before or during the Full Moon on the 10th there's a chance to illustrate your point. There may not be a simple way out of a convoluted situation at home, but from the 7th to 24th Mercury's energy opens the way to find common ground so you're at least talking about what's happening. You may have to wait for the fog of hostility to clear before you feel safe and secure once again. Consider this a test of your capacity to go with the flow—if you can find it.

November

It's a duel between your priorities or needs and the needs of others—but it does not have to be! The lunar eclipse on the 8th adds intensity to the process, since a hidden agenda is exposed, and that can undermine trust. To establish trust once again, you may have to take a tough stance against those who would run roughshod over your feelings. Your goal now is to find balance. Start with the big picture, and tune into how you feel about the give-and-take in your life—in your relationships, at work, at home, and between the inner you and the outer you. Time away from your routine can help after the 12th, when you may also feel more in touch with what's in your heart. The solar eclipse on the 23rd brings everything into focus and the healing begins. That's a reason for celebration!

December

It's quite possible that you've decided to break with tradition this year and try something different. Call it a test of your priorities. You may take a less high-profile option, and decide to use the Gemini Full Moon energy on the 8th the break a destructive habit. You are reclaiming your life. That does not mean you have to write off the people and situations you love, but that you're putting them in a different perspective. At home, take positive action to improve the ambience and comfort of your personal space after the 17th. You're in the aftermath of major change, and need a constructive focus. Express the love you feel, find the place of unconditional acceptance, and put your heart there. Beauty flows once again, and the joy is something you definitely want to share.

Cancer Moon

You may feel a distinctive sense of peace when you glance up and see the Moon. Your Cancer Moon is a natural link to the rhythms of life, which may give you an easy pathway into your inner self. You've always known the value of your intuitive sensibilities, and may feel a deep commitment to the fulfillment of your soul's destiny. Family and home hold the central focus in your heart, but you tend to become intimately involved in all your commitments—at work, with friends, and to your goals. When others seek comfort, they may be innately drawn to your gentle embrace—even if it comes disguised as a bowl of chicken soup.

You understand the value of the things that tie people together: family traditions, heirlooms, gathering around the dinner table, genealogy, or mementos of milestone events. In fact, you may be the family historian, company archivist, or record-keeper for your special interest organization. In relationships, you may prefer to take the initiative, since that way, you can keep your own shields up until you feel safe. Once you establish trust and love is flowing, you can become quite tenacious. Your need to be there for your children is lifelong. Yes, letting go is tough for you, and you may hate the idea that those you love have left the umbrella of your protection. Sometimes, letting go of things is difficult, and you may invest a great deal of sentiment in whatever surrounds you. Your home is likely a reflection of all you hold dear, and you're really into comforting amenities. Your work space needs to be comfortable, too, since when you and others are at ease, you just get more done!

Despite your capacity to dance with the ever-changing rhythm and melody of life, you may feel anxious in the face of change, or when you're heading onto an unknown path. Once you get back into the sway and merge with the river of life, you'll feel the contentment of knowing timeless truth. The eternal ebb and flow cradles your soul, and you are, once again, complete.

After the cycles of the past couple of years, you may be feeling a bit tender, since you've definitely made one adjustment after another. During 2003, your life and your needs come into distinctive focus, and you may feel that you can finally set down a reliable foundation. There are still challenges, although they will be easier to identify, and your options may be more accessible. Changes in the cycles of Jupiter, Saturn, and Uranus stimulate more reliable support, adding a quality of positive awareness of the best ways to fulfill your priorities and needs.

The Year at a Glance for Cancer Moon

The first major change arrives when Uranus slips into Pisces for the spring and summer months, providing a glimpse into the innovations that will mark the years from 2004–2011. This seven-year cycle will bring exceptional breakthroughs your way, so tune in spring and summer to get an intuitive feel for the alterations you want to invite into your life. Also mid-year, Saturn enters Cancer for it's two-year trek on June 3. Saturn's stay in your Moon sign can be extremely stabilizing, and helps you establish a clear set of personal priorities. These are the years of milestone experiences and lasting commitment.

Jupiter's cycles through Leo continues until August 27, and during this time you'll feel a measured sense of optimism and self-confidence. However, after Jupiter begins it's yearlong travel through Virgo, it's easier to open to joy, and your storehouse of joyful experiences begins to grow steadily.

When the longer-lasting planetary cycles—Saturn, Uranus, Neptune ,and Pluto—make contact to the exact degree of your Moon, the influence is strongest. If your Moon is 0–4 degrees Cancer, you'll feel a fresh emotional awakening since Uranus makes a friendly trine connection. You may decide it's time to move or make major alterations at home, and your family is also likely to undergo interesting modifications (like additions!). June, September, and October are key months for significant milestones.

If your Moon is 5–12 degrees Cancer, you'll experience the strongest impact from Saturn's cycle after June and well into early 2004. It's time to evaluate how you feel about everyone and everything, and to eliminate what you no longer need. Commitments made now are likely to last a long time. There can be an emotional heaviness under this influence, but it's there to help you determine your real responsibilities. Plus, if your Moon is 9–14 degrees Cancer, Neptune's influence adds a kind of haze when it comes to feeling connected to your inner self. The stimulus is to turn inside and focus more on your spirituality, but there's a challenge to stay emotionally grounded in the process.

If your Moon is 15–21 degrees Cancer, you're experiencing a bit of inner turmoil while Pluto transits in quincunx aspect all year. Health issues take a higher priority, and alterations in your diet and lifestyle can go a long way toward helping you reclaim your life. In relationships, you'll discover the most significant challenges, and can uncover and heal old emotional wounds that undermine your capacity to experience real happiness.

If your Moon is 22–29 degrees Cancer, you're feeling an undercurrent of unsettled emotions while Uranus transits in quincunx aspect to your Moon. Fortunately, Saturn's cycle helps you take steps to stabilize your life from January through May, and the alterations you make are part of a major life transition. Old habits die slowly, and this year you're getting down to the core drives that may be rooted in past trauma. Now, you can let go, and move forward—even if it does feel like you're dancing the side-step shuffle!

January

Despite the standoff between who's right and who's wrong that's happening around you, there's progress from your own efforts—if you can avoid being distracted. The New Moon on the 2nd heralds a time to define priorities and assign tasks. Since Mercury retrogrades until the 23rd, job descriptions are likely to change before all is said and done, so if there's something on your list you'd prefer to switch, give it a try before the 7th. Your emotional sensitivity is on high alert during the Cancer Full Moon on the 18th, when you'll prefer to be around people who know and understand you. Strange situations can be intimidating and nerve-racking. Agitation arrives on the heels of the Full Moon in the form of lacking cooperation, so clarify expectations before you promise anything—unless you want to be stuck working overtime while everyone else takes a long weekend!

February

Chemistry in a relationship sets sparks flying, and if your love connection is healthy, you can delve into fun-oriented experimental territory with your sweetie after the New Moon on the 1st. A new love needs time for the mystery to unfold, and provides it's own element of risk, although you may decide to play it coy until you feel safe. A disturbance gets on your nerves during the Full Moon on the 16th, when plans close to home will be more to your liking. After the 20th there's a shift toward harmony, but only after the hardliners make their presence known. Negative attitudes can definitely disturb your confidence, even though you may have muttered something like, "Just tell me how you feel." Next time, ask only if you want to know the answer to the question!

March

Get started on a project around the house during the New Moon on the 3rd. You'll appreciate a target for your feeling of increased assertiveness once Mars enters an opposition to your Moon sign on the 4th that lasts the next seven weeks. Buried anger is not likely to stay buried under the planetary instigators, although this is not necessarily a destructive picture. It's just that repressed feelings backfire, so honesty with yourself and others will be much more effective. In fact, during the Full Moon on the 18th you may even resolve issues that have been bottled up for quite some time. It's time to repair anything that's giving you trouble, and you may try to go around the issues and work on the dripping faucet long before you talk about what hurts your feelings. Think of it this way: What can you gain by saying how you really feel?

April

Enticing signals from the right person go a long way toward increasing your confidence when it comes to taking the initiative. Mercury and Venus support your trust in your intuition, helping you make significant headway where it counts. At home, plan dinner parties, a gathering of friends, or time with your favorite person—but keep things simple to avoid getting yourself in a tizzy. After all, Mars continues its high-friction rub, and it doesn't take much to push your buttons right now! Plans for redecorating or moving work out nicely, and if you need to showcase your home for any reason, the best responses come from the 1st to 18th. Once Mercury retrogrades on the 26th, review your plans, but try to avoid major change unless you are definitely satisfied with the options.

May

A rehash of recent developments with someone who's been out of touch can be pleasant, but it can also open a can of worms! Regret can cripple your capacity to seek out new experience, and even if you want to leave the past behind, it can be difficult. Look for common values to help you get through situations involving people newly introduced to your life. You may discover a new friend, or might even mend fences with an old buddy near the time of the lunar eclipse on the 16th. Consider employing the principles of feng shui to alter the flow of energy in and around your home after the 17th, concentrating on drawing more abundance into your life. The discontent you feel may begin to disappear, too—especially if you've been comparing your current situation to a vague set of ideals. It's time to envision and create a space that answers your needs.

June

On the heels of the May 31 solar eclipse, you begin this month ready to anchor your needs more effectively. Saturn enters Cancer on the 3rd, beginning a two-year period of powerful soul growth and enhanced emotional maturity. There's no rush to make everything perfect right away, but you may feel a pressing sense of urgency to at least get started. Clear out the attitudes that inhibit your capability to nurture yourself and others. Get rid of things (and people) cluttering your personal space. What you no longer need will begin to fall away, and your interest in things that no longer fit into your life will wane. By the 19th, you'll feel a renewed sense of purpose emerging. Then, during the Cancer New Moon on the 29th, it's time for you to consciously express your needs, hopes, and wishes. Focus your desires through the lens of your highest needs, and you'll see amazing results!

July

If you hear yourself humming "Oh what a beautiful morning …," it's probably because you can make things go your way. Of course, you have to know what you want, so if you've not yet figured out that part, you'll feel the push to get started. Your capacity to embrace the pure essence of your most soulful self is supported by significant planetary cycles. By the time the Full Moon occurs on the 13th, many of the changes or actions you put into motion last month will peak, and then, you'll be ready for Part Two. Social activities fare best through the 12th, but romance and artistic expressions can blossom throughout July. You're learning to open to the flow of love, and that may simply mean that you finally can allow yourself to be on the receiving end of good things. From there, your heart opens, and giving love is easier, too. Celebrate!

August

Practical matters provide fertile ground for your special talents, even though they may not put you in the spotlight. That's okay, since your enjoyment of someone you love garnering deserved accolades can fill your heart. On a personal note, your confidence in your capacity to speak up about your feelings and needs adds strength to your relationships—and it can't hurt anything at work, either. Most of the bravado that seems to have been the order of the day calms by the 22nd, making room for everyday magic to make a difference. You know—it's the kind of thing that happens when you decide to make your favorite dish, and your best friend shows up on the doorstep. Set fresh goals in motion during the New Moon on the 27th. More magic to follow.

September

Your confidence continues to grow, and that's a good thing. What you have to watch is a tendency to let things slide that fall in the category of restraint! It's so easy to overdo, overindulge, or overcommit. The cost may escape you at first, but you'll feel the pinch later when you're trying to get into your favorite jeans. Look for healthy adventures, including romance that's supports your real needs, until and on the Full Moon on the 10th. Then, seek ways to scale back on your obligations so you can enjoy the fruits of your labors. Someone else's agenda is likely to override your own during the New Moon on the 26th, but that's okay. You're ready to be entertained without the hassle of putting on the show all by yourself.

October

A few awkward moments can leave you feeling silly early in the month. It's the kind of thing that happens when you show up in the wrong attire for a party. The remedy's clear: Double-check details from the 1st to 8th, if you want to keep your dignity intact. After the 10th you're dealing with a different set of circumstances. Focus on activities or social situations then will give you a chance to show off your skills. Still, you may run into someone very attractive, but completely unattainable. Passions run deepest after the 24th, and it's time to improve your capacity to enjoy the fullness of your life during the New Moon on the 25th. Remind yourself: "My life is filled with beauty and love!"

November

Until the 9th, momentum grows strong for you to complete projects at home, or make progress with a personal challenge. Then there's a test following the lunar eclipse on the 8th. Even when you try to consider somebody's preferences, you may still fall short of their expectations. That's when you have to decide whether or not it's worth the effort! There's no need to try to bend yourself into a pretzel shape (unless your yoga practice is going really well). However, flexibility from all sides is important, and the real test is about mutual respect for one another. Once you drag your insecure feelings into the open so you can explore them, you may discover that what you feared is no big deal after all.

December

The balance of attention may seem to lean more toward everybody else, although the give-and-take flow of emotion can gain tremendous momentum if you can keep our heart open. Pressure can build, and the weight of Venus opposed by Saturn early in the month can leave you feeling left out. It's up to you to say "No" when you must, since agreeing to something that does not feel right can be way too depressing. Your capacity to reach out can seem inhibited, but that improves when you're in familiar circumstances from the 1st to 16th. Tensions build after the 15th, especially if you cannot express anger or feel frustrated by someone else. Ask questions. Open up discussions after the New Moon on the 23rd. This is no time to stay in the dark!

Leo Moon

The soulful power emanating from your heart of gold, as your Leo Moon reflects passion, fiery intensity, and uplifting courage, can bring warmth and light into the lives of those you touch, Less than your best is never acceptable, and your most outstanding performance may come when the stakes are highest. When you place your faith in someone, the inspiration you provide can ignite self-confidence when they need it most. Your soul thrives on creative self-expression, and it's your love for life that shines through your remarkable smile.

At home, you prefer to surround yourself with all the comforts, since you definitely believe in that old adage "My home is my castle"—and you can create a fabulous showplace that nourishes the talents of your family and close friends. Even if your surroundings are simple, a quiet elegance always helps you feel most at home. You invest a lot of yourself in those who have your heart, and you can be generous to a fault. At the other end of the spectrum, you can also be extremely self-absorbed, especially when you feel insecure. That's when you get into trouble, and when your willfulness or intractability emerge. Promises are sacred to you, and you expect others to take commitment as seriously as you do. If you are hurt, it can be almost impossible for you to forgive. When you leave room for growth and evolutionary change in your personal commitments, life gets easier. Otherwise, your natural tendency to hold fast can be a bother when it's imperative that you integrate change into your life. Even then, you do have choices about the way you respond, although you prefer to decree change when you feel you want it!

Before you gain control of your life, you may encounter a few bumps along the way. By experimenting with the best ways to express the love in your heart you become more confident, and then your capacity to open the way for others grows. It's through your brilliant talents that you share yourself with the world, and this helps to assure that your bond with a higher power is secure. Never doubt that those who love you find you unforgettable, or that your love-inspired actions and efforts are held in high regard—even when you cannot hear the applause!

The Year at a Glance for Leo Moon

With generous Jupiter gliding through Leo's territory until the end of August, you'll feel that you have a guardian angel watching over you during 2003. The beauty of this cycle is that it's easier to handle almost anything, since it adds a quality of ease and confidence to your emotional well-being. This cycle continues from one that began in August of last year, and marks a time when you may decide to expand your home base, move, add to your family, or travel.

The solar and lunar eclipse cycles for this year do not provide specific challenges to your Leo Moon, although you may find that you are feeling a bit more sensitive to the needs of others. It's best to clarify what someone may want or need from you, since what you think they need might be off the mark!

The slower-moving planets—Saturn, Uranus, Neptune, and Pluto—have the greatest influence during the year they each make a specific contact to the degree of your Leo Moon. Once you've determined your Moon's degree, you'll be able to pinpoint when the challenges and opportunities presented by these cycles will be most powerful.

If your Moon is 0–6 degrees Leo, you're experiencing a series of confrontations with your old habits while Pluto transits in sesquiquadrate to your Moon throughout the year. It's a good time to make a series of adjustments that will help you eliminate excessive clutter or get rid of stale anxiety. Be aware of the way you handle power issues. You may give in to someone or something and regret your choices later, when you realize you feel overwhelmed. Plus, during June and July, Saturn moves into a semi-sextile contact to your Moon, stimulating an even stronger urge to get back on track with your highest emotional priorities.

If your Moon is 7–14 degrees Leo, you may feel that your foundations are dissolving while Neptune travels in opposition to your Moon this year.

While this is a highly creative stimulus, you can be more emotionally vulnerable, and may be tempted to make changes without checking details or facts. Your spiritual needs grow more intense during this cycle, and finding ways to reach out and make a difference in the world can be especially important. Fortunately for you, Saturn moves into a semisextile connection to your Moon in August, and you'll feel you have more substantial options for fulfilling your dreams during the remainder of the year.

If your Moon is 15–21 degrees Leo, it's time to surrender to healing change while Pluto travels in a harmonious trine connection to your Moon. Renovations at home may go quite well, but even more important, renovations in your personal life can make a huge difference. This is a great time to work with a counselor or therapist, and a wonderful time to be part of community projects that transform the quality of life. After May, Saturn moves into a challenging semisquare contact and can bring a few delays in the progress of these changes. Your responsibilities during the second half of 2003 may be larger, slowing the pace so you can handle the extra obligations.

If your Moon is 22–29 degrees Leo, you're feeling a powerful impulse to be free. Uranus completes its transit in opposition to your Moon, but you'll still feel the effects of your need to change throughout the year. Plus, it's time to put the finishing touch on a project at home or to complete a long-term responsibility while Saturn travels in sextile to your Moon until June. After September, Saturn's contact to your Moon can be like a review or a test, just to be sure you've gotten things right. It's like an emotional audit: How do you really feel about your life, your relationship, or your job? This cycle helps you uncover the truth.

January

Your talent for surrounding yourself with capable people serves you well after the 8th, and your work seems easier thanks to their help! Pesky disruptions are a problem from the 5th–17th, when you can be undone by situations out of your control. Whether trouble comes from kids bent on rebellion, or your own need to break out of an unhappy circumstance, the best results arise when you step back and evaluate before you take action. Knee-jerk responses can be harmful. Fortunately, a change during the Full Moon on the 18th leaves you feeling much more comfortable showing just how you feel when somebody asks. Your creative passions run high for the rest of January, and even if your impulse stems from a need to indulge in escape, you could end up on sunny shores.

February

Your flair for the dramatic can ease tensions at home, but may stir up jealousy at work. Power plays seem to come from out of the blue, but you've been watching the storm clouds brewing and have your provisions handy—just in case! Bringing priorities into focus works like magic, and by the time the Leo Full Moon arrives on the 16th, everyone may be singing your praises for saving the day. Of course, you may be off on your own adventure and miss the grand celebration of your success, since romantic intrigue can capture your attention after the 14th. (Like I said, you understand priorities!) Responsibilities close to home require your attention after the 20th, when a family gathering can prove to be more positive than you imagined.

March

Even if you decide to release the reins and let someone else lead, mixed signals can confuse the question about who's in the driver's seat. At home, damage control can drain your resources from the 4th-20th, especially if your rainy day fund has run dry. Your patience with wishy-washy attitudes, or with others who seem to take advantage of your generosity can also be exhausted. Unless there's a balance of give-and-take, you may be looking for a way to exit the situation. Relationships strike a new note after the 21st, although you still will have little tolerance for anybody not pulling his or her own weight. Look to those you trust to fulfill their commitment, since the loyalty test usually shines a light on your most valuable allies.

April

Exciting choices stir your enthusiasm during the New Moon on the 1st, although you may not feel that you're in step with the rhythm of changes surrounding you. Part of the problem can be a difference in values, and you may decide to focus on home projects or close family ties for now—just to avoid the awkward experience of not fitting in with unfamiliar surroundings. Family gatherings have their own surprises, and you may sense that you're not getting the whole story. Most of the mystery is solved by the Full Moon on the 16th, although you may have to bite your tongue to avoid telling someone, "I told you so!" A squabble after the 22nd leaves a bitter aftertaste, since stubborn attitudes prevail. For a diversion, turn your attention to more entertaining possibilities.

May

You'll welcome creative or artistic challenge, and from the 1st until the lunar eclipse on the 16th, you could even discover great allies in the process. Alert! Your eyes are on the realm of possibility and you could miss a costly detail, so postpone major decisions until after the 20th. Behind the scenes, intimate relationship skirmishes arise from the competitive elements of your relationship. While the tension sometimes leads to delightful game-playing, you have to be careful to avoid getting into territory that leads directly to trouble. If you feel mistrustful, explore the reasons. Clear up misunderstandings, as hurts can drive an unnecessary wedge between you. A fresh confidence emerges during the solar eclipse on the 31st, when you're finally on the same page. Now you can get down to business!

June

Extend a helping hand only when you're asked and when it is appropriate, since your offer may be seen as an intrusion if you just step in and take action. No matter what your intention, you could misread the situation simply because you hate the thought of seeing someone you love in trouble—so finesse and understanding are absolute requirements. Part of the problem can be a difference in values, and objectivity can be in short supply until after the 10th. Playful circumstances ease tension, and a romance can soar during the Full Moon on the 14th. However, some changes at home can leave you feeling vulnerable after the 18th, especially if your old familiar stuff is not where you want it. A temporary displacement might be okay if you are remodeling or moving. Otherwise, anybody messing with your property may be in hot water!

July

Too much sentiment can be a bother, particularly if you are accused of "not caring" by somebody whose feelings are worn on a sleeve. You know what's in your heart, but you're not willing to take emotional risks until you feel the climate is right. Your distance protects your vulnerability that you'd just as soon not show to one who is not inside the inner circle. Mercury enters Leo on the 12th, prompting you to talk about your plans, feelings or ideas, but it's not until the 23rd that you may see a situation with sufficient clarity to trust it. At home, disruptions continue to plague your routine. Of course, there is a long list of potential irritants, but whatever the cause, you may feel you've gone above and beyond in your attempts to "be nice." Welcome the Leo New Moon on the 29th. A show of gratitude goes a long way toward satisfying those you adore.

August

Enjoy the last month of Jupiter's travel through Leo's light. Throw a party, attend celebrations, or show your support for your friends and family. With Venus in Leo until the 22nd, you'll feel much more inclined to open your heart and your pocketbook. Just watch your impulses near the Full Moon on the 12th, when you could be dazzled by the glitz and pay more than necessary. Romance may be at the top of your list, but this is also a marvelous time to adorn your home. Of course, you could combine the two, and create the perfect ambience for lasting love! A consultation with a feng shui expert might be just what you've needed.

September

Details. Details. Virgo qualities overtake planetary cycles now, and you might as well take advantage and concentrate on organizing your personal space. Even though you might not appreciate somebody else invading your privacy, you will enjoy the organization and sense of clarity that results. You may feel a bit more vulnerable until late in the month, so you'll need to make sufficient time to retreat when you need it. Health matters may also require more time and attention, and this can be an excellent time to get a second opinion. After the New Moon on the 26th you'll be more inclined to socialize, or to invite others into your home. Until then, a key may be required.

October

Get out of your rut and try something different. Experimentation broadens your optimism from the 1st–9th, especially if it's not likely to lead to anything "permanent." Your fun-loving attitude can be highly attractive, and if you welcome unusual ideas or innovative people into your life, the exposure could enhance your creativity. That part, you'll like! Some confusion may arise during the Full Moon on the 10th, particularly if you are drawn into something you do not want to do. For this reason, you'll need to clarify your "boundaries" before you head into the maze! It's not over, either, since the New Moon on the 25th can bring emotional challenges your way. They are likely to come in the guise of family issues—and I'm not just talking about the Halloween decorations, either!

November

Although you may be worried about whether your resources will stretch to fit your desires during the lunar eclipse on the 8th, your artistry increases. All you have to do is put effort behind your talents. (Ask for help where you need it, from reliable people you can trust.) It's a balancing act, since there may be more demands than you can satisfy, but your desire to maintain harmony prods you ever onward. However, you may feel quite certain about ending your alliance with those who no longer have your affections, since your current focus may offer much more in return. The solar eclipse on the 23rd ushers in a period of positive, healing communication. For the remainder of the month, reaching out brings joy, and reaching closure brings peace.

December

Everyday tasks may seem to require more time, but it's probably because you have crammed so much into your schedule! Still, finding joy in the ordinary keeps you smiling, and your efforts to create an elegant setting for family celebrations can be especially gratifying. Attention to the reasons and philosophy behind your actions can come through a confrontational question during the Full Moon on the 8th. If someone questions your beliefs, consider it an opportunity to honestly explore the source of your ideals. Your attitudes and actions speak volumes all by themselves. After the 17th, you may feel a powerful need to make a difference in your community or to spearhead a family project based on compassion. Whatever your choices, it's a time to reach toward the highest humanitarian ideals—regardless of the season!

Virgo Moon

That internal critic, with running commentary that seems to be constantly making notes, is a manifestation of your Virgo Moon. Even as a child you were an astute observer, and your capacity for dealing with fine details may be unrivaled. You find beauty in natural perfection, and tend to look past surface appearance and into the vital essence of people, situations, and ideas. Your conservative, practical attitude is more discernable to the casual observer, although you are very sensitive emotionally. You just don't like to dabble in the details of your feelings unless it's really important.

You may feel happiest when you're working out the details of a project, analyzing what makes something (or somebody) tick, or fine-tuning one of your designs. Even though you may never achieve what you consider to be true perfection, you strive to get as close as you can to the ideal. One reason your self-confidence can suffer is that you frequently turn your sense of supercritical discrimination against yourself. You may also find that patience is hard to come by when others fail to understand the importance you place on getting things right. Of course, there might be a lesson there—you may need to explore the depth of your tendency to fret too much over the things you cannot control, or the inconsequential details nobody but you notices. (Just keep notes, since you'll use what you learned later on.)

Then, there's your need to keep your surroundings as serene. That's a result of your need to counterbalance the scattered emotions you experience when there's too much tension in your life. You can feel uncomfortable in relationships with "too much emotion," because emotional turmoil or intensity does not fit into your "sensible" category. Or, when someone else messes up your plans, or fails to learn from their mistakes, you can feel strangely unsettled. In your intimate relationship, you need unconditional acceptance, but you must first give it to yourself before you can extend the same to your partner, friends, or family. Compassion for yourself and others begins when you acknowledge the perfection of the moment. From there on, life is much sweeter, and love inspires your words and actions.

The Year at a Glance for Virgo Moon

Although 2003 has a bumpy start, steady improvement comes from maintaining your focus on top priorities. Consider this the year to complete what you've started, and the time to satisfy current commitments. By midyear, the cycles shift, and your responsibilities seem to fit into your life with less intensity. After a slow start this year, the momentum builds, until your life is finally moving along toward your goals and fulfillment of your needs.

The good news is that Saturn moves away from the tense friction to your Moon sign by summer, and then Jupiter heads into Virgo's zone on August 27th, where it will remain until late 2004. These two shifts blend together quite nicely, and if you know you've paid your dues (so to speak), you can see your way clear to spend more time on the things that matter most to you.

The solar and lunar eclipses bring a challenge your way, but come with opportunities to release old burdens that are no longer yours to carry. Specific information on their influences is noted in the monthly sections that follow (check out May and November).

The timing of the influence of the slower-moving planets to your Moon depends upon the degree of your Moon in your chart. When these planets make a connection, you'll feel their impact most intensely.

If your Moon is 0–4 degrees Virgo, you're feeling the brunt of Uranus entering its exciting two-year cycle in opposition to your Moon. However, you may decide that too much excitement gets in the way of your sense of self-control. This influence disrupts the status quo, and you'll feel a powerful impulse to change old habits, or may decide that it's time to move to more promising pastures. These impulses will be most marked from August–October, when Venus, Mars, and Jupiter join the picture.

Saturn's influence brings positive support to your 5–15 degree Virgo Moon. Consider this the year to create a strong framework for your long-term security. After August, Jupiter's energy melds perfectly with your Moon, and you'll feel more confident about your commitments, opening the way for you to take on healthy responsibilities.

If your Moon is 9–13 degrees Virgo, Neptune's cycle can throw a monkey wrench in the works, since you could be blind-sided by others who seem to need you to rescue them. While this is a good time to focus more on your spirituality, there are other cycles at work that will help you keep those spiritual needs in a practical frame of reference.

If your Moon is 16–21 degrees Virgo, you're experiencing powerful transformational change under the influence of Pluto traveling in a tight square aspect to your Moon. This cycle brings old issues to the surface, and it's an excellent time to work with a therapist to get rid of emotional baggage. Ultimately, this can be a time of healing, although you'll still mourn some of the things (or people) you must release.

If your Moon is 22–29 degrees Virgo, you'll begin the year feeling the heaviness of Saturn's cycle in friction to your Moon. There's still a holdover cycle from the wake of Uranus' travels in quincunx to your Moon from last year, with some of the sudden changes you experienced having their strongest impact now. By June, Saturn's cycle ends, and Uranus' influence is also subsiding—so there's a sense of some control and direction. Consider the second half of 2003 your time to rebuild—carefully, and with the idea of simplicity.

All individuals with Virgo Moon are experiencing a year of reflection and insight, with opportunities coming to help with the transformational changes that lead to a sense of inner strength. The foundations you build to support your dreams are strengthened, and that's a good reason to celebrate your successes!

January

The trick to staying connected to your emotional center comes when you effectively deal with the distractions that seem to be everywhere. Although you feel hopeful during the New Moon on the 2nd, and your projects have a smooth start, disruptions can scatter your focus after the 7th – especially if somebody pulls the plug on your support! It's all about reliability, and whether or not to step in and take on responsibilities because another person just can't cut it. Watch for power issues to emerge at home after the Full Moon on the 18th, when a situation that appeared to be quite innocent turns into trouble once you discover a hidden agenda. Part of the problem is the contrast in values, and you must determine where you stand to avoid being pulled into a battle that's simply not yours to fight!

February

Although smoke and mirrors are the traditional trappings of magic shows, you may wish you had such theatrical supplies on hand to deal with those hard-to-convince know-it-alls who don't know the first thing about having fun. Let your practical sensibilities aid you when you present your vision to someone after the New Moon on the 1st, since the bottom line may be the most effective trick of all! Romance takes a sensible turn while Venus moves through Capricorn's dominion after the 3rd, and even if you're feeling amorous, you may not be willing to part with precious resources unless you know you'll get something in return. Shields up during the Full Moon on the 16th, when Mars and Pluto join forces, leaving a potentially devastating mess if you've left yourself open to attack. Remember: It's best not to provide your enemy with ammunition!

March

Now you're cookin'! Despite the series of adjustments you feel required to make (just to keep a few folks happy), you'll feel a consistent sense of accomplishment. Even the wishy-washy types seem more cooperative, or at least you can lead them with less resistance. Before you start feeling too pleased with yourself, though, there's plenty to keep you on your toes. You still have to deal with what seems like passing inspection. Whether it's a job review, an audit, or you're just waiting for the reviews of Sunday dinner—you may feel like you're under extra close scrutiny for a couple of days before and during the Virgo Full Moon on the 18th. Take a good look in the mirror. There's your most daring critic! You might be surprised to discover how much someone else values your efforts. Enjoy it!

April

Support from Mercury and Mars helps you tap into the perfect resources for the job at hand—and just in time! With plenty of projects around the house, you'll appreciate access to the right tools, and a helper might even show up for a while. Yes, you guessed it, you may be on your own when the real work starts. Family matters hit a brick wall after the 14th, when a problem from the past can spell trouble. Reactions can be overblown during the Full Moon on the 16th, but your even-handed manner can help keep the situation under control. You might decide it's better to keep a distance, especially if you can see the possibility that you could be blamed for problems that have nothing to do with you!

May

With everybody else making changes around you, it can be difficult to stay cool. The sense of focus you experience during the New Moon on the 1st helps you stay in touch with your most important goals, and you can inch toward them despite the brewing commotion. Time away from the grind just before and during the lunar eclipse on the 16th can prompt a long, romantic weekend with your sweetheart. Or, it might be more fun to send everybody else away while you enjoy time at home—without work—that is! Loving energy comes your way on the 17th, when Venus moves into friendly Taurus territory, providing substantial support for you to fill your heart. You may not feel a clear sense of direction until after the solar eclipse on the 31st, although your capacity to communicate acceptance and compassion strengthens the connections that mean the most.

June

Even though you might think it's best to avoid talking about how you truly feel, honestly sharing what's in your heart can make all the difference to someone who needs to know. With Mercury and Venus in complimentary contact to your Moon until the 11th, you'll be more at ease expressing yourself. It's easy to get off track during the Full Moon on the 14th, when kids or family may seem to have more pressing needs, or work may simply take its toll. After the 19th, healthy competition actually adds energy, and you may decide it's time to step up your fitness routine, too. Your sense of adventure begins to grow after the New Moon on the 29th, and although you may want to stay close to home, you're likely to see what's around you from a difference perspective.

July

Your imagination is stimulated, creating enthusiasm for change in your relationship, or at home—or both! Passions can drive you beyond your usual practical sensibilities, and you're likely to enjoy every loving moment. With Mars in Pisces, opposing your Moon sign until December, restless dissatisfaction may be your constant companion. If you've been wronged or injured, you'll feel ready to assert yourself, and this is the month to gather facts and line up your allies. After all, some battles are best fought with help from your friends. You may feel an impulse to remodel, make repairs, or pull up stakes and transplant yourself. Action taken before the Full Moon on the 13th meets with the greatest success.

August

You may want to believe an offer or an opportunity, but your common sense tells you to do a background check. Doors are opening, although every one is not meant for you. Fortunately, your analytical mind is working overtime all month and you'll be able to spot trouble when you see it. Enthusiasm from others can work to your advantage, too. But watch out for anybody who promises more than they can deliver near the Full Moon on the 12th. There's no need for you to be left holding the bag, since you definitely have better fish to fry! Venus and Jupiter join the Virgo New Moon on the 27th, ushering in a period of confidence, prosperity, and increasing joy. All you have to do is find the best way to direct it. Pull out your wish list!

September

That overwhelming urge to have more space, pushing you to expand, comes from Jupiter's entry into Virgo, and it lasts for a year. Coupled with the impulses from Mars and Uranus stirring your restless heart, you may simply not know where to start. We all know that appearances can deceive, so it might be a good idea to open the mouth of that gift horse, especially if you have to feed the darn thing. Part of the problem during the Full Moon on the 10th is that you can feel so overobligated that you can't enjoy the fullness of the moment. Looks like you'll do yourself a favor if you set a pace early on, and adjust when necessary. You have a talent for setting the equalizer perfectly, as long as you're tuned in.

October

Why set limits? Your confidence is starting to grow, and your experience and skills work to your advantage. The competition can see your weak points, though, and that could be your downfall. That competitive energy can come from your close relationships, especially if you've not yet resolved an old issue. The problem brewing through the Full Moon on the 10th is that you can be blind-sided if you stretch beyond your capacities. All you need is a safety net, and however you create it, test it out before you think you might need it. Your vulnerability is less marked during and after the New Moon on the 25th, when you can push your capacities a bit with less risk. Changes at home work better then, too.

November

Through the time of the lunar eclipse on the 8th your momentum continues to be strong. You may decide to start more than one project, and there can be success on several fronts. Problems arise later, near the time the solar eclipse on the 23rd, when family matters and situations in the world can bring pressures you have not considered. Use the time from the 9th–23rd to complete details and to troubleshoot problems when they arise. There's no worry about boredom. In fact, you may even wish for a boring day here and there so you can catch your breath! Since the most pressing needs will take priority, and you may have to ask for assistance. Fortunately for you—you know where to look. Now the hard part—ask!

December

The craziness around you may actually inspire your imagination, and you seem to have a solution for just about anything that rolls across your path. You just slip around the corner into your closet of goodies, and voila! Out you come with the perfect fit! Expectations fall into more reasonable categories, and you may feel inclined to renew your commitment to a person or situation—now that you can define where you need to go with it. There's a bit of extra pressure to be perfect from the 4th–7th, and you may have to pinpoint the issues to avoid running into resistance. The New Moon on the 23rd marks a time to focus on love and joy in the acceptance and affection of those you hold dear. It's a two-way street!

Libra Moon

Beauty is your ultimate comfort, and you naturally gravitate toward refinement. Your Libra Moon craves being surrounded by gorgeous colors and sumptuous music, and it reflects your unmistakable grace and refinement. You're drawn to the breathtaking creative and artistic excellence expressed by others, and have a talent for lending peace and harmony wherever you go. Your diplomacy may be in high demand, and more often than not, your fair-minded logic saves the day, when others are swept up in the wake of emotional turmoil.

Despite your capacity for helping others see their perfection, you may have difficulty feeling accepted. This challenge arises from your tendency to compare yourself too harshly against standards that may suit another, but may not reflect your true value or needs. It's your need for symmetry that pushes you toward a desire for a soulmate—someone whose very essence brings true equality and harmony to your own heart of hearts. At its highest level, this emotional drive helps you discover that you need room for human imperfection (including your own!), since this is the true balance required for your soulful existence on Earth. Balance is your primary drive, and that's quite evident when you struggle to make the best decisions for yourself. It's just so much easier when you're advising somebody else! Searching for your ultimate partner can take time, since finding the right ingredients for a healthy relationship often requires experimentation.

You need a home space that you can fill with the things you deem exquisite, and your sense of taste can be quite elegant. Charming people are part of the equation, too, and you may be the consummate party planner. Uncomfortable with hostility, you may look for the nearest exit, although you can take a stand when it's important. Even then, expressing dissent can leave you feeling pretty vulnerable, as it goes against your desire to create peace. To stabilize your emotions, you may require time and space to connect with your inner self. After all, it is the bond you create with your inner partner that mirrors the self-assurance required to attract all that you need from life, including your partner!

The Year at a Glance for Libra Moon

Steps to establish emotional stability benefit every aspect of your life, and can range from career advancement, to commitment in relationship, to a settled move that's just right for your needs. First, it's essential that you decide what you need, and that your goals are clearly in your sights. Uncertainty is more troublesome, yet focused priorities work like magic. Saturn's support helps your ability to manifest your needs from January–June, and Jupiter's energy lends visionary confidence to your emotional outlook throughout the year.

The eclipses of Sun and Moon do not present significant challenges to your Libra Moon during 2003. As a result you may feel that the outside world or demands from others are less likely to distract you from your connection to your inner self and real needs.

Cycles of Saturn, Uranus, Neptune, and Pluto are most noteworthy during the years these planets make a specific connection to your Moon. These influences suggest periods of profound change, so find the degree of your Moon to determine whether or not you're experiencing challenges or opportunities from these planetary transits.

If your Moon is 0–3 degrees Libra, Uranus brings surprising and potentially unsettling changes your way while it travels in quincunx aspect to your Moon. The series of adjustments required to keep up with changes can leave you feeling that your life is a pretzel. Maintaining objectivity is more difficult, but if you keep a check on your emotional boundaries you'll make choices that are less likely to leave you in knots! Guilt or regret about decisions can be a problem during June and July, when Saturn transits in square to your Moon, so watch how you play into the "blame game!"

If your Moon is 4–8 degrees Libra, then this is the year to develop your special talents. Pluto enters a quintile contact to your Moon, and some of the desires you've placed on the shelf labeled "When I have time" clamor for your attention. During July–August, Saturn's square to your Moon can block your sense that others support you or your needs, although this is a good time to become more disciplined where talents are concerned.

If your Moon is 9–15 degrees Libra, your creative imagination takes you to places that seem almost magical since Neptune travels in an easy trine support to your Moon. Reaching into the depths of your inner self brings significant change, and your spirituality takes on new meaning. Alterations at home or within your family have a strong impact, and you may be able to forgive old hurts more easily. After August, Saturn moves into a frustrating square contact to your Moon, testing your capacity to achieve true emotional balance and harmony in your relationships.

If your Moon is 16–21 degrees Libra, you're ready to resolve emotional issues and eliminate unhealthy habits while Pluto transits in a harmonious sextile aspect to your Moon. This can be a great year to remodel or move, but even more important, it's the best time to heal your life from the inside out!

If your Moon is 22–30 degrees Libra, you're experiencing several planetary cycles this year. First, Uranus completes its transit in trine aspect to your Moon, stimulating a powerful desire to express your independence. You're ready to break free from situations that inhibit your capacity for joy, and may move, alter your career, or begin or end a relationship. In addition, from January–June, Saturn's travel in trine to your Moon adds a quality of emotional stability, so that the changes you do make can clarify the best path to take. Your intuitive sensibilities guide you toward the right decisions, and your dreams take flight under the rays of Jupiter during July and August.

January

Despite the tendency for others to grumble, your capacity for finding the silver lining in those clouds puts you ahead of the game. It's out with the old—even if you are working behind the scenes at first. Give those who demand the spotlight room to shine from the New Moon on the 2nd until the Full Moon on the 18th, and then you'll find it's finally your turn. Meanwhile, you have plenty to do on the homefront, and after the 8th, you'll have excellent success clearing away clutter to make room for your fresh project (or the new clothes you score during January sales). Social gatherings can be pure delight after the 18th, but your first priority may be to concentrate on creating the perfect ambience for a romantic interlude after the 21st. You're eager to find out which way the wind is blowing, so give it your best shot, and ask!

February

Cultural pursuits, or an indulgence in your favorite diversion, can lead you to travel or connect with unusual people from the 1st (New Moon) to 3rd, although you may be the most interesting person in the room. Despite the possibility of awkward silence, your charm breaks the ice with even the most conservative types, although it may be a mutual disdain for garish displays that puts you right next to someone whose ideals are much like your own. If you're focused on family events or relationships now, your tolerance for selfishness is tested after the 5th. Open, honest communication brings issues to the table near and during the Full Moon on the 16th, when you'll feel most at ease presenting your side of the story. Put extra effort into home improvement, even if you are on your own when it comes to the actual work involved.

March

Relationships improve dramatically—on every level—thanks to Venus. Still, there's turmoil in the works from fiery Mars stirring up trouble. The thorn in your side could come from trying to keep someone happy when they don't want to be. So, where's the improvement, you ask? It's much easier to walk away, when turning up the heat would only lead to more problems. Plus, your creative energy is aching for direction, and even a small artistic endeavor lifts your spirits. From the New Moon on the 3rd until the Full Moon on the 18th, an opportunity for community or charitable efforts can arise, although you'll have to remember to say "No" to the things you honestly don't want to do. Agreeing just to get someone off your back will backfire!

April

It's almost impossible to hide your frustration with others who sit on the fence when you need an answer. Before you push past the point of no return, consider what you have to gain, since you might end up with egg on your face if you're not careful! Expectations can be a problem, too, and it's possible that you or someone else has been left with the wrong impression. Untangling the mess is tricky, since one issue may lead to yet another hidden problem. This can be fascinating if you're reading a mystery, but when it's your life and you're trying to finish something important, the result is less than wonderful. These energies can be put to good use if you're clearing attics or closets. However, your top priority may be more like "soul clearing" during the Libra Full Moon on the 16th. Just remember: everything does not have to be resolved this minute!

May

Confrontation may be uncomfortable—but unavoidable—through the time of the lunar eclipse on the 16th. Of course, you could cover all the mirrors. But, still, it's difficult to escape from what you feel. You may simply need to explore elements of a relationship (or aspects of your own needs) that you've avoided, and the situations presented now can be the perfect chance to see what would happen if you simply experiment! Mars provides just the right push out of your comfort zone and into the realm of excitement, although you can feel that the ride's going too fast from the 4th to 9th. Seatbelts fastened, you continue on, and remember to breathe (or scream!), and, voila!—you can see the world from a different perspective! It's easier to let go and enjoy yourself after the 23rd, but it's not until the solar eclipse on the 31st that you'll feel you're on familiar ground. Finally!

June

If you're wondering whether or not somebody changed the rulebook, the answer is "Yes!" Saturn moves into Cancer's zone, beginning a two-year cycle that brings more attention to family and domestic issues. At first, the change is subtle, although you've probably felt a shift in the winds already. Positive alterations at home give you breathing room, and there may be more people in and out for one reason or another. Feng shui works like magic after the 11th to alter the flow of energy in your personal space, and even though you may have to get used to the changes, you'll love the results. Love definitely can blossom, although you can also use these cycles to make spectacular change at home.

July

Confronted by illogical options, you may wonder if rational thinking has dissolved. It's just that emotional buttons are very easy to activate, and you can feel like the lone voice of reason in a sea of sentiment. While you, too, might also feel tempted to cling to the familiar past, you'll appreciate signs that objectivity has returned once Mercury shifts signs just before the Full Moon on the 13th. Time spent on artistic endeavors can be your sanctuary. Even if you travel, you may feel an uneasy pang of homesickness if you're missing something or somebody more than you thought. Funny thing:

Feelings don't fit into logical categories. These cycles remind you just how true that can be. Before you slink into despair, reach for moments filled with small wonders. The New Moon on the 29th brings inspiration, and your hope rekindles. Go ahead and let yourself enjoy a warm hug—it may be just what you've longed for.

August

While some folks are huddled together working out plans that are simply of no interest to you, you have a chance to focus your time and attention on a grand and beautiful experience. You might decide to dedicate your energy to thoroughly romantic delights, or you may be more enthralled by a chance to put the perfect touches on a fabulous creation. However, if you ignore the lament from family or friends that they feel left out, you may live to regret it. Fortunately, you have a knack for bringing everyone into the process. A celebration may be in order just before or during the Full Moon on the 12th, when imaginative expressions can be pure joy. It's time to be entertained (or entertaining), and to share playful times that make up sweet memories.

September

Empty promises can be difficult to spot, even though you'll look back and think to yourself that all the signals were there. Close relationships suffer when promises are not fulfilled, and a standoff between Mars and Jupiter can lead to situations that are quickly blown out of proportion. Your diplomacy and grace can ease tension after the 15th, when Venus moves into Libra. Before you volunteer to save the world, first decide if you need to be involved at such a level. You might have better success closer to home. In fact, a move or other improvements can add just the right touch to your personal space on and after the Libra New Moon on the 26th. It's easier to mend fences in relationships then, too!

October

Harmony at home is a welcome change, and expressing heartfelt emotions is easier, and now that Mars is moving forward again, you'll find it easier to make progress on your long list of projects. (It's also easier to get help from others when you need it!) Partnerships or agreements take priority during the Full Moon on the 10th. Complicated situations can emerge close to home, and you might find that you're most effective if you observe for a while before you step in to help create a solution. Vague signals or mixed messages make it tough to figure out what somebody needs, and you may even wonder what you want—since desire and need may be in conflict after the 16th. Honest talk brings issues into the open from the 8th–23rd, but after that, you may be more inclined to keep your lips zipped.

November

Work behind the scenes on festive plans puts you in touch with your true feelings, and by the time the lunar eclipse arrives on the 8th, you'll have a keen sense of what belongs in your life and what needs to go. The time to clear away unnecessary expectations and old hurts begins on the 13th, but you may not feel confident about your decision until the solar eclipse on the 23rd. Talk or write about your feelings and needs with someone who understands your motivations, or give yourself time away from the daily grind to reflect. Travel can be the perfect ticket to sanity after the 14th, but can be a royal pain early in the month. After the 23rd, it's time to turn over a new leaf. Start your resolutions for personal improvement now!

December

Watch out for the stick-in-the-mud types who seem to insist on gnarling your plans. You can decide to get bent out of shape, or you can use your objectivity to stay away from trouble when you see it. Fortunately, there's a bit of mischief afoot during the Full Moon on the 8th, and you can have some delectable fun if you've allowed room for spontaneity. Regrets follow if you go too far, and your sense of propriety (otherwise known as good sense) may save you. You'll feel most generous after the 21st, when a special offering from you goes a long way toward bringing peace when it's needed. Seek out opportunities to give someone else the lead when you can see that he or she is ready. You might enjoy the dance much more.

Scorpio Moon

At the core of your being there's a wellspring of passionate emotion and intense desire fueled by your Scorpio Moon. Captivated by mystery, you feel most alive when you're solving a puzzle or digging into research. You may baffle others who wonder about your capacity to explore the unfathomable. But those very questions and desires are what nourish your prolific creativity. At the least, you radiate intrigue, and you can be very charismatic—even when you may not intend to be!

If anybody prefers to keep emotions below the radar screen, it's you. Oh, you love to probe and may even cajole others into sharing their most guarded secrets—but you simply do not trust just anybody with your innermost thoughts and feelings. Once you do form a bond of trust in a relationship, you prefer to delve into the depths, and there you can build an eternal bond. However, when you do not want to get involved, you can project an untouchable distance. Those who are satisfied with surface emotions will find you confounding, and you may have little patience with anyone who lacks true integrity. You sense the truth, and have an uncanny ability to "read" people. This quality is the source of your ability to heal, since you can be an amazing partner to those seeking to resolve pain and suffering. Through helping others change their lives, you connect with your own spiritual power, and can find work in the healing arts to be quite rewarding. However, there are endless opportunities to transform the world!

At home, you need privacy, preferring a personal space set apart from the clamor of daily life. You might prefer a country retreat, but you can create such a haven in a city, too. It's here that you let go, release and transform yourself. You may absorb or repress more emotions than you express, especially negative feelings like guilt, self-doubt, or unresolved anger, and you need a place where you feel safe to let go and rejuvenate your own life. Your failure to address the debris stashed into the crevices of your psyche can block your ability to experience true joy. Yet, when you surrender to the healing flow and explore the labyrinth of your inner Self, your creative discovery can send you soaring into ecstasy!

The Year at a Glance for Scorpio Moon

This year you'll feel that you are making measurable progress toward fulfilling your security needs. The ups and downs illustrated by the planetary influences to your Moon can challenge your capacity to maintain your focus, but it's becoming easier to determine your priorities, and as you manifest healthy changes, you also strengthen your resolve.

The eclipses of Sun and Moon during 2003 signify that it's easier for you to uncover your true feelings about yourself and your life situation. During May and November, the Moon's eclipses help you reach more deeply into your inner self, and you can feel that you're ready to unlock old fears and open to trust. Foremost, you can trust yourself more fully, and that will ultimately reflect in the positive changes you manifest in relationships.

By midyear, Saturn moves into Cancer, traveling through territory that lends steady support to your Scorpio Moon for another two years. Despite some changes illustrated by slower-moving planets, you'll experience more consistent emotions, and the platform supporting your life grows stronger. However, because Saturn, Uranus, Neptune, and Pluto move very slowly through their zodiacal cycles—this is the year when each of these planets makes a more exact contact to your Moon, and you will make the most significant changes.

If your Moon is 0–4 degrees Scorpio, you'll feel a sense of personal freedom while Uranus transits in supportive trine to your Moon. This is the year to release unhealthy habits, and it's a wonderful time to move or make significant alterations to your home and family. During June and July, Saturn's cycle supports new commitments, and from June–October, Mars adds extra energy to your capacity to fulfill your true needs and desires. However, Pluto's cycle stirs up trouble with a frustrating semi-square to your Moon—so try to maintain honesty about the difference between "want" and "need!"

If your Moon is 5–13 degrees Scorpio, Saturn's cycle is in a frustrating sesquiquadrate to your Moon, and you start the year feeling that you're still not quite on the right track emotionally. It's important to sort through the things you need to do for yourself and the demands or temptations your feel from others. By August, Saturn moves into a supportive trine to your Moon, and you'll feel greater self-assurance.

However, if your Moon is 9–14 degrees Scorpio, you're also experiencing some confusion from Neptune's transit in a square contact to your Moon. This cycle can be mind-altering, and you may wonder what you really do feel about anything or anybody! The answers are found deep within your innermost self. Realize that this period can bring uncertainty, since it is a time to let go of the trappings of the external world and discover the power of the spiritual realms. You may need more time to retreat, since reflecting on what is true and real without undue influence from others is very important.

If your Moon is 15–21 degrees Scorpio, you're experiencing a year of internal revisions while Pluto travels in semisextile contact to your Moon. This cycle requires fine-tuning, and it's an excellent time to make changes that help you feel more expressive. At home, you may decide to take advantage of feng shui as a means to enhance and strengthen the flow of energy in your personal space.

If your Moon is 22–25 degrees Scorpio, you're completing a cycle of adjustments that began last year. Saturn ends its cycle in quincunx aspect to your Moon in June, and after that time, you'll feel more centered.

If your Moon is 26–29 degrees Scorpio, you're still experiencing a bumpy ride emotionally, since Uranus is transiting in a square contact. There's good news: It ends this year! The unsettled experiences from this cycle test your capacity to eliminate what you no longer need while avoiding the temptation to burn your bridges while you're still on them.

January

You're inspired to get things moving forward with the New Moon on the 2nd. Huge progress can be made on the personal front by addressing your needs and concerns in a close relationship, or on improvements at home. Alert! You may be attracted to something (or someone) that throws you into an emotional tailspin. Despite your fascination with unusual possibilities, existing commitments can overrule your desire to make a sudden change. This unexpected disruption can divert your attention just before the Full Moon on the 18th, although a flexible attitude will provide you with some emotional leeway. A knee-jerk response can lead to unnecessary difficulties, and feelings of frustration when you are not in charge are understandable—especially if you're worried about someone you love.

February

Vague or misleading actions from others may leave you scratching your head, wondering what the heck is going on during the New Moon on the 1st. It could be that they're just dreaming out loud, and you were within earshot! Your creative focus gains momentum after the 3rd, when your special touch adds the perfect ambience at home. Contact and communication with a trusted friend can inspire you to make positive life changes. Despite power struggles involving others in your immediate vicinity, you may feel blessed to have a constructive focus for your time and energy. However, you could be baited into joining a battle that's not yours to fight during the Full Moon on the 16th. Concentrate on more harmonious options after the 20th, when finding peace is your priority.

March

If you're hoping for a quick exit from an uncomfortable situation, it will be easier to slip away gracefully during the New Moon on the 3rd. Differences in values can prompt you to question your preferences or decisions, although you might determine that a little clash of color adds just the right spark, and decide to stay involved, but with less visible commitment. (Call it your safety net!) Despite an uneasy feeling that you're not being told everything, you have your sources and can do some research behind the scenes from the 5th–20th. Take care about sharing information or showcasing your prime ideas from the 11th–16th, since you could be duped into giving away the farm. Fun-filled gatherings are a healthy distraction from the humdrum just before and during the Full Moon on the 18th, although you might also have a great time with family or friends from the 29th–31st.

April

You may feel a need to refresh your relationship with your sweetie, or for change around the house. Whether you seek an adventure away from home or decide to dig for gold in your backyard, it's time to uncover hidden resources or bring out the beauty of your rare collectibles. Change at home is most enjoyable from the 4th–20th, especially if you have time and space to exercise your creative artistry. Now is the time to choose exquisite paint or wallpaper, or to find a fabulous treasure in that out-of-the-way shop. After the Full Moon on the 16th you may decide to pull in the reins a bit to avoid stretching your time and energy beyond your comfort zone. A small family crisis may require more time to resolve than you first thought.

May

With all the ammunition flying about, you may wonder how you got into the battle zone. Of course, you know, but might not want to admit your own culpability! Now, all you have to do is keep your shields up long enough to find safe cover, so you can hide out until the fighting stops. If you've been honest about your feelings in a relationship, all the fuss may be the result of someone else needing to let off steam—especially if you've announced that you no longer want to play a useless game. The turmoil might just be a result of repairs or a move, but it might feel like somebody opened Pandora's box, and the lid has definitely blown away! In any case, there's a lot of emotional tension during the Scorpio lunar eclipse on the 16th. By the time the solar eclipse arrives on the 31st, there's still dust in the air, but at least you can see where the arrows are coming from.

June

All that business about fair fights seems to be the stuff of fiction, since you are witnessing the lowest common denominator when it comes to dirty tricks from the 1st to 10th. If you're lucky, the trouble will just be what's reported on the news, but if the stink's coming from your backyard, it can be more difficult to maintain your composure. The attacks are the result of frictions from Mercury, Venus, and Mars—and they're not playing nice! It's tempting to throw some mud of your own, but you can see an opportunity to resurrect mutual respect after Saturn moves into Cancer on the 3rd. Some civility returns during the Full Moon on the 14th, but you may not feel that you're in safe territory until after the 17th. With Mars joining freedom-loving Uranus, you'll feel more confident about bidding farewell to situations you no longer need. Begin your journey toward more productive growth during the New Moon on the 29th.

July

Your patience proves its worth, and now things are finally going your way. A move or renovation can be revitalizing, and through the Full Moon on the 13th, the momentum toward starting fresh continues in your favor.

You'll still make progress, but might decide that you want to give more time and focus to strengthen and fine-tune the relationship issues or work on personal projects you find most fulfilling. Love blossoms from the 4th–28th, when a flirtation can lead to powerful passion, or rekindled affection can heal wounds with your soulmate. It's time to make the most of your resources and to share what's in your heart with someone you trust.

August

That old adage "All that glitters is not gold" seems to ring true, and your ability to peer beneath a false façade serves you well when others may be distracted by the flashing lights. You may be quietly working on the things that matter most to you, ignoring the inconsequential. However, the allure of change can be tempting, and might even be worth exploring—just to see what's really there. It's unlikely that you'll invest time or energy in a situation that costs more than it is worth. Design plans, but wait until the New Moon on the 27th to break ground. Jupiter joins the New Moon and Venus in harmony with your Scorpio Moon, and you'll feel a surge of confidence knowing that you have the support when it counts the most.

September

Despite Mercury's retrograde that lasts until the 20th, you're feeling in the groove. Practical tools and assistance from trusted friends give you a boost, and during the Full Moon on the 10th you can feel satisfied with progress you've made. Weak points are exposed from the 4th–7th, and once you've made repairs, you'll feel good as new. (Yes, those could be your physical weak points, so pay attention!) This is also a good month to concentrate on relationship, and to allow ample time to enjoy those you love. Affections provide marvelous glue, and help you hold together what you need the most. The tide turns within an old family issue on the 26th, and you'll breath a big sigh of relief!

October

Get used to adulation, since your talents gain the notice they deserve! Acts of kindness work like magic to heal old hurts, although apologies that come your way may seem a bit awkward. Beautify your home after the 8th, when Venus dons Scorpio's attire and enhances your ability to attract the perfect elements for your personal space. You may have romance in mind, but the end result you create can be a delectable comfort – romance or no romance! Misdirected signals can confuse an issue with your sweetheart from the 15th–19th, but if your sense of humor is intact, you'll weather it just fine. Even though you may not always be a party person, you might enjoy hosting a festive event during or after the Scorpio New Moon on the 25th. Of course, a party for two is not a bad idea, either.

November

Peaceful moments early in the month lead to more passionate exchange during the lunar eclipse on the 8th. Extend a helping hand when you can, since your efforts will be long remembered by a friend or family member, who may get in over his or her head. However, you can get into an itchy situation if you stick your nose into something where it does not belong— so be sure you're invited before you arrive with your tools and casserole dish. Scattered energy is on the agenda for the solar eclipse on the 23rd, and you may need a lasso to help bring the herd back in line. Of course, you could just leave them wandering around, but then they would miss turkey dinner!

December

More than just the season, you actually feel inclined to do all you can to share heartfelt wishes and abundance with others. Your storehouse of goodies seems more than adequate to cover what you desire to do for everyone else. Just remember to speak up when it comes to letting some-body know what you need or want from them, since after the 16th, you may feel that you get the short end of the stick. There's room for positive change during the New Moon on the 23rd, when innovative changes to tradition can bring others closer. You're ready to laugh, and may surprise a few people when you start the fun and games. Of course, those who know you have been holding their breath waiting in anticipation.

Sagittarius Moon

A quiet confidence burns in your heart, since you know that life is filled with unlimited possibilities. Your Sagittarius Moon relishes the exhilaration of the quest—whether the adventure is an exploration of far-away places, inspiring people, or just a search for the persistent need to ask "Why?" You need independence and will resist attempts from anyone to contain your boundless spirit. Philosophical by nature, you thrive on a steady diet of ideals, wisdom, and spiritual truth. That's one reason others look to you for inspiration when they need light along their own pathways.

For you, home may not be a particular place, but is, instead, a feeling you carry in your soul as you journey through life. Your Sagittarius Moon makes it easy for you to adapt to different environments, cultures, and ideologies, as your restless yearning to expand your understanding of man's relationship to the Source demands that you keep an open mind. You can stay up for hours enjoying a heated debate and thoughtful conversation, but you do not appreciate those who hold extreme prejudice or keep their minds locked against truth. In relationships, you can be demonstrative and passionate, and you appreciate a partner who understands your need to occasionally wander. You'll be most committed to situations that nurture your higher values and spirituality, but can be fearful of commitments that impair your ability to continue your life exploration. You find comfort in a place where you can dream and nourish your visionary sensibilities, and will adore sharing life with a mate whose ideals harmonize with your own.

The uplifting experience of soaring to the heights of understanding can happen when you're in a forest, or on a mountaintop, although you can just as easily take flight amidst the hustle and bustle of a city, or in the confines of the old books section of a library. Wherever you experience harmony between your spirit and your heart, and can surrender to the embrace of truth, you have found your home. Your connection to the universe may provide more questions than answers, but that's what motivates you when you greet each new dawn, and when your sense of wonder inspires others to believe in tomorrow.

The Year at a Glance for Sagittarius Moon

This can be a landmark year for you, with abundant opportunities to advance your aims and fulfill your needs. Your confidence grows, and it's your sunny attitude that attracts the most exciting possibilities. Travel, writing, or education may play a significant role in your advancement, too. Persistent effort helps you maintain your focus, and although your flexibility will be helpful as you adapt to greater responsibility, excessive distraction can be costly.

The solar eclipses have strong significance for you during 2003, and during the months of May and November you may make the most marked changes. From January through April you may be more in touch with your deeper motivations as a result of the cycles involving the eclipses. It is this awareness that can help you plot a more steady course toward your goals.

Jupiter's cycle through Leo sheds a confident light in your life from January through September. Despite resistance or hardship from other pressures, your optimism helps you find your way. When Jupiter moves into Virgo on August 27th, for its yearlong cycle, you'll need to watch your awareness of your limitations, since you can easily overextend.

The influence of Saturn, Uranus, Neptune, or Pluto is most noticeable during the year these slower cycles make a more exact contact to your Moon. If your Moon is 0–5 degrees Sagittarius, you'll feel inclined to make radical changes under the influence of Uranus moving into a square aspect to your Moon. This two-year cycle can seem like a carnival ride, since there can be lots of emotional ups and downs. The resulting uncertainty can undermine your confidence, but if you determine to release what you no longer need and to explore your motivations for change, your faith in yourself will improve. Be particularly attentive during November, when the solar eclipse helps you find the most significant thing you must focus upon as you positively alter your life.

If your Moon is 6–14 degrees Sagittarius, you will experience two strong cycles this year. First, you are feeling the stimulus to give your spirituality and creative expression more room in your life, signified by the cycle of Neptune in sextile contact to your Moon. However, beginning in July, Saturn moves into a yearlong quincunx aspect to your Moon, testing your ability to be more attentive to your real feelings and needs. You may need to make significant changes in your lifestyle that will better support your health, but your relationships may also be in need of positive repair. Saturn's influence will help you bring your spiritual needs into a practical frame of reference.

If your Moon is 15–21 degrees Sagittarius, you'll experience profound changes while Pluto travels in conjunction to your Moon during 2003. This cycle can happen only once in a lifetime, with the resulting experience of rebirth transforming your connection to your soul. Whether it's a move, renovation, career change, or major alteration in your family, the end result can be a feeling that you've left one part of your life behind and are now on a radically different path.

If your Moon is 22–29 degrees Sagittarius, you're laying the groundwork that will allow you to experience a powerful sense of free self-expression. Uranus' cycle in trine contact to your Moon indicates that you're ready to let go and move on toward different horizons. However, from January through May, Saturn's opposition to your Moon may require that you stay close to home to deal with your responsibilities. Once you've satisfied those obligations, you'll feel you can truly move ahead. In relationships, career or lifestyle choices—it's important to close out the old before you give birth to the new!

January

Create the map you intend to follow on your next adventure during the New Moon on the 2nd. (The map may be a plan to redesign your kitchen!) Guidelines can restrain your tendency to go off in several directions at once with the stimulus of Venus in Sagittarius that starts on the 7th. The good news is that your wish list is easier to fill, and expressing what's in your heart can bring magical results. Once Mars moves into Sagittarius on the 17th, your patience may run out and you'll feel an eager impulsiveness to charge out of the gates—and knowing about the track will tell you how fast you can travel. Your intuitive sensibilities are strongly activated after the 19th, although a few folks will still feel nervous about your activities. You may barely glance back at others stunned by your departure, although those who love you may be right by your side—seatbelts fastened, of course.

February

Your dreams during the New Moon on the 1st can awaken fresh possibilities, and may prove to be visionary. Even if you cannot recall the details, more attention to your dreams provides valuable insights. Despite your own faith, doubt can undermine your ability to trust what you need. Your courage helps you get to the source of your fear, and even if the challenge to overcome your obstacles seems huge, persistent effort cuts it down to a manageable size. Opportunity peaks during the Full Moon on the 16th, when your ideals shine a hopeful light that also inspires others to follow your lead. At home and in your relationships, your straightforward honesty clarifies the most significant issues. There's nothing like the power of truth!

March

Talk about what's bothering you, but if you truly want to communicate, take time to listen to the concerns expressed by others. You may discover that your ideals are irreconcilable, but at least you know when to step out of the way or when to support your rights to be different. Tests of tolerance may not be much fun, but you certainly understand their value. Communication can be testy near the Full Moon on the 18th, when stubborn attitudes block progress. After the 21st, there's more room for diversity—but that could be due to the fact that you've turned your attention to something (or someone) completely different—without malice. At home, a change in décor or rearrangement can alter the flow of energy so that you feel more creative and expressive. Romantic ambience can have a wonderful impact after the 22nd, and social events can be quite productive, too.

April

Too much sentiment can prompt you to slip out the nearest exit, especially if you feel that someone's holding on when you want to let go! The prompt from the New Moon on the 1st is about initiating change, and anything that seems stuck can seem almost intolerable. While this can symbolize a lack of evolution to you, your understanding and patience may be necessary to help someone else deal with his or her pain. Acknowledging your own limits helps, too. And it's perfectly fine to ask for help when you need it! You may simply be at your wits' end, and if you need a break, the universe complies after the 20th; although, you're still juggling a large stack of responsibilities.

May

With a flair for fun, you can foster a lighthearted approach to the things that may be weighing heavily on the hearts of others. From the 1st through the lunar eclipse on the 16th, you're ready to clear away clutter and to give yourself more breathing room. You might move, or decide it's finally time to go through the piles of mail stashed in the corner awaiting your attention. Your temptation to rush can lead you directly into trouble, since you can easily overlook details, or may throw away valuable goodies. Mercury's tense connection with nebulous Neptune can leave you lost in a fog. Despite the effort, concentration on a more mindful attitude can save you headache and heartache, since you can send mixed signals and may not even know it! The writing's on the wall during the solar eclipse on the 31st, when another's responses tell you what you need to know. Look up!

June

Your frustration with others, whose pace seems more like the tortoise, probably shows on your face, particularly if you feel that your needs are lost in the shadows of more vocal complaints than yours. To escape the frustration, time away from the scene can do you a world of good. Besides that, it's easier to reflect on your real feelings and to let go of negative emotion without being under such close scrutiny. The Sagittarius Full Moon on the 14th can place you squarely in the bull's-eye for those who may be upset with you, and while you might want to hold your tongue, it can be a real trick to accomplish. Tension at home can seem to come from out of the blue after the 18th, but if you take a closer look, it's clear what's behind the hostility. The question is whether or not you can do anything about it.

July

From now until mid-December, feisty Mars is swimming through Pisces, and you can feel emotionally drained as a result. The problem arises when you try to assert your needs, and you can feel that your efforts to express your true feelings are simply clumsy. Part of the difficulty comes from the way you respond to others who may be adrift in what seems like too much sentiment. This can be quite noticeable during the Full Moon on the 13th, when you may decide to make yourself scarce if you're uncomfortable with demands you feel from others. A trip can be a positive escape, although situations close to home can tug at your heart. It's easier to get away during the New Moon on the 29th, when more favorable pathways are open to you.

August

The road to contentment may be a little bumpy, but your confidence gets a boost from someone you love or admire, adding a rosy glow to the challenge of navigating emotionally charged circumstances. Your efforts to beautify your home can keep you smiling through the 22nd, and could be prompted by a party or gathering of friends. It's probably a good idea to avoid loaded subjects unless you really want a debate, and even then, a situation can get out of hand before you know it. Practical considerations take top priority after the 23rd, when you may have to shelve your plans in order to take care of business close to home. Your challenge may be to determine when to get involved with disagreements and when to steer clear. Choose carefully after the 26th.

September

Differences in taste can lead to disagreements at home and escalate into feelings of estrangement during the Full Moon on the 10th. Before you assume that you have to give in and eat your spinach and tofu after all, first explore what's eating you! Solutions don't have to be complicated—even when your options all seem to come with fine print. Whether you're repairing a relationship or fixing a leaky faucet, your tension over the little things may have reached its capacity. Mercury's retrograde plays into the craziness, too, since old issues you thought were resolved are back on the table until after the 20th. Finally, fresh options arrive on gentle breezes of acceptance during the New Moon on the 25th.

October

Logic goes only so far, and then you have to contend with the fact that feelings are feelings after all. It's easier to find the positives in a sticky situation through the time of the Full Moon on the 10th, and after that time, sentiment or resentment can warp objectivity. Fortunately, communication flows nicely from the 6th–23rd, although you may have to choose your consorts carefully. It's a good time to do people-watching—since observations help you maintain your objectivity about what's really going on. You may discover a common thread that allows you to understand why certain triggers are in operation at home or at work. Even if everyone else does not see the larger picture, your awareness makes a dramatic difference.

November

You're raring to go when it comes to getting a project off the ground. Containing your feelings can be an act of futility, and with Venus transiting through Sagittarius until the 27th, there's no reason to hold back your affections. What can be a problem is knowing how far to go before you step over a sensitive boundary, and if you pay attention to the signals sent your way during the lunar eclipse on the 8th, you'll see signals that tell you how much give-and-take is at play. Still, careful maneuvering is required from the 9th–19th, when the standoff between Mars and Jupiter can put you in the line of fire in a fight that clearly belongs to somebody else. Fresh opportunities arise during the Sagittarius solar eclipse on the 23rd, although a definite power play can leave you speechless.

December

Fine-tune your sense of humor. There's plenty of material to keep everyone in stitches during the holiday hustle. The trick to staying out of trouble is to locate the proper situation to share your observation, since you could step on the wrong conservative toes during the Full Moon on the 8th. Mars finally moves into friendly territory on the 16th, giving you relief from the agitation you've felt since summer. Your passions need room to roam, and after the 21st you may have the perfect excuse for a getaway with your favorite person. Closer to home, you might decide to retreat to your den or workshop so you can unleash a creative passion. In either case, expressing yourself takes a positive turn, and joy finds a comfy seat at the dinner table.

Capricorn Moon

The self-respect you feel when you're standing tall in the light of your accomplishments feeds your Capricorn Moon. You're driven toward your aims, and you take your commitments seriously. For that reason, you have little patience for things you consider to be a waste of your valuable time; although, you'll gladly make room in your life for those who have proven their merit. Even as you stand at the summit of achievement, your desire to fortify your security prompts you to reach toward new peaks. It's this process of growth and productivity that feeds your soul and inspires the admiration of others who share the circle of your life.

With your eye on the prize, you may feel oddly useless when work is insufficiently demanding. If anybody can be addicted to work, it's you, as you naturally assume responsible roles and prefer to be the one in charge. As a result, you may grapple with feelings of resentment when others head off to play and you burn the midnight oil. To minimize such negative intrusions on your productive life, you'll appreciate surrounding yourself with others who are capable of taking on responsibility of their own. You may even have a knack for identifying special abilities, and you can certainly be a marvelous teacher for your children or others who need your guidance. However, you can be a strict taskmaster, and may insist on the same excellence and commitment you expect from yourself. Once you extend your approval, someone knows that they've done well. The smile of satisfaction you offer is further proof.

Your preference for the practical is apparent at home, where you favor surroundings that reflect quality, functionality, and simplicity. You may love mountains, tall trees, and rocky cliffs—and might want to incorporate such natural elements in your home space. Family and security are top priorities for you, and establishing a safe home may be among your top priorities. In relationships, you can seem reserved with your feelings— although your wicked sense of humor is one of the things your family and friends love about you. In fact, you do love to play, but can feel guilty about it if the work is not done. To strike a balance between work and play, you may nave to give credence to your sensitive side, and allow the flow of joy and love to penetrate your walls of self-control. Your need to protect yourself can be a detriment when you honestly want to share your deeper feelings, and it may take the tender love and laughter of a child to remind you of the priceless qualities you truly cherish about life.

The Year at a Glance for Capricorn Moon

With a renewed sense of commitment to your responsibilities and goals, you'll feel a strong desire to establish a firm base of operations. You'll appreciate the defined direction emerging this year, since the distractions from your focus are less troublesome. It's a year to set priorities, and to let go of burdens that are no longer yours to carry. At the same time, you may take on increased family obligations, or may expend more energy and attention on matters close to home. Your determination, coupled with applied effort, can lead to a period of progress at home or in your career.

While the Solar and lunar eclipses do not activate challenges to your Capricorn Moon, their influences may extend to other planets in your astrological chart. Jupiter's planetary cycle does make connections to your Moon this year, and from January through August the expansive quality of Jupiter can tempt you to reach beyond your means. This can create dissatisfaction with the status quo, and filling the need to change can be costly if you simply respond to outside influences instead of listening to what you truly need. On August 27th, Jupiter moves into Virgo, and until late 2004 this cycle stimulates more productive changes.

The slower-moving cycles of Saturn, Uranus, Neptune, and Pluto are most profound when these planets make a more exact contact to your Moon. If your Moon is 0–14 degrees Capricorn, you'll feel a strong desire to slow your pace beginning in June, when Saturn moves into an opposition to your Moon. This influence will last about a year, and can be the overriding drive in your life. Your desire to settle into a lifestyle that helps your build a more secure platform can extend to establishing a permanent home, or you might be more inclined to make a deep commitment to a career path or relationship.

If your Moon is 0–4 degrees Capricorn, you're experiencing a year of breakthrough, since Uranus travels in a supportive and stimulating sextile contact to your Moon all year. This influence helps you let go of unnecessary things. It also marks the perfect time to eliminate unhealthy habits, and to become more freely expressive of your desires and needs. Your impulses to move or make changes, coupled with Saturn's grounding influence during the months from June–September, can signify a powerful life change.

If your Moon is 9–15 degrees Capricorn, you'll feel a nagging desire to let go and forgive under the influence of Neptune traveling in semisextile contact to your Moon. Your creativity, imagination and spirituality all take on greater significance, and after Septemter, practical Saturn challenges you to integrate your spirituality and artistry into your daily life so that you feel more connected to your inner self.

If your Moon is 15–21 degrees Capricorn, the subtle influence of Pluto transiting in semisextile connection to your Moon prompts you to explore your deeper motivations. As a result, techniques like behavior modification therapy or work with a counselor can help you clarify your drives and intentions. At home, you may decide it's finally time to get rid of clutter—the same thing you're doing with your psyche!

If your Moon is 22–29 degrees Capricorn, you begin the year in the completion of a cycle that began last year. Saturn continues its influence in quincunx contact to your Moon, and until June you'll feel that you're putting the fine-tuned touches on changes in your life. Uranus is also completing its eighteen-month cycle in quincunx aspect to your Moon (not over until December), and with these two cycles happening at the same time, you'll feel more connected to your destiny. Situations can arise that seem to put you face-to-face with evidence of your life path, and your choices can set you on a path toward greater personal fulfillment.

January

Even if you're not one for resolutions, the influence of the Capricorn New Moon on the 2nd can prompt you to set goals that provide the framework for a productive year. You may even get around to projects at home that have been waiting for your attention for far too long. Retrograde Mercury in Capricorn until the 22nd could bring an old acquaintance to your door, but it may also prompt you to get back in touch with someone you've missed. At the least, you'll feel inclined to get through that "to do" list that's been posted on the refrigerator for the past six months. Reach out with love until the Full Moon on the 18th, since acts of affection can solidify trust. Work is likely to demand more attention after the 20th, when you'll have to make a deliberate effort to stay in touch with personal matters.

February

Good things flow into your life, and the rewards fill you with satisfaction. With Venus welldressed in Capricorn's rays, you'll feel more tenderhearted and your powers of attraction can be uncanny. Surrounded by control issues, you'll have ample opportunity to observe struggles and to determine who's in charge. However, you can keep your boundaries well protected and concentrate on what's important to you. It's a good idea to define what others expect from you, though. Your failure to meet those ideals could lead to complications later on. Vague signals can muddy the water after the Full Moon on the 16th, and agreements made with only a handshake may not be worth a hoot.

March

Repairs, building projects, a move – anything constructive – show signs of progress when Mars enters Capricorn's zone on the 4th for its six-week stay. If you're unhappy with the overall "feel" of your home, use feng shui to improve the flow of energy within your personal environment (or at least consult a talented decorator!). Establish agreements during the New Moon on the 3rd that define your priorities and give others helpful guidelines to understanding what you need from them. Then, get to work on your top-drawer priorities. An anticipated change of the guard can alter your focus during the Full Moon on the 18th. You'll be most comfortable with a direct approach in your personal relationships, although it's easy to run rough-shod over the most sensitive types. To avoid alienation, watch for signals that tell you if your demands have gone too far.

April

Remind yourself that kids will be kids, since the distractions from the more impulsive types can prove frustrating during the New Moon on the 1st. Your tender side shows to those who share your personal space, but you may keep a fairly closed exterior when you're out in the world. It's your protective side that's activated, since anything or anyone precious to you will be under your close watch if you sense the vulnerability involved. Your focus now is on establishing foundations that will stand the test of time, and your innate sense of structure and appreciation for quality serve you well. Love and support are there if you need them, and the value of heartfelt gestures is definitely not wasted from the 1st to 21st. Tune in to the expressions that will be more appreciated by others, then you'll find it easier to show gratitude when it's appropriate.

May

Renew friendships or significant commitments during the New Moon on the 1st, when promises are likely to hold fast. Likeminded allies may be hard to find, and reaching out to them can help you feel more at ease in a world filled with changes. While you may appreciate the value of liberal ideas, those who carry them too far can get under your skin, although it may simply be their lack of experience that seems to contrast with what you see as an unworthy level of power. The lunar eclipse on the 16th emphasizes the situations that will be most open to your participation, although you may have to take the initiative if you want anything to change. By the time the solar eclipse arrives on the 31st, you're involved with a project that makes the best use of your resources.

June

An easygoing pace works best until the Full Moon on the 14th. You'll appreciate a chance to adapt to the shift in the cosmic structure, when Saturn moves into its two-year opposition to your Moon sign on the 3rd. You can almost feel the chill of increasing responsibility nipping at your heels. It's not necessary that you take on the burden of the entire world, but since your tendency is to take up the slack, you might be tempted—especially if you worry about somebody else making a mess of things. Part of the lesson is about allowing others pass their own tests—without your interference or shield of support. Concentrate on forming solid working partnerships during the New Moon on the 29th. That's a balance of power—not a loss of it.

July

Consider this a time when you learn to dance to a different rhythm. You don't like dancing? Well, somebody's likely to issue an invitation, and cooperative actions may require that you step lightly in time with their music! Your life can be positively enhanced when you open to receive affection and appreciation, and even if you are not entirely comfortable as the recipient, your grace with the process can bring its own rewards. The Capricorn Full Moon on the 13th can be a test of your ability to take your lead from someone else, when honesty about your true needs makes a huge difference. At home, it's time to make repairs or to renovate. However, a move might end up placing you in a disruptive situation. Take another look at that option after the New Moon on the 29th.

August

"Too much flash and not enough substance" can be your complaint during the Full Moon on the 12th. If you can find the practical side to a situation (or a person), your tolerance increases, but you simply have no patience for anything flimsy. With your immersion into a pet project or involvement in family matters, you'll feel more content, although you may resent anyone who begs your attention when you do not want to give it. While increased tension flies around your backyard, there are signs of progress during the New Moon on the 27th. Your direction or guidance help things move along when they get stuck. To maintain a semblance of harmony and order, you may have to keep your comments about the paint or furniture to yourself, though.

September

Good things land on your doorstep, and with Jupiter's cycle bringing abundance, you may decide it's time to celebrate your good fortune! Your acknowledgment of the accomplishments of one of your brood goes a long way toward strengthening the bonds of love. And during the Full Moon on the 10th you may thoroughly enjoy being the power behind the throne. Surrounded by family and friends, you may feel a wondrous sense of renewal. Your efforts to enhance the comfort of your home fare best from the 1st–14th, and even though Mercury retrogrades until the 20th, you may not feel like waiting to indulge, and make at least a few changes. Since you probably appreciate working within a budget, you might stay out of trouble. Still, costs can run over estimates, so be sure to make allowances before you finalize the deal.

October

Back to the drawing board, you may decide to revamp plans before you put them into motion just before the Full Moon on the 10th. If you run into objections, your first response might be to fight back, although the logic of someone's argument might convince you to reconsider your decisions. Your patience pays off, since the New Moon on the 25th ushers in a highly productive period, when any time you may have lost while dealing with details or interruptions seems to vanish in the wake of progress. Love surrounds you, and your own feelings of tenderness flow freely when you are in a safe place to let your heart lead the way. It may even be the most practical choice.

November

A combination of hard work and good timing serve you well from the 1st through the lunar eclipse on the 8th, when you may finally get a chance to enjoy the fruits of your labors. Changes in your family can be a reason for a party, as long as you still have ample time to concentrate on the "serious" business still demanding your attention. Arguments over differences of opinion can seem a bit silly to you, although the persistence of human folly always gives you a chuckle. You may be off in your own world working on a project that requires most of your time once the solar eclipse rolls around on the 23rd. There's a lot to do behind the scenes, and you may have big plans for next month.

December

While some suspect that you have a tender heart, there's ample evidence of your compassion during December. An enduring love grows stronger under the constancy of Venus traveling through Capricorn's domain, and your desire to express your affections can solidify those bonds. Since your finances may improve, too, your expression of affection may come with a valuable gift. Whether you're on the giving or receiving end, you'll expect some kind of reciprocity. Remember: The smallest box may hold the most precious goods! Of course, you could have your aim set on something more practical—like the deed to the house of your dreams. Manifesting your dreams and desires works like a charm during the Capricorn New Moon on the 23rd. All you have to do is to decide precisely what you want. The rest sails downhill from there!

Aquarius Moon

Your soul resonates with the truth that we are all one people; your need to find the common threads of humanity is a reflection of your Aquarius Moon. Despite this drive, you love to know that you're different and you cherish your independent way of thinking. Your visionary sensibilities challenge you to develop your ideas and your talents, and you may be a trendsetter. Your friends feed your soul, yet you can be a loner as you travel the untrodden path toward self-realization. Your paradoxical nature challenges others to stay on their toes, since you are not likely to slack off when it comes to your push toward evolutionary change!

Despite your preference for logical solutions, you've experienced the profound value of your intuition over and over again. You know that a mix of logic and intuitive insight leads to innovation, and when you're at the peak of awareness you can see how these qualities blend. The aloof quality of Aquarius takes its toll on your emotional self, however—since your attempts to fit your feelings into logical or rational ideas can be a real headache! You may "know" that emotions are not logical, but that does not stop you from trying to make sense out of what you feel. Ultimately, you are challenged to adopt an air of unconditional acceptance, and it is this quality that makes you such a valuable friend and partner. In relationships, you need someone who'll value your eccentricities and will understand your need for independence. Those who require continual input may have to be content watching from the sidelines as you launch into your various plans and ideas.

Your home may be filled with all sorts of gadgets and technological innovations, and it's here that your inventive ideas need to take root. You may also welcome a wide assortment of friends into your personal space, and appreciate the value of communal sharing as a way to make the most of all your resources. Yet other paradoxes arise from the fact that you can also be highly conservative, and that you may nurture an idea or way of life with bold determination—seeing it through the its end as a means of understanding whether or not you were right. The paradox of finding unity through diversity is your ultimate challenge, and it drives you to remain open to the experiences that shatter the boundaries of the ordinary.

The Year at a Glance for Aquarius Moon

With an expanded sense of confidence and bright visions for the future, your emotional center glows with hope. The year 2003 marks a time of growth and opportunity, when you build a secure platform from which to launch your dreams. You may have to make a few adjustments in order to avoid overreaching your limits, but somehow dancing on the edge of possibility keeps you feeling more alive than simply waiting patiently for the light to change.

This is the last year for Uranus to transit through Aquarius, and after seven years of rekindling your true needs and feelings, you're ready to spend extra time developing some of the brilliant ideas that have kept you awake at night. However, Jupiter does continue its cycle in opposition to your Moon sign that began last year, so until the end of August, you'll feel an urgency to explore, expand, and reach out. This cycle serves as the launching pad, and with focused clarity you can generate a tremendous enthusiasm that aids in the fulfillment of your dreams.

The eclipses of Sun and Moon draw your attention to the need to bring a better balance between home and career, and your awareness of the strengths and weaknesses in these areas will be more marked during May and November. To determine if Saturn, Uranus, Neptune, or Pluto will make a significant impact in your life this year, pinpoint the degree of your Aquarius Moon. The influence of the slower-moving planetary cycles to your Moon will be most noticeable during the year these planetary cycles make an exact contact to your Moon.

If your Moon is 0–2 degrees Aquarius, you're stepping on to a different platform for your emotional fulfillment this year while Uranus moves into a semisextile contact to your Moon. Many of the choices you make will be reflected in simple changes—like alterations in your diet or routine. However, you might also decide to make basic renovations to your home, or move to a place that's more convenient to work.

If your Moon is 3–7 degrees Aquarius, you'll dig into your motivations and eliminating negative emotional drives while Pluto travels in semi-square aspect to your Moon. This cycle signifies a time when you may feel less connected to your past and more focused on where you're heading. Of course, the key to working through the challenge is to remain mindful of where you are "now!" That will be easier from July–September, when Saturn travels in quincunx to your Moon, stimulating a series of emotional adjustments.

If your Moon is 8–14 degrees Aquarius, you'll feel an urge to let go and get into the flow while Neptune merges with your Moon and helps you erase your resistance to your highest needs. This is an excellent creative stimulus, and your consciousness expands. From January through June, Saturn's cycle in sesquiquadrate to your Moon tests your capacity to maintain healthy emotional boundaries, since you could feel tempted to try to save the world! Of course, that's not a bad idea, but you might find that it's easier if you're not entirely alone!

If your Moon is 15–21 degrees Aquarius, you'll experience a powerful need to heal wounds from the past while Pluto transits in sextile contact to your Moon. Under this influence, renovations at home can be more easily accomplished, but your relationships and life path are also under reconstruction.

If your Moon is 22–29 degrees Aquarius, then this is your year to put the finishing touches on major changes. From January through May, Saturn's cycle in supportive trine to your Moon adds a quality of emotional stability and marks a positive time to make commitments. However, it's the cycle of Uranus in unified conjunction to your Moon that stimulates your desire to answer your truest needs. You may break away from inhibiting situations, and certainly will be ready to let go of outworn attitudes. During July and August, you'll feel the most urgent need to change, but might want to be sure the parachute is working properly before you start the final countdown to launch!

January

Stubborn resistance from someone who feels deeply invested in a situation can thwart your progress, especially if your ideas or actions fly in the face of convention (and they probably do). Part of the problem is pure emotional prejudice—otherwise known as fear. Your encouragement and enthusiasm can be highly persuasive after the 7th; although, you may not have more than a few standing by your side until after the Full Moon on the 18th. At home, repairs or renovation can be a real headache, and unless you simply must, avoid starting new projects until after Mercury turns direct on the 22nd. Repairs are one thing—renovation is another! Travel can be just what you need to break the tension in a relationship, although a romantic dinner or weekend enjoying your favorite things can put the blush back into a stale relationship after the 22nd.

February

Consider the Aquarius New Moon on the 1st to be a truly special fresh beginning. Even if you renew a vow, you'll feel that you're starting on higher ground. It's time to surrender to the whisper of your soul, and if that involves a different approach to a love relationship, then you might be more inclined to admit a few of your hopes and even some of your misgivings. However, you may feel that you need some time alone, and a retreat or time away from the everyday grind can reawaken your perspective on your needs and choices from the 13th–22nd. Previous commitments might call you back during the Full Moon on the 16th, although this is a marvelous time to share your passions with your lover.

March

Your heart sings more freely, and you'll need more time to devote to a creative project, a special family gathering, or your dearest relationship. Venus lends her lovely light to your Moon, and from the 2nd–27th you'll feel much more at ease expressing your affections. This is also an excellent time to beautify your home, although a move will be most fortuitous from the 1st–5th or after the 22nd. An event or party scheduled from the 12th–16th can be riddled with innuendo, and might actually be amusing unless you're the one caught with your hand in the cookie jar. After the 24th you may have a change of heart and decide to explore different options. Although this can seem innocent, someone may take your decision personally unless you go out of your way to explain.

April

Your preference for independence is in overdrive, and it can seem that demands from others are closing in around you. Part of the problem can be that there's not enough of you to go around—or at least that's the perception. Clarify expectations during the New Moon on the 1st, since unspoken assumptions can turn a reasonable situation into a free-for-all from the 10th–16th. Practical matters take highest priority now, so theories about what might work may just be a waste of time. Of course, you'll still have all those ideas shooting through your mind, but will not enjoy wasting them on others who'll scoff. After Mars enters Aquarius on the 21st you may feel more inclined to assert yourself and your ideas. Then, too, you could just be spending more time in your workshop!

May

With plenty to do, you're less likely to get into trouble. Of course, someone who resents your independent attitudes may launch an underhanded attack during the lunar eclipse on the 16th! Surreptitious actions on your part can work against you, although it's prudent to protect a sensitive idea, special project, or something that's not yet ready to be released to the world. It's crucial to deal with anger honestly for the next six weeks, since Mars is bumping against your Moon. Align yourself with others who understand and support you, and quietly build your network. After the 21st you'll feel more comfortable "in the open," and during the solar eclipse on the 31st you'll see the strength of your true allies. Go easy with repairs at home, since elements like plumbing and wiring can be troublesome. If you're not an expert, consider calling one.

June

Closed-mindedness can tick you off from the 1st–10th, but by the Full Moon on the 14th your audience is much more receptive. It's a good time to explore your own stubborn attitudes, since even though you think of yourself as an innovator, you can definitely get stuck in a stubborn rut. You may just need more playful activities, and after the 9th, there's every reason to seek out the most enjoyable options first. Whether you spend more time with friends, or just pull out the games to share with your family—you're ready to focus on what you have in common instead of singling out your differences. Love relationships can undergo a powerful transformation, although there may be a press for more traditional options instead of experimental ideas. All things in their time.

July

Sentimental attachments wash against your objective, logical shores, and can wear away at your patience, undermining your cool composure. You simply cannot make sense out of less-than-objective reactions from others. You are witnessing the logic-defying power of emotional attachment. You might even feel a bit weepy, or you could have trouble tossing out an old scrapbook that's little more than dusty debris. It's time to dig deep and allow more room in your life for others to feel the way they do. For the remainder of the year, Mars will cycle through Pisces, triggering deep-seated emotional insecurities. Little by little, you'll be prompted to let go of your resistance to the realm of the intangible. This month it starts with your relationships and those blasted sentimental and romantic elements you simply cannot escape. Surrender!

August

The buildup leading to the Aquarius Full Moon on the 12th can be purely delightful—unless you decide to fight it. Even so, a part of you feels the passions of your soul, and if you're involved in an intimate connection you'll feel the challenge of surrendering to love. Trusting emotion has never been your strong suit, but love is more than emotion. It permeates the essence of your being and transforms all that you are, leaving an eternal flame glowing in your own heart. Your creative or artistic endeavors may take on a more ethereal quality, and at home, you'll need more space to experiment with your inventive impulses. Practical matters capture your attention during the New Moon on the 27th, although you may still decide that delving into the transformational quality of love fits into that category.

September

It can be a trick to steer clear of disputes, although you may have excellent insights about the best way to resolve deep-seated differences. Emotionally- charged arguments escalate during the Full Moon on the 10th, and while the trigger might be money, the issue is probably something more profound. It's easier to interject your observations after the 15th, although you may just have better things to do if there's too much resistance. Improvements at home take a higher priority, and whether it's re-arranging furniture, a renovation, or a move, the New Moon on the 26th inspires a fresh perspective. A family gathering or a party for friends can change the tone and give everyone more creative options for their attention.

October

Cooperative ventures prove successful through the time of the Full Moon on the 10th, but after then you may be on your own since everyone seems to have an agenda. Fortunately, communication flows nicely when it counts the most, and reaching an agreement keeps your projects moving along until the 25th. By the New Moon on the 25th you'll have to contend with family matters, whether you want to or not. The manner in which you participate is up to you, and the emotional boundaries you've set may have to be re-evaluated in the light of the needs of others. The pressure could come from work—but either way, you can be dragged into a maze of complexities.

November

Your patient attempts to connect with the right resources pay off, although you may end up paying more than you intended (one way or another!). Before you give up that pound of flesh, take another look during the lunar eclipse on the 8th to determine if it's absolutely necessary. Selfish attitudes from others garner little sympathy from you, and you may decide to make yourself scarce if you know your efforts will go unappreciated. Your creative energy moves into high gear this month, and a heart-warming project gains exceptional momentum after the solar eclipse on the 23rd. Travel can play a huge role in the changes you follow this month, since you're eager to expand your horizons on several levels. Who you take with you is another story!

December

Progress moves like a locomotive. The slow start tests your faith, although staying focused on your aims helps you hold fast to your vision. A celebration honors significant achievements near the time of the Full Moon on the 8th, and you might feel more inclined to step aside and offer up the spotlight to your steadfast supporters. Your artistry is renewed, and gifts from your heart go a long way toward healing a relationship after the 18th. Home can become your sanctuary, and reflections about the changes you need to make that will extend or enhance the flow of energy in your personal space can lead to major changes. Draw up plans after the 22nd, when Venus moves into a union with your Moon and it will be easier make just the right changes.

Pisces Moon

When you close your eyes and tune into the way the world ought to feel, peace on Earth is a natural state. Your Pisces Moon yearns for tranquility, and your sensitivity helps you reach into spiritual and artistic realms that are purely magical. Other people are drawn to your kind and compassionate energy, and your faith feeds the inspiration that keeps you flowing through the journey of life. You may have a special radar that draws you to outstanding drama, music, photography, and art, because there is a part of you that continually resonates with the realm of uncorrupted imagination. It's that same otherworldly quality that permeates your creativity and permeates your tender caresses.

The shimmering delight you feel when you have a chance to reach out and make a difference can be contagious. Whether you're involved with charitable efforts, deeply engrossed in your artistic expression, or padding around the kitchen—you're happiest when you know you are "in the flow." You need a home space that gives you plenty of room to let go, and may take special care to create a sleeping space that invites you to dream. Plus, you'll enjoy living near water. (At least make sure that you have a fabulous bathtub!) In relationships, your deep desire for a soulmate urges you to search for a partner whose ideals and sensibilities are in harmony with your own. You trust that love endures beyond time and space, and it is your capacity for boundless love that endears you to others. Since you prefer to express tolerance in the face of bigotry, and to extend kindness when others are steeped in misery, you may cross into territory that causes the calloused to turn away. This same quality can lead you to sacrifice your own needs in favor of the pressing demands you feel from others.

Urged to rise above the limits of the physical plane, your need to escape the bounds of the earthly plane can stimulate your creativity—but you can also fall prey to addictive behaviors, or may be drawn into traps set by those whose hearts are filled with deceit. For this reason, you need to create a kind of emotional filter, and you will benefit from activities that serve to ground your energy. Meditation, dance, yoga, journal-writing—all can help you stay clear and focused so the flow of love can move into your life with greater purity. Your ultimate goal—to become unified with the Source—is achieved moment by moment, allowing eternal love to flow through you and into the world.

The Year at a Glance for Pisces Moon

This year, you begin a breakthrough cycle and may feel that you are on a more satisfying life course. Even the surprises that come your way can lead to situations that are more fulfilling, although adaptability will be necessary if you are to make the most of changes that are beyond your control. Fortunately, you have a knack for finding the flow and surrendering when you must, and others may take their lead from your trust in the ultimate good.

The most exciting cycle that begins in 2003 is the seven-year journey of Uranus through Pisces. During this period, you may feel that you're more in tune with the ways of the world—a nice change from what may have caused you to wonder whether or not you were on the right planet during the last several years! Just as with the cycles of the other slow-moving planets, the most significant impact and sweeping changes from the Uranus cycle will happen the year Uranus makes an exact connection to the degree of your Moon. However, since this planet is now in the territory inhabited by your Moon, the entire seven-year period will be filled with life-altering experiences.

Expansion is the name of the game with Jupiter, and until the end of August, Jupiter's influence to your Moon tests your adaptability. You can be tempted to stretch your limits—physically and emotionally—especially if you are allowing others to lead you into unhealthy directions. On August 28th, Jupiter moves into Virgo, the sign opposite your Moon, and while temptation may still haunt you, you can see it more clearly!

Other significant changes involve the cycle of Saturn, since it moves into a zone that much friendlier to your Moon in June. Check the paragraphs below to find the degree of your Moon and review whether or not

Saturn is presenting particular challenges. To determine the impact of the eclipses of Sun and Moon to your Moon, refer to the notes for May and November below.

If your Moon is 0–4 degrees Pisces, you're in for a wake-up call! Uranus joins your Moon this year, bringing a desire for far-reaching personal revolution. You may decide to move (or a move could be decided for you), and alterations in your family are an almost sure thing. In late June and during most of September and October, Mars and Uranus join together to stir your urge to make sweeping change.

If your Moon is 5–13 degrees Pisces, Saturn's cycle adds some stability from September-December. These are the best months to make commitments, since your trust in your judgment improves and your resources and energy are more reliable.

If your Moon is 9–14 degrees Pisces, maintaining your focus can be difficult since Neptune's cycle infuses your life with emotional fog. Your creativity can be enhanced, but your drive may difficult to activate.

If your Moon is 15–21 degrees Pisces, you'll experience deep-seated emotional changes this year while Pluto squares off against your Moon. This is a healing cycle, although some of the things you must eliminate in order to heal your life can leave a kind of emotional hole. As you move through the pain of repairing your life, you rekindle your faith in ultimate Truth. Health issues need care and attention, but your relationships may also require a series of adjustments.

If your Moon is 22–29 degrees Pisces, you'll complete the tests that began last summer. Saturn continues its cycle in square to your Moon until June, and this marks the time when you'll complete some of your obligations and major challenges. Uranus also stimulates your Moon, altering your personal habits and helping you let go of what you no longer need.

January

Your calm composure helps you contain your creative focus, and with fresh inspiration during the New Moon on the 2nd, you're eager to move forward. Progress and easy flow are more probable until the 16th, when Mars moves into irritating contact to your Moon. While romantic tension might be wonderfully delicious during the Full Moon on the 18th, you'll feel less than satisfied if you are not on the same wavelength with your lover. Trouble can come from friction in the outside world—and if that's contaminating your personal life, then you may have to take a look at how much you're bringing home that really belongs back at the office. However, if the big issue is what's happening behind closed doors, it's time to air your grievances and look for the ties that can bring you closer. At home, repairs can be a real pain, so if you are in over your head, call in the experts!

February

If you're feeling thin-skinned, it may be necessary to create a buffer zone between yourself and the world. Friction from Mars continues, and you may feel that your vulnerabilities are completely exposed. Meditation might help, but an intense workout at the gym could prove more effective—especially if there's somebody you want to confront, but know you cannot! Talk about your feelings with someone you trust from the 1st–14th, but give yourself plenty of time to indulge in creative pastimes, too. Despite your frustrations, your heart-centered needs take a high priority (or is that the source of your tension?). Your tolerance, understanding, and hopefulness are enhanced after the 18th, when circumstances around you are slightly calmer.

March

With the battle zone farther away, you can let down your guard and enjoy yourself during the Pisces New Moon on the 3rd. This cycle marks the perfect time to envision your ideal life. Go ahead—tune in to your favorite dreams, let your imagination go wild, and step into the flow of your inner self. It's like trying on shoes. You never know how they feel until you slip them on your feet and walk around the room. Now, it's time to try on your desires and wishes. Find out what fits. Make alterations. The self-assurance that follows opens the way for you to manifest a reality that is more "you." You may decide to target change in your relationship, too, and during the Full Moon on the 18th can "test drive" your improved approach. Benefits start slowly, and love begins a beautiful blossoming after the 28th.

April

The support you feel may come from others, but it's your capacity to trust yourself that's confirmed. Under the amiable glow of Venus in Pisces, you're much more at ease when you express your honest feelings—at home or at work. Constructive change flows best from the 1st–20th. Alterations at home can give you more breathing room, but you might want to go further and consult a feng shui expert to help you redirect the flow of energy in your personal space. Beautify your life in every way you can, since you're attracting what you need, and it suits you wonderfully well! Others can become more demanding after the 22nd, and to avoid difficulties you'll want to clarify expectations and confirm appointments—just to be sure you show up and the right place wearing the right outfit!

May

Solid commitments stabilize your priorities during the New Moon on the 1st, although promises need careful definition since agreements made now will be likely to stay with you! The impatient types around you can drive you nuts—particularly if you feel that they are heading for disaster despite your advice. Significant improvement in a close connection amplifies your real feelings, and during the Lunar Eclipse on the 16th you may need time away from the press of everyday hassles to enjoy the comforts of love. A fascinating change or an unusual person captures your attention and can spark your creativity after the 16th, but the truth of the situation may not emerge until the solar eclipse on the 31st, when you can better see the whole picture. Still, the process itself can be delightful!

June

A much-needed project at home may not go smoothly from the 1st–10th simply due to disruptions you did not anticipate. Simple plans work best, and unless you have everything in place, you might prefer to get started during or after the New Moon on the 29th, when you feel more settled and there's less traffic running through the house. Until then, consultations with experts or personal research gives you the data and guidance to feel more confident about your choices. A huge change, like a move, might be in order, and by spending more time closing out details of your "old" existence you make way for a smoother transition. Mars enters Pisces on the 16th, and until mid-December the high-energy planet supercharges your Moon. Restless feelings make it difficult to pace yourself, but when you do, you'll have more energy to make necessary changes.

July

Emphasis on the home front is huge—family gatherings, a celebration for friends, or more time at home with your sweetheart—all give you a chance to open your heart to others. However, you might also spend significant energy beautifying your home, adding the touches that finally bring your dream house to life. You can make a difference—not only for yourself, but in the lives of others—and during the Full Moon on the 13th, you're right in the middle of the creation of lasting memories. Your artistic expression can also be a strong emphasis now, since this is the time to start from your heart and follow the flow. A love relationship takes on new meaning, and vows made before the 13th can shape a fresh direction for your life.

August

Consistency works to your advantage, and even if you're tempted to follow a distraction from someone else, limiting your availability for such options keeps you on more solid footing. Voice mail has its perks—so if you're focused on a project and need to stay in the flow, let the call go there and check messages later! After the New Moon on the 27th you may feel more inclined to focus your attention on demands and needs from others, although it's also the beginning of an excellent cycle for cooperation and sharing. Jupiter's shift into an opposition to your Moon amplifies the best and the worst when it comes to give-and-take in relationships. Objective observation helps you determine what's out of harmony.

September

Stretched beyond your capacity, you can feel emotionally exhausted, and that's certainly a possibility if you've martyred yourself for an unapprecia-tive recipient. Although you may not get everything you want or need, the challenge from the 1st–8th is to ask for help when you know it's necessary, or to step out of the picture if your efforts are met with too much resist-ance. The tests in your relationships at home and at work are about drawing boundaries and staying with them. If you mean "No," then say it. Otherwise, how will anybody get the point? Just as important, expressing who you are and what you need can be a tough exercise, since differences in values can leave you feeling vulnerable. Resolutions come when you uncover your own limitations and honor them.

October

Now that Mars has moved into direct motion, you'll feel that you are accomplishing something. Digging a deep rut may have left you spent and frustrated last month, but now you can rise up with fresh perspective and renewed confidence. Family ties are strengthened by close communica-tion, and a gathering of the clan can work wonders after the 11th. You'll feel that the things you need flow into your life with greater consistency, however you may not want to initiate a project or a major change until the New Moon on the 25th. Use the time in between to draw up plans, gather supplies, and line up the right people for the job. Then, break ground on the 26th!

November

The Lunar Eclipse on the 8th can signify the culmination of major change in an intimate relationship. Change in the family hierarchy may have resulted in greater responsibility for you, but your ability to determine an equitable balance of power may be challenged by those with more selfish needs than your own. Work situations may reflect the same inequities, and rampant greed from others can prompt you to disappear from the picture. Your philosophies are called to the fore, and during this test of what you feel is right, you may decide that you can no longer participate in situations that are not harmonious with your highest needs. No announcement is necessary, since you absence will speak volumes!

December

Your comfort zone is definitely more comfy, and an intimate gathering can be the perfect setting to cuddle up with your sweetheart. Your foundation grows stronger, especially since you've eliminated factors that would undermine the integrity of your base of operations. Even the minor power plays you see during the Full Moon on the 8th are not likely to ruffle your feathers, since your focus is clearly set on the priorities that serve your real needs. This is different from pure selfishness—call this a "self-full" time, when replenishing your needs will enhance your capacity to give to others. Your creativity is in high gear during the New Moon on the 23rd, and for the remainder of the year, you may sink below the radar screen and dance into delightful whimsy or deep spiritual retreat.

About the Author

Your personal Moon sign descriptions and forecasts for this book were written by internationally renowned astrologer, author, and teacher, Gloria Star. She has been a contributing author of the *Moon Sign Book* since 1995 and wrote the *Sun Sign Book* for Llewellyn from 1989–2002. She is the author of *Astrology & Your Child* (Llewellyn, 2000) and *Astrology: Woman to Woman* (Llewellyn, 1999). She also edited and coauthored the book *Astrology for Women: Roles and Relationships* (Llewellyn 1997). She has authored two astrological computer software chart interpreters: *Optimum Child* (for Windows) was released by Astrolabe in 2002, and *IO Child* (for MAC) was released by TimeCycles Research in 2001. Her column, *Astrology News,* is a feature in the *Mountain Astrologer* magazine. She has also written online for several websites and has authored numerous astrological columns over the course of her career for various periodicals.

Listed in *Who's Who of American Women* and *Who's Who in the East,* Gloria is active within the astrological community, where she has been honored as a nominee for the prestigious Regulus Award. She has served on the faculty of the United Astrology Congress (UAC) since its inception in 1986, and has lectured for groups and conferences throughout the U.S.A. and abroad. She has served on the Board of the United Astrology Conference (UAC), and is a member of the Advisory Board for the National Council for Geocosmic Research (NCGR). She also served on the Steering Committee for the Association for Astrological Networking (AFAN), was editor of the AFAN newsletter from 1992–1997, and is now on the AFAN Advisory Board. She currently resides in the shoreline township of Clinton, Connecticut.

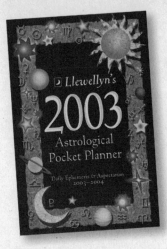

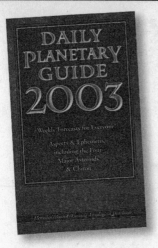

Still the Most Trusted Astrological Calender

Find out why Llewellyn's *Astrological Calendar 2003* is the oldest and most trusted astrological calendar. It just keeps getting better. Colorful, contemporary art by MoonDeer kicks off each month in 2003, and monthly horoscopes by Cathy Zornes provide the most rewarding and challenging dates for each sign. More features include:

- Global forecasts by Claudia Dikinis
- Financial and travel forecasts by Bruce Scofield
- Best planting and fishing days
- Monthly ephemerides and major daily aspects
- The Moon's sign, phase, and void-of-course dates
- Graphic retrograde table
- Quick reference guide for each month, symbol key on each month, and times included with aspects

LLEWELLYN'S *ASTROLOGICAL CALENDAR 2003*
48 pp. • 13" x 10" • 12 full-color paintings
ISBN 0-7387-0069-X/J070 • $12.95 U.S.
To order call 1-877-NEWWRLD

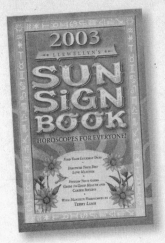

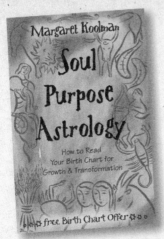

Visit Us
on the Web

www.llewellyn.com

Explore Llewellyn's *New Worlds of Mind and Spirit*. Find out what our authors are doing. See our latest releases. Click on any book for more details—or click ONLINE BOOKSTORE to refine your search.

¿Habla español? ¡No hay problema! Visite LLEWELLYN ESPANOL.

Click FUN & INTERACTIVE for cool things to do, such as a quick tarot reading or a magical personality quiz.

Learn more about our company or even contact us at LLEWELLYN.COM

Discover *The Llewellyn Journal*, our new online magazine—it's free! No memberships. No dues. No clubs to join. No passwords. *The Llewellyn Journal* is designed to be free of banners, pop-ups, pop-unders, and outside advertising. Click on THE LLEWELLYN JOURNAL or go directly to www.llewellynjournal.com.

Everyone's invited—and we're expecting you!

Notes